ABOUT THE AUTHOR

Marvin J. Wolf, who lives in California, has lived and worked in the Far East for several years. He has written about Japan and the East for many publications, including *Japan Times* and *Asia Magazine*. He has served as a commissioned officer in the USA, in Korea and Viet Nam and has travelled to Japan many times on editorial assignments. Marvin Wolf is a member of the American Society of Journalists and Authors.

THE JAPANESE CONSPIRACY

The Plot to Dominate Industry Worldwide –
and How to Deal with It

Marvin J. Wolf

NEW ENGLISH LIBRARY

First published in the USA in 1983 by Empire Books

First published in Great Britain in 1984 by New English Library

Copyright © 1983 by Empire Books

First NEL Paperback Edition September 1985

NEL Books are published by
New English Library,
Mill Road, Dunton Green,
Sevenoaks, Kent.
Editorial office: 47 Bedford Square, London WC1B 3DP

Typeset by Hewer Text Composition Services, Edinburgh

Printed and bound by Cox and Wyman Ltd, Reading

British Library C.I.P.
Wolf, Marvin J.
   The Japanese conspiracy : a stunning analysis
   of the international trade war.
   1. Japan—Commercial policy
   I. Title
   382'.0952   HF1601

ISBN 0–450–05866–2

For Sara, the Munchkin Queen,
who lovingly unmixed my metaphors
and widened my paradigm.

Acknowledgements

I am indebted to the following people, each of whom freely contributed their views and their special knowledge.

In the U.S.: Ilene Birkwood, Hewlett-Packard; Dr. John Calhoun, manager, business development, Intel; Chris Carlson, JETRO; Stuart Chemtob, U.S. assistant attorney; Dwight Clark, Director of Volunteers in Asia; P. Phillips Connor, attorney for Houdaille; Richard D. Copaken, Washington attorney; Dr. Jim Cunningham, Advanced Micro Devices; Dr. Michael Dertouzos, MIT Computer Laboratory; James Ellenberger, AFL-CIO international specialist; Ellie Engelmore, Stanford Computer Laboratory; Dr. Edward Feigenbaum, Stanford University; Joseph Franklin; Mark Fruin, professor, California State University, Hayward; Robert Gaertner, Cray Research; Richard Green, E. F. Hutton; Peter A. Gregory, Cray Research; Tom Hinkleman, executive director, SIA; Herbert B. Hoffman, U.S. assistant attorney; Tom Howell, Washington attorney for SIA; Keiko Kadota, Nippo Marketing; W. J. Kitchen, Motorola Semiconductors; Chris Langer, Control Data; Jack Latona, Houdaille Industries; John Markoff, writer for *Infoworld*; Margaret McCloud, FBI, San Francisco; William Nail, Zenith spokesman; John J. Nevin, chairman, Firestone; Steve Newhouse, Caterpillar spokesman; Larry Norris, Energy Conversion Devices; Joseph Podolsky, Hewlett-Packard; Clyde V. Prestowitz, U.S. Commerce Department; Pascal Redburn, court reporter; Robert Rutishauser, Control Data; Jerry Sanders, president, Advanced Micro Devices; Bill Shaffer, Control Data; Leonard M. Shanbon, ITC import compliance; Lennie

Siegel, director, Pacific Study Center; Sara Siegler; Charles Signor, Zilog; Elliot Sopkin, public relations, Advanced Micro Devices; John Taylor, Zenith public relations; Lloyd M. Thorndike, Control Data; Rebecca Wallo, Intel communications facilitator; William Yates, president, Avco Financial, Japan.

In Tokyo: Shigeyoshi Araki, Japanese Foreign Press Center; Kazuhiko Bando, MITI; Mike Benefiel, Commerce Department, U.S. Embassy, Tokyo; Ronald N. Billings, Japan Soft Bank; W. John Child, U.S. Embassy; Takako Doi, House of Representatives; Koichi Endo, managing director, Fujitsu laboratories; Hugh Hara, assistant press attache, USIA; Dr. Hisao Hayakawa; Shigeki Hijino, editor, Britannica Japan; Fr. Pius Tetsuro Honda, O.F.M.; Hiroko Horisaka, translator; Kotaro Horisaka, Sophia University professor; Dr. Tsutomu Hoshino, Tsukuba University; Dave Jampel, president, Imperial Press; Kinji Kawamura, Japanese Foreign Press Center; Tadao Kitigawa, farm cooperative director; Yuichi Kitigawa, farmer; Jimpei Kamuro, hotel handyman; Koichi Kujirai, counsel to the MITI minister; Dr. Kaneyuki Kurokawa, director, Fujitsu laboratories; Carol Ludwig, press attache, USIA, Tokyo; Hiroko Maki; Yuzuru Matsumoto, Universal Public Relations; Masao Mitsui; Yuri Momomoto, Fujitsu public relations; Kunihiro Morita, Sugal Creative Productions; Koichi Muramatsu, UNI literary agency; Soichi Nagamatsu, MITI electronic policy division; Tatsuko Nagasawa; Chinatsu Nakayama, House of Councillors; Hideo Ogata, Mitsubishi public relations; Yasuhiko Ohmori, president, Japan Soft Bank; Hirotaka Okaniwa, Nissan Motors spokesman; Masayoshi Sakisaka, Epson U.K.; Shigeru Sato, deputy general manager, Fujitsu computer; Shigeru Sawada, Nissan Motors spokesman; Takayoshi Shiina, president of SORD; Lester Slezak, U.S. Embassy, Tokyo; Shinsaku Sogo, JETRO; Yoshio Taketomi, Japan UNI Agency; Masako Ueda, Japan UNI Agency; Yuki Wakayama, Toshiba public relations; Jon Woronoff, author; Yoichi Yamada, SOHYO international affairs; Fujiya Yamagata, JETRO; Kenzo Yanigada, senior

Acknowledgements

researcher, Fujitsu laboratories; Yasuhisa Yazaki, head assistant to Ms. Nakayama.

The writing of this book would have been impossible without the assistance of many others. While I cannot list everyone who helped, I would like to gratefully acknowledge the contributions of Julie Hall, my principal researcher, who was generous with her time and her many perceptive insights; Belle Ballantyne, who gathered much invaluable research material; Gail Nekunam, who offered hospitality and encouragement. Fred Hahnfeldt was indefatigable and innovative in solving the problems attendant to the electronic transfer of large portions of the manuscript by computer. Nancy Hahnfeldt sacrificed much of her evenings and weekends while keyboarding the remainder of the manuscript.

In Tokyo, Robert Kirshenbaum of Pacific Press Services was unreservedly generous with his time, his staff and his facilities. I am grateful to Noboru Shimizu, Kayoko Kudo and Tomoko Yamamoto for their kindnesses and translation services. Tatsuko Nagasawa was equally generous with much good advice and penetrating insights. Nobuatsu, Tomoko and Kenji Tsutiya provided invaluable favors and introductions. Bob and Lois Paolinelli gave their sage advice and still other introductions. Osamu Sakashita provided assistance in translations and interpreting. Professor John Boccellari and Tetsuro Muto of Tsukuba University were generous with many small favors. Lennie Siegel of Pacific Studies Center offered unrestricted access to his research files.

Contents

1 The Japanese Conspiracy

JAPANESE BUSINESS has come to be universally regarded with a near-mythic mixture of fear and admiration, even envy. Demigods of trade, the Japanese are seen as mysteriously energetic, tirelessly shrewd, part of an irresistible tide. In America, in Europe, Latin America, the Middle East, Southeast Asia, throughout the developed and undeveloped world, the West watches passively as the Japanese seize one market after another.

In scarcely a dozen years Japan has increased its annual exports of high-tech products more than sevenfold, to more than $40 billion. Many estimates, including those by the American Productivity Center and by the Japan Economic Council, predict that Japan will surpass the United States as the world's leading economic power by the year 2000. The JEC, an advisory group to the Prime Minister's Office, has already outlined Japan's conquest in simple terms. By the turn of the century, now barely fifteen years away, the per capita income of the Japanese will be $21,200, compared with only $17,000 in the U.S. and less in Western Europe.

The trade statistics in Japan's favor are startling and growing in awesome proportions each year. In 1970, Japan's balance of payments surplus with the United States was only $1 billion, a meaningless sum to a nation the size of America, then exporting some $150 billion a year to the world. By 1980, the $1 billion had magically mushroomed to $10 billion, a large, significant trade imbalance, but still not one that threatened the economic sanctity of America, or the West.

But within two years, the force of the Japanese export onslaught would be fully felt throughout the world. In 1982, America's trade deficit would rise to $30 billion,

1

most of which – $21 billion – would be with one nation, Japan. Staggered by that red ink, Americans were soon to learn that 1983 would be considerably worse. As Japanese computers, television sets, radios, pharmaceuticals, cameras, cars, video recorders, stereos, bicycles, subway cars, tractors, and motorcycles flooded the American markets, estimates of the 1983 Japanese trade balance with the U.S. – initially $30 billion – rose to $35, even $40 billion and more.

Along with these deficits have come increased unemployment in America and Western Europe, as more and more workers move from assembly to unemployment lines. The Japanese trade surplus accounts for the direct loss of over 1,000,000 American jobs, and as many or more in Western Europe. Ultimately the toll is much greater as the industrial infrastructure of the Western world is weakened.

'No industry is immune from trade deficits,' Alfred E. Eckes, chairman of the U.S. International Trade Commission, warned in August of 1983. Each $1 billion in trade deficits, he reveals, is equal to about 25,000 U.S. jobs lost. 'Problems that have hit footwear, apparel, steel, and autos may soon impact the chemical industry, pharmaceuticals, and other high-technology sectors,' Eckes says. France, Sweden, West Germany, and other European nations are suffering these same trade deficits with Japan as that nation assaults their domestic markets.

Surprisingly, many Americans and Europeans believe that the Japanese deserve their success. Almost four out of five polled by the *Los Angeles Times* in May 1983, felt that the prime reason for the success of Japanese products is 'cheaper labor costs,' followed by superior management. 'Our management is old-fashioned,' is the common complaint. If the Japanese are beating the Western nations, this argument states, it is our own fault. We've been unwilling to work as hard; we demand wages that are too high. After all, our Calvinist consciences mutter, the Japanese demonstrate unrivaled energy and skill; it is no wonder their productivity is the envy of the world. They are shrewd bargainers, but out-maneuvering your opponent has always been the essence of good business. We must learn to do better; we must emulate the Japanese, say many. We need to adopt quality circles and other storied Japanese management techniques.

There is obviously much to be learned from the Japanese. But their skill and productivity, though impressive, is not the major reason for their stunning international success. Behind their massive penetration of foreign markets is a system of business activity which can best be described as *economic totalitarianism*, a government-directed enterprise in which all the energies of Japan have been mobilized to overwhelm the world competition. It is a national conspiracy directed from a central command post, a squat eleven-story building in Central Tokyo, the headquarters of MITI, the Ministry of International Trade and Industry. The elements that comprise the conspiracy come from every facet of Japanese life: unelected bureaucrats; industrialists; *shinko-zaibatsu*, the reconstituted cartels; labor union officials; politicians; and submissive workers. Even co-opted Americans and Europeans contribute to the new power of Japan.

The Japanese themselves have termed their centrally run operation the 'Bureaucratic-Industrial Complex,' one that is becoming as potentially dangerous to world stability as the military-political threat of the Soviet Union. But while Russian dissimulation seems to persuade only the naive, the Japanese have brilliantly disguised their conspiracy in a convincing cloak of free enterprise. They thus confound and confuse those in the West who have become unwitting partners in Japan's economic aggression.

Although Japan now boasts a democratic political system not unlike America's and Western Europe's, its business methods bear little resemblance to free-market capitalism, or even the demisocialist-style capitalism of France, Great Britain, and Italy, which still follow the conventions and ethics of international trade.

Business the Japanese way is unique and often difficult to understand for those not familiar with its nuances. From the Western viewpoint, it regularly flouts the rules of ethical behavior, yielding to the obsessive need to win at any cost. Joseph J. Sullivan, a former employee of Sony, has repeated a telling conversation with Japanese industrialist Akio Morita, president of Sony. 'Sullivan San,' Morita said, 'militarily we could never defeat the United States, but economically we can overcome the United States and become number one in the world.'

Individual Japanese industries are efficient, but not to the degree the world has been led to believe. Much of their advantage is based on unsavory practices. Japan has 'borrowed' or copied foreign technology, or acquired it through joint-venture agreements which it has later disavowed. When this has failed they have resorted to bribery, industrial espionage and outright theft. Its industries often act in concert, as did the prewar Japanese cartels, the *zaibatsu*, targeting their competitors in other nations and dumping their products at a temporary loss in order to win larger and larger shares of the world's markets and eventually achieve monopoly positions. The Japanese educate their scientists and engineers in American and European universities; they then return home to use their new skills in a trade war against those who educated them. Japan, it is now becoming clear, is winning the trade war because it refuses to play by the rules.

The desire to become *itchiban* – No. 1 – has created a tense, uneven, and unfair relationship between Japan and its trading neighbors. Not only does Japan insist on imposing Byzantine import barriers to shield its domestic market from outside competition, but its export trade policies include predatory pricing, secret government subsidies, the targeting of advanced technology industries in America and elsewhere, restrictions on direct foreign investments, and a grossly undervalued currency.

In addition, intervention by MITI forces Japanese firms to 'Buy Japan,' to purchase exclusively from domestic suppliers despite price and quality disadvantages, and to pursue an over-aggressive export policy with the world. On one occasion, a group of Japanese television manufacturers found cheating the U.S. government claimed that MITI had 'compelled' them to do it. These, and still other methods, are at the core of a privately owned but

4

state-directed form of capitalism modeled after a military campaign.

Japan has been portrayed as a worker's paradise in which employees are perpetually grateful to a benevolent management. In fact, Japanese corporations exploit many of their workers, particularly women and millions of temporary and part-time workers who are denied the much-heralded Japanese corporate benefits. Early 'retirement' at age 55 forces skilled, mature workers with inadequate pensions back on the job market, usually starting all over at the bottom. Instead of true labor unions, the Japanese employ 'company unions,' which are used less for collective bargaining than to enforce discipline and boost productivity.

Some in the West – including government leaders who could act to confront this worldwide industrial conspiracy – are reluctant to see our Japanese allies in a negative light. But contemporary history demonstrates that whenever it has been convenient for them, the Japanese have bent, distorted, and abused existing American, European, and Japanese legislation and contractual arrangements in order to gain corporate and national advantage. Where avoidance, obfuscation, and shrewdness have failed, they have lied to achieve the defeat of their industrial partners and to further their quest for what they believe is their national manifest destiny – economic supremacy.

The Japanese industrial conspiracy has numerous layers of complexity, which, as we shall see, involve every aspect of the Japanese and world economy. One is a hypocritical, but effective, policy which insists on free trade for Japan throughout the world, while Japan uses every possible device, from tariffs to truculence, to close its domestic markets. America and the European Economic Community (EEC) have complained, often bitterly, that Japan does not practice what it preaches. Japan's response, for more than twenty years, has been to deny that there are any restrictions, and then to promise to 'liberalize' the particular ones that trading partners point out.

'Trying to move the Japanese on trade is like peeling

an onion,' said William Piez, who directed the U.S. embassy's Tokyo trade office in early 1983. 'You start taking the layers off, but you're never sure if there will be anything inside at the end. The whole thing is a rather zen experience.' Piez was referring to the fact that behind the formal trade barriers that Japan had officially 'lifted,' there is a maze of informal ones, including standards and inspection procedures that crudely, but effectively, block imports.

In 1982, Foreign Minister Yoshio Sakurauchi claimed that 'Japan is one of the most open markets in the world.' A few weeks after that comment was made, the Japanese ambassador to the U.S., Nobuhiko Ushiba, told reporters: 'There is no example in recent history of a nation liberalizing trade policy as fast as Japan.'

The reality is just the opposite. European Economic Community spokesman Gilles Anouilh places it in perspective: 'Japan with a population of 117 million, imports no more manufactured goods than Switzerland, with a population of 6.4 million.' The Japanese answer, sounding ridiculous by contrast, comes from Norishige Hasegawa, chairman of a committee 'to promote' trade with America. 'We're already importing what we need; Parker pens, Cross pencils, and French neckties,' he says with no trace of irony.

Japan's protectionist policy, which insures the basic strength of its domestic industries against fair competition while it assaults foreign markets with its exports, is not an *ad hoc* program. It has been carefully orchestrated by MITI, which by persuasion and arm twisting, manipulates Japan's import and export strategy, down to the behavior of customs officials. 'We enable the Japanese to bring in everything they want when they don't even give us the right of entry,' said Charles L. Nicolosi, an analyst in the New York offices of Dean Witter Reynolds.

As the world's leading manufacturer of automobiles, for example, Japan sells millions of its cars in the U.S. and Europe but imports few. Before a car is shipped to the United States, each Japanese manufacturer certifies that it meets U.S. product and safety standards; America accepts its certifications and freely admits the Japanese imports. But the Japanese view every import into their market as currency lost in the war of trade balances.

In a guerrilla war of harassment, certifications by foreign manufacturers are disregarded by Japanese customs. Every car, every baseball bat, every foreign product attempting entry to Japan is subject to elaborate testing, and those not meeting standards must be reworked to meet them before entry is allowed. The handful of U.S. cars imported in Japan are sometimes virtually rebuilt in Yokohama harbor before leaving the Japanese customs area, a cost born by the importer.

If a foreign product does finally penetrate the protectionist barriers, the Japanese respond with elaborate tactical maneuvers. The cigarette war is an excellent illustration of their ingenuity in blocking imports. Achieving even a minuscule 1.5 percent share of the Japanese cigarette market required American manufacturers to absorb a prohibitive 35 percent tariff. But the official tobacco monopoly was still worried that some Japanese might prefer a foreign cigarette to a cheaper, if inferior, homegrown brand.

A six-page battle plan was issued by the Japanese cigarette industry to thousands of distributors and retailers, detailing such tactics as placing limits on the stocking of foreign brands, actually removing them from small vending machines, and eliminating point-of-purchase displays for foreign cigarettes in prominent locations. Compliance by retailers is assured: the Japan Tobacco and Salt Corporation (JTSC) has absolute control over the licensing and supply of all tobacco products in Japan.

In early 1983, in response to American diplomatic pressures, Japan made a great show of lowering cigarette import duties to 20 percent. But Japan's trade defenses are mobile. Almost immediately after this seeming concession, the price of all cigarettes was uniformly raised by nine cents, wiping out much of the tariff cut's effect on imported cigarettes.

Despite facetious comments about 'Parker pens,' Japan has enormous need for at least one American commodity

– food. It would not only help correct the U.S. trade imbalance, but would be a boon for Japanese consumers, who are victimized by Japan's inefficient agricultural industry. A Tokyo housewife must expect to pay $35 a pound for the best sirloin steak while Japanese 'ranchers,' whose average 'herd' consists of 2.5 cattle, get only 7 percent of that price, or about $2 a pound. The rest of the money is eaten up by an archaic distribution system of as many as two dozen middlemen, most of whom never see a live cow, a beef carcass, or even a raw steak. If a foreign supplier of beef – American, Australian, Argentine, or otherwise – should attempt to maneuver past these legions of middlemen, Japan has a final revetment: import quotas on foreign beef are kept so low that Japanese farmers sell virtually all their production at exorbitant retail prices.

The Japanese face no such restraints in their trade with the West, who openly welcome most Japanese imports because of their price and quality, unaware of the permanent disruption it creates in their economies.

Japan starts out with an enormous advantage in reaching its goal of industrial conquest. Unlike America, Germany, France, the Soviet Union, or Israel, Japan does not pay for most of its own defense. Former U.S. Senator Paul J. Fannin of Arizona calls it a $70-billion-a-year subsidy from the United States, the sum they would spend if we did not protect them from potential aggressors. 'With this tremendous advantage,' says Fannin, 'the Japanese now dominate one after another of our markets. Radio, TV, recorders, small calculators, motorcycles, bicycles, sporting goods, and now the manufacture of automobiles, farm machinery, road equipment and electric generators, is suffering from this subsidized competition.'

World reaction to the Japanese capture of world markets has varied from numbness to shock to impotent outrage, and even despair. Responding to a 1983 poll by Opinion Research Corp. of Princeton, New Jersey, three-fourths of 500 American opinion leaders from business, labor, Congress, academia, and the media stated that

Japanese trading policies systematically violate internationally accepted business and trade practices.

More than two-thirds of Americans surveyed by the *Los Angeles Times* poll said U.S. policy should restrict imports to protect American industry and American jobs. American politicians from the President down have tried to persuade Japan to impose restrictions on its exports and to open their own markets to American goods. But it has been to little avail. The Japanese response has been a cascade of cosmetic changes and a public relations blitz incorporating blithe denials of wrong-doing along with righteous indignation. Japanese trade policy, they maintain, is strictly a matter for the Japanese to decide.

Many Japanese, exultant at their new world prominence, are immune to criticism about their business methods, but some do express anguish over Japan's reputation. 'Our mercantile image has once again been tarnished,' says Kinji Yajima, a retired Tokyo Institute of Technology professor. 'We Japanese are now being regarded as a scheming bunch of villains around the U.S. It will take years for us to improve our image to what it had been before.

Japanese political commentator Akira Sono has warned his fellow Japanese of the friction that their economic war is beginning to generate worldwide. Trade relations between the U.S. and Japan, he says, have deteriorated to the point where 'the Japanese people are reminded of the pre-World War II ABCD (American-British-Chinese-Dutch) encirclement of Japan, and European Community nations are taking an equally high-handed posture.'

This has happened, Sono explained, because 'Japan has been treating foreign products like unwanted stepchildren. Japanese politicians and bureaucrats seem incapable of demonstrating a spirit of fair play. Consumers seldom criticize the economic structure that causes them hardship through high commodity prices. The people cannot appreciate economic democracy because they have not assimilated the political democracy that was forced on them as a result of defeat in war.'

Sono adds: 'Perhaps the Japanese will reach maturity

for the first time when foreign countries shut out Japan's exports. Recent Japan-U.S. relations resemble those of the spring of 1941. The free nations of the world might come to look upon Japan as an outcast. The result might be more disastrous than the defeat in World War II.'

The seriousness of the problem and the need for a Western counterattack to protect its own economic health is the thesis of this book. To understand the dimensions of the problem, we need to see the Japanese conspiracy at work, as it targets one world industry after another for conquest.

2 Green Tea and Dirty Tricks

JAPANESE IS a language well-suited to circumlocution, to airy discourses on subjects seemingly only tangential to the purpose at hand. In spite of this, or perhaps because of it, Japanese businessmen like to talk. They talk endlessly at meetings, often designating junior members to take copious notes of what transpires. To make sure of what was said and how they felt about it at the time, some will return to their offices or homes and confide the meeting's proceedings to their diaries.

At a typical business meeting, much of the early conversation will seem like a vague exercise in polite ambiguity. But after a time everyone present has had a chance to stake out his own, or his department's, or his section's territory. It is done gently, without forcing an opinion on the group. It is only after this exercise that the real conversations take place, with compromise and consensus achieved after long hours of meandering and exceedingly tactful discourse.

From time to time, *o-cha* – Japanese green tea – is served, usually by an attractive, well groomed, perpetually smiling but traditionally mute female functionary. The more complex the issue, the more tea is required. The Japanese chide one another that if what is being discussed involves bargaining, the side that walks away with the best concessions is the one with the most bladder control.

'We don't argue much among ourselves, we rarely have open disagreements,' explained Masayoshi Sakisaka, a London-based marketing executive with Epson, part of the Seiko Group. 'The reason is that we all believe strongly that our point of view is correct, and the other fellow will eventually come to accept it if he just has all the information we have. Therefore we must meet often, and the meetings usually last quite a while.'

Nothing about the meeting at Tokyo's once opulent Palace Hotel, directly across the moat from the emperor's residence, on the warm, smoggy Tokyo afternoon of September 10, 1964, would have seemed unusual. Those attending the meeting were businessmen, most in their late forties or early fifties. All were dressed in conservatively cut Western-style suits of muted blue and gray hues and wore long-sleeved, French-cuffed white shirts, the Japanese corporate uniform. These were powerful men, television manufacturing experts, upper level executives of Japan's six leading consumer electronics manufacturers: Hitachi, Matsushita, Mitsubishi, Sanyo, Sharp, and Toshiba.

Along with their retinues of key assistants, the group met behind closed doors. Tea was served, not, as usual, by the hotel, but by a smiling young woman from one of the companies represented. The meeting went on for nearly three hours before breaking up, still giving most of its participants time to return, in company cars, to offices in distant corners of Tokyo before the evening rush hour paralyzed traffic on the city's narrow streets.

It was a most productive first meeting. Of course, most of the men knew each other; they had gone to the same schools, were of the same age, and had served in similar units and with approximately the same military rank during the Great Pacific War. Over the years they had had a certain amount of contact at electronics industry association meetings. But at this meeting they had an opportunity to learn more about each other's feelings and desires for success, more about each company's management, its business outlook and its future plans. Little was accomplished in a substantive way; what was significant about this gathering of the six leading Japanese television manufacturers was that it took place at all.

The group met again on the 10th of the following month. Now that personal contacts had been solidified, the group moved to business issues, the most important of which was: At what level should they fix the 'bottom' prices of their TV receivers in Japan's domestic markets?

It was a difficult question. A bewildering variety of models was coming off each of the companies' assembly lines, and each firm was a little wary of the others. These firms had been competing for years; several of their parent companies had been competitors for decades. But now their top management, the presidents and chairmen of the giant conglomerates, the new *shinko-zaibatsu*, had secretly agreed that it was better for a time *not* to undersell each other in marketing their television sets, both in Japan and abroad. No longer would one company's models become best sellers while the sets of others sat on the shelf, ignored. The men in the room knew that such management directives were easily made but not readily put into practice. If their collusion was uncovered, the Japan Fair Trade Commission might take action under Japanese law.

But illegal or not, their company leaders had decided to price-fix their merchandise, and it was not up to loyal 'salarymen' – the Japanese executives – to question the decision. Many in the room had already had their say on the matter in meetings with their superiors; now their assignment was to find ways to make it work. It was not merely a matter of pricing. There was also the question of profit margins; each company's costs were somewhat different. They had to smooth out the fluctuations of the marketplace and decide how much profit was to be made on each unit, and how many units each could sell. The participants found the business of price-fixing so complex that they decided to meet at the same hotel every month, on the tenth day. Thus the Tenth Day Group was born.

The Japanese consumer paid dearly for this collusion. The Tenth Day Group was so successful that it and other secret groups of these leading Japanese manufacturers were responsible for maintaining the high prices of TV sets in Japan, which in a few years were selling for almost twice as much as comparable Japanese sets in the United States. A Japanese color set whose 'bottom price' was $700 in Japan would be sold retail for less than $400 in the

United States. The members of the Tenth Day Group had come together for a purpose that was more important for their companies – perhaps, they felt, ultimately more important to the Japanese nation – than the inflated profits the six companies received. In fact, the profits would not line the pockets of the Tenth Day Group or be offered as dividends to Japanese stockholders. The money was to be used secretly to offset the losses that their companies expected to suffer as they drove most of the American television manufacturers out of business.

This astonishingly successful plan, which crippled the American television manufacturing industry, is minutely documented in reports prepared by the Japan Fair Trade Commission (JFTC). The reports are based on the diaries of some of the participants, on the depositions and statements of several of its members, and on minutes of dozens of meetings held by the Tenth Day Group. Later, the record of their actions would become part of a lengthy civil antitrust suit against these Japanese television manufacturers and some of their American distributors.

The Tenth Day Group continued to meet monthly at least through 1977. But despite their intentions, the Tenth Day Group was not able to resolve all the problems. They were continually running into such policy matters as how individual Japanese manufacturers could outwit U.S. Customs officials when they violated American law by exporting their sets at prices far below fair American market value.

These matters were relegated to more senior men who comprised the Palace Group, the managing directors of the six companies. The Palace Group, which usually met monthly at that hotel faced the knotty issues members of the Tenth Day Group could not resolve. To prepare a cogent agenda for the Palace Group, staffers formed the Palace Preparatory Group to screen issues for Palace Group meetings. Their notes and the minutes, like those of the other groups, were to be periodically destroyed.

But some were not. Toshiba's representative, a man named Yajima, failed to destroy all the pages in his notebook, which included this cryptic entry:

To leave women's lockers alone.
To burn old documents.
Will not take minutes. Burn all documents.
Also, change the place of meeting.
Report at the next meeting.
Name get together meeting concerning TV (10th Day
  Group).

The Tenth Day Group, together with the Palace Group
to which it reported, represented Japan's industrial elite,
the largest diversified companies run by Japan's clubby
insiders from firms that traced their corporate roots to
prewar Japan, to the *zaibatsu*, the ruthless industrialists
who wanted Southeast Asia's raw materials and China's
markets so badly they were willing to start a world war.

There was a third arm to the conspiracy, the Okura
Group, also named for the hotel where they met, Tokyo's
prestigious Okura. The group had been formed in 1963 at
the behest of Kinosuke Matsushita, septuagenarian
founder and president of Matsushita Electric Industrial,
often regarded as Japan's most influential businessman.
The Okura Group, which included the managing directors
of these six largest Japanese electronics manufacturing
companies, ratified – or sent back for more study – the
decisions reached after agonizing consensus, and much
green tea, by the other groups. When the Japanese
authorities wondered why these top executives of ostensibly competing electronics firms were meeting so regularly
– and if it was related to the TV models selling in Japan for
outrageously high prices – members of the group cast
about for a plausible story.

'We are a social group,' they would later tell the
Japanese Fair Trade Commission during its investigation.
When the JFTC investigators questioned that response,
they offered the excuse that the group was a private club
of men with similar interests.

The JFTC confiscated mounds of papers, reports,
diaries, and minutes, and then brought in the minor participants for questioning. More deferentially, they asked the
powerful members of the Okura Group to chat, at their

convenience. The JFTC had accumulated an enormous amount of evidence, but in the contemporary Japanese tradition industrialists have extra-legal powers. When the situation looked grim, patriarch Kinosuke Matsushita intervened. 'We apologize,' his embassy told the JFTC. Matsushita had elegantly side-stepped the issue, but the authorities were reassured and the matter was closed. Meanwhile, the American television industry has never recovered from the monthly meetings of the Tenth Day Group.

❊

'Dumping' is a term which has come to mean selling a product in another country for less than its fair market value. FMV is not an esoteric or subjective concept. It can be measured by comparing the prices of indentical or similar products sold in the country of manufacture. Dumping, which is undoubtedly as old as manufacturing, was made illegal in the U.S. in 1916. In 1921, the U.S. Treasury Department was made responsible for assessing special penalty duties on goods believed to have been dumped.

Dumping has historically been practiced by the Japanese – and other nations – as an unethical way of gaining a disproportionately large share of the market. The objective is usually to force domestic companies out of the market by offering imported products to consumers at prices so low that domestic manufacturers cannot match them for long. Domestic competitors are then either forced out of business or must abandon the market as unprofitable. This paves the way for foreign dumpers to dominate it with their own products, whose prices are then gradually increased back to profitable levels.

In 1964, several Japanese companies, including Matsushita, Toshiba, Sharp, Mitsubishi, Sanyo, and Hitachi, began to dump enormous quantities of table model and portable color television sets on U.S. markets at prices so low that no American manufacturer could compete. 'This was just one phase in a stage-by-stage assault on the U.S. markets,' says Arnold I. Kalman, a

Philadelphia attorney who specializes in antitrust and dumping cases. 'You can trace back the Japanese companies which are today involved in the semiconductor business to the companies which were in the business of making TV sets, and before that, radios.'

Kalman's firm, Blank; Rome, Comisky and McCauley, has been representing two American firms, Zenith and National Union Electric (NUE). NUE, makers of no-longer-manufactured Emerson television sets, and Zenith, one of the few remaining American firms in the industry, have pressed a lawsuit alleging that Japanese TV makers conspired with American importers to dump their products in the U.S., to the detriment of the entire American TV industry. Eight American manufacturers, and several smaller firms, were driven out of business with an estimated loss of 70,000 jobs, billions of dollars in profits, and increased American trade deficits.

Zenith is one of America's pioneer electronics manufacturers, and for many years was the leading U.S. maker of color TV sets. In 1977, for example, it sold $957 million worth, about 22 percent of the U.S. market, and employed about 20,000 people to make them in the U.S. Zenith was badly injured as a result of this Japanese dumping. NUE, which still makes Emerson air conditioners, Eureka vacuum cleaners, and Tappan kitchen ranges, among many other products, has abandoned TV manufacture. The lawsuit, filed in 1971, has yet to be tried on issues of merit. In 1981, a federal judge granted summary judgment, dismissing the case against the Japanese defendants, which include all of the companies mentioned above, their U.S. subsidiaries, and several U.S. retailers, on technical grounds. The plaintiffs have appealed that decision and the case is inching its way through the appellate courts.

The assault on the American television market was not just the result of hotel room intrigue. In 1963, high-level representatives of the Japanese TV-manufacturing companies, with the approval of MITI, met publicly to create a legal cartel. The document signed by the participants, including the men who would later become the Tenth

Day, Palace and Okura group members, created the Television Export Council and the Television Export Examination Committee. Their purpose was to regulate the conditions for the sale of TVs in the U.S.

Perhaps the most significant result of their work was the 'check price,' the lowest price, determined by complex calculations, by which a Japanese-made TV set could legally be imported into the U.S. and still avoid a dumping fine. Although the exported sets included hundreds of different color and monochromatic models ranging from five to 18 inches in screen size, models with vacuum tubes, with transistors, and hybrid models with a panoply of technical variants, the cartel managed to reduce all sets to just ten different check prices. As soon as the legal cartel had established their own regulations, the secret industry groups – the Tenth Day, Okura, Palace and others – set out to find ways to circumvent them.

It was archetypical Japanese business behavior. It required numerous meetings and the ingestion of even more tea. The first step was obvious. Every television set exported had to be valued at the check price, the equivalent to fair market value. But it was the manufacturers themselves, through their cartel agreements, who determined those check prices. As part of their long-range plan, they sharply raised their prices in Japan and set them extraordinarily low on sets exported to the U.S.

The American government was typically slow to respond. But in 1970, after millions of cheap Japanese sets had already flooded the American market, the U.S. Treasury Department did ask Matsushita to verify how the domestic price was calculated. Their answer was a model of sophistry. 'We gave out various discounts, rebates, and allowances to each of our distributors, and they were all different, and always changing,' a Matsushita executive told the investigators. 'And we also had to pay some expenses to distribute the sets.' The expense categories listed by Matsushita included selling, warehousing, delivery, office, financial, and administrative expenses, credit terms, bad debt costs, service trailing costs, and payments made to retailers to cover costs for construction of store fixtures, promotional programs, financing, advertising, life insurance for the retailers, and casualty insurance for the stores.

For the American investigators, Matsushita's attorneys produced 70 linear feet of documents for each of Matsushita's 186 distributors, more than two miles of paper. They told the American government that it was difficult to determine the exact costs of their merchandise, but Matsushita and its partners had no trouble calculating them for their Japanese commodity tax returns, a form whose definition of production cost virtually duplicates that of the U.S. Customs statute of fair market value. 'It was a good story,' says attorney Kalman. 'Now, if you buy that one, I have a bridge I would like to sell you.'

Sanyo developed an even more elaborate argument to becloud U.S. investigators, but it, too, was transparently thin. In Japan, where wages are based primarily on seniority, two workers laboring side by side on a TV receiver assembly line might earn very different salaries based on their age. (If one were a woman, of any age, she would earn less than either of the men.) This became the rationale for the Sanyo explanation. They claimed that they used older, experienced workers on domestic models, and paid them more than the younger, less experienced workers who worked on export models. Therefore, they said, it was natural that their domestic sets would sell for more than those that were exported. No one who has ever visited a Japanese TV assembly factory would find this story credible.

With check prices firmly established, the Japanese were ready to start dumping. At the check-price levels, Japanese sets would undercut U.S.-made sets by an average of 40 to 60 percent. But some Japanese conspirators were concerned that it was still not low enough to achieve their objective: the destruction of the American television industry. Perhaps, the Japanese worried, American television manufacturers would compete by cutting profit margins and improving productivity or by going offshore for partial assembly. Since the Japanese were losing money on every set exported to the U.S., it would thus cost more to drive out the competing U.S. companies. The answer to that threat was simple: falsify the U.S. Customs documents. The declared price would have to be at the check price, but they could circumvent the customs procedure by granting a rebate to their U.S. buyers. Since this was illegal, the money would have to be dispensed under the table.

No one can undermine a nation's industry without the cooperation of its own business people. Systematic Japanese dumping in the U.S. required the active participation of American merchants. For the scheme to succeed, importers of lower-than-fair-value (LTFV) goods must cooperate with the dumpers. The Japanese searched for such merchants and rapidly discovered a welcome outlet, 'Where America Shops,' at Sears, Roebuck and Co., the nation's largest retail merchant. Sears apparently was willing to severely bend federal regulations to increase their profits, even if it resulted in the crippling of an American industry. But Sears was not alone; the Japanese eventually sold their dumped color TV sets through some 80 U.S. retailers.

Sears's products are merchandised in nearly 900 retail stores in the U.S. and through over 1,500 catalog sales offices. Sears is also the largest single U.S. importer of television sets. In a 14-year period (1963–1977), the firm imported over 6.5 million television receivers from Japan worth more than $700 million. In fact, between 1960 and 1975, Sears sold over 60 percent of all the Japanese color television sets produced for export. But why would Sears get involved in such a scheme? 'Sears's motive was the enormous price advantage it obtained,' says Kalman. 'Sears admitted in its brief that it negotiated substantially lower prices with Sanyo and Toshiba. These prices, Sears conceded, gave it a "definite price advantage" over other U.S. sellers who did not participate in the conspiracy.'

Japanese prices were set so low that over the years Sears eagerly bought an increasing percentage of its television receivers from Sanyo and Toshiba. Between 1963 and 1975, these Japanese brands crowded Sears display cases, replacing American-made sets, particularly those manufactured by Warwick Electronics, a regular supplier of Sears. In a legal brief Warwick's management filed with the Securities and Exchange Commission, Warwick – which had once supplied Sears with most of its TV sets – attributed its loss of Sears's business to the predatory pricing of sets made by Toshiba and Sanyo. Soon after Sears stopped buying its products, Warwick went out of business, its assets purchased by Sanyo at liquidation prices.

Many of the Japanese sets were being sold with American labels. Beginning in 1963, Sears began retailing Sanyo and Toshiba TV sets as Sears's private brand at heavily discounted prices. The sets were being sold below even their check prices, though the documents filed with the U.S. Customs indicated otherwise. A Sears senior buyer, Jerome Brennan, wrote a memo to his bosses describing exactly how the Japanese manufacturers had colluded on pricing levels, acknowledging that virtually every Japanese TV exporter was involved in the scheme. Brennan's memo outlined the method by which funds were transferred back to the U.S. wholesale buyers.

A handwritten note about a telephone call to Tokyo made by Mr. Ijima at Toshiba asks if U.S. Customs agents were questioning Sanyo executives about double invoicing:

> *Toshiba Murao says he heard* CUSTOMS *was questioning* SANYO *on double invoicing?*
> SANYO TOP LEVEL SAYS NO – not at present time. Sanyo feels we should wait on divulging system. Trigger off new investigation last for years.
> *Very dangerous – would re-open whole new case.*
> Sanyo feels Customs already knows of double invoicing and would gain nothing – tell truth when asked.
> *RE: Toshiba – will we have to divulge how we over and underbill with them – would we have to reveal system if asked by customs?*

Files subpoenaed from several other American importers described the Japanese methods. Sanyo had devised a 'loyalty discount' formula in order to disguise their rebates, a formula found in Sears's files, as well as in those of General Electric and Magnavox. Sears was apparently aware that the scheme was common to all of Sanyo's U.S. customers. Handwritten notes from Sears's buyer Brennan spelled it out: 'Sanyo already using procedure with all other customers.'

Midland, another retailer that purchased TV sets from the Japanese, wrote a letter to Sharp in 1968:

> As you know, we are buying television sets from different manufacturers in Japan. We have talked to you and other manufacturers about how we can receive the money that is owed to Midland because of the pricing of television sets. The manufacturers that we have talked to have proposed to us to rebate this money to us in the United States if we would sign the enclosed agreement. We have signed this agreement with different manufacturers, and they have already started rebating money to us in the United States.

The rebate money found its way back to the U.S. in devious, if not original, ways. Sears was receiving some of its secret rebate money from Japan through a Swiss bank. In 1971, Sanyo established a special numbered account with Swiss Banking Corporation in Basel, the picturesque financial capital on the Swiss Rhine. Starting in January of that year Sanyo deposited monthly checks to its Swiss account, usually in excess of $150,000, and reaching as high as $420,000. A few days after each deposit, the Swiss bank's New York office would issue a check in an identical amount to Sears. Sanyo's name never appeared on the checks drawn in the U.S., but an emissary from Sanyo personally delivered each check to Jerome Brennan, the Sears buyer. In court documents, Brennan admitted that he deposited a check in a special Sears account created for these funds. Toshiba, Matsushita, and NEC used similar techniques with each of their U.S. importers.

The use of a Swiss bank intermediary was romantic, but some Japanese firms were more direct in their payoffs. Toshiba offset some of Sears's 'overpayments' simply by giving Sears credits on other merchandise it purchased. By 1968 the arrangements were in danger of being discovered by U.S. Treasury agents, who were responding to dumping complaints by American manufacturers. The investigation also prompted discussion among the Japanese television suppliers at their trade association, the Electronics Industry Association of Japan (EIAJ).

Since the Japanese had artificially inflated the prices of television sets sold in Japan, American TV manufacturers reasoned that they could recoup some of their losses by competing in the Japanese market, where domestic sets sold for twice as much as their American counterparts. But the Americans had yielded to the Occidental temptation to underestimate the Japanese.

When Zenith attempted to market TV sets in Japan in 1961, MITI became sorely displeased. Zenith first enlisted two major Japanese trading companies, C. Itoh and Nichimen, but neither was able to get MITI permission to export dollars to buy the U.S. products. In 1963, Zenith tried again, and Nichimen spent a sizable Zenith budget for advertising and publicity in the hope of selling a mere 500 sets. Nichimen reported back that although they had tried hard, the Japanese manufacturers had asked MITI to intervene against Zenith.

According to a report by the office of the U.S. Comptroller General, MITI had pressured Japan's leading department and appliance store chains and had jawboned Nichimen 'not to indulge too aggressively in the distribution of Zenith Products.' The ministry's implicit power soon became evident. In 1975, when Japan sold 5.5 million of its own overpriced sets in its domestic markets, it imported only 11,644 sets, or two-tenths of one percent. By 1978, the Japanese purchase of imported sets was down to 485 units, less than the number many individual Sears stores sell in one year.

Another major American company, Motorola, also became involved with the Japanese TV dumpers, to their chagrin. In recent years Motorola has spent millions advertising its competitiveness with Japan, accurately pointing out that Japan's trade policies are unfair and ethically dubious. A recent two-page Motorola advertisement proclaims, 'When Japan Waives the Rules, Japan Rules the Waves.' The text castigates Japan for 'extreme protectionism at home and collective efforts permitting targeting abroad.' The chief executive officer of Motorola, Robert Galvin, has been active in speaking on this theme to the government and industry groups. 'Motorola finally got religion,' says Arnold Kalman, 'but they sure got it late.'

Motorola, now the largest of America's dwindling roster of semiconductor manufacturers, has long been a leading U.S. producer of consumer electronics, including TV sets. Motorola established a branch office in Tokyo in 1959 at the dawning of Japan's reemergence as a powerful industrial nation. This first office evolved into Motorola Service Company, Ltd. Later, Motorola formed a second Japanese subsidiary, Motorola Semiconductor of Japan, Ltd., and joined with Alps, a relatively small Japanese concern, in a joint venture known as Alps-Motorola.

In 1973, Motorola was hoping to conclude a deal with Aiwa to sell color television sets in Japan. Aiwa, a smallish company controlled by Sony, proudly announced it would market Motorola's big Quasar color consoles, made by the American company in Japan, to retail at 330,000 yen, or about $1,500. It was an attractive price alongside comparable models which Japan Victor and Matsushita were then selling for between 480,000 and 570,000 yen. But rival Matsushita, an enormously influential firm in Japan, decided that such a large American company as Motorola could not be permitted to gain a toehold in Japan's protected markets. The presence of an American company selling sets to Japanese consumers for less than inflated Japanese prices would not only endanger their high domestic prices but expose them to dumping charges in the U.S. Somehow, Motorola must be stopped. It was accomplished through an offer Motorola could not refuse.

In March 1974, Matsushita purchased Motorola's

Japanese television manufacturing interests for $100 million in return for which Motorola agreed to abandon all its television manufacturing, including its plants in both the U.S. and Taiwan. Matsushita and Motorola announced plans to jointly pursue other ventures in 'growth industries' at a later date. Motorola had received a sizable sum for a business that was only marginally profitable, and Matsushita had eliminated its only possible American competitor in Japan.

When the Japanese TV makers held their first clandestine meetings at the Palace and Okura hotels, Japanese imports accounted for less than 5 percent of U.S. television sales. By 1971, the U.S. Tariff Commission noted, the Japanese cartel-member companies controlled more than half the U.S. market. They had driven ten American TV makers out of business by denying them profits, simultaneously destroying tens of thousands of American jobs.

John J. Nevin, former head of Zenith and now chairman of the board of Firestone, is vocal in his anger at both the Japanese television industry for its deceit and at the American government for failing to stop the illegal practice. He outlines the catastrophic results of this Japanese dumping conspiracy on American television manufacturers.

'Five of America's best-known television manufacturers were forced into acquisitions or liquidation. I told the [Los Angeles] grand jury that about 60,000 or 70,000 American jobs had disappeared,' Nevin explained when interviewed. 'All the scholars want to talk about "the dumb American management." Let me tell you what really happened in the American TV industry as a result of the Japanese dumping. First of all, Admiral went belly-up or was on the verge of going belly-up, when it was bought by North American Rockwell, a really first-rate firm. They have to liquidate Admiral about two years later. They lost so much money they can't keep it going. Ford Motor Company buys Philco, and they liquidate Philco. Motorola, which is the leading U.S. semiconductor manufacturer, sells its television business to Matsushita and goes to the Justice Department and says, "If this sale isn't permitted, we will shut down the business, we can't make money in it." So that's Motorola being acquired, Admiral and Philco going out of business.

'At the time of the Motorola acquisition, Magnavox is also in trouble. They sell out to Phillips. Phillips is *the* dominant television and electronics manufacturer in Europe, and they have got an enormous position elsewhere in the world, except in Japan. They buy Magnavox, and after about three years, they go to the Justice Department along with GTE-Sylvania. They say to the Justice Department, "If you won't let Sylvania and Magnavox merge [which the Justice Department ultimately did], both the businesses will have to be shut down." GTE-Sylvania, an American company, Phillips an international company, are both top-flight, yet they can't compete in the face of this Japanese dumping.

'In the 1960s Sears was buying its television sets from Warwick,' Nevin continues. 'Warwick, in turn, is an affiliate of Whirlpool, the company which supplies Sears with all of their washers and dryers. Sears at this point in time also begins to buy television sets from Japan, principally from Sanyo, and they start forcing Warwick to meet the Sanyo prices. And that forces Warwick into very serious financial trouble. They ultimately work out a deal where Sanyo buys the Warwick assets from Whirlpool. So in effect, of all the U.S. television producers who were in place in early 1970s when color television was invented, three survived: Zenith, RCA and General Electric. GE's survival was by accident. They tried to merge their TV division with Hitachi, and the U.S. government wouldn't let them.

'In the middle seventies, RCA took such enormous losses in their television business it would have forced a Zenith, or anybody else, out of business. But RCA is receiving license and technical agreement payments from the Japanese that exceed their U.S. television manufacturing profit. RCA had decided to sell their technology and know-how for television to the Japanese, and they entered into license agreements that provided them with an enormous flow of revenue. That's why, through this whole row, you've got everybody else in the U.S. television industry screaming like hell except RCA.

'The bottom line today is that as a result of this, the smaller companies were bankrupted, forced out of business or forced to sell out to the Japanese, and that a whole mass of jobs has disappeared from the U.S. Zenith was the single undiversified company that managed to survive,' Nevin says.

Nevin is convinced that MITI was aware of, and probably involved in, the plot to destroy the American television industry. He believes that it was regular custom for most major Japanese television manufacturers to offer rebates to American distributors, part of what he calls 'phony billing.' 'Now, you only reach one of two conclusions from that,' says Nevin. 'Either the Japanese companies conspired to avoid the Japanese law, which stated that any individual Japanese company which violated the check prices was subject to enormous fines, and kept all of this a secret from MITI. Or, the other, more logical conclusion is that MITI knew exactly what the hell they were doing all along, just like the American buyer and the Japanese seller did. You can't have a market in which purchasing agents expect to buy at check prices with a big rebate and not have the ministry know what's going on. You've got to conclude that MITI knew all the time that these check prices were not the basis of actual transactions, but were really false prices that were simply submitted to U.S. Customs.'

Nevin sees the Japanese television collusion as one designed to protect the high prices of sets sold in Japan itself. 'Let me give you another little number, in terms of conspiracy,' Nevin says. 'There are three major Japanese television companies that built plants on Taiwan. They did that to get major labor cost savings, which is legitimate. Yet there is no record of any television set made by a Japanese company in Taiwan ever going back into Japan. In other words, keeping the price high in Japan so you can sell at low prices overseas is the name of the game.

Console television sets, the big 25-inch furniture sets, sell for $2,000 to $2,500 in Japan, three times what they sell for here. Now Matsushita buys Motorola, Sanyo buys Warwick, Sony creates color TV plants in the U.S., yet *no* Japanese TV manufacturer who is making console TV receivers to sell in the U.S. market for $800 or $600 ever ships one into Japan to compete with the $2,500 prices there. Conventional wisdom says the reason Zenith didn't sell in Japan is it didn't try hard enough and its executives didn't speak Japanese. That's obviously ridiculous. The Japanese companies didn't ship TV sets back to Japan, and the reason they didn't is there is no interest in breaking the price fix over there.'

Nevin's rancor is equally directed at the government of the United States, which refused to enforce the law against Japan until it was too late. 'The three years between the submission of the dumping complaint in 1968 and the Tariff Commission's injury finding in 1971 were years of financial crisis for American television makers,' Nevin points out. 'In 1968, nine of the 16 American companies lost money. In 1969, eight of the remaining 15 U.S. producers lost money. In 1970, ten of the 15 lost money.

'In 1974 and again in 1975, the U.S. trade deficit with Japan totaled $1.7 billion. In 1976, the deficit rose to $5.4 billion, and in 1977 $8.1 billion; in 1978 it totaled $11.6 billion,' Nevin states. 'Apparently Americans have been led to believe this was a result of the superior Japanese productivity. It wasn't. It was because the Japanese had been able to violate American antidumping statutes with impunity for more than a decade.

'The television dumping case,' Nevin continues, 'provided instances in which the U.S. Treasury itself has been as deceitful as the importers and as responsible as they for long delays in the enforcement of the law. In 1977 the customs service finds out that there's fraud. And they go out and start a major investigation. They know there's massive fraud and President Carter signs an agreement with the Japanese limiting television imports. *Secretly* they tell the Japanese that they will stop the ITC investigation of customs fraud and of dumping and that the Department of Justice – and this is incredible – will remove itself from any investigations of antitrust activities that are associated with dumping, because dumping is Treasury's prerogative.'

This covert American promise to the Japanese is contained in a letter dated May 20, 1977, over the signature of U.S. Ambassador Robert S. Strauss to Fumihiko Togo, Ambassador Extraordinary and Plenipotentiary of Japan. 'That letter was read into the Congressional Record because Danny Rostenkowski, who was then on the Trade subcommittee, asked Strauss during his testimony if it was true that such a letter existed,' Nevin says. 'The only reason Rostenkowski found out the letter existed is that when the Japanese protested the dumping assessments, they described them as being completely inconsistent with the side letter given the government of Japan by the government of the United States. So the Japanese blew their own cover.'

Nevin does not believe the federal government gave American corporations a fair hearing, a deficiency he attributes to the government in general, and to certain individual federal employees involved in the Japanese television case. Joseph S. Wright, Nevin's successor as chairman of Zenith, has made public a letter from the U.S. Embassy in Tokyo to a high official in the U.S. State Department in 1978. The revealing document, which supports Nevin's contention, reads as follows:

'On June 8 I had dinner with an official from MITI's [Ministry of International Trade and Industry of the Government of Japan] American Bureau.

'I congratulated him on his part in devising the GOJ [Government of Japan] negotiating tactics and scenario on the color TV dumping issues in late March and described to him our perceptions of the tactics (see my June 1 memo to you).

'He accepted the compliment and confirmed that the tactics were as I described them. He added that MITI, the Ministry of Foreign Affairs, and the Japanese TV industry had met for two days solid in March – with sessions extending late at night, to develop tactics. They were not very confident that they would succeed, he said, but they were very happy with the outcome. He ascribed the GOJ [Government of Japan] success to approaches to the most senior USG [U.S. Government] trade policy officials, who could then make a "political decision." '

On a larger scale, Nevin believes the American government's attitude toward the Japanese is based on an unsophisticated reaction dating back a generation in American history, and not updated by contemporary reality. As Nevin has stated: 'The attitudes of American leaders on foreign trade questions continue to be based on a Marshall Plan mentality that sees Europe and Japan as being so weak in economic matters as to require continuing American concessions and that sees the United States as so strong as to be immune to economic injury no matter what trade concessions are made by its government.' He summarized the government's handling of the TV dumping case as 'only one example of the American government's willingness to wink at unfair and unlawful acts in foreign trade in order to avoid diplomatic confrontation.'

In trying to determine the actual value of the millions of dumped sets, U.S. investigators spent several years exploring a labyrinth of blind alleys, hobbled by the uncooperative Japanese as their guides. The U.S. Customs Service had finally found the Japanese guilty of dumping. In an internal memo they stated: 'The U.S. Customs Service has at present in its possession documented evidence that Japanese producers of television receivers in concert with certain U.S. purchasers, have engaged in double-invoicing to circumvent the provisions of the U.S. anti-dumping statutes.' In setting the fine, the investigators gave up trying to determine the fair market value price of each dumped set, and, with misgivings, accepted the check price, which at a conservative estimate represented about half the actual cost of manufacture and export, as their benchmark. Using that as a basis for calculating the extent of the damage, customs officials assessed an $800 million duty on the Japanese companies, covering all color TV dumping from 1964 through 1979.

It was an admirable attempt at restitution, but it was not a practical fine in a world in which the Japanese have economically intimidated major nations. In 1980, officials in the Commerce Department, which had inherited the case from Treasury during the Carter Administration, reduced these duties to a mere $67 million, plus an $11 million fine. The relatively small settlement has been challenged by both American and Japanese TV manufacturers, and will likely drag on in the U.S. courts for years, though it seems the U.S. is apparently bound to uphold the $67 million sum.

There are American participants as well in this economic tragedy, companies whose greed made them willing collaborators in this grandiose, and successful, scheme. In March 1979, Alexander's, Inc., the department store chain, pleaded guilty in New York City to U.S. Customs fraud, the first conviction of a U.S. importer in the Japanese dumping scandal. According to David W. O'Connor, the federal prosecutor, Alexander's received 13 shipments of about 2,000 TV sets each, which were marketed under Alexander's private brand name. All were manufactured in Japan by General Corp., which according to court documents secretly rebated $25 of the declared $72 wholesale price on each set.

The major American perpetrator allegedly was Sears, Roebuck, which the U.S. government is currently prosecuting. On February 26, 1980, a federal grand jury indicted Sears for conspiracy and 12 counts of customs fraud in filing false documents on TV sets Sears bought from Sanyo and Toshiba. 'The case first came to court in June 1980,' explains U.S. government attorney Herb Hoffman, who prepared the case against Sears in Los Angeles. 'Sears's pretrial motions to dismiss the indictment were denied in October of 1980, and Sears appealed these rulings to the Ninth Circuit, which stayed the case until March of 1981, when the government's case was argued. In May, the Ninth Circuit upheld the ruling, and the case was scheduled to be tried in June of 1981. In the meantime, because the first judge had removed himself from the case without stating a reason, a new judge was appointed. On the first day of trial, Sears renewed the same motions they had earlier made. The new judge granted a motion to dismiss the indictment.

'This case has been pending since June 1981, over two years in a pretrial case,' Hoffman explains. 'It is going to be very difficult to put this together for the trial, three years after we indicted, over ten years after all this occurred. The witnesses are going to claim lack of recollection – it's going to be difficult. There are old witnesses, some with health problems, and that sort of thing. Delay always works in favor of the defendant because the burden of proof is on the government. We're waiting to see what the Ninth Circuit does, and we sent them a letter that any further delay puts our case in jeopardy. But my intention is to go forward with it. I feel that strongly about it. I'm not going to drop it. I'm going to give it my best shot.'

Hoffman's persistence may soon be rewarded. In September 1983, the Ninth U.S. Court of Appeals reinstated the criminal charges against Sears, Roebuck, which, the government claims, concealed rebates from Japanese manufacturers from June 1968 to August 1972, and also filed 12 falsified customs declarations between December 1974 and July 1975.

But in the final analysis, the Big Six conspirators of the Tenth Day Group have had their way. Amortised over the 15 years that the Japanese firms dumped sets in America, the $78-million fine, which they have yet to pay in full, amounts to much less per company than the kickbacks Sanyo gave to Sears through their Swiss bank in only one year. For a petty cash expenditure, and the ingestion of considerable amounts of tea, Japan had taken another major American industry.

The television conspiracy was an elaborate case of destroying the enemy by dumping. Japan does not have an exclusive franchise on dumping, but it is clearly the one country in the capitalist world that does it systematically. 'You want to know about Japanese dumping?' asks Stuart Chemtob, an attorney in the Foreign Commerce Section of the U.S. Justice Department. 'Here's a partial list of Japanese commodities or products which have antidumping findings and orders in effect.' He began to read:

'Spun acrylic yarn
Birch 3-ply doorskins
Melamine in crystal form
Ferrite Cores (type used in consumer electronic
    products)
Television receiving sets
Roller chain
Portable electric typewriters
Carbon steel plate
Fish netting
Large power transformers
Pipe and tubing . . .'

The full list is current through only October, 1982, but it itemizes 28 separate incidents of Japanese dumping. In the dumping of steel, an activity that has made depression towns of several once-thriving American communities, the Japanese trading firm Mitsui is a leading culprit. On July 21, 1982, 'Mitsui pleaded guilty to 21 counts, 20 of them substantive, and one count of conspiracy,' explains Herb Hoffman, who pressed the government case. Mitsui, federal investigators agree, was only the latest 'big' offender; Japanese steel dumping had been going on for a long time before Herb Hoffman caught up with Mitsui. On Stuart Chemtob's list of 28 confirmed dumping incidents, there are five other steel product dumping orders in effect, and undoubtedly many more have escaped prosecution.

Japan began a systematic program of dumping steel in the U.S. in the early 1970s. The goal was the same as that of Japan's TV manufacturers: to drive American competition out of business by selling their steel cheaper than

U.S. makers could afford to price theirs. In 1971 Japanese steel imports into the U.S. reached 18.3 million tons, all of it at the expense of U.S. steelmakers. When they complained to the federal government, the Japanese agreed to a 'voluntary' curtailment of steel imports. A Trigger Price Mechanism (TPM), a list of minimum prices for imported steel, was established by U.S. authorities. Once again the federal regulation was a challenge to the ingenious Japanese, who found ways to circumvent it.

In Detroit, in 1973, a customs inspector intercepted a shipment of steel coil valued at $1 million that had supposedly been produced in Canada. When the inspector examined a few coils, he noticed that the stenciled weight on each coil was marked in kilograms. It was obvious that the claim was false: Canada, like the U.S., uses pounds to measure such products, while Japan uses kilos.

About the same time, other customs inspectors reported that shipments of steel entering the country from both Canada and Mexico had been marked with Japanese lettering. Through a London broker, a New York importer purchased flat-rolled steel sheets ostensibly made in Taiwan; but at the time, Taiwan had no rolling mills. 'It reminds me of the story about the woman who found a fish in her milk,' a Bethlehem Steel executive angrily commented. 'She couldn't prove anyone had watered the milk, but then how else would the fish have gotten there?'

This infraction took place in 1973, when the U.S. steel industry was still comparatively strong. Today it is a rusting hulk. Dozens of steel mills and blast furnaces have been torn down and 300,000 American steelworkers are unemployed. Even with its reduced capacity, the U.S. industry is operating at only a 60 percent level.

Mitsui, whose 1981 total worldwide sales were $45 billion, began their illegal campaign to evade the trigger price sometime late in 1977. Their strategy was simple: They listed the steel's price on customs declarations at just above the TPM, then arranged under-the-table kickbacks to their U.S. buyers, the same technique used in the television conspiracy. As a major Japanese trading company which sells a variety of products, Mitsui does not manufacture steel, yet it handles some 40 percent of all Japanese steel sold in the U.S. 'Mitsui has ten offices in the U.S. and each has a steel department with between two and seven people working in it,' Hoffman points out.

Dumping is an effective technique for a nation like Japan which is unencumbered by Western notions of business morality. Cases are hard to prove because most of the documents needed are buried in the files of the domestic buyers, who are not anxious to admit they have benefited from unscrupulous Japanese tactics. But after Hoffman started his investigation in 1980, he learned how to make these vital pieces of paper appear almost magically.

'I brought officials or employees of Mitsui's customer companies before grand juries, or I sent customs agents to their offices on informal visits to question them,' Hoffman reveals. 'This became an embarrassment for Mitsui. After a customer has been before a grand jury or has a couple of agents drop over and question him about Mitsui's pricing, they tend to avoid buying from Mitsui.'

Using promises of immunity from prosecution, Hoffman's investigators built a case against Mitsui; the evidence was the testimony and files of companies that had received kickbacks. Faced with this evidence, Mitsui pleaded guilty to 20 counts of filing fictitious invoices and one count of conspiracy. The criminal penalty was $210,000, or $10,000 per count, the maximum the law allows. But Mitsui also agreed to pay $11 million in dumping penalties, the heaviest fines levied in the 194-year history of the U.S. Customs Service.

A few months later, Hoffman's office struck again, this time against Marubeni, another large Japanese trading company. 'Marubeni was the company that actually paid the $2 million in bribes to [former Japanese Prime Minister Kakuei] Tanaka in the Lockheed case,' remembers Hoffman. Marubeni had also been convicted a few years earlier in connection with the Alaska Pipeline project, when they distributed bribes to get their bids accepted. Hitachi Cable Ltd. was convicted in the same case. During that investigation, the U.S. government developed an informant inside Marubeni who told the

U.S. attorney he thought Marubeni was also filing false customs invoices on steel.

'Marubeni operated a little differently than Mitsui,' Hoffman continues. 'National Can Company was purchasing two types of products from Marubeni, tin plate and aluminum. White tin plate was covered by TPM regulations, aluminum was not. Therefore, Marubeni fictitiously increased their prices on tin plate to get it above the TPM, and offset it by charging decreased prices on the aluminum. This went on for months until customs went in and told National Can they'd like to talk about it.'

A grand jury investigation followed, and in October 1982 Marubeni and National Can agreed to negotiate. Marubeni pleaded guilty to ten counts, National Can to one. The fines were again the maximum, $10,000 per count. 'Marubeni also agreed to pay $2 million in civil penalties,' said Hoffman. 'But even at that price, it doesn't seem to be much of a deterrent. Perhaps the law should be changed to allow some kind of suspension of all trade in cases like these.'

The Japanese, a strongly law-abiding people at home, seem unconcerned about the laws, rules, and conventions of Westerners. In August, the U.S. Commerce department ruled that 59,000 Japanese pagers, small portable radio receivers used to call people to a telephone, were sold at unfairly low prices. The pagers, made by Matsushita and NEC, were valued at $7 million. In 1979, the Japanese firm Pioneer Electric was fined $2.9 million by the European Common Market's Court of Justice in Luxembourg for secretly establishing a protected market for its consumer electronics products in France. Pioneer's marketing arms in England and France had sought to block the imports of lower-priced competitive goods made in Germany and England. In May, 1983, after reviewing a petition from Kaiser Cement Corporation, the U.S. Commerce Department ruled that Japanese-made cement was being sold in Oakland, California at less than fair value.

One of the most attractive targets for classic Japanese marketing techniques has been the portable typewriter.

In 1973, there were four American manufacturers of portable electric typewriters, employing some 25,000 people. Shortly after, the Japanese targeted this market. In 1974, U.S. Treasury Department officials ruled that Japanese portable typewriters were being sold at less than fair market value. But the following year, the ITC ruled that Smith-Corona, which had brought the complaint, had not been injured by the dumping. Between 1976 and 1978 Japanese-made portables doubled in annual volume to 500,000, and in 1979, Sears, Roebuck dropped Smith-Corona as its principal supplier in favor of Japanese firms.

In 1980 the Commerce Department finally agreed that SCM had been injured and set antidumping tariffs of between 36.5 percent and 48.7 percent. Following that, Brother and Silver Seiko, two leading Japanese typewriter makers, appealed the Commerce decision, claiming to have since raised their prices to competitive levels. In August, Commerce lowered the tariffs to between 4.3 percent and 14.9 percent. Smith-Corona appealed. So did Japan, claiming there should be no dumping tariffs at all.

Annual imports of Japanese typewriters into the U.S. grew from 144,000 in 1971 to 603,000 in 1981. Between 1973 and 1980, the Western competition – Olympia, Royal, and Underwood – were forced to buy or assemble their typewriters in Japan, Taiwan, and other countries. It had taken the U.S. government five irreplaceable years to decide that SCM was being injured, but by that time it was too late. Twenty-one thousand American jobs were permanently lost.

Stanford Ovshinsky is a brilliant inventor whose work in optical electronics rates an entry in *Webster's New Collegiate Dictionary* under a newly coined word, *Ovonics*. In 1970 Ovshinsky patented a remarkable system for storing data on a computer memory disk. Using a laser, the Ovshinsky device can place 100 times as much information into the same space as conventional magnetic storage methods, and it can be erased or changed at will. Even though IBM was not sure what products might result from the process, in 1972 it bought a license from Ovshinsky's company, Energy Conversion Devices. ECD is a small firm based in Troy, Michigan, primarily devoted to R&D. It has fewer than 300 employees and less than $21 million in sales, but it has been very active in licensing Japanese companies and in forming joint ventures with them.

'We've had very good relationships in Japan up to now,' explains Larry Norris, a senior VP with Ovshinsky's firm. 'We have a joint venture with Sharp Corporation in the field of photovoltaics, which is now in production making solar electric cells from our amorphous silicon technology. And we're now going into calculators. We have several Japanese licensees with a chemical company and Fuji. We also have a Japanese subsidiary, and a wide range of business associates, partners, and licensees. In fact we have more business in Japan than we have in the U.S.'

In April 1983, Ovshinsky was shaken to see an elegant press kit distributed by Matsushita, a $45-billion-a-year conglomerate which proudly claimed that it had produced 'an erasable optical disk for the first time in the world.' Ovshinsky's firm promptly filed suit. 'IBM is a licensee under this patent which is being infringed by Matsushita,' says Norris. 'IBM did the right thing. In 1972 it took out an insurance policy and put it in the bank. "If we ever use the process, we'll pay you a royalty," they told us.' In Norris's opinion, 'Matsushita went ahead and just grabbed it without paying us a cent.'

But why would a giant company like Matsushita just take someone's technology? Norris has no theory. 'I can't understand this behavior. They've invested a lot of money in development, probably as much as $100 million. Then to go out and jeopardize the whole damn thing by just blatantly infringing somebody's patent – to me it doesn't represent rational business behavior. It's stupid.'

But in Tokyo, Shigeki Hijino does have a theory to explain Matsushita's behavior. Hijino is the 42-year-old editor-in-chief of *Britannica International Yearbook* and a prominent social critic. 'Matsushita is an octopus. Everybody knows it. It's just out to grab whatever it can,' he says.

Norris of Energy Conversion Devices is still shaking his head. 'We took a very aggressive stance. A small company like us could have written them a letter and gotten into their corporate bureaucracy, and we could have been there for ten years, and they would just put us on hold. Maybe that's what they were relying on,' Norris says. 'Stan wasn't going to be put in a position like that. That's why we filed our lawsuit, and held a big press conference. They were stunned.'

A few weeks later, Ovshinsky and Norris went to Congress to testify about the case before the Dingle Committee. 'We talked for an hour, and Matsushita got raked over the coals,' recalls Norris. 'I'm sure that they didn't think that a little company of two or three hundred people was going to give them that kind of anguish. Maybe they're in a mood to talk business, now that we have their attention.'

They do seem to have captured Matsushita's attention. While Matsushita continues to publicly deny that it has done anything wrong, they have initiated talks with ECD, and Ovshinsky has gone to Japan to negotiate with the giant electronics firm. 'We've got a patent infringement case and if they take a license from us on reasonable terms, that should settle the matter,' says Norris. If Matsushita does not agree to terms, however, it could take a long time for Ovshinsky's firm to get anything out of Matsushita. Japan has comparatively few courts and only 11,000 lawyers in the entire nation. Their judges have caseloads five or six times heavier than those of U.S. federal district judges, which makes litigation an impractical avenue for corporate redress.

One of the most popular components in home computers is a chip called the Z80, developed in 1976 by Federico Faggin, one of the maverick geniuses of America's Silicon Valley. Faggin founded Zilog to manufacture the chip, and after a few years sold his company to Exxon, returning to devote more time to his research. As personal computers rose in popularity, more and more manufacturers chose the Z80 as the CPU or 'brain' of their computers. Zilog licensed three companies, including Sharp in Japan, to make the Z80 and collected a small royalty on each Z80 chip these companies sold. Several of the newest home computers are being produced by such Japanese companies as Nippon Electric Company (NEC), SORD, Fujitsu, Sony and Hitachi, and many of them have chosen to use the Z80. This chip allows software manufacturers to easily adapt many programs written for other, mostly American, computers.

In early 1983 Zilog came upon a new chip called the PD 780 produced by NEC, which was becoming a best-seller in Japan's awakening home computer markets. When Zilog took the chip apart and examined it carefully, it seemed to be an identical copy of the Z80. 'There are three legitimate alternative sources – companies we licensed – for the Z80. But we are contending that NEC, which is now rivaling us for market share, is illegally producing our chip,' says an angry Chuck Signor, spokesman for Zilog, which has sued NEC in the U.S. federal court. 'They just went out and copied the chip and it's selling like crazy – mainly in the Japanese markets, but now also in the U.S.,' Signor claims.

The Japanese are skilled, and noted, for 'reverse engineering,' taking someone else's product apart to see how it works, then building something that does virtually the same thing as the original. 'They have their top engineers, maybe the best 5 percent of their force, working on nothing but reverse engineering,' claims Ronald N. Billings, an American who has worked in the Japanese computer industry for 14 years and is now a consultant to Nihon Soft Bank, Japan's largest software company. Apparently the technique is legal, or almost so. 'It's a tricky business because historically reverse engineering has been considered a valid situation, even on patentable areas,' says Zilog's Signor. 'A person opens your chip and looks at it and tests it and tries it out. Then he goes to his R&D people and says, "Can you put out a chip that does the same thing?" They start from scratch and they go do it. That's considered allowable in this business.'

The problem, says Signor, is that he is convinced that the NEC chip is not a product of reverse engineering. 'They photographed it, warts and all, the errors are still in there,' he contends. 'Federico Faggin, the guy who designed our chip, says it's all still in there. It's a direct copy and not an engineering development. Other companies we've licensed have paid several million dollars for the right to be a second source.'

In addition to the lawsuit, Zilog has brought a complaint to the International Trade Commission, which has accepted the case. But in Japan, Zilog is powerless. 'We can't prosecute them over there,' says Signor. 'But if we can get an ITC ruling in our favor, the ITC will stop all imports of products with that chip in it. The ITC will settle it in nine months to a year. Unfortunately, the U.S. courts will take three to five years. That's why we went to the ITC.'

After Zilog presented its claims, NEC countersued Zilog, contending that the Z80 is a copy of the NEC chip, not the other way around. 'They claim to have patents on their chip,' says Signor. 'But we'll agree to their suit, if they'll agree to ours. Their claim is worth about a million bucks. Ours, in our opinion, is worth $40 million. Even if they could prove their suit, they would receive very little in damages. On the other hand, we've had tremendous damages.'

Even if the ITC ruling is in Zilog's favor, hundreds of thousands of products with NEC's chip will have been sold around the world, each representing a sale lost to Zilog. And more will be sold in Japan, where Zilog can neither block sales nor hope to get a court settlement.

Before personal-size microcomputers went on sale in retail stores, the word 'computer' was usually preceded by the initials 'IBM.' Big Blue, as IBM is affectionately known in the industry, was the dominant presence. IBM was no less dominant in Japan, where its share of the market for large, business-oriented machines hovered near 75 percent for most of the 1960s and into the early part of the next decade. The reasons were obvious: IBM made the best computers for the tasks required; IBM provided reliable software; IBM's service was first rate.

But by 1970 MITI had decided it wanted to foster a domestic computer industry that could compete with, and ultimately replace IBM. This was a key reason behind the MITI campaign to match and pass the U.S. in semiconductor technology. But Japan's computer manufacturers found that competing with IBM was not easy. 'We tried to sell our own machines,' recalled Taiyu Kobayashi, chairman of Fujitsu, in 1982. 'However, the installed base of IBM is so large and the users, quite naturally, want to use the software base they have built up over the years. The relative value of software in the computer system has risen to in excess of 70 percent of the cost of the system. Being compatible was the only way to get started in the computer business.'

Kobayashi confirmed that the Japanese sales strategy – compatibility with IBM's hardware – was the keystone of an effort to cut into IBM's share of the market. But in the early years, plug-compatible Japanese-made computers were not received well, even in Japan. Despite the unpopularity of their products, the Japanese industry continued its efforts to improve them. 'MITI put out R&D funds and brought together the various companies for joint development projects,' confirmed Kobayashi. 'When domestic makers began building products and it wasn't clear whether what we made would work or not, MITI went around to the industries that had benefited from its patronage – automobiles, steel, etc. – and said, "Here, use these."'

While they set about rationalizing the Japanese computer industry, MITI also restricted the import of foreign-made IBM computers. 'There was considerable pushing and hauling about how to restructure the Japanese industry to compete with IBM,' Kobayashi explained. Some in Japan wanted to merge all the companies into one giant computer corporation, but a decision was finally made to align the companies into three groups. Fujitsu was paired with Hitachi to pursue large computer development. And just about that time, someone important quit at IBM.

Eugene Amdahl was one of IBM's top computer engineers, chief architect of the team that had designed the IBM 360. When he left IBM to form his own company in 1970, Fujitsu saw an opening. 'We got word that Amdahl had quit IBM,' recalled the former Fujitsu chairman. 'That was the time when Fujitsu was feverishly attempting to get hold of IBM's architecture. The friend of one of our top people at the time was a close friend of Amdahl, and Amdahl was intending to make machines that would use IBM's software but offer higher performance for the money. We couldn't afford not to get in on this.'

In 1971, Fujitsu built a research laboratory in a corner of Amdahl's building, and two years later they bought 24 percent of his company's stock. Several managers at Fujitsu opposed the plan to go IBM-compatible, partially because of the huge investment, and also because of fear of legal retaliation by IBM. Kobayashi decided to seek a partnership on the project with Hitachi and met regularly with his opposite member at Hitachi. 'We felt around, asking whether Hitachi would care to join us,' Kobayashi remembered. 'Hitachi said "No, we'll go our own way."'

To place Japanese business ethics in American perspective, one must imagine that this conversation had taken place between the presidents, say, of Intel and Advanced Micro Devices. 'That alone would be enough to put both of them in jail,' says John A. Calhoun, a senior officer at Intel.

By 1974 Fujitsu had acquired enough computer technology to introduce its Model 370M, which ran twice as fast as the IBM 370 and used the same software. Hitachi, too, belatedly adapted the IBM-plug-compatible approach in its new products. By 1979 IBM's share of the Japanese market had declined to 27 percent. To put this into context, outside of the United Kingdom, where Big Blue provides 43 percent of the business computers, and the communist countries where its products are not sold, IBM's market share is at least 50 percent in every country in the world. Fujitsu passed IBM to become *itchiban* in

1979, trailed at a distance by Hitachi. IBM's immediate answer to the Fujitsu 370M was a machine called the 3033, which was better than its own 370, but which represented only incremental improvements in technology.

But IBM, the competitor, was not yielding the Japanese market. This was only an interim machine for Big Blue, something to keep it in the market until its next generation was ready. IBM's new series of highly advanced machines was being developed in great secrecy under the code name Adirondack, and known collectively as the 308X. The first of this generation, the 3081, was scheduled to be delivered in October 1981.

When a computer company decides on a business strategy of developing machines that imitate those of a competitor and run on the competitor's software, it is in a classic good news/bad news situation. The good news is that it can reap the considerable benefits of not having to invest in expensive R&D. It can wait for the competitor to bring out his computer, buy several, and through reverse engineering get the benefit of most of his efforts for a few cents on the dollar. It can then build machines that cost far less to develop, correcting the inevitable minor design errors that find their way into anything as complex as a computer system. The result is a product that can be sold to the competitor's customers for substantially less than the competitor can sell his own, and at a substantial profit.

The bad news implicit in this strategy is that the company has to wait for the competitor's product to appear before it can build a copy. That can take three or four years, by which time the competitor might have another technological shoe to drop. But if, by some means, the rival company can get advance information on the competitor's new generation of computers, it can reduce the time spread. Even a few months' head start is worth millions in sales.

Fujitsu was in an enviable position in that it employed many former IBM employees. But Hitachi, which had turned down the opportunity to join Fujitsu, would have to wait for the new IBM machine to appear, or it would have to find some other means.

When ten of IBM's 27 secret workbooks describing the 308X series illicitly came into Hitachi's possession, they realized their value and set out to get the rest. Those ten workbooks, each a three-ring binder of 40 to 200 looseleaf pages, were, according to federal prosecutors, spirited out of IBM by Raymond Cadet in November of 1980. Cadet, then a 45-year-old computer scientist, left IBM's research labs at Poughkeepsie, New York, and was next employed by National Advanced Systems (NAS), a Silicon Valley subsidiary of National Semiconductor. Cadet's boss at NAS, an Iranian named Barry Saffaie, learned about the ten IBM workbooks and allegedly made several photocopies of them. In the summer of 1981, Saffaie flew to Japan, where, says the Justice Department, he delivered one set to Hitachi, whose computers are marketed by NAS in the United States. The indictments against Cadet and Saffaie were later dismissed when the government refused to produce certain documents.

Kenji Hayashi, then 40, is a very thin, bespectacled man somewhat taller than the average Japanese, a man with a fifties crewcut and what a U.S. Justice Department attorney describes as a 'hideous' laugh. Hayashi was one of Hitachi's senior engineers. A few weeks after the stolen IBM workbooks were delivered to Hitachi, he inadvertently acknowledged their existence to Maxwell Paley, a San Jose, California, computer consultant. Paley, another former IBM employee (21 years with Big Blue) had offered Hayashi, his regular contact at Hitachi, a legitimate study of the 308X project, a report that his consulting firm had developed from other sources. Hayashi told Paley that he didn't need the study; he had volumes 1, 3, 4, 8, 9, 10, 11, 12 and 15 of the Adirondack series. If Paley had other workbooks, Hitachi was interested. Paley was immediately aware that something was quite wrong. The notebooks, his 21 years at IBM told him, were not supposed to be at Hitachi.

Approximately 20 percent of the business of Paley's firm, Palyn Associates, was with Hitachi, but loyalties to his country and his former IBM colleagues proved stronger. Paley phoned a close friend at IBM, Bob O.

Evans, a vice-president in charge of engineering, programming, and technology. He told him that he was sure that Hitachi had somehow acquired IBM's 'crown jewels.'

IBM is a company that spends 'substantially more' than $50 million a year just on security. Learning that Hitachi had the notebooks galvanized Big Blue into action. IBM's top troubleshooter, a rugged, silver-haired ex-Marine captain, ex-FBI agent, and ex-T Man (Bureau of Narcotics), Richard A. Callahan, was put in charge of the initial reconnaissance operation. It was important to IBM to verify that Hitachi actually had the notebooks in their possession before going further. To gain access to Hitachi's Hayashi, IBM enlisted Paley, who agreed to act as a double agent for IBM.

Paley telexed Hayashi that he might be able to deliver more of the secret IBM notebooks, and set up a meeting in Tokyo for October. With an associate, Robert Domenico, and IBM's Callahan, Paley flew to Tokyo. On October 2, Paley met Hayashi in a room at the Imperial Hotel, where Paley gave Hayashi a handwritten index to the whole set of IBM workbooks. He also told the Hitachi engineer that while his firm was not in the business of securing confidential, proprietary information, he might to able to find someone who could. But, Paley told Hayashi, he needed to know precisely what Hitachi was looking for. What did these notebooks look like, exactly? Could Hayashi get him some to look at, so he would know if what his contact brought in was the genuine article?

Hayashi could. On the 6th of October, Hayashi brought Paley three of the ten notebooks. He also brought him the first in what would be a long series of 'shopping lists' – the IBM items that Hitachi desperately needed to get their copycat computer system up and running so it would compete with IBM's. When Paley turned the notebooks over to Callahan, he was immediately able to identify them as stolen IBM property.

Now that IBM's security people were assured that Hitachi did indeed have its 'crown jewels,' they were left with three courses of action. They could ignore the theft. They could sue the Japanese company in civil court for damages. Or they could turn the case over to the Justice Department for possible criminal prosecution. If they had chosen to ignore Hitachi's theft, it would encourage others to steal. For this reason, not incidentally, IBM has long followed a hardnosed policy about theft of its secrets. The policy was well known: IBM goes after those who steal from it with a vengeance. It prosecutes.

The second course of action, a civil suit, would be appealing only if there was a certainty that IBM could get justice. But if Hitachi were sued in the U.S., it might take years to resolve the case. To sue them in Japan might well take decades, assuming a Japanese court could be expected to render a judgment against one of its own companies. Moreover, initiating a civil suit might encourage Hitachi to settle out of court, a settlement that would also likely include a 'no publicity' provision. IBM wanted Hitachi to get all the publicity it deserved.

IBM decided to go to the Justice Department with its evidence. The FBI and IBM were old friends. IBM was then training FBI agents how to act like legitimate electronics purchasing agents for an FBI sting operation, whose cover was Glenmar Associates in San Jose, California. The FBI was investigating the 'gray electronics' market, where stolen electronics components, including computers, are bought and sold. The operation, code-named PENGEM (Penetrate Gray Electronics Market), had already begun; the machinery to incriminate Hitachi was in place. The emphasis, the Justice Department decided, would be temporarily switched from theft of high-tech items destined for the Soviet bloc countries, which was PENGEM's initial focus, to similar goods headed for Japan.

In November 1981, Hayashi left Tokyo and came to Las Vegas, where Paley introduced him to IBM's Callahan, who was posing as a somewhat disreputable, but very able, retired lawyer. A few hours later Callahan introduced Hayashi to 'Al Harrison,' as a source who might be able to get him the secret IBM materials. Al's real name was Alan Garretson and he was an FBI agent.

The FBI went out of its way to impress on Hayashi, and each of the Hitachi employees he brought into his scheme, that what they were doing was illegal. Transcripts from hundreds of hours of video and audio tapes make it clear that Hitachi's people were fully aware of this, but it did not reduce their zeal to make the company, and their nation, *itchiban* in the computer market.

Theft did not preclude bargaining, something the Japanese cultivate with the same patience they devote to the art of *bonsai* dwarf trees. Not only did Hitachi want IBM's secrets, but they wanted them at the lowest possible price. Hayashi and his fellow Hitachi conspirators bargained endlessly with the FBI agents. They held out the inducement of future employment to the federal agents if they did good work. To Paley, whom the FBI had deftly moved aside as soon as he introduced Callahan under the cover name 'Richard Kerrigan,' they displayed the stick. In a letter to Paley written on December 7, 1981, exactly forty years after Pearl Harbor, Hayashi wrote: 'I have no idea to pay your travel fee if you don't have the suitable information for us.'

Hayashi revealed his business instincts later, when the filched information and hardware were being shipped back to Hitachi's headquarters in Japan by another person drawn into the conspiracy, Tom Yoshida, a U.S. citizen and president of a small American firm. As a faithful Hitachi salaryman, Hayashi directed Yoshida to send the stolen goods out on Japan Air Lines and intentionally undervalue the shipping documents. 'From $10,000 the usual cost, for example, to $500 . . . if he say "$10,000," you must pay more taxes in Japan,' Hayashi told the FBI's Garreston in a videotaped conversation. Stealing secrets was risky business, illegal business, but it was still business.

Initially, the FBI thought they could close the case in 'two weeks or so.' But as it unfolded it became apparent that it would take more time to draw the maximum number of Hitachi employees into the FBI net. This meant that IBM would have to continue supplying trade secrets and hardware beyond their original intentions. Some of the information Hitachi requested was now available from IBM customers. One evening in November 1981, FBI agents 'bribed' their way into a secret-filled room at

Pratt & Whitney's Hartford, Connecticut plant to allow Hitachi's Jun Naruse to photograph a new IBM disk drive memory device installed there for testing.

Other information was less accessible. IBM was understandably hesitant about continuing to supply Hitachi with its trade secrets, but Callahan and the FBI told IBM officials that to make an airtight case, and to demonstrate publicly that the conspiracy had reached Hitachi's highest management levels, IBM would have to satisfy Hitachi's 'wish list.' IBM reluctantly agreed. Between November 1981 and June 1982, when the FBI arrested Hayashi and Isao Ohnishi, a Hitachi software expert, Hitachi paid out some $600,000 to the ersatz spies. In return they got substantial amounts of IBM hardware, software, and proprietary information, secrets that IBM had spent hundreds of millions of dollars developing.

The passage of time made each secret a little less valuable to Hitachi. But once the first few secrets had made their way across the Pacific, Hitachi's demands grew more insistent. This made IBM even more anxious; the requested material was scattered among research labs, customer sites, and various manufacturing facilities. Each time it had to be collected without alerting IBM employees who, for security reasons, were not aware of the FBI operation. By June, a concerned IBM told the FBI 'no more.' In any case, they explained to the FBI, much of what Hitachi still wanted would be legally available through purchase in a few months.

The FBI agents were convinced that the Hitachi conspiracy was not just the work of over-eager low-level employees. They were sure that the highest echelons of Hitachi were involved in the plot. To learn which top Hitachi executives were controlling the scheme, Callahan and Garretson offered enticing bait. They told their Hitachi contacts that they were able to get their highly confidential hardware, software, and manuals out through IBM's thick security blanket through a pair of *passeurs* who were very senior IBM execs about to retire. As it often happened, the FBI told Hitachi, both had access to virtually anything the Hitachi people wanted.

These high-level IBM executives, Callahan insisted, could not compromise their identity. 'One is on leave from IBM and is president of a college,' he told Ohnishi and Hayashi. 'Which college?' Hayashi asked, several times, but Garretson and Callahan sidestepped the question. These IBM men, they said, were interested in a steady extra income for a few years, but 'only if they could be paid in cash,' Callahan stressed. 'They have to pay a lot of taxes on their retirement funds, and they want to avoid taxes on this money.' But, Callahan added, the IBM men would not agree to the deal unless they could meet a Hitachi official of comparable rank. They would have to have his personal assurances of confidentiality. Hayashi agreed and suggested payment by bank check sent by air express. 'No good,' said Callahan. 'Wire the money directly to the bank, it's faster.'

Hayashi concocted an elaborate strategem to bring Dr. Kisaburo Nakazawa, head of Hitachi's computer factory at Odawara, into contact with Garretson and Callahan. He was careful not to alert anyone at Hitachi who was not already privy to the scheme. It was arranged for Nakazawa to make a trip to Hitachi's San Francisco offices; a full schedule of activities was published as a cover. They met at the St. Francis Hotel where Callahan, in an effort to learn who else at Hitachi was in on the plot, asked Nakazawa to draw diagrams of the Hitachi organizations. Callahan also professed concern about keeping word of the stolen materials from getting back to IBM. Nakazawa assured the FBI agent that he would personally handcopy the information from the pilfered documents, each marked with the red ink 'IBM SECRET' stamp. No photocopies would be made.

As the scheme gathered momentum, the volume of IBM materials grew. Computer tapes inscribed with IBM's new software package were to be provided to Hitachi, which paid $250,000 for a program they could have bought openly for $100,000 if they had waited a few months. Tapes were smuggled into Japan by Ohnishi, who left his country with blank tapes on IBM reels, which he then told Japanese Customs 'had a value of only $10.' On his return to Japan, Ohnishi was to carry the same reels with the IBM tapes, and show the customs document to prove that he had brought the same number of tapes out of Japan. 'Very clever, very smart, good job,' said Garretson when Ohnishi told him what he was going to do. But Ohnishi never had the opportunity. On June 22, 1982 he and his Hitachi colleagues were arrested at the FBI cover office in San Jose.

But at times the Hitachi thieves were surprisingly inept. An IBM tape was 'stolen' for the weekend and would have to be 'returned' on Monday. Hitachi had one of their San Francisco people come down to HAC Semiconductor to duplicate the tape. 'It took your man seven hours to do a five minute job,' Garretson complained to Ohnishi and Hayashi.

On another occasion, Nakazawa asked for a large piece of hardware called a backboard. 'It's too big to sneak out of the IBM lab at Poughkeepsie,' complained Callahan. 'It's *this* big,' he said, demonstrating with his hands far apart. 'How you gonna sneak that out? Should I get somebody with a big overcoat?' Nakazawa giggled and shrugged.

The FBI investigation revealed direct participation by a total of 11 Hitachi executives, ranging from Ohnishi and Hayashi up to Nakazawa. 'Hayashi told the FBI undercover agent that he had the authority to spend up to $1 million,' says special prosecutor Herb Hoffman. 'Nakazawa is Hitachi's leading computer developer.'

No decision has been made by the Justice Department concerning whether it will seek to extradite to America the nine Hitachi employees who had returned to Japan before the arrests. 'As soon as the charges were filed, Hitachi filed five binders full of motions. The essence of them was that IBM had set Hitachi up, that it was strictly an anticompetitive situation, that the U.S. government joined hands with IBM and let IBM control the investigation for competitive reasons,' says Hoffman. He then asks: 'What does that say about Hitachi's credibility when they made all these allegations, then before the motions were heard by the judge, they plead guilty. What does that say about their credibility?

'When it was time for sentencing, the judge said he would not have the individuals put in jail. This was a situation in which Hitachi employees were acting at the behest of their superiors. It was very important that the company be convicted,' Hoffman points out.

Ultimately, however, Hitachi paid little for its transgressions. In San Francisco, on February 8, 1983, Judge Spencer Williams fined Hayashi $10,000 – the maximum fine – and Ohnishi $4,000. He also levied a fine of $10,000 against Hitachi, which paid its employees' penalties. The total cost in damages was only $24,000. 'The only thing they could be convicted of was stealing trade secrets, since IBM gave them everything they took out of the country,' says Hoffman. 'But the important thing was for Hitachi to stand up there in court and admit that they were guilty of trying to steal IBM's plans.'

In the early fall of 1983, Hitachi settled the civil suit brought by IBM for the theft of their trade secrets. The agreement included the return of all the stolen IBM materials in its possession, and a provision that IBM would have the right to inspect all new Hitachi data-processing products before they are released for sale during the next five years. They also agreed to disclose the identities of all the individuals who offered IBM secrets to Hitachi. But Hitachi has yet to admit that any of IBM's secrets were used in the development of new products, and they have not yet compensated IBM for the huge expenses involved in settling the case.

The Hitachi 'operating expenses' for the conspiracy were only $600,000, a pittance compared to the value of the technology gained. None of the other Hitachi employees involved were tried here or in Japan; they were merely transferred to other jobs. Even Yasukichi Hatano was allowed to keep his seat on the board, though he was relieved of his duties as head of computer operations. 'Mr. Hatano is now a "director without portfolio,"' commented Yasushi Sayama, a Hitachi spokesman. Nor did Hitachi suffer much loss of face in Japan; perhaps even the reverse. The Japanese press, which tends to act in concert with official policy, saw the case as evidence of an attempt by IBM to frame Hitachi. 'Jap-baiting,' most of the influential dailies complained.

Since 'sting' operations are illegal in Japan, except in drug cases, the Hitachi theft of IBM secrets provided a good opportunity for a discussion of America's loose morals. The Japanese papers insisted on calling it the 'IBM industrial espionage' case, as if IBM had been the offending party. Shoichi Saeki, a Tokyo University professor of American literature, reported the comments he overheard in the sauna of his sports club. 'It was a really filthy trick,' said one man. 'It was entrapment. The Japanese government must protest against this,' said another. 'The American methods go too far,' said a third. They were criticizing IBM for having Hitachi's spies arrested.

Saeki himself likened the FBI operation to the activities of a con man. 'The FBI set up a bogus consulting company. This is an old trick of con men,' he said. 'In America, where many ethnic groups coexist and the restraining influence of traditional social ties has weakened, con games are widespread.' He added, 'My experience in the United States convinces me of this. . . . In many areas of American life, tricky methods similar to con games are used. . . . Modern advertising and public relations, with their hypes and hidden persuasion, originated in the United States.'

The theft of IBM secrets apparently did not tarnish Hitachi's image as an innovative company. In fact, the editor-in-chief of *Nikkei Computer*, a prestigious Japanese bimonthly, reported that 'many users of IBM machines have told me they're thinking of switching to Hitachi.' Hitachi's sales actually rose in the months following the revelation that Hitachi had stolen IBM's secrets. The U.S. Social Security Administration, which had been shopping for computers, bought two Hitachis for $7 million. 'They were cheaper, and performed equally' to the IBM models a U.S. government spokesperson explained.

On June 18, 1982, four days before the IBM case made headlines around the world, Fujitsu's two-page ad in the *Nippon Keizai Shimbun*, a trade newspaper, announced that it had completed a new model computer, which was compatible with the new IBM 3081K. *Nikkei Computer*, in its July 26 edition, quoted a former Fujitsu employee as saying that virtually all of IBM's secret documents were in Fujitsu's possession. 'The era in which many little stars revolve around the great IBM sun is coming to a close; thus a new era in international business is dawning,' said Taiyu Kobayashi, Fujitsu's chairman.

The New Era of Japan has arrived, much to the confusion and detriment of the businessmen and workers of the Western world.

3 MITI, the Bike Races and the Great Machine Tool Debacle

IT WAS 1977, one of those stultifying August days when the cloud of pollutants in Los Angeles seems to have abrasive teeth and develops into what locals call an 'episode.' Driving through this smog in a rented car on the crowded, unfamiliar freeways between his airport hotel and the industrial area east of downtown, P. Phillips Connor was unaware that the air was only the first unpleasant surprise of the day. Connor, then a 43-year-old Chicago attorney, was on his way to Japan. He had stopped off to visit the Los Angeles offices of Burgmaster, a machine tool manufacturing company and a division of Houdaille Industries, an important Fort Lauderdale, Florida, client of Connor's law firm. He was to be present when an attorney representing a Japanese firm took a legal deposition from Al Folger, Burgmaster's president.

Connor's second unpleasant surprise occurred later in the day, around noon. As he remembers it, a secretary interrupted his meeting with Folger to tell him there was an urgent call from the Japanese consulate in Los Angeles. It was 'something about his visa.' Connor excused himself and took the call. 'It was the consul general, and after he apologized a couple of times, he told me my visa for Japan was canceled,' Connor recalls. 'I was very surprised. I asked him why, but all he said was that it was canceled. He was "very sorry," but I would not be allowed entry into Japan. My first reaction was suspicion that Yamazaki had interceded with the Japanese government to block my discovery procedure.'

Yamazaki, a Japanese machine toolmaker, was the defendant in the lawsuit Connor had filed for his client, Houdaille. Connor was surprised that the Japanese were using their diplomatic power to thwart his investigation of

55

how Yamazaki was allegedly violating its licensing agreements with Houdaille. The Japanese government was not interceding on behalf of one of its behemoth cartels, a *zaibatsu* with billions to protect. Yamazaki Machine Works, Ltd. was only a small maker of machine tools with a plant in Oguchi, an industrial city near Nagoya. In June 1970, Yamazaki had entered into a ten-year contract with Houdaille, and in return for license fees on the sale of each machine, Houdaille had furnished the relatively unknown Japanese firm with thousands of drawings, technical details, and a great deal of proprietary information.

Since these trade secrets were the essence of Houdaille's business, the terms of their agreement with Yamazaki included restrictions on where Yamazaki could sell the machine tools it would build from the Houdaille plans. The contract restricted Yamazaki to Japan and the Far East and also provided that the technology Houdaille had furnished was confidential and for Yamazaki's exclusive use.

For several years, the Japanese licensee appeared to perform according to the prevailing Western stereotype of the Japanese corporation – polite and correct. But in August 1976, Houdaille's management was astonished when they came across trade advertisements for a line of horizontal and vertical 'machining centers' offered by Yamazaki's U.S. marketing subsidiary in Florence, Kentucky. These machines appeared to Houdaille to be identical to the very products they had licensed Yamazaki to manufacture and sell solely in the Far East. But Yamazaki was selling them in Houdaille's own country, the U.S., and at considerably lower prices than Houdaille.

After inspecting the machines, Houdaille's technicians concluded that the machines were indeed copies of their own, except for the Yamazaki label. 'Any time you design a thing as complicated as a work station, you're bound to realize when you're finished that you could have made a little change here or there and made it a little better,' explains Jack Latona, a Houdaille vice president. 'But these were identical to our Burgmaster machines, right down to the design mistakes we made. It wasn't old wine in a new bottle. It was old wine in an old bottle. The same wine in the same bottle, and they didn't even bother to clean up the bottle when they put their label on it.'

When Houdaille complained to Yamazaki, the Japanese denied violating their contract, insisting that the technology was their own, a qualitative improvement on the state-of-the-art. Since it was their own design, Yamazaki claimed, not only had they not violated their contract by marketing in the U.S., but they no longer felt it was necessary to pay royalty fees to Houdaille. After months of fruitless negotiations with the Japanese, Houdaille's officers, their patience exhausted, filed a complaint with the U.S. International Trade Commission. After hearing Houdaille's evidence, the ITC decided the matter should be investigated.

Legal procedure in such cases involves a process known as 'discovery,' in which attorneys from the complainant and the respondent – in this case, Houdaille and Yamazaki – are each given the legal right to collect evidence from the other's files and to take depositions from the various people involved. The ITC requested a Japanese administrative law court to permit Houdaille to conduct its discovery at Yamazaki's plants and offices in Japan. It is a routine legal request, one regularly honored throughout the capitalist Western world. Connor felt confident that after his Japanese journey, the Houdaille case would be clinched.

Phil Connor first went to the Japanese consulate in Chicago and obtained a visa, then notified Francis Sogi, an attorney representing Yamazaki in Chicago, of his intention to go to Japan. The visa was issued the same day. Connor's office reserved a room for him at the Nagoya Castle Hotel and booked a seat on Varig Airlines, with a scheduled arrival in Tokyo on August 7. He then headed out to California to see Al Folger of Burgmaster.

Alerted by Connor's notification to Sogi, the Japanese moved rapidly to deal with the American attorney. Telexes were soon criss-crossing between Tokyo and Chicago; Yamazaki's top managers were on the telephone to their friends in the government ministries of Tokyo. The result was not long in coming: on August 5th, the Japanese government canceled Connor's visa. The outraged Houdaille attorney returned to Chicago, where he called upon the Japanese consulate to demand an explanation from Mr. Italu Murata, the official who had originally issued his visa.

Murata was frank: He told Connor that his visa had been canceled on orders from his superiors at the Japanese Foreign Ministry. Their decision was ironclad: Connor would be allowed to enter Japan on business only if he agreed to certain restrictions. 'I couldn't take depositions, and I couldn't speak to anyone that Yamazaki didn't want me to speak with,' explains Connor, who is still incredulous about the case. 'The only documents I could see were those that Yamazaki "presented voluntarily." Under the circumstances, I didn't see what purpose a trip to Japan would serve.'

Although Connor and Houdaille complained to the ITC, the decision to admit someone to Japan ultimately rested with the Japanese government, who were apparently using their full sovereign powers to frustrate one American corporation. The U.S. State department joined the complaint, and through the Japanese embassy requested entry visas for two ITC investigators.

But the Japanese government was adamant. Connor could not come to Japan if he expected to conduct any legal activity against Yamazaki. In an August 15, 1977, letter over the signature of Koichiro Matsuura, a ranking Japanese foreign service official, the Japanese government overruled the administrative law judge who had granted Connor authority to investigate Yamazaki. Matsuura said his government would allow the ITC investigation to proceed but only if the U.S. agency would 'neither order to produce nor search any documents against the will of Yamazaki.' He added: 'They should also refrain from taking any written statements from Yamazaki. Any information obtained through the contacts with Yamazaki in Japan may not be used as evidence in making any administrative or judicial decision.'

It was obvious to Connor that he had been blocked. The Japanese restrictions made investigation of Yamazaki, or any subsequent litigation against them, hopeless. But Connor still could not understand the official Japanese intervention. Why would the Foreign Ministry of the Japanese government be so concerned about a business conflict between two firms, neither of which is an industrial giant?

The American machine tool industry has for generations been a core activity, much as computers are becoming today. These metal-spinning lathes, die stampers, and drill and punch presses were the machines that made America such a formidable foe in World War II and provided the manufacturing base of America's postwar expansion. Much has since changed in the machine tool industry, but they are no less vital. New machines, especially those used in defense industries, are far more complex than those in use only a decade or two ago; new alloys give metals properties that allow greatly improved performances. As technology advanced, as the material changed, the sizes of the parts being machined grew smaller, and tolerances finer. It became more difficult for a man to make the cuts or holes at a precise angle in a block of metal, and to do it quickly and accurately time after time.

The answer was an American invention, a numerically controlled (NC) metal-working machine run by a computer-generated punch tape that makes it possible to perform the same task as a man, but with greater precision and at higher speeds. It was a machine tool, and it revolutionized manufacturing. As computers became miniaturized, and faster, several machine tools could be controlled by a single computer generating numerous punch tapes and turning out vast numbers of precision products. The value added was magnified enormously because one worker could create thousands of identical products in a single day. Designed by white-collar workers, built and serviced by blue collars, these industrious machines are sometimes called 'steel collar' workers.

A modern machining center is huge, six or seven feet

tall, eight feet wide, 15 feet deep, and weighs several tons. They are also expensive and therefore a prime target for Japanese exports. 'It would be hard to find one for $100,000,' says Jack Latona. 'You can pay $350,000 to $400,000 for certain machines; $250,000 is sort of a ballpark price. A punching machine tends to be even larger, because it's working on a big sheet of metal, as opposed to a block, and so its bed is larger. Their prices range from $85,000 to $400,000. We also sell a punching machine with a laser, which costs quite a bit more than a plain punching machine.'

A 1982 Air Force study places the importance of these gargantuan products in sharp focus: 'Nearly all manufactured products are made with machine tools, or are made on machines that were in turn built by machine tools; thus the machine tool industry is one of the key elements in our national productivity network, and its influence is much larger than indicated by the small proportion of the GNP it represents.'

The Japanese planners understood this as well. If they were to maintain their aggressive industrial posture worldwide they would have to supplant America and Europe as the main producers of machine tools, an industry that grosses $1.8 billion a year in the U.S. alone. They were not beginning from scratch; their course of action had already been tested in other targeted industries. First they would acquire the most advanced Western technology and duplicate the product. Then they would undersell American and European competitors in their own countries. The final step would be to take over their market shares, both in the U.S. and elsewhere, and stand by as their foreign competition died an unnatural fiscal death.

Though the Japanese began this process in the late 1950s, it was not until 1980 that they were ready to actually challenge American and European machine tool manufacturers on their home ground. As late as 1976, the Japanese were a negligible presence in the U.S. machine tool market, holding only 3.7 percent of it, and about the same level in Europe. But their opportunity came in the late 1970s when worldwide demand for these products slumped as world economies headed into a prolonged recession.

While U.S. and European manufacturers were cutting production, laying off workers, and in general retrenching, Japan's machine tool makers did something unusual – and seemingly irrational – from a traditional business viewpoint. With an enormous amount of new funds supplied from some unknown outside source, they expanded their production. They turned out thousands of numerically controlled (NC) machine tool products even though they could not sell them. Akimitsu Ohko, research director of the Japanese Machine Tool Builders Association, reported that in 1981 there was an inventory of 1,000 unsold Japanese-made NC machining centers in the U.S.

At first it looked like a planning gaffe, but the Japanese had actually moved sagely. As the recession ended and demand for these machines increased, Japanese machine tools were being unloaded cheaply in America and elsewhere at discounts of up to $100,000 per machine. By the end of 1981, the targeting campaign bore fruit: Japanese makers of NC machining centers, the leading component of the machine tool market, had taken over a 50 percent share of the American market.

Bloodied by Japanese discount competition, many of the smaller American firms moved toward bankruptcy, while even such larger companies as Houdaille began to feel the impact of Japanese imports in dwindling profits and smaller market share. 'It's our impression that everybody in the U.S. machine tool industry has been hurt, pretty much across the board,' says Jack Latona. 'There may be some small outfits that are making highly specialized stuff that haven't been hit as hard, but basically everybody's had the same swipe. We closed a plant in August 1983, the Die-Acro plant in Lake City, Minnesota. The product line is being consolidated in another plant. Almost 500 people worked there, at its peak, and 250 people when we announced our closing.'

Today, the victory is near complete. The Japanese control about 60 percent of the numerically controlled machine and 30 percent of the entire U.S. machine tool market, and a similar share in Europe. An even larger threat sits in warehouses in the form of an inventory of Japanese machines waiting to be sold in the United States – an inventory that keeps rising. By early 1983 there were, by Houdaille's estimate, about 2,400 Japanese machines in the U.S., or more than a peak year's total of U.S. sales. Meanwhile, American manufacturers, with only 60 percent of their capacity in use, were losing money despite increased productivity. The six largest firms reported that their 1982 net earnings were down by more than a third from 1979, which itself had been a poor year.

Even Washington, which is usually indifferent to the state of failing American industry, became concerned. 'The Japanese will completely control these high-technology markets and industries within a few years,' warned U.S. Senator Chuck Grassley (R. Iowa) in a December 1982 speech. 'This will bankrupt the U.S. machine tool companies, and throw their skilled employees out of work.'

Unfortunately, Grassley was one of the few in the capital who understood what was going on. Washington bureaucracy has been largely unresponsive to American machine tool makers, mouthing shibboleths about the failings of U.S. technology. 'The conventional wisdom in Washington, even among some of our so-called friends, is that the U.S. is behind the times in machine tool technology,' says an angry Jack Latona of Houdaille. 'It makes me want to roll around on the floor, chew, and foam at the mouth. The damn *Japanese* machine tools are nothing but *U.S.* machine tools! They've even copied some of our mistakes, things that if we were redesigning we would now change. But here are those bozos walking around like it was *their* invention. By God, those flexible machine tools were designed, developed, and promoted *first* right here in the United States. What the Japanese have done, very skillfully, but with the help of their government, is copy them. And then our own government acts as though the U.S. machine tool industry was some old-fashioned, obsolete, smokestack industry. They think of us in the same way that they think of the steel industry. That's pure nonsense!'

Faced with the specter of Japanese machines built mainly from American technology being sold at a 25 percent discount in the Western markets, Houdaille decided to initiate a private probe of the Japanese machine tool industry. It hired a Washington attorney, Richard D. Copaken, who in turn secured the assistance of the Japanese law firm of Nagashima and Ohno; Nagashima is a fellow Harvard Law School alumnus of Copaken's and an occasional lecturer at Harvard on international law. Their investigation, which focused not only on Yamazaki but on the influential Japanese Ministry of International Trade and Industry (MITI), revealed aspects of Japanese business methods and ethics that eventually brought the case before the U.S. Cabinet. Before Copaken was finished, he had uncovered startling information on the Japanese that provided the basis for a 1983 petition addressed to President Reagan.

Copaken is a well-connected attorney, a magna cum laude graduate of Harvard Law and a former White House fellow in the Johnson Administration. His efforts, backed by nearly $1 million spent by Houdaille, have provided the West with the first detailed inner view of how MITI masterminds the Japanese export economy and builds their multi-million dollar trade surpluses with measures that are often illegal, even by Japan's comparatively loose ethical business standards. Although Houdaille's probe was focused only on the Japanese machine tool industry, it reflects much of the ugly underside common to almost all Japanese industrial activity.

The Yamazaki incident was not just an example of the abrogation of trust between two companies doing business together while 7,000 miles apart. As the Houdaille investigation was to show, it was a small segment of a larger Japanese government plan to take over the vital numerically controlled machine tool market, the latest

American and European-developed industry targeted by the Japanese.

The plan was carefully orchestrated in Tokyo by MITI, which, as far back as 1956, set out to protect their own fledgling machine tool industry from American and European competition. The Japanese initially relied on strict tariffs and quotas, measures which were effective. But over time, in response to growing pressure from their trading partners, the Japanese implemented several 'liberalizing' plans which supposedly removed formal import barriers. As it turned out, these 'liberalizing' laws were a Japanese *shoji* screen designed to divert criticism away from their entrenched, protectionist 'Buy Japan' policy.

As Houdaille's investigation showed, 'Buy Japan' is, despite Japanese mouthings of 'free trade,' still the nation's covert policy. 'Officials of the Japanese National Railways told us they have *never* purchased any foreign-produced machine tools, even though they've purchased five or six Japanese-made tools in the last three years,' says attorney Copaken.

Once their machine tool industry was protected by a Buy-Japan policy, the Japanese could move to their next step, a program to 'rationalize' the industry by reducing the number of firms that would compete against the world. In effect, Japan was recreating the giant cartels that the U.S. Occupation authorities believed they had destroyed after World War II.

Like their U.S. counterparts, most Japanese machine tool companies were family-owned businesses too small to achieve economies of scale and too numerous to avoid duplication of R&D. MITI began 'encouraging' mergers between smaller companies, and starting in 1961, new laws were passed virtually exempting merging companies from taxes, a practice that continued until mid-1978. The MITI plan worked. In the first year after this law was enacted, 93 mergers were recorded in the industry, more than twice the number in the preceding year; in 1968 they reached a high of 122. When the number of companies had been cut to what MITI felt was the proper competitive size, the old law was reinstated; but by that time Japanese machine tool companies with small market shares had been weeded out. 'Their market shares were turned over to a limited number of more successful producers,' says Copaken.

The next step was to organize the remaining firms into an effective fighting force, legally empowered to work like a cartel. Even in Japan, there are supposed limits to the collective activities in which firms can engage, limits ostensibly set by Japan's MacArthur-imposed Anti-Monopoly Law. But with typical Japanese legal obfuscation, this statute has been selectively interpreted by MITI. In recent years, Copaken's investigation revealed, MITI has used a little-known loophole in Japan's Cooperative Association Law (CAL) to make its Anti-Monopoly Law into a tasteless economic joke.

CAL was supposedly designed to serve the same 'small and medium-sized' firms, enabling them to form co-ops to conduct virtually any joint business activity – R&D, marketing, exchanges of confidential information about foreign technology, loaning or borrowing money. This statute has enabled Japanese trade associations to act as though they were functioning cartels and still be exempt from the Anti-Monopoly law.

If membership in these associations were truly limited to small firms, the cartel-like collusion might be tolerable. But there is a hidden provision in CAL that makes it possible for a large company to join one of these co-ops without violating the Anti-Monopoly Law, provided that the Japan Fair Trade Commission – JFTC – is notified of it within thirty days. The JFTC will entertain complaints about its action, but since the identity of individual members of cooperatives is kept secret, that process is virtually impossible.

Once MITI had created its protected machine tool cartel, the next step was to direct it to expand production of the NC machines and sell them at discount prices. 'MITI successfully pressed the Japanese machine-tool manufacturers to act jointly to concentrate their efforts in developing and producing NC machine tools,' explained

Phillip O'Reilly, Houdaille's president. 'Each company in the cartel was directed to increase to 50 percent the NC share of its total production.'

But MITI still needed one more ingredient to make their scheme work: money. Enormous amounts of capital were required to subsidize the new cartel while it was under-selling the competition. Some of the funds could be pro-vided by tax incentives, but when you ask a manufacturer to sell his products abroad at giant discounts, that manu-facturer needs a cash flow to stay in business. Much of this charade was for the benefit of Japan's trading partners. The Japanese government had to maintain the appearance of a free enterprise economy; it could not openly grant subsidies equal to the losses created by dumping goods in an unprotected foreign market. Subterfuge was essential in the transmission of state capitalist funds, a kind of nation-to-company 'laundering.'

By the mid-1950s MITI had already invented the off-budget subsidy, one which never shows up on government books. In the case of the machine tool industry, MITI initially found its hidden source for money in a most unlikely place – the sugar import industry. Houdaille attorney Richard D. Copaken explains this early MITI maneuver. 'MITI gave to certain officially favored export industries, including machine tools, valuable licenses to import raw sugar,' Copaken says. 'This highly profitable arrangement enabled them to purchase sugar at prevailing world prices and sell it in the domestic Japanese market at prices that were artificially inflated [\$40–\$150 per ton higher] as a consequence of the government's sugar import quota. As MITI officials explained it to me, by utilizing this price differential "the government could compensate the exporters for their deficits attributable to dumping in foreign countries."'

But this ingenious ploy was eventually discovered by Japan's trading partners, and when they screamed, MITI was forced to look elsewhere for a secret source of dump-ing funds. It was discovered in a most extraordinary place, one that seems anomalous to the world of serious business. The money, enormous amounts of it, was found in gambling, specifically in the billions of yen being wagered on a modern Japanese craze, bicycle and motorcycle racing.

In any organized gambling scheme, legal or otherwise, the only sure winner is the house. MITI moved to take over that lucrative role, the same one that has built Las Vegas, Monte Carlo and Atlantic City. By promoting and expanding bicycle and motorcycle racing, and taking an exorbitant 25 percent cut of the gross, MITI siphoned off hundreds of millions of dollars from the bettors. Suddenly MITI was awash in subsidy cash.

In the early 1980s, after persistent questioning by foreign newsmen who had heard rumors about the scheme, MITI admitted that some funds from bicycle races went to help subsidize their machine tool industry. But, they insisted, these funds were small – less than a half million dollars a year. And that, they said, was distributed among several types of machinery makers, not just those who made machine tools.

The potential scandal blew over: a half million dollars could do very little to prop up a billion dollar industry. During the Houdaille investigation, a MITI official was asked about these figures, but he repeated the earlier assertion. Copaken was not convinced, intuitively feeling that MITI was 'misleading' him. There had to be more gambling money involved than the Japanese were admitting to. But he had no recourse; he couldn't even make reasonable inquiries. When he asked MITI to arrange a meeting with officials of the betting authorities at Japan's Bicycle Rehabilitation Association, they refused. A frustrated Copaken returned to the United States.

Then in May 1982, Copaken stumbled upon a way to break through what he was convinced was an official wall of silence. When Copaken learned that NBC was planning to do a one-hour documentary on Japan, a program entitled 'High Tech Shootout,' he saw a chance to focus American public attention on the problem of unfair Japanese competition.

'After speaking to the producer, it was clear their intention was to do a piece based on the notion, "How Japan makes better widgets than the U.S. and why they're so superior to the United States,"' Copaken recalls. He suggested to an NBC executive that there might be more to this story than met the eye. 'I thought they should look into why if Japan was producing superior widgets, what kind of effort lay behind it, particularly how fair was the competition that was shaping up between the two countries.'

But the network executives were not interested, a disappointed Copaken learned. He decided to speak directly to James Gannon, the producer actually filming the documentary in Japan. In mid-May 1982, Copaken caught a plane to Tokyo to make his appeal in person. 'I kept on bugging Gannon until finally I said, "You're going to be meeting with MITI. Please, just ask them about cartels and about the Houdaille case. If you're not intrigued by the responses you get, I promise to leave you alone."'

Gannon did ask, and, according to Copaken, the question immediately turned a calm interview with MITI officials into pandemonium. The MITI bureaucrats, he says, 'kind of threw up their papers and started running around, got very excited, and spoke in Japanese to each other for quite awhile. The NBC crew didn't know what was going on – so much for Oriental stoics.' The MITI people asked for a short break, and after conferring, coolly asked the Americans to turn on their camera and ask the same question again. When the cameras were rolling, a Japanese spokesman calmly replied, 'We don't think we should comment while this is before U.S. decision-makers.'

Hours later, with the interview concluded, a senior MITI bureaucrat took Gannon aside. Could he have his assurance that NBC would use only the last response to the question about Houdaille and cartels? Gannon replied that since the whole interview was on the record, he could not do that. Besides, MITI's first answer was really more interesting.

'The MITI officials immediately called Kyoko Kato,

a Japanese woman working as a researcher for NBC in Tokyo, and put it to her very strongly. It was her patriotic duty to persuade NBC, her employers, to use only the footage with the second answer,' Copaken reveals. When Kato dutifully tried to do what she could, it naturally had the opposite effect. 'Of course it only whetted NBC's appetite. The Japanese did for me what I couldn't do for myself,' Copaken adds.

All this had taken place on a Friday. Copaken told Gannon that since there were a couple of days without scheduled shooting, perhaps they could look into the mystery on the weekend. 'I said, "Humor me, let me show you what a great visual image it would be for your piece to see this great big giant bicycle wheel that rotates above the marquee of the Bicycle Racing Association offices."' When Gannon agreed Copaken bought a small Hitachi video camera and recording unit to take along.

'They humored me,' Copaken continues. 'It was only a few blocks from the hotel. We walked over and I started videotaping the giant bicycle wheel on the building. The Japanese government had never allowed me to meet with these officials, even though I'd asked to several times. But I decided, "What the hell, as long as we're here, let's go in and ask a few questions."'

Out of this chance decision came an incisive insight into the true workings of Japanese government-business alliance. 'We went up the stairs and I kept the camera running,' Copaken recalls. Inside the Bicycle Racing Association office, Copaken asked the first person he met, 'Where do you keep your documents on the money you raise for the Japanese machine tool industry?' The people he asked gave no response and just walked away, but he stubbornly kept repeating the same, seemingly inane, question until a uniformed man arrived. He listened to Copaken, then in broken English and with gestures, he bade the two Americans to follow him.

'I figured, "The jig is up, he's taking us to some sort of paddy wagon, and we're going into the pokey,"' says Copaken. But he kept his video camera rolling as they were led down the stairs and out a back door and into a back alleyway. Instead of being arrested, they were led into the next building and up three floors to another office.

Their uniformed escort spoke sharply to a clerk, who promptly stood and bowed deeply to the two visitors. Copaken and Gannon bowed back and were led up another flight of stairs to a locked and darkened office. 'They opened the room, turned on the lights, opened a safe, and started bringing out documents and handing them to me,' Copaken recalls, commenting on his surprise at the sudden, inexplicable Japanese cooperation. He kept his video camera rolling while leafing through documents showing how the bicycle race proceeds were distributed.

'The numbers they showed me proved they were controlling something in the neighborhood of $104 million a year as a flow-through to the machinery industry,' Copaken says. Speaking in English, supplemented with gestures, Copaken asked for copies of the documents, which were immediately provided, some in English, some in Japanese. Copaken took these documents to his Japanese law colleagues for translation. 'Lo and behold, we were dealing with at least $104 million a year, whereas the Japanese government was telling me it was only some $200,000 to $300,000 a year.'

On the next day, Copaken and Gannon went to 'the den of all these cartels,' a Tokyo office building where the associations were headquartered. Copaken's extraordinary luck held. Although it was Sunday, there were a few people working in the offices. 'They showed us right in. I kept on asking people, "Where is the laboratory that receives all these moneys from the bicycle racing and spends them on developing machine tools?"' In response, Copaken was given a brochure describing the Technical Research Institute of the Japan Society for the Promotion of Machine Industry, which included the laboratory's address in a Tokyo suburb.

While Gannon and his TV crew went on to film bicycle races in Nagoya, Copaken had his hotel telephone the research institute. He identified himself as an American visitor interested in how the Japanese were developing the machine tool industry in Japan. Could he visit them? 'Apparently, they'd never had a request like that before,' said Copaken, 'and they agreed.'

Copaken caught a train to the laboratory, bringing along his video camera. 'I just laid it over to one side, but these technocrats were fascinated with this latest, state-of-the-art Hitachi video camera,' he recounts. 'They started asking me about it, and I showed them how it worked. I just kept it running for the rest of the day. I got a fantastic interview and was able to record all the joint anti-competitive research they were conducting and how it was financed with bicycle racing funds.'

The institute's director surprisingly revealed that his facility alone got some $13 million annually in direct grants for joint research for member machine tool companies. This research, the director proudly explained, was shared with the entire machine tool industry, in order to promote its technological development. At the very moment Copaken was conducting these interviews, the government of Japan was submitting a diplomatic note to the U.S. State Department in which it asserted that subsidies from bicycle racing to the Japanese machine tool industry had never exceeded $500,000 annually.

After his return to Washington, Copaken spoke to James Murphy of the U.S. Trade Representative's office, who told him they had received a diplomatic note denying all Houdaille's charges. 'I told them that it was very interesting, but I said, "Let me show you some tapes."' The next day in a government office building across from the White House, Copaken played his videotaped interviews to an audience of a dozen officials, senior staffers from the Trade Representative's office, from Justice, Defense, the National Security Council, Commerce, Treasury, even from Transportation. The evidence on the tapes was conclusive.

Copaken's own efforts to get a response from MITI had been met with silence, but after the meeting and a second formal U.S. diplomatic inquiry, Japan finally responded on their bicycle race connection. 'If you carve away all the verbiage and get down to the crux of it, they essentially said, "We concede the $100 million that Mr. Copaken documented. But we won't confirm anything beyond it,"' Copaken relates. 'Of course, this told me that I hadn't done a very thorough job. If they were going to admit to $100 million – then there *must* be much more. I decided I'd better get the hell back to Japan and find out exactly what the total was.'

Once more, Copaken flew to Tokyo, where with the help of the Japanese law firm, he obtained statistics published by the Ministry of Home Affairs as well as other incriminating material. 'I discovered that it wasn't $104 million a year, it was $985 million a year,' Copaken now says. His new documents included a list of the machine tool companies receiving bicycle race grants and subsidies, and the amounts. When executives of several grantee companies agreed to meet him, Copaken asked each about the subsidies and videotaped their answers whenever he was permitted.

On his return to Washington, Copaken put together a second show on Japanese business methods for U.S. cabinet staff officials. On April 15, 1983, Houdaille's petition to President Ronald Reagan for relief from Japanese machine tool imports was discussed by several members of the U.S. Cabinet, who met for two-and-one-half hours. After considering Houdaille's carefully constructed case they were in agreement on almost all points raised by the American machine tool maker.

In a statement labeled 'Agreed Facts,' the cabinet members confirmed that MITI had annually subsidized its machine tool industry with nearly a billion dollars in gambling revenue from bicycle and motorcycle racing. MITI had also conspired to weed out the smaller, less profitable companies in the Japanese industry, forcing mergers and jawboning companies with only limited production to switch to other products. Japan had turned an officially blind eye to clear violations of its own anti-monopoly laws by machine tool manufacturers. MITI had encouraged the machine tool cartel to price their exports below fair market value, allocated market segments to various companies and worked to prevent the import of foreign machines. Simultaneously MITI had provided huge tax incentives, subsidized R&D, and provided below-market loans.

The cabinet members had agreed that Japan had severely damaged the U.S. machine tool industry, but they could not agree on a course of action. According to Copaken, Secretary of Commerce Malcolm Baldridge supported granting Houdaille's petition, which called for denying American purchasers of Japanese-made machine tools the valuable investment tax credit. U.S. Special Trade Representative William Brock agreed. Representatives from other departments were divided on a course of action. The final decision, they agreed, would have to rest with President Reagan.

Copaken had proved to be a formidable opponent of MITI, but the Japanese were not giving up. In the last moments of the struggle, they displayed great ingenuity in protecting their multibillion dollar export business. Kazuhiko Otsuka, an affable, high-level trade specialist in the Japanese embassy in Washington, had heard of the crucial cabinet meeting in advance. Knowing how important it was to learn the cabinet's conclusions before President Reagan did, Otsuka camped out in the antechambers of the U.S. Trade Representative William E. Brock while Brock was still at the cabinet meeting. When Brock returned, Otsuka rushed up to him and prodded him into blurting out that the cabinet had agreed that Houdaille's petition was accurate. Otsuka excused himself and immediately got on the telephone to Tokyo.

Before President Reagan could be properly briefed on the details of the cabinet debate, he received two urgent messages from Japanese Prime Minister Yasuhiro Nakasone. Nakasone reminded Reagan that he was facing a challenge in the forthcoming elections of the House of Councillors, the influential upper house of the Diet. He also told Reagan that he and his government had gone on record for increasing Japan's military defense capabilities, as the U.S. had requested. Perhaps the President might focus on the broader considerations involved when he pondered the Houdaille petition.

Soon after, despite the unimpeachable evidence against the Japanese, President Reagan turned down the Houdaille petition. A high U.S. official said that a ruling against Tokyo would have been grievously undiplomatic at the time. 'They told us they would consider a finding of unfair trade practices as the equivalent of branding Japan, America's foremost Pacific ally, as an enemy,' stated the Administration official. This statement is understandable only when it is recalled that many of the illicit activities MITI had either sanctioned or instigated took place during the period when Prime Minister Nakasone himself was the head of MITI.

Houdaille and America and the Europeans have thus far been losing the major battle, but Houdaille has had a pyrrhic victory of sorts. Under threat of an ITC ruling that would have denied Yamazaki permission to market its machines in the U.S., Yamazaki finally settled with Houdaille. 'They gave us a substantial sum and we terminated our licensing agreement,' said Jack Latona. 'The whole thing was a screwing. You settle things, in part, because of what it costs you to get any kind of protection from your own government even though you've been wronged. The only reason we got what we did was because the ITC made it quite clear that they would come down on our side.'

Meanwhile, there are thousands of new Japanese NC machine tools in U.S. warehouses waiting to be sold at huge discounts, an inventory that threatens the survival of that American industry. These are machine tools that were designed, in many cases, with American technology copied or stolen by the Japanese. Machine tools built by Japanese companies that received massive government subsidies from gambling profits. Machine tools built by Japanese cartels that have never had to face American or European competition in their home markets.

The Houdaille-Yamazaki case is vitally important, not only because it involves another key American and

European industry threatened by the Japanese, but because it demonstrates the ingenuity of the Japanese in pursuing their unethical, state-directed economic aggression – one that has targeted one industry after another for conquest.

4   Deluge at Silicon Valley

As 1978 drew to a close, the industrious chipmakers of California's Silicon Valley reflected on their achievements. It had been a vintage year for semiconductors, a year of rising sales curves for their tiny chips, each containing tens of thousands of miniature transistors etched into silicon wafers smaller than a fingernail. It had been an especially profitable year for the dozen American companies whose immaculate 'clean rooms' produced 16K memory devices, the so-called dynamic Random Access Memory chips, or RAMs.

Silicon Valley was proud of its new product, a technological triumph which had brought prosperity to the communities in the lush Bay Area of California. The new ICs, or integrated circuits, were micro marvels, each able to remember more than 16,000 individual pieces of information and provide any one of the bits, or any combination, on demand to the microprocessor, the chip that is the brain of a modern computer.

Its pride was justified. Designing chips with tens of thousands of individual components, was a distinctive national accomplishment. It was the result of the confluence of peculiarly American elements: brilliant technical innovation, money risked by thousands of investors, and the hustling but largely ethical entrepreneurism displayed by the founders of a youthful industry just reaching adulthood. 'The semiconductor industry was born in the Bell Labs, and developed almost exclusively by American firms,' boasted Warren Davis, an official of the Semiconductor Industry Association.

Only American industry was strong enough to make and sell semiconductors, rich enough to fund the relentless obsolescence in technology, large enough, smart enough, competitive enough to find the scientists, workers, designers, marketers, and managers to accomplish the task. Perhaps most vital, only in America were there companies willing to risk their capital, even their entire futures, to gamble on making the semiconductor revolution a reality.

Silicon Valley's computer scientists, technicians, chemists, marketing and financial executives toasted 1978. Many celebrated recent raises and promotions in their ranch-style homes in the cool hills above Silicon Valley, in such expensive suburbs as Campbell, Los Gatos, Menlo Park, and Palo Alto. Others drove their imported sports cars to Santa Clara's Decathlon Club, where the Valley's elite tilted their Perrier and Zinfandel glasses in celebration of all that RAM chips had done for them, and to all the good things to come. Even in the stagflated American economy of the late seventies, semiconductor product sales were rising 22 percent a year, and the sales curve seemed to be getting steeper. By 1978 revenues had reached more than $5 billion a year, and 1979 promised more.

Silicon Valley resonated in harmony with the ever-growing demand for more RAM chips from giant computer makers like IBM and Control Data. More modest-sized firms such as Digital Equipment and Hewlett Packard were also buying them for use in their most powerful mini and mainframe computers. Electronic and videogame manufacturers were devouring truckloads. Young companies like Apple, as well as such mature firms as Tandy, the parent of Radio Shack, were creating new home computers around the miracle chips. Automobile and home appliance makers were discovering novel applications for microchips in models yet to be built. Millions of chips were gobbled up by calculator and watch makers; the telecommunications industry hungrily ingested hundreds of thousands for switching systems, avionics, navigational and communications equipment.

If 1978 had been a good year, 1979 would be even better, Silicon Valley insiders were convinced. As for 1980, they knew that better memory chips would soon be coming out of research clean rooms. Scientists were already exploring the technology required for a 64K RAM chip. This latest triumph of American know-how was a silicon wafer no larger than a breakfast bran flake, a memory chip four times as powerful as the 16K, a chip with *hundreds of thousands* of transistors, which could store more than 64,000 bits of data.

Its elegant, innovative design approach was a model of American ingenuity; it would be ready for mass marketing early in 1981, or a little sooner. Product development teams at several companies were pondering applications for the new chips, designing new products and new uses for a device all but unimaginable only a decade earlier. Not WIN buttons, slogans, or arcane economics, but semiconductors, devices as American as baseball and Chevrolets, were going to get America moving again as the high-tech revolution shifted into miraculous gear.

Optimism and faith in self and America so permeated Silicon Valley as 1978 ended that few in the semiconductor industry bothered to glance at the Pacific horizon, where a small black cloud, almost obscured by distance and the bright glow of success, a black cloud made in Japan, rose in the East.

Japan, which would pass the U.S. to become the world's leading car maker in 1981, had already set its industrial sights higher than automobiles. In the early 1970s, Japan's MITI, the Ministry of International Trade and Industry, acting in concert with the six leading Japanese electronics firms, had forged consensus on an important dimension of national industrial policy for the coming decades. The future, they correctly inferred, would belong to those who could organize and control knowledge. Translated into industrial action, this meant that the future would belong to the nation that could lead, then dominate, the computer industry.

The key to industry dominance, the Japanese reasoned, was mastery of the multitude of complex techniques that are used to build microchips. The most important chip to build initially, using the most advanced Metal Oxide Silicate (MOS) technology, was the dynamic memory chip, the RAM. 'Dynamic RAMs lead MOS technology. Period,' explains Wally Rhines, a senior vice-president of Texas Instrument's Semiconductor group.

MITI was also aware that RAM chips in themselves were destined to become a multibillion dollar business. Whoever could produce the best RAMs at the best price would quickly carve out the largest share of the rapidly expanding world market. Obviously, some Americans were aware of this too. 'Semiconductors are the crude oil of the 1980s,' was a phrase coined by Silicon Valley's W. J. (Jerry) Sanders III, the feisty, flashily dressed president of Advanced Micro Devices, a leading manufacturer of integrated circuits. It was a phrase reiterated, usually without attribution, by publications worldwide. The pithy economic truth was echoed by *Japan Economic Journal*, which stated candidly that 'semiconductors are very likely to determine the level of a country's computer, telecommunications, robotics, aerospace and other high-technology industries of the future.'

If the Japanese could control the RAM market, they would then have access to the technology and revenues that would in time assure dominance in all other microchip manufacture. Within a decade, this supremacy would provide the financial and technological underpinning needed to first achieve world leadership in the knowledge-intensive industries, and then become *itchiban*, the number-one economic power of the world. In 1975, MITI and Japan doggedly set out to become the Saudi Arabia of semiconductors. It was a terribly ambitious undertaking.

If tomorrow a space ship from another galaxy were to crash on earth, yet remain sufficiently intact for our scientists to determine its nature, purpose and function, we would have a situation analogous to Japan and America in the 1960s. Our science has evolved to the point where the materials used in this alien machine could be analyzed, and the molecular structure understood, but it is unlikely that Earth scientists could quickly make a copy of that sophisticated vehicle. While they might be able to perform reverse engineering – that is, take it apart and discover the principles on which it operates – they would not know how to make the tools that made it. In all probability, they would even lack the tools to construct the tools to make the space ship.

In a way, Japan's chipmakers found themselves in a similar situation at the end of the 1960s. Sony, then a struggling, almost unknown, Japanese electronics firm, had in 1955 acquired a license from Western Electric for a mere $25,000 to manufacture that seminal American invention, the transistor. Surprisingly, it was done over the initial objections of MITI, whose officials now like to point to that failure in foresight as proof that it cannot control the actions of one small company, let alone a major industry. In actuality, Japan, still suffering the disastrous effects of the war, had not yet grasped the long-range economic implications of semiconductor technology. And Sony's president and cofounder, Akio Morita, then an outsider in an insider's country, was not intimidated by his government.

Sony first used the transistor, which Western Electric had put in hearing aids, to turn out small portable radios, which millions of young people, including American soldiers stationed in Japan and Korea, found attractive. Some of Japan's insider companies, the horizontally and vertically diversified *zaibatsu*, were envious of Sony's success and rushed to make transistorized products of their own.

By the time this technology was being developed into a high state in the U.S., Japan's electronics manufacturing industry had grown into a dominant force. Japanese-made radios, cassette and tape recorders, hi-fi equipment, television sets, and microwave ovens had flooded the world's markets, forcing many American and European giants out of business. The old Japanese prewar cartels, the *zaibatsu*, had more than recovered their prewar pre-eminence, and the newer *shinko-zaibatsu* – the same companies efficiently reorganized – rivaled them in every way.

Although the conglomerates that controlled Japan's leading electronics firms were rich and powerful, none seemed willing to risk the major expenditures of capital required to keep up with the state of the semiconductor art practiced by American companies. The few integrated circuits brought to market by Japanese companies had been of poor quality, not unlike earlier Japanese-made automobiles. Nor had they sold well. Gearing up to compete with American industry involved too many hazards, and there was no guarantee of success. Japan's large electronics companies were making money with their multitudes of existing products; why undertake something that was difficult and expensive, and uncertain of success? Risk is not a characteristic usually associated with Japanese business; the *zaibatsu* wanted assurances from their government.

In December 1971, MITI pressured Japan's six largest electronics manufacturers into joining in a cooperative effort to target the American semiconductor industry. It was accomplished through the promise of subsidies, low-cost loans and preferential tax treatment, and the threat of government foot-dragging in areas of vital concern if they failed to cooperate. To 'minimize duplication and share costs,' MITI paired Nippon Electric Corporation (NEC) with Toshiba; Oki with Mitsubishi; and Fujitsu with Hitachi.

Considering the point at which these firms had started, the technological results were significant after a period of only three years. But in the marketplace, Japan's 'knowledge' products were still unimpressive. Its computers, and the semiconductors within them, were overpriced, imitatively designed, low-quality items that could not compete. If the Japanese electronics manufacturers wanted state-of-the-art quality and price, they still had to buy American integrated circuits.

In America, innovation was king and entrepreneurs were flourishing. New electronics firms were sprouting like grass after a spring rain, thriving in industrial parks, garages, and even on kitchen tables, all nurtured by the fertile soil of Silicon Valley. Other new companies were started when the restless talents of more established firms quit to pursue their own dreams.

A classic example is Intel, now one of Silicon Valley's largest chipmakers. In 1968 Intel began as an offshoot of Fairchild Semiconductor, one of the Valley's oldest companies, which began operations in 1957 when Gordon Moore, then only 39, left to cofound Intel with Robert Noyce, then 41. Noyce, an Iowan with an MIT electronics doctorate, is the coinventor of the integrated circuit. At the start of his career, Noyce was a disciple of the American coinventor of the transistor, Bell Telephone Lab's Nobel laureate William Shockley. Moore is a San Franciscan with a Cal Tech doctorate in physics and chemistry. Together, Moore and Noyce, who account for some 20 patents on semiconductors, typify what people in the semiconductor industry mean when they refer to someone with 'the right stuff.'

Intel began with only a handful of people and quickly acquired a reputation for innovation. In late 1969 a now defunct Japanese calculator manufacturer named Busicom asked Intel to produce a set of 12 microchips for a line of high-performance, programmable calculators. Intel's researchers decided that while they could make chips to perform the required functions, the Japanese design would lead to a clumsy, expensive device. In search of other solutions, they were inspired by the lean architecture of a large mainframe computer the company used to perform scientific calculations. The big computer sparked a novel design approach that begat an entirely new kind of chip. The new Intel microchips reproduced the functions of the large, expensive, power-hungry mainframe computer on tiny, inexpensive silicon wafers that used only small amounts of power.

It was a revolutionary achievement and led to the reproduction of an entire computer on just four silicon chips. By 1971, Intel had acquired about 500 employees and was annually selling about $9 million worth of their semiconductor devices, including chips with permanent 'read-only memories' (ROM) containing instructions that were issued repeatedly to the computer's central processing unit (CPU), its brain.

By 1976 Intel had learned how to further shrink the size

of individual chips. With miniaturization, the number of transistors on each chip increased, as did the complexity of their functions. Intel produced the world's first computer-on-a-chip, the 8048, a wonder that virtually duplicated the functions of the far larger computer which had been used to design it. Cramming tens of thousands of transistor devices onto a single, postage-stamp-size chip represented a new breakthrough in chip design and in construction of the machines needed to manufacture it in mass quantities.

Intel was at the forefront of world semiconductor technology. Its success sparked a number of American competitors, and by July 1976, 54 different microprocessors had been announced by a rapidly expanding industry. Dozens of special-purpose chips were invented by American companies, and suddenly everyone, it seemed, was selling chips or making new products that took advantage of the capabilities of these marvelous devices.

In Japan, MITI regarded the technological genius and explosive growth of the American semiconductor industry with envy. Clearly, America's lead, together with the financial benefits it conferred, was lengthening. Unless the Japanese began immediately, it would be too late for them to achieve parity with America in semiconductor manufacture, much less eventual dominance of the field. It was time for the Japanese to make their move.

America had naively given Japan a start by licensing more than 30,000 patents for U.S. semiconductor technology to Japanese firms between 1950 and 1975. But Japan still had to acquire the newest technology in a short time. First, Japanese scientists would have to unlock the secrets of Very Large Scale Integration (VLSI) design architecture, a process requiring mastery of the highly advanced chemical and physical processes needed to make the silicon wafers. They would have to learn how to make photolithographic systems that could reduce a fine line drawn on a wall-size design blueprint to a few ten-thousandths of a millimeter's width on a chip measuring only a few millimeters. They would have to learn to make and use not only the machines that made the chips but also the highly sanitized workspaces where the machines were installed. And they would have to recruit, train and manage a large, expensive work force.

All this required enormous sums of money. It would come from both private sources – Japan's banks and participating electronics companies – and typical Japanese public sources: low-interest government loans, subsidies, grants, tax credits. The project was so ambitious, so costly, and MITI's timetable so brief, that research would have to be conducted jointly by the government and private industry. Like many projects of the state capitalism of modern Japan, it was organized much like the U.S. Manhattan Project that built the atomic bomb during a wartime emergency. Only this time the payoff would not be military victory, but jobs and market share.

There was neither time nor money to waste on duplication of effort by various companies. MITI would have to organize the whole project, parceling out various tasks to the company or government lab best suited to each job. And MITI would have to supervise the use of the technology yielded, ensuring that after the research was conducted, no company would get a jump on the others. It had nothing to do with conventional capitalism or free enterprise. It was a state project – Japan against Intel and the rest – with all the advantages in mobilizing resources that governments have over individuals.

The first goal was to achieve parity with the leading semiconductor manufacturers in the United States. Then they would seize a majority of the market, crippling the American firms that had spent decades risking their stockholders' money and the careers of their management to achieve their present technological leadership.

'In April 1975, MITI organized Hitachi, Fujitsu, and NEC into a team to develop large scale integrated circuits,' explained Alan William Wolff, a partner in a Washington, D.C., law firm specializing in trade issues. To bring maximum scientific effort to bear, MITI next went to Nippon Telephone and Telegraph (NTT), the state-owned telecommunications company, and insisted that NTT join with MITI's own electrotechnical laboratory. Tackling VLSIs would require all the technical expertise then available in Japan. Its scientific legions marshaled, in July 1975 MITI launched the VLSI project.

Attorney Wolff addressed an angry crowd of executives at the Semiconductor Industry Association's Long Range Planning Conference in a plush Monterey, California, hotel, the Del Monte Hyatt, in late November of 1982. He explained how MITI organized the Japanese electronics concerns to defeat their American competitors. 'MITI and NTT agreed to consolidate their efforts in the creation of the VLSI Association to share information, divide developmental tasks, and reduce R&D costs,' Wolff said. 'The basic research would be done in the cooperative laboratory that it had in NEC and Toshiba, who were working on non-IBM compatible components. These two units were working on applied research; the MITI laboratories and NTT laboratories were also working on basic research, with coordination . . . done in the VLSI organization.'

Initially, the Japanese government funded the project with $132 million in *hojokin* loans, loans that are actually government subsidies because they bear no interest and are to be repaid only when and if the private companies turn a profit on products resulting from the technologies developed. At this writing, not a yen of these loans has been repaid. In addition to government money, about $190 million in nominally corporate funds was invested, though there is evidence that the source of these funds, low-interest, below-market rate loans channeled through an industry association, were actually another disguised subsidy. 'The results were a thousand patentable technologies,' said Wolff.

This government activity freed the participating firms to use their own money to expand manufacturing capacity. By pooling their efforts the six Japanese companies also avoided the costly duplication of research that normally occurs because competing firms want to keep their discoveries secret until a product is ready for sale. A senior Japanese semiconductor company official later publicly boasted that participating in the VLSI project had saved his firm 80 percent of what it would have spent to acquire the same technology on its own.

The fruits of the MITI project were quickly passed to its Japanese participants. But unlike American research 'imported' by Japan, none of this technology was permitted to leave Japan. Until Japanese companies had achieved MITI's goals, licenses for new semiconductor technology were denied to foreign manufacturers. Japan would continue to buy, or steal, technology from the West, but it was very important that the American companies not learn what MITI was planning until it was too late.

The small inclement cloud that had appeared on Silicon Valley's horizon in late 1978 was beginning to hover ominously. Japanese chipmakers, who had turned out small numbers of 4K RAMs of indifferent quality for domestic consumption in late 1974, harvested the first results of the MITI-VLSI project in 1978 in the form of 16K chips. These new Japanese chips were of markedly better quality than the preceding generation. But they were not mainly the result of original Japanese research. They were based on the best American designs; some say that they were simply stolen from American technology. 'Their 16K chip was a photographic copy of the Mostek chip,' declares John A. Calhoun, Intel's tall, lean, bearded director of business development.

At first, most of these new Japanese chips were bought by other Japanese factories, later to emerge inside electronic products destined for local consumption. Almost none were exported. As a result, very few in Silicon Valley were aware how big the offending Japanese cloud was and how imminent was the attack on their industry.

Japanese tend to cluster each type of business in a separate district. In Tokyo, near Akihabara Station, there are several square blocks of stores, shops, wholesale warehouses, and distribution centers for the consumer electronics industry. Packed into these few blocks are thousands of individual companies, great and small, which sell everything from transistors, microchips, wire and batteries, to refrigerators, tape players, microwave ovens, rice cookers, high fidelity amplifiers, and the latest home computers.

A few blocks away is a smaller district of rug and floor-covering merchants, two streets of shops where virtually anything available in Japan for floor covering may be found. Not far away, in the streets between Jinbocho and Ochanomizu stations, are hundreds of stores selling new and used books; sales points for virtually all of Japan's thousands of magazines and every one of Tokyo's dozens of newspapers; wholesale warehouses and the offices of circulation companies; literary and book agents; and the publishing companies themselves.

Just as electronics and books have their own centers, so does government. The government district is a vast region of huge, monotonous, look-alike office buildings stretching for miles around the moats guarding Japan's nominal seat of government, Emperor Hirohito's sixteenth-century palace. Japan's plan for dominance of the knowledge-intensive industries through an assault on the U.S. semiconductor industry was conceived under the harsh overhead fluorescent lights of frugally furnished offices on the upper floors of MITI's ugly stone headquarters, a few minutes' walk from the Diet, the Japanese parliament.

MITI's plan was organized in four parts. The first was to master semiconductor technology. Such a huge project could hardly escape detection abroad. Accordingly, the VLSI project and its technological goals were actually announced by MITI and greeted with polite yawns in overconfident, burgeoning Silicon Valley. This indifference was partially understandable because the second, third, and fourth parts of the MITI project were never announced, and have yet to be fully acknowledged by the Japanese government. The CEOs and the rising execs of Silicon Valley, which owed its very existence to American-style entrepreneurism and the rough-and-tumble of the marketplace, could not see how Japanese companies could compete. But, as they incredulously and painfully learned, there was a way.

The Japanese Conspiracy

In every army, soldiers are taught the value of delaying tactics in defensive strategies. Space is traded for time, time needed to gather new strength and mount a counter-attack. And this strategy to protect Japanese industry from superior imported American microchips, was the second element in MITI's plan.

'U.S. semiconductor companies lost about $15 billion in revenues as a direct result of Japanese protectionist policies in the sixties and early seventies,' Robert Galvin, CEO of Motorola, America's largest chipmaker, told a Senate Foreign Relations Committee investigating trade barriers in Japan. But that was after the damage was done.

'U.S. semiconductor sales to Japan's domestic markets in 1973 were 8.9 percent of the total chips sold in Japan,' a spokesman for Silicon Valley's leading market research firm told the Semiconductor Industry Association (SIA). Between 1974 and 1978, this share hovered between 9.1 and 10.5 percent. As the VLSI project neared its final, crucial phase, MITI's minions needed state-of-the-art chips for their development equipment, chips that only the U.S. makers could supply. The American share of Japan's market rose to almost 15 percent in 1979, the last full year of the VLSI project, then declined rapidly. By the end of 1981 it was again back to just over 9 percent.

'The problem is one of Japanese firms having every reason to collude,' asserts Alan Wolff, the Washington trade attorney. 'These large, vertically integrated firms produce only about 18 percent of their microchips for their own use. So they are selling to one another, and that's a very cozy relationship. They are encouraged [by MITI] to buy Japanese.'

To ensure that the Japanese manufacturers would not have to go abroad to fill their chip needs, MITI 'rationalized' the new Japanese chipmaking companies by reorganizing the industry into complementary, largely noncompeting elements. It 'encouraged' each chipmaker to specialize in one or two types of chips. The only chips the Japanese industry would have to buy abroad were small numbers of highly specialized ones, those that they could not economically produce themselves.

Deluge at Silicon Valley

Japan had erected a series of formal trade barriers to American chips through quotas and import tariffs prior to 1973. Partly in response to American diplomatic pressure, most of these official barriers were dismantled between 1974 and 1976. Tariffs were reduced to a negligible level, just over 4 percent, to correspond with the U.S. level, and quotas for different kinds of chips were reduced in stages or eliminated. But these so-called liberalizations did not stimulate free trade. In fact, they had exactly the opposite effect. As MITI announced each 'liberalization' in a campaign to defuse criticism of its import policies, each barrier that was withdrawn was replaced by another, invisible one.

The new protectionism was so carefully coordinated that a few Japanese could not resist bragging about how well it worked: 'Protection has been provided those industries that are in need of protection because of their newness and their fragility as emerging industries. Thus protection is negotiated for the semiconductor and computer industries, and telecommunications. . . . This allows a nurturing of technology in the domestic market until competitive scale and sophistication are achieved.' This candid disclosure was made in an advertisement in *Scientific American*, paid for by 16 Japanese firms, including Toshiba, Matsushita, Sony, and TDK. But by the time it had appeared, in October 1980, there was no longer any need for secrecy. By then the Japanese cloud over Silicon Valley was raining RAM chips.

The first appearance of Japanese-made 16K RAM chips in U.S. markets came at a time when Silicon Valley was selling virtually every 16K chip it could make. Orders were running first weeks, then months, ahead of deliveries, but almost none of its companies could raise enough cash to expand production capacity. A senior official of the semiconductor association explains: 'With the whole U.S. economy basically flat – no real growth between 1973 and 1975 – the cost of borrowing money was quite high, and the equity markets were depressed, so there was little incentive before 1978 for chipmakers to expand capacity. Who can expand their work force and build new plants in the middle of worldwide stagflation?'

MITI had already answered that question when it put together the VLSI project. The answer was the Japanese government. The third part of their strategy was an elaborately disguised, massive infusion of capital subsidies to Japan's infant chipmaking industry. To maintain a facade of Western capitalism, most of this money did not flow directly from the government. Instead, MITI shrewdly channeled loans from the Japan Development Bank (JDB) to the Japan Electronic Computer Company, a private consortium acting as a financial godfather to the giant firms involved in the VLSI project. 'The concept of free trade is made a mockery of by subsidies and nurturing, targeting and protection of markets the Japanese have practiced for the last decade,' an angry Jerry Sanders now says. 'The Japanese subsidies have been in the billions – at least \$2 billion, probably more, between 1976 and 1980.'

The subsidies, which were disguised behind a bewildering web of artifice, were only the beginning. The active intrusion of the Japanese government into the new semiconductor industry made it a very attractive investment for private lenders. MITI's loans were a signal to Japan's bankers that the investment was secure. The U.S. General Accounting Office spelled this out in a 1979 report on trade issues with Japan: 'Commercial banks [in Japan] were able to get a specific "reading" of the industries which the government wished to favor from noting the companies to which JDB made loans. The government made no attempt to supply all the needs of companies. . . . the JDB loan meant that the large commercial banks would then give these firms priority for funds.'

The final stimulus from MITI was a tax giveaway. Because semiconductor technology moves ahead in spurts which transform today's state-of-the-art machines into antiques in three years, MITI provided a generous tax policy for VLSI participants. They permitted deductions of up to 60 percent of book value – the *list* price of the machines – for purchase of production equipment in their first year alone. They then added generous tax deductions for R&D costs and for exports.

The result was predictable. Supported, coddled, and motivated, the Japanese semiconductor industry was able to forego the necessity of normal capitalists – producing a profit – and moved relentlessly into the American market with an improved chip, which it sold at prices below American cost. In 1979, Silicon Valley felt the storm from the East. Japan's six chipmaking companies launched their first export drive and rapidly captured 42 percent of the U.S. market for 16K RAM chips.

Japan is a chain of volcanic islands, a small, mountainous, overcrowded country with virtually no natural resources. The homes of most of its 118 million people, as well as their places of employment, are crowded into a narrow strip of relatively flat land between Osaka and Tokyo. Riding the *shinkansen*, the bullet train, through this strip, the visitor looks out on an almost surrealistic landscape. Multitudes of apartment houses, small homes, shops, and factories are jammed together higgledly-piggledy, with no apparent plan. Huge steel mills stand next to the tiny shops of a small town. Chemical refineries sprawl against railyards. Smokestacks incessantly pour steam and industrial effluvia into the air, and that whole dense industrial strip of land resembles an ecological underworld covered with thick layers of grime.

Even the tiniest space between buildings is put to some use, whether for a single-row garden or storage. When a structure becomes too old, it is pulled down and a new one promptly erected on the same lot. When a building no longer serves its original purpose, it is recycled. If necessary its innards are gutted and a new interior installed. When Fujitsu Electronics needed more lab space for its part of the VLSI project, they chose a small plot of land in Kawasaki, a drab suburb 90 minutes by train from central Tokyo.

Kawasaki is home to dozens of large, depressingly ugly factories and small shops. Most of its daytime population is made up of workers who live elsewhere and spend up to three hours commuting to and from work. Fujitsu's chip labs and clean rooms were installed in a recycled building not far from the train station, a low, uninspired, white structure soon smudged into the prevailing gray of Japan.

But as the Japanese VLSI project moved rapidly ahead, MITI planners realized that the haphazard, all-but-gridlocked industrial zones in and around Tokyo, Nagoya and Osaka would not be adequate to the growing demands of the new knowledge industry. Once again, they copied America. Japan's answer to Silicon Valley is its own self-styled Silicon Island, the island of Kyushu, southernmost of the main islands of the Japanese archipelago. In recent years, most of the new microchip factories have been carefully seeded in the semirural communities around Kyushu. In Kumamoto Prefecture, the hub of Silicon Island, the dominant feature of the terrain is fire-spitting Mt. Aso, a live volcano that has been the island's main attraction for centuries. By 1980, the factories of NEC and Mitsubishi were spewing chips by the millions, $263 million worth in that year alone.

While Silicon Valley U.S.A. was struggling to keep its factories open in the recession of 1981–82, the four huge Japanese chip factories in Kumamoto set off an unprecedented local boom. Nodaichi Soy, a sleepy soy sauce factory, changed its name to Nodaichi Electronics, spruced up its grounds, hired 200 people, and started making components for Mitsubishi's RAM factories. Haraseiki, which had eked out a bare profit as a footwear wholesaler with a handful of workers, increased its work force to 500 and became one of Mitsubishi's largest subcontractors.

Other local firms hired software engineers, many just out of school, to design programs to run on the microchips pouring from the giant factories. Still other factories added new lines or converted entirely to making equipment that uses microchips, including robots, automated office filing systems and numerically controlled (NC) machine tools. Prefecture officials worked assiduously to plan the controlled growth of their cities, where they estimated at least 110 new companies would start in the next few years. The new Japan of world industrial domination, unlike the old, would be planned from the ground up.

The original Silicon Valley, the heart of America's semiconductor industry, is in California's spacious Santa Clara Valley. The valley starts in the suburbs of San Jose, at the foot of the great San Francisco Bay, some 40 miles from the city. It is an area of small towns nudging snugly one against another. Cupertino slides into Santa Clara, then melts into Sunnyvale, then sprawls into Mountain View. Along the main thoroughfares, the names of the shops and stores offer a familiar roster of everyday American commerce: Thrifty, Longs, and Save On; McDonald's, The Sizzler and The Colonels; Sears, Kinney, and K-Mart.

The residential streets curving behind the stores and shops have names like Oak, Grape, and Plum, in tribute to the rich farms, orchards, and vineyards that covered this area until after World War II. Or they are named for some real-estate developer's grandchildren: Jennifer, Jerry, and Joan. Silicon Valley's tracts of one-story frame, stucco, and siding homes, and its rows of monotonous apartments are relieved by the happy coincidence that conifers, palms, and leafy trees all thrive at this latitude. Lawns are littered with children's toys, driveways clogged with clunker cars, gaping garages filled with the familiar accumulations of the typical American.

Many who live in these apartments and tract homes are the families of the 180,000 people who make up Silicon Valley's hourly wage contingent. Supervisors and managers reside a little closer to the foothills, in towns like Palo Alto and Campbell. Top management, largely the self-made men and women of the entrepreneurial class, live in the cooler climes of the green, leafy hills. But the silicon in Silicon Valley is not in evidence. It is carefully hidden behind miles of manicured, tree-lined boulevards a few miles away, roads accessible only via a half-dozen freeways criss-crossed by spacious express roads with synchronized signals to speed Silicon Valley's commuters to and from work.

Insiders sometimes call the American computer and

semiconductor industry 'IBM and the seven dwarfs.' IBM is headquartered in Armonk, a quiet town in suburban New York. A few other large companies, including Texas Instruments, are located near Dallas. Others are congregated along Highway 128 near Boston. But most of the seven dwarfs, and their retinues of peripheral manufacturers, vendors, subsidiary and contractor companies, are concentrated here in Silicon Valley, reposing in lowslung concrete buildings that seem like endless variations on a single theme, all somehow resembling titanic versions of tiny transistor assemblies.

Smaller companies are situated in sprawling industrial parks, most differentiated only by logotypes displayed on near-identical signs set at uniform angles to the road. But big company or small, most Silicon Valley factories or office buildings are replete with mammoth parking lots and visitor lobbies where strangers sign in to receive color-coded badges proclaiming their status as outsiders. Departing strangers' briefcases or purses are routinely examined for purloined papers or other sensitive company material. In the highly competitive environment of Silicon Valley, security is tight. In 1980, after six Japanese chipmakers shared 42 percent of the American market in 16K RAMs, security became tighter than ever.

Inside the labs and clean rooms of Silicon Valley, America's top semiconductor researchers were hard at work on their response to MITI's 1979 surprise. They were working on the 64K RAM, the chip with four times the capacity of the 16K, the chip expected to sell in the millions of units, and sell for about four times the price of the 16K. The 64K was important not only for the revenues it would bring, but for the manufacturing expertise that producing such RAM chips teaches. 'Dominance in memories allows you to advance the technology, which is the precursor for dominance in the other fields,' explains Jerry Sanders. 'The other fields require more innovative solutions, but if you have a more precise foundry – which is what memory manufacturing gives you, the ability to build very large scale integration devices – then you have a more effective tool for building the other products. Putting it another way, if you want to consolidate your position, the first thing you make sure you have is the most powerful tools.'

In 1980, more than a dozen of America's leading chip-makers were digging into their corporate pockets to finance expanded production capacity and to design the 64K RAM chip that would maintain their preeminence. They had been frightened by the 16K onslaught from Japan. Now they were in for an even nastier surprise.

The Japanese 64K chips which appeared in mid-1980 shocked the Valley. By the end of that year, when U.S. companies were beginning to ship samples of their elegant new designs in 64Ks, the Japanese were already selling their chips here in commercial quantities. 'The Japanese chip was a brute force product, forced together from the American Mostek 16K design,' says Intel's John Calhoun. 'It wasn't a sophisticated design effort. Six Japanese companies produced 64K circuits within a very short time of each other, all looking identical. It wasn't very elegant, but it worked.'

What of the elegant American chips still under development? 'We screwed up,' admits Tim Propeck, director of product marketing at Mostek. Adds Calhoun: 'We were trying to be *too* elegant, and maybe *too* smart. And we let the market window disappear on us.'

As 1980 turned into 1981 the rain of Japanese chips became a torrent, then a monsoon. And as world markets were inundated by Japan's 64K RAMs, their price dropped precipitously, far below what Silicon Valley makers could sell at and still make a profit. Between December 1980 and January 1982, Japanese companies booked orders for 64K chips at the lowest prices in the world. In early 1981, while the market price was between $25 and $30 a chip, Fujitsu offered the 64K for $15. As prices fell again during 1981, the Japanese companies led the decline by keeping their prices $5 *below* the lowest U.S. seller's price. By the end of the year they were selling 64K RAMs for less than $8; by early 1982, four of the six Japanese companies were quoting a figure of $5 a chip. One even offered to sell 64K RAMs for delivery in late 1982 for $4.25 apiece. Americans were being priced out of the market, and eventually out of business, by profit-insensitive Japanese firms directed and subsidized by MITI.

'With most semiconductor products there's a 70 percent learning curve, e.g., every time you increase production volume by 70 percent, you can lower the market price 30 percent,' says W. J. Kitchen. Kitchen is Motorola's Phoenix-based manager for strategic projects, which include semiconductors. 'When the Japanese came into the market with the 64K RAM in mid-1981, they stood that curve on its head. They had a 20 percent increase in volume but an 80 percent reduction in pricing,' he adds, angrily. 'That drove most of the American companies out of the business. They just couldn't afford to stay in, so they cut their losses and ran. And it made it much harder for the companies that did tough it out to find the funds for R&D on other products. As long as the Japanese government is subsidizing these companies, they can afford to cut their prices to those levels. They can afford to give up all profits in exchange for market share, and no American company can compete with them.'

His view is widely shared by leading American manufacturers. 'Clearly our industry has been deprived of hundreds of millions of dollars – more like into the low numbers of billions – of profits, because of Japanese predatory pricing, resulting from their protected home market and their subsidies,' complains Jerry Sanders.

The Japanese strategy of crippling Silicon Valley and permanently taking its share of the market was working. That was the fourth part of the MITI campaign: to have Silicon Valley's balance sheets hemorrhage red ink. Japan would sell its chips at prices so low no U.S. company could compete. MITI's subsidized Japanese chipmakers reached through the American 64K RAM market window and took the lion's share, forcing most American and European manufacturers out of the semiconductor business. By 1983 Japan had taken 70 percent of the world market for the 64K RAM devices.

'We kind of gave the 64K generation to the Japanese,' said a rueful Jack Carsten, Intel's senior V.P. for components. The effect on Silicon Valley was devastating. Three-fourths of the dozen U.S. semiconductor industry manufacturers bailed out of commercial RAM manufacture as unprofitable. The firms that gave up in frustration, and disgust, include Advanced Micro Devices, National Semiconductor, Signetics, Zilog, Intersil (a division of GE), and American Microsystems. Only Motorola, Mostek, Texas Instruments, Intel, and Fairchild Semiconductor remained. All of TI's 'American' production was actually imported into the States from plants it had established in Japan a decade earlier with the intention of selling to Japanese customers. Mostek, a Texas company with a highly-creative management team, attempted to follow Japan's cut-throat pricing strategy, but was so enfeebled by the fight that it turned to a white knight to avoid bankruptcy. The white knight was United Technologies, a huge, diversified Connecticut company, which absorbed Mostek. 'It's pretty terrible when you've got to sell your company to save it,' said Tom Hinkleman of the Semiconductor Industry Association.

In 1979, venerable Fairchild, at the time the fifth-largest U.S. chipmaker and once a Valley giant, was taken over by Schlumberger, a French-owned multinational oil exploration company, for a mere $400 million. Another American chipmaker, Signetics, was absorbed by Dutch-owned Phillips, while several other, smaller companies were acquired by such diversified companies as Honeywell, Gould, and GE.

Even Intel was in serious trouble. Even Intel – whose management and technical innovation were the envy of Silicon Valley, whose young engineers spoke proudly of having graduated from 'the University of Intel,' and whose chairman, Gordon Moore, is universally referred to as the Valley's 'guru' – had felt the power of Japanese economic totalitarianism. By the end of 1982 Intel's long-term debt had ballooned alarmingly as the company desperately sought to maintain funding for its renowned R&D efforts. Intel was so starved for cash that in early

1983, they turned to IBM, who bought 12 percent of the company's stock for $250 million and took options on another 18 percent.

It was the end of an era, the end of Silicon Valley's two decades as the leading site of American-style start-it-on-a-shoestring venture capitalism. It was the victory of a well-managed, unethical, military-like economic onslaught by a major industrial nation on a handful of independent American companies.

But Silicon Valley's agony was not over. Japan's subsidized chipmakers now came out of the closet. Openly confident of victory, an executive of Nippon Electric Company (NEC) cheerfully admitted the goals of MITI's price-cutting strategy. 'The Japanese perspective is that when you're still making inroads into a market, you can't afford the luxury of making money,' confided Keiske Yawata, president of NEC Electronics USA, a new division of Japan's largest chipmaker. NEC commenced U.S. marketing operations long ago; now it is building a California factory.

In early 1983, another shoe fell. Fujitsu, one of the VLSI project participants, brought out samples of its new RAM, precursor of the next generation of chips, the 256K. Its early introduction seems to guarantee that the few surviving U.S. 64K RAM makers will not have the opportunity to continue selling their current chips through 1986, when they might expect to start earning their first real profits to offset massive losses on their 16K and early 64K chips.

'The Japanese have won what they set out to win,' says AMD's Jerry Sanders. 'It was to have a competitive manufacturing technology, competitive to American industry. They got this through protectionism and subsidies. They're playing a different game, a game called "gain market share." That's typical cartel mentality. Drive the others out, then you can price accordingly.'

Tom Howell, a Washington, D.C., attorney who represents the Semiconductor Industry Association, says that although some American firms are doing research on the 256K RAM, most have given up and are leaving the vital RAM field to the Japanese. 'The people in the industry are a lot more pessimistic about this chip than even the press accounts say,' Howell reveals. 'It leads you to believe that what's going to happen in 256K is as Jerry Sanders said, "What battle? A battle implies there's two sides."

'Typically the semiconductor companies invest a certain amount of money in R&D for the next generation product, as the companies that did the 16K and 64K RAMs. But the big bucks come in when you set up your production lines and commit to mass production. A lot of firms have now held back on doing that. "If the bottom is going to fall out of the price, why bother?" they ask.

'We feel that the Japanese have picked this area, and they've decided it's very important. They're going to pour a lot of resources into it, and as a result, most everyone on our side of the water has said, "Well, since they've picked that, we're just going to have to find somewhere else to work. We don't relish the prospect of a bloodbath." That was the gist of the 64K problem. Somebody like TI or Motorola can probably take the losses. But some of these other guys feel "Why bother? We can do other things with our money."

'This episode with the 64K RAM was bad,' Howell continues. 'The RAM is a mass-produced memory device that is a key part of our whole investment strategy. We learn from making these things, and what we learn we can translate into improvements in other products, plus we can make a lot of cash because these things are big sellers. Knock that out and not only do we lose some money immediately, but we are worried about the long-term effects. Motorola, who is staying in, is saying, "We've got to keep making them. We know it's a loser, but because we have all these other products, we're concerned about losing them. If we stop making RAMs we're going to start falling behind all across the board. So what you're looking at here is a process that may span ten years."

'There's sort of an alarm going up now,' Howells says.

'Look out, if they beat us here, the next thing you know they're going to be moving into some of the other product areas like logic, or the other memory areas, like EPROMs. They're going to show us up there, and before you know it, we're going to be disinvesting completely.' Disinvesting by Americans, is of course a euphemism for what had been foreseen by the modern Japanese state.

The beginnings of an American response although small, are in a cooperative industry organization, the North Carolina-based Semiconductor Research Corporation, SRC. Most of America's semiconductor and computer companies have contributed funds to support it. SRC does no research of its own but coordinates grants for fundamental semiconductor technology research at U.S. universities. The president of SRC is Erich Bloch, who is also an IBM vice-president. In 1983, SRC will channel about $11 million to academic researchers; they plan to increase this to $15 million in 1984 and by 1986 to more than $30 million. This is far more than the $7.5 million which the National Science Foundation spent in 1982 but far less than MITI pumped into Japanese research during the VLSI project. 'It has finally dawned on the country that this is one technology we can't afford to hand to the Japanese,' said John D. Shea, president of Technology Analysis Group, Inc., a California research firm.

Japan, meanwhile, is moving ahead rapidly with the production of the 256K chip. The design and manufacturing technology for Fujitsu's new chip has been transferred, virtually without cost, from Japan's state-owned Nippon Telephone and Telegraph Co. not only to Fujitsu but to Hitachi and NEC as well. A fourth Japanese firm, Oki, has announced plans for a new, 75,000-square-foot plant to house a pilot production line for their 256K chip. In the same way the 64K chip meant smaller, more efficient, cheaper products, the 256K will initiate a cycle of even smaller and better computers, robots, telecommunications, and manufacturing equipment. With sales of the 256K chip expected to reach $2 billion a year toward the end of the decade, the new generation of microchips will be the best-selling product in semiconductor history, another milestone on the road to what analysts project will become a $90-billion-a-year industry – ten times the size it is now.

The U.S. response to this latest Japanese chip is feeble. Western Electric, corporate descendant of the Bell Lab which gave birth to Shockley's transistor, is boasting about its own 256K chip, but many in the semiconductor industry are pessimistic. 'That's another brute-force product,' says Intel's Calhoun. 'It won't be a long-term, commercially viable chip.' Advanced Micro Device's Dr. Jim Cunningham, vice-president of the company's advanced technology division, also takes a dim view of this chip. 'It's a joke. It's prohibitively big,' Cunningham says. 'Cost is a very strong function of die size, and the Western chip will cost too much to make to price at a reasonable level. The Japanese chips are startup sort of numbers. They'll get the die sizes down and take them from there.'

'We've developed an entirely new kind of design for our 256K RAMs,' says Toshiba's Yuji Wakayama, the English-speaking head of the giant company's international public relations effort. 'The way to make a profit from chips is to increase the yield of each batch. With the high level of integration required, often one or two memory cells on a chip will be defective. Then the whole chip is defective. Now we've started putting a few extra memory cells in the corners. During inspection, if we find a defective cell, we'll use our new optical laser to burn out that cell and we'll replace it with one of the spares in the corner. This increases the yield.'

Toshiba began shipping these 256K chips to U.S. customers in early 1983. 'The U.S. mainframe computer makers are very pleased with it,' says Wakayama. 'So our engineers are very proud of this chip. It's proof that in this development race, Japan can win. We're already using this kind of technology on one megabit [1 million bits storage capacity] and four megabit RAMs, which we'll be making soon. After we make our profit on the 256K, of course,' he added with a smile.

Now that Japan's chipmakers lead in RAM technology,

their next step is obvious. 'We want to be a major U.S. semiconductor supplier, and there's more to the industry than memories,' says NEC's Yawata. His colleagues at NEC headquarters in Tokyo are even more specific. 'Our research effort is now directed at microprocessors,' says Tomihiro Matsumura, a senior vice-president. And Toshiba, another beneficiary of both the VLSI project and the NTT 256K technology transfer, has already introduced chips made with CMOS, complementary metal oxide silicate.

CMOS technology was invented in the U.S. and used widely in battery-powered devices such as digital watches and calculators. But when Japan took almost all this business from the U.S. in the early seventies, American companies abandoned research on it. Now Japan's chipmakers are introducing new chips with low-power – and low-heat – requirements for very high integrated or high speed circuits. Other Japanese chipmakers are bringing out dazzling new gate arrays, large, high-speed switching devices with an expanding panoply of applications as computers grow in power and shrink in size.

The Japanese continue to increase their production, adding pressure on their marketing men to take an ever larger share of the world business. In midsummer 1983, Toshiba announced it would double its capacity, to produce ten million VLSI chips per month by June 1984. A new plant in Iwate Prefecture, about 260 miles north of Tokyo, will be built at a cost of $123 million.

In July 1983, NEC announced construction of an $84 million plant to make three million 256K RAM chips a month in Kumamoto Prefecture, on the southern part of Silicon Island. The plant, which will begin production in July 1984, is to be adjacent to the world's largest semiconductor factory, owned by an NEC subsidiary.

Meanwhile a race is underway to develop the 'super chip,' a RAM chip that will store from 15 to 20 *million* bits of information. While the state-of-the-art in 1983 is a 256K chip, Japanese firms are working on a chip that will drastically shrink the size of larger computers and all computer-related devices, speed up their operations, and increase memory capacity. American firms are also doing research in this area, but the momentum of production and marketing in the RAM field has shifted so strongly to the Japanese that Americans may never recapture it. 'We'll easily take a good position over our American competitors,' predicts Tomihiro Matsumura of NEC.

Jim Cunningham of AMD is plainly worried. 'The Japanese are out to dominate the total electronics business, and it's going to be pretty hard to stop them. The only company I'm sure is going to make it is IBM. I'm not sure anyone else has the power.' His boss, Jerry Sanders, is bitter. 'America still leads in innovation, but we have to be present in the memory business in order to develop the technology and get down the learning curves. It means large capital investments. The Japanese have an advantage in this because they have access to cheaper capital. The solution the Japanese put forth is to tell us, "Well, there's just no room for small companies in this industry." Therefore National, AMD, and Intel should all be acquired by somebody, and so forth. But we have a history of diminution of influence in our field when companies are acquired. Fairchild and Mostek are just the most obvious examples of companies that at one time had technological leadership and once acquired by a larger company went into decline.'

Toward the end of 1983, American-owned semiconductor companies had been reduced to 53 percent of the $9 billion world market, while Japanese companies had reached 41 percent. But even these figures – which annually show an increase in Japan's percentage – hide a stark reality: the U.S. share includes Texas Instruments, most of whose chips are made in Japan.

A recent University of California at Berkeley study puts the Japanese threat in worrisome perspective. 'The Japanese successes signify much more than a loss of profits for U.S. firms in particular categories in a single industry,' it stresses. 'They indicate the potential for an irreversible loss of world leadership by U.S. firms in the innovation and diffusion of semiconductor technology, which will be at the center of competition in all industries which incorporate electronics into their products and their production processes.'

The Japanese have also set their national sights on the equipment to make semiconductors, a vital component of the international race. Japanese microchip manufacturers, once largely dependent on U.S.-made equipment, are now switching to Japanese. Nippon Kokagu, makers of the celebrated Nikon camera, entered the market with their own 'stepping' machines to make the wafers, which are later sliced into chips by diamond saws.

Nikon succeeded in the camera business after World War II by copying Germany's Leica and Contax models and selling them for considerably less than the originals. Using the same technique with complex stepping machines, Nikon has found a model – and target – in an American firm, the GCA Corp., now the world leader in the manufacture of stepping equipment. Nikon, whose machines perform almost as well, is selling their steppers for up to 30 percent below the GCA machines. The Japanese acquired the technology for almost nothing, a Japanese expert concedes, by 'reverse engineering' the American models.

Protected by complex import barriers, Japanese-made steppers now provide about 70 percent of Japan's domestic consumption, and the Japanese are working feverishly to upgrade their technology. 'It's a critical technology that has a lot to say about the future of the semiconductor industry,' acknowledges James Wolpert, vice-president of L. F. Rothschild, Unterberg, Towbin, a semiconductor industry analyst.

As 1984 drew near, the chipmakers of Silicon Valley looked back on 1978 with fond nostalgia for the good old days when every new year looked brighter than the last. It was a time when a dozen technological miracles were taking shape in their clean rooms, when Japan was just a country it was hard to sell to, when innovation was rewarded and the marketplace could make you or break you. In 1978, no one was frantically searching for some small niche in the market that the Japanese would not bother with.

In 1978, Silicon Valley was the knowledge industry's most important, most promising national resource. But in 1983 Dr. Jim Cunningham of Sunnyvale's Advanced Micro Devices, could candidly tell a visitor: 'I think that in five years Silicon Valley could be decimated. Like Detroit. Like Bethlehem Steel. A lot of the companies here will be absorbed by the Japanese multinationals. We'll probably do the R&D for them.'

5   The Japanese Ethic

'ALL WARFARE is based on deception.' This maxim, written by Chinese General Sun Tzu Wu in 500 B.C., has been taken to heart by the Japanese, who call upon it in their daily contacts with the West, with whom they believe they are in a life-and-death mercantile war. To win that war, they have made masterly use of Wu's admonition to deceive.

The lie is a universal tool. While a form of guilt is attached to it in Western cultures, the Japanese ethic makes it easier for a Japanese to tell an untruth. 'They have a clear distinction, which they call *tatemae* and *honne*,' says Jon Woronoff, who has been living in Japan for more than a decade and is author of several books on Japanese society. '*Tatemae* are things the way they should be: "everything's fine, we cooperate, we help one another." The *honne* is the real truth.

'Whereas, we in the West would see this as rank hypocrisy – and in some ways it obviously is – the first reaction of a Japanese person is to say the good thing, the nice thing, the appropriate thing, the suitable thing, even if he knows in his heart it isn't true. Even when they know each other very well the Japanese will first say the *tatemae*, and then, maybe after a few drinks, the *honne*.'

The Japanese have no guilt about this duplicity. 'It's a social practice,' Woronoff explained when interviewed. 'In fact, they would feel guilty about doing the other thing – they would feel very uncomfortable with truth. It's not entirely conscious; it's simply done that way.' For much the same reason, the Japanese are obsessively secretive. 'The *honne* are the things they don't want to tell. We are brought up to be truthful and to express our feelings; they are systematically brought up to repress – not to let people know anything. There is absolutely nothing they will volunteer. They won't tell anyone anything unless he specifically asks, and even then, if they feel it's something that they should not share with others, or makes them or others look less good, they won't do it.

'And they're not overly curious about others, either,' Woronoff continues. 'In Japan, you are punished for being inquisitive. If a Japanese person is curious and wants to know something, he finds it's so damn much work that after a time he just says: "The hell with it, I've got enough to worry about without finding out." It all fits together, part of a cultural mindset that is completely different from ours.'

The Japanese language seems designed for the speaker who wants to deceive. In Japanese, the verb is always placed at the end of a sentence, a syntax that can be artfully manipulated. It permits the speaker to state the subject and object of a sentence first, perhaps at great length. Meanwhile he monitors the reactions of others present and at the very last moment, inserts the verb. The verb he has chosen may not be the one he originally had in mind, but it now serves his purpose.

A hard verb may be substituted for a soft one, a conditional verb for an absolute, or even a negative for a positive. The speaker can thus completely reverse his statement before the utterance is completed. Since harmony is the highest priority, a Japanese can thus wind up saying what he thinks will please the listener by gauging his reactions. The Japanese listener will often understand this verbal flipflop for what it is, and as he hears one thing, he understands another. The Japanese language, in effect, allows him to speak from both sides of his mouth at the same time. On learning Japanese, St. Francis Xavier, the sixteenth-century Jesuit, called it 'the devil's tongue.'

Foreigners who are used to language as an instrument of direct communication, become confused when dealing with the Japanese. In any given conversation, a Japanese may be telling you the truth, not telling you the whole truth to protect you from unpleasantness, telling you two diametrically opposed ideas to convey indecision, or contradicting a previous sentence because he has observed either a pleasant or unpleasant reaction on your part. Unless you have learned the Japanese language, you will never – despite a bevy of translators – know what the speaker actually means. Only later, by his actions, will it become clear; but by that time it might be too late.

Written Japanese is just as complex and subject to as much vagueness as the spoken language. Just as the Japanese import technology today, they brought over ideograms – stylized representations of a thing, a place, or an idea – from China in the sixth century and set about modifying about 50,000 of them to their own needs. If a person knows the original Chinese, it is easy to understand the Japanese modification – called *kanji* – though not the other way around.

About the ninth century, a system of phonetic writing, *kana*, evolved to denote personal and place names, as well as peculiarly Japanese ideas for which *kanji* proved inadequate. Later, a second, more stylized *kana* was invented specifically to accommodate foreign terms. The first *kana* is called *hirakana* and the second, used somewhat as italics are used in English, *katakana*. As almost all Japan's modern technology is imported, *katakana* became even more important, especially as a way to transliterate the name of something that had no previous existence in Japan. A taxi became a *takesi*, rush hour became *rushawa*, and the first Western-style men's shirts, which at the time of Japan's initial exposure to the West were all white, became known as *waishatsu*. If a Japanese wants a pink man's dress shirt he asks for a *pinku waishatsu*.

There is another way of communicating in Japan, and it has been developed to virtually an art form. It is called *haragei*, loosely meaning 'belly talk.' It consists of a well-defined body language coupled with deftly inserted silences. For example, a government leader, a corporate executive, or a bureaucrat may wish to prove that he has indeed honored the letter of the law. In spoken conversation, the speaker will use all the appropriate words.

'Be sure that all assembly line workers are given the free choice of accepting overtime or rejecting it,' a company executive might tell a foreman. That is for the record, for others to hear, if someone should ever question why all 10,000 of a factory's work force 'voluntarily' worked overtime, and why none decided to decline management's 'request.' The executive and the foreman might each return to their offices and write a memorandum of the meeting, or make a diary entry of what was said, but they will not record the belly talk that took place. The belly talk in this case might be a subtle but clear message that the law notwithstanding, it was important to company goals that discipline be maintained; that production continue for several hours beyond the normal end-of-shift; that no worker be allowed to plead personal business as an excuse to leave.

There is no exact Western equivalent for belly talk, but if one can imagine two people having a conversation in a room they both know is 'bugged,' then a smile, a wink, a nod, or a shake of the head can render all words spoken into their exact opposite meaning. There are many other forms of *haragei*, including simply not answering a question at all, or grimacing at hearing a request. To a Japanese, this is as clear and unmistakable as the spoken word – perhaps even more so.

Those who deal with the Japanese are often frustrated by their seeming vagueness. This is a product not only of the general culture, but of the Japanese language, which shapes the Japanese ethic far more than the English language influences the attitudes of an American or an Englishman. 'English is intended strictly for communication. Japanese is primarily interested in feeling out the other person's mood,' states Masao Kunihiro, a Japanese anthropologist. Japanese is vague where English is precise, Japanese is oblique where English is direct.

Because of this obliqueness, much can be lost in translation. The most common reply to a request or an opinion is rendered by the word *hai*, which is often, inaccurately, taken for *yes*, signifying agreement. In fact, in typical usage *hai* merely means 'I have heard and I understand what you said.' Similarly, the phrase *zensho shimasu* literally means 'to handle (something) as well as possible.' Often this is used to mean 'let's talk about something else,' while a Westerner, hearing the literal translation of that Japanese phrase, might take it as a person's promise of action.

The Japanese language is used with a studied degree of understatement in nearly all situations. The gravest crises are described by the Japanese as if little is amiss; but this should not be interpreted to mean that the gravity of the situation is not having its full impact on the speaker. When Emperor Hirohito spoke on Japanese radio in August 1945 to announce Japan's surrender, for example, it was the first time his subjects had ever heard his voice. His speech was brief, lasting only a few minutes. When he described Japan's defeat, he merely said: 'The war situation has developed not necessarily to Japan's advantage, while the general trends of the world have all turned against her interest.'

It was unnecessary for Hirohito to mention that 200,000 people and most of the cities of Hiroshima and Nagasaki had been vaporized; that three million Japanese soldiers had died in China, in New Guinea, in the Philippines, on Okinawa and a hundred nameless Pacific islands; that Tokyo had been firebombed with impunity. It was enough to say that 'the war situation has developed not necessarily to Japan's advantage.' The seriousness was understood at once, merely because the person of an emperor had broken 2,600 years of silence.

Japanese are supremely status conscious, each constantly aware of his own niche in the system and who is both above or below him. Conditioned from birth to maintain harmony at virtually any cost, they feel an order from a superior is to be obeyed promptly and to the best of one's ability. Unlike the West, where hierarchy is fragile, even suspect, and orders are usually made emphatically, it is rare to give orders in Japan with much emphasis. It is simply enough to give the order for it to be obeyed.

Since status is extremely important in society, the

Japanese have developed highly stylized ways of expressing status in their speech. A company president speaks in
a certain way to his peers, in another way to senior subordinates, and in a third way to the rank and file. The
differences are in the choice of words, even in the tone of
voice.

Japanese is tailored to the status of the speaker *and*
the person spoken to while English does not take the
speaker's status into account. In English one describes
oneself as either 'I' or 'me,' but in Japanese the social
status of the '*I*' is explicit. For example, a woman might
say *watashi* or *watakushi* or even *atashi* in speaking about
herself. It depends on whether she is speaking to her
husband or to her father, to a woman friend, or to a child.

To avoid the difficulties involved in correctly determin-
ing status, the first-person pronoun is often omitted in
Japanese conversation. It is simpler in business to establish the status of all present if at first meetings there is an
immediate exchange of business cards. After the cards are
placed on the table with suitable ceremony, everyone
knows the pecking order of the hierarchy. The conversation can then proceed without anyone's being offended by
someone unknowingly granting too much, or too little,
status to another person.

In dealing with the Japanese, one is often lost in trying
to determine the true meaning of their statements. They
are quite capable of exquisitely camouflaging one intended meaning with its diametric opposite. Take the
common situation of a subordinate who fails to execute
orders to his superior's satisfaction. In an American company, the boss might well raise his voice, threaten the
employee with some sanction. 'Can't you even follow my
instructions! Do that again and you're fired!'

When a Japanese executive wishes to communicate the
equivalent, he will not display his emotions. He will not
embarrass his subordinate by calling him a name. He will
not reveal his anger, for to be publicly angry to a subordinate is usually taken as a sign of weakness. Instead the
Japanese executive will elevate the tone of his speech,
change to the honorific suffixes and most-exalted case.

In an exaggeratedly polite manner, he will speak to the employee as though he were supremely important.

He will beg that this personage attempt the desired task, one so trivial as to be far beneath the exalted one's concern. He might say: 'If it is at all possible, if it will not trouble you excessively, it would please me very greatly and I will be forever indebted if you would consider attempting this very inconsequential task some time soon.' Such speeches are accompanied by all the nonverbal signals appropriate to the situation, such as pouring a subordinate's tea, or offering him a cigarette, and by avoiding direct looks. Soon afterwards, of course, he may demote the employee, reduce his bonus, or see to it that he is not promoted.

This same technique is often used by Japanese on foreigners to display contempt or scorn, a ploy that is usually misunderstood by the outsider. When a Japanese seems to be much more polite than the situation warrants, a Westerner should immediately be on guard. In such cases, the most suitable outward response for the foreigner is to reciprocate the behavior. Contempt for another may be displayed by excessively low bows, excessively polite greetings or farewells. For a Japanese, whoever makes the first public display of discourteousness has lost the argument.

Japanese are not like Americans and Europeans in the way they perceive and react to events and ideas, nor do they necessarily share the same sense of right and wrong. A popular film in the early seventies, *Red Sun*, featured respective symbols of American and Japanese culture, an American cowboy gunfighter, played by Charles Bronson, and a samurai warrior, played by Toshiro Mifune. The samurai and the cowboy represent the most enduring values of each nation's cultural heritage. In the film, two capable men, each bound to different codes of honor, are adversaries in a desperate situation. To survive, they make a truce, and each learns to admire and respect the other.

It is well enough for a film, but to consider the realities behind the stereotypes is to learn much about how the Japanese mentality differs from that of the West. The cowboy of myth was strong, unusually self-reliant, a loner, rarely well-educated. Like all Americans, he lived in one small area of a huge, barely explored continent. This sense of roominess, of unlimited prospects, conveyed a freedom to choose that is ingrained in the American character – the opportunity to find another town, another ranch, another career.

Though a cowboy might carry a gun, he was nominally a Christian, and if he shot someone, even in self-defense, he would have to justify his act in a court of law. The few who flouted this ethic were shunned as outlaws. Even though there were never many real cowboys, Americans revere the cowboy's code of independence and justice, identify with it, perpetuate it in many modern ways.

In contrast, the word *samurai* comes from a root meaning 'man of service.' For nearly a millennium the samurai were ubiquitous throughout Japan, but lived mostly in urban areas near the seats of local authority, in a country that even four hundred years ago had a far greater population density than does American now. At the height of samurai power, about one Japanese in six belonged to this class and was comfortably supported by rice raised by the other five.

The samurai was comparatively well-educated. Unlike most rice farmers – and most cowboys – he had leisure enough to learn to read and write. Samurai customarily went armed in public; while all other Japanese were forbidden even to own a weapon, their two swords were symbols of their class and status. But if a samurai felt the need to draw sword or bowstring, he rarely did so against another samurai. If he killed or injured a peasant, he usually incurred no guilt or penalty. The samurai served only their feudal masters and were not accountable to the peasantry.

The society of the samurai was one of limited horizons. Everything depended on growing enough rice to feed the population, and nearly all cultivated land belonged to the feudal lords. Individual upward mobility was virtually unknown; a rice farmer's son would not dream of growing up to be a samurai. And even the samurai were bound to village, town, or city by kinship and feudal obligations. Since a samurai without a master was a samurai without income, a samurai would die defending his lord's fief. Many took their own lives rather than endure the shame of defeat, though a few chose the wandering life of the masterless samurai, the ones called *ronin*.

The end of Japan's long feudal period, and of the samurai, came soon after the Emperor Meiji ascended the throne in 1868 and instituted a series of reforms intended to bring Japan into the modern age. After quashing a revolt by the Satsuma clan in 1877, the samurai put away their swords and distinctive garb, and gave up most of their special privileges.

But beneath the veneer of Western dress and mastery of the technical and scientific, the Japanese psyche still echoes with feudal, samurai values. Some of the most successful units of Japan's mercantile army, Mitsui and Mitsubishi, were founded by samurai clans. The authoritarian hierarchy that served the warrior class was transferred intact to Japan's commerce and industry after the end of the samurai era. The idea of a rigid chain of command also defined the new order: *shacho*, the corporate president, directed numerous executives, including *bucho*, *kacho*, and *kakaricho*; *hancho*, the squad leader or foreman, then supervised *shain*, the worker.

The language of Japanese business, as reported in its own press, is replete with military terminology. Goals are objectives, actions to meet them are maneuvers. Markets are attacked, beachheads are established on foreign shores; competitors are outflanked, surrounded or beaten back; hard times call for digging in; success is victory. A 'salaryman,' the Japanese term for worker or executive, may wear a suit and carry a briefcase, but for the Japanese, business is the moral equivalent of war.

The samurai influence and the Japanese sense of honor and morality are illustrated by one of the most enduring stories of contemporary Japan, *The 47 Ronin*. First in

Kabuki, later in novels, and today in film, the tale is told and retold and echoed in countless derivative works. It is the factual story of a seventeenth century samurai named Oishi whose master committed *seppuku* – suicide – after being disgraced by a high official of the shogun. Swearing secret revenge, Oishi spent seven years pretending to be a dissolute drunk. He gathered a force of 46 other *ronin* and in a blinding snowstorm, seized the odious official's house, beheading him. Oishi took the head to the temple where his master's ashes were enshrined, after which all 47 *ronin* committed ritual suicide.

Japanese love this story; it has betrayal and treachery, drunken debauchery, violence, cunning revenge, and a dramatic mass suicide. Akiro Kurosawa, one of Japan's great filmmakers, used it for his 1950s film, *The Seven Samurai*, now considered a minor classic. Ironically, an American film based on the Kurosawa epic – *The Magnificent Seven* – transposed the story to the American West, where the samurai became cowboys. They were drifters and outlaws, but they rode not for revenge but to protect defenseless citizens of a small Mexican town from bandits. When they at last triumphed, the surviving cowboys did not, of course, commit mass suicide, but rode off into the sunset.

As the films demonstrate, the Japanese concepts of right and wrong are not the same as those of the West. Western logic admits of no contradictions. Precision is valued, proofs to theories are offered, axioms and corollaries accepted. While Japanese accept these principles in scientific applications, they reject them in human relations. To a Japanese, life is a natural contradiction; people are good *and* bad. Contradictions in life are not meant to be resolved, as in Western drama. Rather, they are harmonized. In fact, a man without apparent contradiction is considered a simpleton. A man with many is a hero or a villain, or both, depending on how he achieves harmony in life.

A Japanese may play many different roles, all honorable. If he is confronted by a far stronger opponent he may survive honorably by playing the fool, as did Oishi, the samurai of a disgraced lord, and Hirohito, the emperor of a defeated Japan, who went on Japanese radio to disavow his own divinity. If, later, he somehow defeats this adversary, his pretense of foolishness becomes admirable. When the adversary is more powerful, virtually *any* means employed to overcome him is justifiable, even murder. So throughout Japan's bloody history, the assassin, if he murders for principle – perhaps to right some grievous wrong or to bring some issue before the public – has been regarded with sympathy, even admiration. If his victim is an important man, as was the official whose head was taken, it is assumed that he must somehow have been lacking in some virtue. How else could the assassin have succeeded?

According to a 1982 Japanese poll taken by *Sankei-Fuji*, a communications conglomerate, a majority of Japanese perceive America as a lion among nations. If he who tames the lion is admired, then when a large foreign corporation, or the foreign nation itself, is humbled, it must somehow have deserved its fate, no matter what means were used to defeat it.

Unlike the Westerner, who prides himself on individuality, the Japanese always operates from within a team or a group. His ethics are situational ethics, values and morals submerged in those of a group from which no one can be singled out for responsibility. The goals of the individual Japanese are the group's goals, his methods the group's methods, his rewards the group's rewards. While a Japanese may belong to several groups simultaneously – an alumni group of his former university, a sports team, a school of martial arts, a religious sect – no group is nearly as important as the employment group. In the Western experience, the nearest comparison of this strong psychological attachment might be that of an individual to a fanatical religious cult, such as the Hare Krishna, the Unification Church (Moonies) or the Jonestown group, which demonstrated its obsessive loyalty by committing mass suicide.

Within the confining and traditional strictures of Japanese society, the group provides the only psychological outlet for each person's pent-up aggressions and competitive urges. 'Since there must be peace within the group, at all costs, the aggression must be directed somewhere else,' says Jon Woronoff. 'It's usually against a competing company, or nation.'

The dominant group purpose is to win. This seems little different from the Western aim, where corporations and football teams fight indefatigably for victory, either in the form of profits or by playing in a Super Bowl. But in Japan, the desire to win is considerably more obsessive. Winning is the only thing. The group, and the individual in it, must struggle to win at *all* costs, an obligation that can strain the limits of normal morality.

'There are lots of reasons why Japanese want to win,' says James N. Ellenberger, an international specialist with the AFL-CIO. 'Obviously they think they're better than anyone else. After you've been in Japan a while you can sense that immediately. They seem to have an inferiority complex, but a lot of that is put on. When they deal with foreigners they will purposely try to leave that impression, but amongst themselves, they're saying: "Gee, these jerks we have to deal with are incredible." This isn't much different than it was during the reign of shogun Tokugawa, in some ways. If you look at Japanese feudalism, you'll find an uncanny resemblance to a lot of things that are current.'

Woronoff concurs. 'This idea of winning goes back over two thousand years,' he explains. For the twenty centuries of feudal society that preceded the present era, the competing *daimyo* of each fief could only expand his influence at the expense of some other warlord. Today's *daimyo* is the corporation's president, and the fief is the corporation itself.

'When you're working for a company, and you know that if it goes under, you'll never get a job that good, you *have* to win,' Woronoff continues. 'If you're working for an American company, a European company, a South American company, and it's doing poorly, you quit and go to another. But a Japanese, in effect, *can't* leave his company. He must stay with the one that first hired him. If he leaves, it's almost impossible for him to get a job with a major firm. And so, if the company goes under, he not only loses his job, he loses his status, he loses his retirement benefits. He feels it would surely be utter destruction for him. Which, to some extent, explains the desperation with which the Japanese will fight for his company.'

Just as in feudal times, company victories come at the expense of their competitors, domestic and foreign. 'For Japanese, market share is important,' says Woronoff. 'But it's not just off-handedly important. It's crucial. There are books which list companies by market share, and even the newspapers and magazines do this once a year. For Americans, who are worried about profit, they couldn't care less about market share. They know you have a good year, then you have a bad year. It's not the end of the world. For the Japanese it's extremely important that if your company is number five, you don't become number six, this is a loss of face, a loss of prestige. It's a zero sum game. If I get one extra percent of the market I've got to take it from someone. My profit may or may not affect yours, but as soon as it comes to market share, it's impossible for someone else to gain without me losing. In addition, if you start at 30 percent and go to 28 percent and then to 26, the Japanese can imagine a doomsday scenario in which they will get down to zero.'

In developing skills that will help his company to win, the Japanese salaryman follows the path of his samurai antecedents. One of the 'bibles' of the Japanese management is *The Book of Five Rings*, the work of the samurai Miyamoto Musashi. Musashi was born at the beginning of the Tokugawa shogunate, in the late sixteenth century, and grew to adulthood at a time when the country had been unified for the first time under a military dictatorship. The way of the warrior was the rule by the strong of the weak. At the end of his life, Musashi set down the principles he felt would lead to victory in a military society.

Despite the passage of time and the formalized pretenses of Japanese-style democracy, Japan's present executives consider themselves heirs to Musashi's legacy. They study his book with great intensity, seeking new meanings for these ancient teachings – insights that will help them on the battlefield where export drives have replaced swords.

The Japanese draw on their feudal era for the 'secrets' of *bushido*. The term is written with three characters, *bu* (military), *shi* (man), *do* (way). *Bushido* is the code of the military man. Like most Japanese concepts, it is borrowed from foreign sources. From Zen comes stoicism, indifference to suffering, scorn for the weak and for death itself. From Shinto comes love of country. Shinto is the nationalistic religion that invests the sacred fields, rocks, mountains and lakes with spirits of their own. And from Confucianism comes the social ethic of the five relationships, of which the most important is the debt owed by subject to king, or in the Japanese system, by retainer to *daimyo*, by salaryman to president.

Japan's continuing fascination with its recent feudal past is illustrated daily in every bookstore, each of which devotes a section to the samurai. Among the most admired books are those about Japan's first shogun, Ieyasu Tokugawa. According to Yuzo Yamamoto, author of four business books drawing on *bushido* for source material, much of what Ieyasu put into practice is finding relevance today.

Ieyasu demonstrated, for example, how to manage a work force when it was impossible to grant adequate wage increases annually. Ieyasu separated wages from position and prestige. He granted his principal vassals vast authority, powers of decision-making that could affect the lives of all their subjects, and paid them low salaries. That sounds suspiciously like the middle echelons of most Japanese companies today. Ieyasu, who is widely believed to have achieved power simply by outliving all his rivals, is held up as an example of the virtue of patience, another characteristic of the Japanese corporate hierarchy.

Another role model eagerly imitated by the salarymen, especially those above the age of 40, is found in the young samurai who wrested power away from the last Tokugawa shogun, resulting in the Imperial Meiji Restoration and the beginnings of modern Japan.

Toyotomi Hideyoshi, who never took the title of shogun but whose military campaigns unified Japan for the Tokugawa shoguns who followed him, is considered as an exemplary Japanese. Hideyoshi was a master of deception who rarely displayed his true feelings or thoughts. While other warlords mercilessly put their vanquished foes to the sword, Hideyoshi spared defeated lords and was often able to achieve victory while avoiding bloody battles. Hideyoshi invaded Korea in 1592, the first step in his plan to conquer the world. Korea was considered the doormat to China. But the Korean Admiral Yi, using an ironclad 'turtleship' rowed by hundreds of oarsmen, routed Hideyoshi's naval forces and the boats carrying his reinforcements. The Koreans severed Hideyoshi's naval supply line to Japan. Isolated on the Korean mainland, Hideyoshi's Japanese Army was finally defeated by the Chinese Army in a crucial battle at the Yalu River. The underlying bitterness that characterizes Japanese-Korean relations to this day can be traced partially to that failed invasion.

Hideyoshi also confiscated the arms of the Japanese peasantry, drew a sharp distinction between the samurai class and the peasants, and after initiating the first land survey for all of Japan, fairly apportioned fiefdoms to his *daimyo*. Between them, Hideyoshi and Ieyasu provide all the necessary precedents for the current Japanese approach to corporate management.

The ways of *bushido* are taught to Japanese management just as they were once taught to the Japanese Army. Mid-level executives, with enough seniority to be earmarked for top jobs, are sent to special schools which teach, in effect, applied *bushido*. Junior executives are sometimes sent to training camps run by the Japan Self Defense Forces, for mental and physical toughening, and for additional self-discipline. Other firms use such schools as the Kanrisha Yosei Gakko (literally, management training school), in Fujinomiya, about 50 miles from Tokyo.

Kanrisha Yosei Gakko is the corporate equivalent of an officer candidate school except that it is a condensed course of only two weeks. Approximately 20,000 Japanese executives have graduated from Kanrisha since 1979, at a cost of about $1,000 per student. The point of the training is to fortify the strong and eliminate the weak. Companies sometimes fire those who fail to meet the school's strict standards, but they promote those who pass with distinction.

The curriculum is a lesson in rigor and self-abasement not unlike the most severe hazing found at military academies. Corporate executives take nocturnal forced marches of 25 miles, go without meals as punishment for substandard performance, humble themselves by loudly singing embarrassing songs on street corners at mid-day, humiliate themselves by confessing their inadequacies to a room of fellow students. One man was forced to declare that he was sexually inadequate, only to be told by his instructor, 'You're not even a human being.'

Students rise daily at 4.30 A.M. for strenuous exercise followed first by ancient samurai rituals, then by systematic hazing. Every morning before breakfast, the trainees spend 20 minutes bent double or on their hands and knees looking for nonexistent weeds. The purpose of this exercise is to teach the trainee how to react when given a senseless task, to teach 'inward calm.'

Outwardly, Japan is a modern society, but the Japanese still conduct their daily affairs as though they were a tribe in which everyone is supposedly related, a tribe that has its strict, often unwritten taboos, its well-defined hierarchies, its overwhelming concern for the welfare of the group. Since the only way to join a tribe is to be born into it, a streak of xenophobia permeates the Japanese ethic. Its source, like so many things in modern Japan, is rooted in its past. The Japanese have come far technologically, but they have made the change too rapidly to shrug off the feudal and oligarchic mentality that chains them.

They still worship their old gods, of whom the Emperor Hirohito is but one, and still cling to the belief that brought the present emperor's grandfather, Meiji, to power in 1868: 'Venerate the emperor and expel the barbarians.'

The arrival of American naval officer Commodore Matthew Calbraith Perry in Tokyo Harbor in both 1853 and 1854, with his black ships and technologically advanced weapons, disgraced the Tokugawa shoguns who had ruled Japan for two and a half centuries. By allowing the Western barbarians to enter the country, establish treaty ports, and exempt their citizens from trial by Japanese courts, the shogun and his supporters showed themselves to be impotent. Despite more than a million samurai under arms, the shogun had been unable to uphold the most important law of Japan: Keep the foreigners out.

Disgraced, the shogun was toppled; the power of the emperor was restored in 1868. Meiji's mandate was to take from the barbarians the three hundred years of technology that Japan lacked and use it to make Japan strong enough to remove the insulting presence of foreigners from their midst. Meiji abolished the hereditary fiefs, state salaries, and special privileges of the samurai, encouraged the growth of commerce and industry, and mobilized his entire nation under the slogan *fukoko-kyohei* – rich country, strong army. He died in 1912.

His son and successor, the Emperor Taisho, reigned only a few years before the first of a series of strokes incapacitated, then killed him. Meiji's grandson, Hirohito, was selected from among the princes royal, and trained by his uncles and their chief vassals to be an emperor in the tradition of Meiji. In a broad but accurate sense, Japan's leaders followed the vision of Meiji. 'Venerate the emperor, expel the barbarians.' This was the basis of the events that brought about Nanking and Pearl Harbor. If they could win, and they thought they could, then all Asia, which Japan claimed as its empire, would be rid of the 'barbarian' West.

'You could say, in a certain sense, that the same

struggle continues today,' says Shigeki Hijino of Japan's *Britannica Yearbook*. 'This arrogance, of considering ourselves Japanese and therefore better than any other nation, is insufferable. It poisons our dealings with others. I see these same signs of self-righteousness when dealing with trade issues.'

This self-righteousness is demonstrated in recent Japanese complaints that Western reaction to their mercantile success is rooted in racism, that we would not be as concerned with their success if they were not Orientals. But, in fact, any study of Japanese culture and history reveals that it is the Japanese who are the racists. Some prominent Japanese businessmen have even publicly stated that the reason for their success is the 'purity' of their race; Western nations, on the other hand, are human 'mongrels.' This belief underlies Japanese attitudes towards foreigners, an echo of the racial policies of the Axis alliance of Germany and Japan in World War II, one that attributed superiority to the 'pure' race and racial inferiority to those of mixed ancestry.

This concept of Japanese racial 'purity' is, of course, nonsense. The Japanese themselves are a very mixed people, a racial amalgam that was fixed less than twelve hundred years ago, a millisecond in genetic history. It would be as if someone took America's ethnic mixing today as the sign of the beginnings of a new 'pure' race.

Successive waves of immigrants came to Japan from different regions of China, while others came from Korea, and still others from the sub-Arctic areas of Siberia. Linguistic similarities and physical characteristics also indicate that some of the early progenitors of the Japanese were proto-Polynesians. In Japan, these groups mixed with the aboriginal Ainu, a Caucasoid race that still exists in Japan's northernmost islands. Until only a few hundred years ago, intermarriage with high-born Koreans was much desired, but since the eighth century there has been no major influx of foreign genes into the Japanese islands. This illusion of racial purity is something the Japanese have gone to great efforts to maintain.

This Japanese racial consciousness is not just jingoistic

propaganda. It is the basis of a set of onerous and discriminatory laws restricting Japanese citizenship to those of Japanese racial ancestry. Even if a person is born in Japan he is not eligible for citizenship unless his father is Japanese. An interracial couple, the Weatheralls, sued the Japanese government in 1983 to obtain Japanese citizenship for their children, who were born in Japan and live there today. 'The ideas of the Ministry of Justice are extremely conservative,' says Chinatsu Nakayama, who is on a Diet legislative committee dealing with immigration. 'How can they be so ruthless, the law is so cold-blooded, I often think.' This particular policy may soon be modified. There is legislation pending that would award Japanese citizenship to the Japan-born children of Japanese mothers, a law that Nakayama believes will pass the parliament.

This does nothing, of course, for the children born of foreigners in Japan. In most countries, citizenship is based on birthplace. Even in the Soviet Union, Russian-born children of foreigners can be granted citizenship if their parents remain in the country. But to racist Japanese, a foreigner is one with whom his tribe, or 'race,' has no connection, no past, and hence no future.

While Japanese deal with foreigners with formality and politeness, there is rarely warmth and never an assumption of equality. A foreigner employed by a Japanese firm can never be granted coveted 'permanent' status. For example, Professor John Boccellari, an American from Staten Island, New York, is a Japanese-speaking graduate (Ph.D in Japanese literature) of Tokyo University. He teaches comparative culture at Tsukuba National University but can never hope for tenure, nor the promotions and retirement settlement that accompany it. 'I'm a foreigner, so they can only renew my contract for one year at a time,' he told me. Boccellari is married to a Japanese scholar, and they have a young child, born in Japan, who is not a Japanese citizen. Should he want it, Boccellari himself can never hope for citizenship.

Foreigners are virtual outcasts in Japan. Even if born in that country, and without any other true homeland, they must submit to fingerprinting when applying for overseas travel documents. Most foreigners are also excluded from subsidized housing and must rent in a seller's market, where a three-room apartment in Tokyo can go for $3,000 a month, or more. While it is possible for a foreigner to buy a house through an intermediary, if he wants to own it in his own name he must breach bureaucratic obstacles so formidable that Westerners usually do not bother. The Japanese government does not want ownership of sacred Japanese land to pass into the hands of the 'barbarians.'

To belong in Japan, one must be Japanese. But even then, belonging is enhanced by being a member of a close-knit group, one that can provide the protection of the ancient village, which gave group identity to its members and provided social control over anyone who might seek to break out.

In feudal times, villagers were organized into 'five-man groups,' which could in fact be composed of as many as a dozen families. If one of the members of a 'five-man group' committed a crime, even a minor one, everyone in the group was punished equally. In some villages, if a crime such as gambling was committed in one household, the heads of the households on either side were considered equally responsible and punished along with the offender, even if they had no knowledge of the crime. Punishments consisted of banishment, fines, ostracism, and public apologies.

Banishment meant not only a lifetime among the outcasts; it condemned the descendants of the offenders to this same status. Ostracism, *mura hachibu*, which still occurs today in the rural areas, meant that no one in a village would associate with the family of the guilty, except, possibly, in the case of fire or a death. In general, there were only two punishments for major offenses: life imprisonment or death. This of course engendered a deep-seated social control, and a sharing of responsibility that persists in modern Japan.

The largest, most powerful contemporary group is the

corporation, which rewards and disciplines its employees just as if they were all residents of the same village. Once ensconced in a corporate job, most of the new elite, the university graduates, spend their first few years learning how their company works. Typically, they are rotated from department to department every six months or so, gaining exposure to a wide variety of activity, perhaps simultaneously receiving the education that most U.S. and European university students get before they graduate.

In the Japanese system, everybody works in one huge, unpartitioned office, where everything that is said or done is seen or heard by everyone else. Working without privacy – even family photos on desks are frowned upon – and under constant supervision, the process of conformity that began in childhood is honed. The college graduate, no less than the blue-collar worker on the factory floor, is systematically taught that what is best for the group is best for him. Since individualism is the worst heresy, people are addressed, not by their first names nor even, usually, by their family name. Instead they are referred to by their position.

Meetings are held frequently, often in a space cleared in the center of the office. The nominal objective of these meetings is 'consensus.' But while everyone is permitted to state an opinion, new arrivals soon learn that the prudent thing to do is to watch the others, state facts as they know them, and avoid strong positions until the leader has made clear what his own opinions are. To demonstrate loyalty to the group, personal sacrifices must be made, uncomplainingly and publicly. Thus while office hours might officially end at six in the evening, few will leave until 7:30.

When, after several years with an organization, a salaryman finds his career track within the company, he may start to make his opinions known at these meetings. This is done only in the most tentative way at first. The group dynamic is such that while eventually a real discussion will take place, it will not be until many hours have passed, or even until many meetings have been held. Once an idea is accepted within the group, the group becomes its author, and whoever first voiced it is deliberately forgotten. Thus no one is singled out; while no one is given credit for success, no one is responsible for failure, either.

At higher levels, proposals may be circulated – often hand-carried by one of the firm's newest junior *juyaku*, executives – to nearly every official who is in any way involved with the proposed action. This is called *ringi*. 'You agree or disagree, but more often you agree,' said one senior executive. 'By the time these papers come to your desk you will be already briefed and fully persuaded by the initiator of the document, and your stamp of approval is merely a formality, an official confirmation of what has been informally agreed upon through various means of maneuvering, bargaining, compromise-taking, concession-making.'

If someone strongly dissents, it is always done well before the document is circulated. 'The dissenter usually can be persuaded – given a small compromise concession – without destroying the integrity of the decision sought,' said the executive. 'That's usually the way, and enough time is given for accomplishing it.'

The Japanese corporate system rewards conformity by tying promotions to seniority for all but those in the highest levels of the organization. A salaryman who does not 'stick up' – and who is therefore not 'hammered down' – will be promoted along with the men who joined the company at the same time he did. Since virtually all these men are university graduates who came to the firm a few weeks after graduating in April of a given year, each becomes part of a 'class' of salarymen who rise almost in lockstep until they near the first 'cut.' At this point, the few who will go on to become directors – the Japanese equivalent of vice-presidents – are selected, usually by those vacating these positions.

The also-rans stay on for a few years until retirement age, then fade away. This leads to a lot of dead wood, middle-level executives with few responsibilities, men with little to do but stare out the window. But they also dare not leave, for they will lose their high salaries if they start at the bottom elsewhere, and their lump-sum retirement settlements are based on years of service and salary at retirement.

'My father died ten years ago,' explained Yuji Wakayama, a 38-year-old public relations executive for Toshiba and a graduate of Tokyo University. Wakayama had just celebrated, with suitable corporate ceremony, a formal dinner on the anniversary of his fifteenth year with the company. He was trying to answer my question about whether he would remain with the company until retirement. 'My father was an unsuccessful trader,' he told me. 'He went from company to company, and each time for a bigger salary, but his position did not rise, and so he never got the titles and the extra privileges. He wasn't considered successful, though he worked quite hard all his life. I will stay at Toshiba until my retirement, because it is a great honor to serve such a good company.'

Outsiders are almost never brought in to fill high positions. Awarding the presidency of an established firm to someone who did not start with it would cause mutiny in even the most disciplined executive ranks. But though a man may harbor ambitions for high office, he must keep them bottled inside, or manifest them only as a desire to better serve the company. The path to the top is lubricated by family ties, school connections and personal relationships with government. In a few very large companies, the top posts are reserved for the families of the founders. Thus, at Matsushita Industrial Electric, the chairman is the founder's son. Often a brother, cousin, or a son-in-law is elevated to the top post to carry on a family tradition. Once a man is selected for the presidency, his rivals for the pinnacle post are expected to quietly retire. Sometimes they are rewarded with a top post at one of the company's subsidiaries.

Unless he is a member of the founder's family, a company president, unlike those in American corporations, will serve only a few years, to make room for someone from the class below. But during his tenure as chief executive his decisions will go unquestioned. Even if the company suffers terrible times under his leadership, it is highly unlikely he will be replaced until he is ready to retire. To do so would be tantamount to regicide and set an unhealthy precedent for those who follow. Accordingly, even if a president makes a horrendous mistake, someone, or more likely, a group, will come forward to accept responsibility.

Like other senior executives, a president's perquisites are at least as impressive as those for the top executive of any comparable American company. And while his salary will seem modest in comparison to what his American counterparts are paid, his untaxed expense allowances may exceed his salary. He will also be likely to serve as a director for several companies, with additional compensations, often in the form of stock options. The president will usually retire upward in the firm to become chairman, while the preceding chairman, if his health permits, will keep his private office, together with some honorary duties.

Because of the long and close association between a salaryman and his company, there develops a special feeling of kinship which the Japanese call *amae*, indulgent love. It is the kind of relationship that begins in infancy between the child and the mother, a relationship of absolute trust and dependency. *Amae* is, as the noted Japanese psychiatrist, Takeo Doi, described it, the 'oil of life.' It means complete trust and confidence are exchanged between two people.

The Japanese do not feel comfortable about relationships that exclude *amae*. They tend therefore not to have 'casual' friendships, and the relationship between a man and his wife, usually devoid of Western-type romance, will often develop into this sort of *amae* relationship, with the wife usually assuming a mother role toward her husband. The *amae* relationship is established among individuals who work for the same employer, and eventually the *amae* is transferred from the individuals to the company itself. *Amae* is one of the reasons that Japanese salarymen will do almost anything their comany requires of them.

Under the bonds of *amae*, mistakes, even serious mistakes, are always forgiven, unless they are the unthinkable type of mistake, gross disloyalty to one's *amae* partner. That is the reason why once a salaryman leaves a company that has employed him for any length of time, no other large company will hire him in an important position. They assume that no matter what the reason, no matter what the provocation, if a salaryman was so disloyal as to dissolve an *amae* relationship, he is likely to be similarly disloyal to his new employer.

Given the absence of an *amae* relationship, the Japanese tend toward *enryo*, to hold back, to 'consider things from a distance.' It is precisely for this reason that Japanese do not feel comfortable with Westerners who speak Japanese well. As long as he can hide behind language, a Japanese does not feel threatened by a foreigner with whom he has no *amae* relationship. But if that barrier is pierced the Japanese will become uneasy. 'Japanese deal in a very friendly manner with foreigners who can't speak Japanese, but they feel threatened by foreigners who can, and tend to keep them at a distance,' said Professor Sumiko Iwo, a social psychologist at Keio University.

With an *amae* relationship, however, all things, legal and illegal, ethical and unethical, merciful and punishing, are possible. It is between people with such close bonds that all the extralegal transactions are made that keep Japan's economy rolling. *Amae* established by family friendships, or in university, remain strong ties for a lifetime. MITI bureaucrats, for example, often remain in contact with their old university friends in the major firms with whom they have established an *amae* relationship. They may suggest to one of these friends, now an officer with a large company, that some particular MITI *gyosei shido*, 'administrative guidance' is the proper course of action. The *amae* partner *must* trust him without reservation. This 'oil of life' makes it possible to form cartels among companies that would normally compete with each other.

Contracts made between *amae* individuals at different

Japanese companies are purposely vague and brief, for there is no need to set everything down in writing. If there is a problem later on, they will sit down and straighten it out. In the Western world, a contract is a contract, and if one side violates the agreement, the other will turn to the law to force compliance or exact a penalty. When a Japanese company contracts with a foreign company, the *amae* relationship is rarely present. The foreign company is untroubled by its absence, but the Japanese note it as significant and try to wring concessions to balance its absence. After protracted negotiations, a contract may be signed. But if, after several years of continuing close association, the Japanese begin to perceive that an *amae* relationship has developed between individuals of the two companies, they may feel free to tamper with the contract. It does not trouble them, because in *amae*, everything will be forgiven for the sake of continuing the relationship.

Because of *amae*, the Japanese are emotionally spoiled in their close relationships and experience a 'victim' syndrome when rebuffed. 'The Japanese suffer from an unusually strong, built-in susceptibility to injury as a result of *amae* expectations – which give them an almost overwhelming tendency to become totally dependent on others,' says author Boye De Mente. 'They experience *giseisha* [victim syndrome] anytime anybody or anything hinders or interferes with their aims or efforts. This feeling is most likely to be triggered when someone, some company or some country, does something they feel is against their interests.' Then, as Dr. Doi points out, '"victim mentality" carries with it an underlying need to get revenge to wipe out the "insult."'

Revenge may take strange, even violent, forms in Japan. Since there is no mechanism within the tightly-controlled Japanese group to channel rage into acceptable actions, and since one of the worst things a Japanese can do is to publicly display anger, these feelings are usually repressed. But not forever. When an individual Japanese can no longer bear this emotional overload, he may explode into the most virulent behavior. When some particular Japanese company or industry feels they have been beaten, and hence victimized, the eventual expression of revenge may take the form of some particularly unethical behavior. In large groups, and within the largest group of all, the tribal Japanese nation, this explosion can take the form of ritual suicide, violent demonstrations, or even war.

In the present economic war against the West, there is an element of revenge, one designed to compensate for Japan's devastating defeat in World War II. As a Japanese businessman or tourist stands in the center of the West, in Times Square, New York City, and looks up at the giant Japanese advertisements for Mitsubishi, Toshiba, Ricoh, and Sony, which dominate the area, he may consider that he has finally achieved retribution.

If a Japanese person is the offending party in an insult and has caused someone else to become a victim, he must do Japanese penance, *meiwaku*, literally, an apology or an annoyance. The offender is expected to humiliate and abase himself, accept full responsibility and make restitution. In business, this is usually done with money. Because of the danger of disappointing someone with whom an *amae* relationship exists, Japanese try to avoid making any kind of direct statements or direct promises that they cannot keep.

The objective is to avoid any behavior that will cause friction or disturb the *wa* or peacefulness of another. Thus a Japanese is likely to respond to direct requests with oblique assurances. They try to present their *honne to tatemae*, the 'framework of their thoughts,' which is used to give someone else the lines to read between. If things do not then work out, everyone can reasonably claim that no direct promises were made and no offense should be taken. This does not always prevent 'victim mentality,' but it does make the offense seem less deliberate.

In feudal times, if a vassal went over the head of his samurai to approach the lord directly, he stood to lose his own head for it. But so did the samurai, whom the lord now saw as a weak leader. This custom is retained in business. A junior will almost never go over the head of his boss, even when he knows his boss is wrong, and even if something more important than his own job is at stake.

Japan is a formal society where introductions are essential to life and business. When a Japanese wants to meet someone he does not know, he goes about it by finding a middleman who does know him. There has arisen a class of professional middlemen, people who know almost everyone of importance, or know someone who does. For a fee, they will arrange an introduction. If someone wants a favor from someone he does not know, the usual method is to find someone to whom that person is somehow socially indebted. The middleman in this case will simply write a few words on the back of a business card: 'Please try to help so-and-so,' or something similar. This is usually sufficient for a small favor, but the one who grants it thereby incurs an obligation from both the one who asked the favor and the one who sponsored him.

Gifts are an important lubricant in Japanese life. When a Japanese wishes to gain a favor, he customarily gives his hoped-for benefactor a gift whose importance is directly related to the nature of the favor asked. Custom also dictates that these gifts always be wrapped; the recipient will never unwrap it in the presence of the giver since neither giver nor receiver should have to suffer embarrassment if the gift is inappropriately small. It is understood that the larger the gift the more important the favor that will be asked. For this reason, many Japanese are unwilling to accept large gifts from Westerners. They do not want to incur an obligation to someone they neither know well nor trust.

Another type of socially accepted 'gift' is a bribe, *sodeno shita*, literally 'under the kimono sleeve.' It may be an envelope full of money, such as $2 million accepted by former Japanese Prime Minister Tanaka. More typically it is a fancy party, an expenses-paid vacation, a prepaid visit to a courtesan, or some other very personal gift. For the American or European trying to do business with the

Japanese it is wise to beware of Japanese bearing gifts; their motives are usually suspect. If a gift is accepted and the subsequent request refused, the Japanese may feel *giseisha*, the victim mentality, with its accompanying desire for revenge.

At the same time, it is almost impossible to get things done in Japan without the help of someone with influence. The notion of sponsorship is indigenous to the culture, such as gaining an important first position with a large company. In feudal times, a samurai might ask his lord to appoint a nephew or family friend to a post. If the appointee failed to discharge his duties with appropriate efficiency, the *onjin*, 'obligation person,' was responsible. He might pay for a serious lapse with his own life. Accordingly, the beneficiary of an *onjin* incurs a lifetime obligation to his sponsor. This custom continues in modern Japan. It provides one more measure of control, one more incentive to win at any cost. To fail in an important job is not merely to fail for your company but to fail for your sponsor.

The group consciousness of the Japanese business fraternity, tied together by *amae* and other complex human relations, arms the Japanese businessman for an important aspect of contact with the West. It is negotiation, a war game at which he is particularly adept and determined to win at all costs. The Japanese play it as a full team, rather than as individuals, which is the Western way.

When dealing with the West, a Japanese company will make elaborate preparations, including many meetings to establish the best advance strategy. Individuals will commit reams of statistics to memory and develop strategies for all anticipated 'enemy probes.' Negotiations are planned in advance and negotiating positions are developed to be phased in at various stages. Nothing will be given away beforehand. All planned concessions are treated as 'ammunition,' to be expended only at the most propitious moment. And as master strategists, they often mistakenly attribute to the 'enemy' all the capabilities and strategies which they themselves possess.

Richard Copaken, the Washington attorney who investigated the Japanese machine tool cartels for Houdaille Industries, gained experience dealing with Japanese negotiators while representing the government of the Marshall Islands. His task was to negotiate a tuna fishing treaty and an economic assistance package with the Japanese on behalf of the 20,000 Marshallese living on two tiny archipelagos 2,500 miles north of New Zealand.

Copaken gained great insight into how the Japanese bureaucracy viewed the U.S. government as a negotiating partner. 'The same people who were negotiating with me on tuna fish by night were negotiating automobile issues with the U.S. government by day. And they tended to let their hair down with me, a bit, and tell me about how they perceived the U.S. side,' he recounts.

'I discovered that the Japanese tend to attribute the same kinds of comprehensive, integrated, thought-out responses to the U.S. that they used in negotiating themselves.' Copaken, of course, knew that Americans usually conducted negotiations in a more haphazard manner. 'I knew that it was 99 percent accident and 1 percent error – and minuscule amounts of intelligence. The Japanese perceptions of events were quite at odds with what was really going on, way out of kilter with reality,' says Copaken.

A few years later, engaged in his own negotiations with the Japanese on behalf of Houdaille, he was able to use this knowledge of how they work to his advantage. 'It occurred to me that in the Houdaille context, the Japanese government might well jump to the wrong conclusion – that I was some kind of cat's paw for the U.S. government. If they did, I might be able to parlay that. And that is exactly what happened. When I arrived I had a series of meetings at MITI. They were quite surprised that we had done enormous amounts of homework, and that we were not satisfied with the superficial answers that they normally gave and which seemed to satisfy everybody else. We had all the follow-up questions that they didn't want to answer.

'After a day of this, and hundreds of questions we had prepared in advance, we were notified that this was all the time they could afford to spend for one private attorney representing one private company. Of course, they told us, "If it were the government of the U.S. that were asking for this information, it would be a very different situation." But since we were not, since we were only a private outfit, that would be the end of it.

'Essentially, what they were doing was trying to flush out into the open what they were convinced was a fact – that this was a trial balloon by the U.S. government, and not just a legitimate private party pursuing a private case. With considerable malice aforethought, I added to their discomfort by truthfully insisting to them that I was just one lawyer representing one small company. This, of course, convinced them that the opposite was truth. It was a wonderful situation, filled with irony, where the only way to persuade them that I was actually a secret agent of the U.S. government was to flat out deny it,' he said.

Copaken was playing the Japanese game of deception simply by telling them the truth. Using this warped Japanese perception of his real status, Copaken was then able to convince the MITI bureaucrats to continue holding their meetings with him. The lesson of this episode is that the Japanese do not look on important negotiations in the same spirit of give-and-take that most Westerners do. Nor do they negotiate business deals with the same set of ethics.

Another example of the Japanese approach comes from the experiences of Dr. David L. Cocke, formerly chief research chemist for a Chicago-based petrochemical consortium that develops catalysts. Their most vexing customers are the companies in the Japanese petroleum industry. 'We have learned that they will begin negotiations by softening us up six months ahead of time. That's when they start complaining of problems with the catalysts they previously purchased from us. It will be one little problem, then another little problem, and after a while it's a problem every week. We never get to find out if they're actual problems or not, because they always tell us that they've solved it, for now. But when we sit down at the bargaining table, they've got all these documented "complaints," which they use to set the stage for negotiating on *their* terms,' said Cocke. 'Last time we wound up selling them new catalysts at our actual costs, just to keep the business relationship from going to another country. At the bargaining table they're all smiles and polite, but inside you know every one of them is J. P. Morgan, gobbling up another poor railroad.'

The traditional Japanese approach to a meeting is to send a negotiating team, rather than one or two individuals. It is not uncommon to schedule an appointment with an executive and to have the meeting in a large conference room, surrounded by as many as a dozen Japanese negotiators. The Japanese feel more confident in numbers. One or two junior members of the team can be sent scurrying to dig up some forgotten paper; two or three team members can excuse themselves and visit the rest room while the meeting continues; one fellow can talk for a time until he is tired, and then be replaced with a fresh negotiator; proposals submitted for consideration can be discussed at great length by various team members until the person who submitted it has quite forgotten why he wanted it.

An explanation for this mentality comes from Jiro Tokuyama, a director of the Nomura Management School. 'Because opportunities are such a precious commodity in Japan, they are entrusted to groups rather than individuals,' he explains. In practice the team approach prevents anyone from giving away too much, and it presents a formidable obstacle to the other side, which has to contend with an entire spectrum of counterproposals. Even after a bargain has been struck, after 'the enemy' has accepted a proposal put forth at a meeting by a group member, if subsequent events show this to be a poor bargain, the Japanese may simply later disown it. They insist that it was merely an individual's idea, not the official company proposal.

A popular spectator sport in Japan is *sumo* wrestling, in which a pair of 300-pound, near-naked leviathans attempt to shove each other out of a circle marked on the floor. The wrestler who wins most often is the one who can resist his opponent's opening shove, then take advantage of the brief moment when his opponent is off balance to throw him out of the ring. This is not unlike a Japanese negotiating session. *Bushido* teaches that patience is a virtue and a weapon. A Japanese team will delay, after initial greetings and introductions, and instead of an opening proposal offer only silence. They will sip their tea and wait. As the silence deepens, a Westerner may find it awkward, and step in with his opening proposal. This is a triumph for *bushido*, because the modern samurai has learned his adversary's position without revealing his own. From this point, it is much easier to shove him out of the ring and achieve victory.

Shortly after he became the principal editorial cartoonist for *Asahi*, a national daily newspaper, Ranan Lurie, an American, came up with the character Taro San, which he proposed as the cartoon symbol for Japan. Taro San, Lurie hopes, will become as familiar to the world as England's stout, muttonchop-whiskered John Bull, or America's star-spangled, top hatted Uncle Sam. Taro San, who has the blessings of Prime Minisiter Yasuhiro Nakasone, is a young man with a shock of long black hair bound back from his forehead with the sort of white cloth headband that was worn by the *kamikaze* pilots of World War II, and which is still worn by students of the martial arts or by those about to take school exams.

The headband bears the two *kanji* characters of Japan. Taro San is wearing a Western-style business suit jacket, a white shirt and a tie with Japan's red sun, and flowing, traditional Japanese trousers. On his feet are what most Americans would refer to as shower shoes, the flat, open-toed *geta* sandals, worn over white stockings. This is a collection of marvelously appropriate symbols, for Taro San is indeed a complex amalgam of details that epitomize modern Japan. Despite his Western suit jacket and tie, his feet and his head are rooted firmly in Japan's feudal past.

In 1983, I met a man who had known a samurai, had in fact known several. He had seen them, spoken with them. Mr. Kitagawa had done this, of course, in his youth. He was 90 years old when we met, but his mind was lively and his senses intact. When he was born, Meiji was a 40-year-old emperor, an infallible Living God who had reformed feudal Japan, including the elimination of the awesome power of the samurai. Samurai had put away their ornate costumes and cut the top knots from their hair scarcely twenty years earlier. Now Kitagawa, a farmer, lives with his wife, son and grandsons in a hundred-year-old farmhouse, on land his family has owned for eight generations, a few miles outside of Shimada, a sleepy farm town two hours from Tokyo by *shinkansen* bullet train. Within a few miles radius, he told me, there were about two hundred families, among them 32 men and women between the ages of 80 and 104.

There are many such aged men and women in Japan. There is, for example, Nobousuke Kishi, 87, architect of MITI, economic czar of Manchukuo, godfather of Nissan, World War II minister of munitions, former prime minister, the archduke of Japan's conservative nationalists. And there is Kinosuke Matsushita, 89, the 'Henry Ford of Japan,' who still keeps office hours at the manufacturing behemoth he founded, now controlled by his son-in-law. There are tens of thousands of such old men in Japan who know first-hand what the code of the samurai meant and what it means now. It is not merely that Japan has long-lived people, with an average male life expectancy of 74.22 years, the longest on earth. Japanese women, with a 79.66 year life expectancy, are second only to Iceland's women. More importantly, these men and women are living reminders of Japan's feudal past, the lingering remnant of the influences that continue to control so many facets of Japanese life.

'Japan suffers from a national strait jacket, an incredible arrogance on the part of our leadership and the press,' says Shigeki Hijono. 'I'm frightened by the revisionist tendencies in Japan today. Now there are people saying that Japan did *not* surrender unconditionally in World War II, that only the Army and the Navy surrendered, that the people have never surrendered.'

While I was in Tokyo in 1983, a four-and-a-half hour film, *Tokyo Trial*, ostensibly describing the events leading to the International War Crimes Tribunal of 1946–48, was playing to packed audiences. The film juxtaposes footage of U.S. military actions in Vietnam and the atomic bombing of Hiroshima with carefully selected scenes from the trial. Only about two minutes of the film deal with the conduct of the Imperial Army in Nanking. It seeks to equate the conduct of American forces in Vietnam with the war crimes for which a handful of Japan's wartime leaders were convicted. More than 400,000 Japanese have paid to see this film. While it was showing, a legal symposium in Tokyo concentrated on an analysis of the courtroom proceedings. The film asks, 'Was not the verdict of 35 years ago an arbitrary punishment imposed by the victors?'

'There's a lot of talk like that now, things that a few years ago were only whispered, but now are said aloud,' says Hijono. 'And there are people publicly praising the emperor for his single act of stopping World War II. But, if he could stop it with a single act in 1945, he could have stopped it in 1941 as well. Nowhere have I seen an objective book or even an article on what really happened in Nanking.'

In 1937 a Japanese army under the command of General Iwane Matsui captured the Chinese city of Nanking, 170 miles up the Yangtze River from Shanghai, and for six weeks raped, murdered, and tortured its citizenry in a systematic orgy of terror and violence. Before they ended this nightmare, more than 5,000 women and girls had been raped – and then murdered – and 190,000 innocent and unresisting civilians butchered. Entire sections of the city were torched, and virtually everything of value was carried away. Before the Warsaw Ghetto and before the Nazi death camps, Nanking became known as the most heinous atrocity in history.

'The authorities are revising the textbooks to make little mention of Nanking,' Hijono adds. 'The revisionists are taking things out of context, magnifying the details and claiming injustice. For example, now they're saying that censorship during the occupation was demeaning, insulting, and outrageous. But they're saying nothing about how ten million Japanese would have starved to death, except for the Americans who fed us. That's a sign of total disregard for our history.'

The Japanese are in a strange, conflicted position in modern society. They are still not fully comfortable with the Westerners who forcibly pried open Japan's door to the West only 130 years ago. The Westerners were at first regarded as barbarians and viewed as oddities. While maintaining their racist sense of superiority to this day, the Japanese have never overcome the shame of Commodore Perry's easy victory in 1854, when he sailed unopposed into Tokyo Harbor to demand the opening of trade. Because they are still culturally smug and xenophobic, the Japanese are uneasy about foreigners who have convincingly demonstrated the superiority of Western science and technology. Some believe that the Japanese are still awed by the West, a feeling they desperately try to hide. 'The Japanese as a whole feel a deep inferiority complex toward foreigners, especially Caucasians,' said Ichiro Kawasaki, former Japanese ambassador to Poland.

Even now, most Japanese find it hard to believe that Japan is within a decade or less of matching the American GNP. While driven to become number one, they often still think of themselves as a poor relation to the West. 'America has a land area 27 times as great as Japan's and possesses vast supplies of energy, natural resources, and food. Its population is almost twice that of Japan,' said Jiro Tokuyama. 'Japan differs greatly from the United States in that 80 percent of its land is mountainous. Japan lost its colonies as a result of defeat in World War II, a defeat which triggered the decision to renounce war as a means of resolving international issues. To feed a large population in a small and mountainous land, the only alternative is foreign trade.'

As the Japanese move toward becoming *itchiban*, they still feel that they are the underdogs in world competition; they continue to worry about starving to death as a nation. The feeling that they are constantly teetering on the edge of national disaster – that they are perpetually at the mercy of the West – enables them to wage economic war without rules, to rationalize almost any unethical behavior in dealing with foreigners. In this they are not unlike the Soviets, who out of supposed fear of another invasion of their homeland, seek to conquer the world.

Their national plan for worldwide economic domination is a natural outgrowth of the Japanese ethic. It enables the Japanese to band together in tight corporate, tribal groups. They speak obliquely and with eloquent vagueness. They mask their true feelings and confound their enemies. In mercantile battle, they follow the code of *bushido* laid down by fierce warriors who ruled a feudal police state.

They approach business transactions with the ferocity and tactics of an army on the march. To make their competitive lives bearable, they take refuge in the childlike behavior of *amae*, demanding that wives and close friends indulge them with sweet permissiveness no matter how they err. They respond with savage vengeance when rebuffed. They discriminate against all who do not possess their 'pure' blood, and extol the virtues of a feudal past that few outside Japan can appreciate.

The Japanese ethic is not one that the West can, or should, emulate. But this singular perspective of life and values is one that Westerners must learn to understand if they are to survive the economic war being waged against them by the Japanese.

6   Targets for Tomorrow

'WE ARE a small country, a poor country. We haven't any oil. We have no minerals or other natural resources. But we have many people. So many people. People are our only natural resource so we Japanese must mobilize the energy of our people. Then we can do almost anything,' said Hiroko Horisaka. She is an attractive woman in her late thirties, the mother of two small children, a housewife and freelance translator, and outgoing by Japanese standards. Her husband, formerly the Latin American correspondent for Japan's leading economic newspaper, is a professor of economics at Tokyo's Sophia University, and her father-in-law is a retired MITI bureaucrat. What Horisaka says is what virtually every Japanese has been taught since childhood to believe.

'We have a saying, "When America sneezes, Japan catches cold." You have such a big country, such a rich country. How could Japan ever hope to match America?' she asked. Her sincerity cannot be doubted; Hiroko's statements reveal the fundamental dichotomy that dogs the Japanese, the innate belief in the superiority of their own race and the simultaneous insecurity about their future. 'The Japanese are a nation of worriers,' said the late Herman Kahn, who has also answered Hiroko's question: 'The postwar Japanese have made economic growth into a popular religion.'

Their growth has been phenomenal. Behind it is not just Hiroko's confidence that the Japanese can 'do almost anything,' but a calculated and unremitting practice of targeting numerous industries throughout the world to force them to yield to Japanese competition. The methods, in addition to hard work and planning, are, as we have seen, unfair business practices, state subsidies,

143

dumping, copying, and theft of products. The result is first an increased Japanese share of market, then the eventual demise of many of their international competitors.

Japan is not limiting its conquests to the fields of electronics, supercomputers, and autos. In their continuous examination of new areas in which to expand Japanese industrial power, MITI has found many promising industries, some new, others well-established, which they have targeted for the near future. Just as their assault on the semiconductor field was initially mounted in silence, then suddenly became front-page business news, so Japan is now quietly preparing its campaigns for tomorrow.

One of the most promising targets is the aircraft manufacturing industry, the pride of America and a major U.S. export product. In July of 1983, I asked MITI's Koichi Kujirai, one of the ministry's senior bureaucrats, if Japan presently has plans to enter the field of aircraft manufacture. Kujirai, as is typical of MITI officials, at first denied Japanese interest in the industry as too risky. He then went on to admit the beginnings of activity reminiscent of all previous targeting campaigns.

'Japanese aircraft makers are now aiming at international collaboration with aircraft manufacturers overseas, and they are discussing the feasibility of such collaboration in the 150-seat market, medium-sized airliners,' Kujirai admitted. A less senior MITI official has also conceded that Japan is eyeing the skies. 'We think aerospace will be the industry of the future,' Akira Yamazaki, deputy director of aircraft and ordnance, told the press.

The aircraft industry is peculiarly suited to Japan's style of economic warfare. Productivity in the U.S. industry has inched ahead at a bare one-tenth of one percent per year, compared to 2.3 percent for all U.S. manufacturing, making American aerospace 'a large, stationary target for the Japanese,' in the words of Wolfgang Demisch, a First Boston Corporation securities analyst. The financial condition of the largest U.S. aviation companies has been cyclically precarious. Those who work in the industry are accustomed to extended layoffs as their companies go through hard times.

Americans aerospace companies, including Boeing, which depends heavily on civil aviation rather than military orders, have been particularly vulnerable to cost competition. The high costs of American aircraft are due in part to the cyclical nature of the business. It is expensive to stop producing an item, disband the work force, and then later reexpand, reacquire machinery and equipment. But given the structure of unsubsidized, competitive American industry, with requirements for short term profits, these cycles are accepted as inevitable in the U.S. But that is not true in Japan, where MITI helps maintain a consistency in those domestic firms slated to target foreign competition.

Japan has demonstrated its ability to turn out high-quality aircraft. 'The ability they've shown to build high-quality autos and hi-fis carries right over into their defense industry,' says Frederick Carment, a Tokyo-based official of the Grumman Company, a large American aerospace firm. Japan's new research in supercomputers will make computer modeling and computer-assisted design of engines and airframes considerably easier for them.

An early, essential step in targeting an industry is the acquisition of technology; and despite pious claims to the contrary, Japan has already begun to do that in the aircraft industry. 'We are ten years behind the European level and fifteen to twenty years behind the U.S.,' claims Masayoshi Oiso, a defense analyst at Tokyo's Nomura Economic Research Institute, who could have made the same statement about Japanese semiconductor technology in the early 1970s. MITI's VLSI project solved that problem in four years. 'In another ten or twelve years, they'll have all the tools in place,' believes First Boston's Demisch.

This may prove to be a conservative estimate. Japan has already made an impressive start in developing aviation technology. Ironically, the Japanese are getting their head start from their future competitors – the naive American aerospace companies. It is the same pattern Japan followed in electronics, semiconductor, auto, computer, and machine tools, where they gained expertise, design, and technology from American and European competitors.

Japan is already producing some $2 billion worth of aerospace products a year, including 15 percent of Boeing's top-of-the-line 'Airliner for the Eighties,' the new 767. Three of Japan's largest companies, Fuji Heavy Industries, Mitsubishi Heavy Industries, and Kawasaki Heavy Industries are junior partners with Boeing in the project, ideally suited to learn American aviation know-how on the job. Fuji makes fairings, the complex-shaped metal panels that join wings to fuselage; the other two companies make body panels.

Britain, too, is contributing to Japanese expertise. In 1980 Britain's nationalized aerospace leader, Rolls-Royce, sought out Japan's leading aircraft manufacturers and entered into a joint venture with Ishikawajima-Harima Heavy Industries (IHI), Mitsubishi, and Kawasaki to build jet engines. The three Japanese giants put up a total of $500 million and formed Japanese Aero Corporation, which, with Rolls-Royce, has already produced a test-bed engine called the RJ500.

Pratt & Whitney, a division of United Technologies, together with West Germany's Motoren-und-Turbinen Union (MTU) and Italy's Fiat Aviazoni, has created International Aero Engines to 'develop a new engine for future 150-seat airliners.' Japan's triumvirate will have a 40 percent share of this project as well, which by 1988 is scheduled to deliver a new engine with a thrust of 20,000 to 30,000 pounds, but with 14 percent improvement in fuel efficiency. The Japanese will thus take one more long step 'on the learning curve of Western aerospace technology,' as the British publication *Economist* put it. In the meantime, Great Britain's aircraft industry work force has been reduced by some 6,500 workers, or about 8 percent of the total force, since 1981.

Even giant Nissan, the illegitimate offspring of the Japanese Army born to build tanks, trucks, and guns in Manchuria and now the second-largest of Japan's auto-makers, is craving to put some of its cash overflow to work in commercial aviation. 'The agreement is not final yet, but we think Nissan will be Boeing's partner in the YXX project,' said Nissan's Shigeru Sawada. The YXX, also known at Boeing as the 7-7, is another entry in the popular 150-seat market.

The Japanese have already gained the expertise that enabled them to brake their *shinkansen* bullet trains from 125 mph down to a dead stop without derailment. The design is based on the U.S. Airforce F-104 Starfighter's brakes, which keep the very powerful fighter from flipping over onto its stubby wings during a 150 mph landing. The Japanese acquired the technology when the F-104 was built under license in Japan to supply the Self-Defense Forces during the 1960s. Other technological transfers include puncture-proof rubber fuel tanks from military jets, now used in Japan's growing fleets of small executive jet airplanes.

The joint venture, the siren that brings American and European companies hat-in-hand to the Japanese with technology and experience, is their favorite method for gaining technology. McDonnell Douglas has entered into such a joint project with the Japanese Aero Corporation. McDonnell will build a 150-seat aircraft, designated the D3300, and has asked the Japanese to become 'equal partners' in the project. McDonnell is also sharing subcontracts with JAC on airframe components for its Super 83 and Super 90 airliners, larger craft based on their successful DC-9 design.

McDonnell Douglas has great faith in the Japanese aviation industry. They have licensed Mitsubishi to manufacture their F-15J, currently the U.S. Air Force's hottest fighter, for the Japanese defense forces. The fighters cost Japan about $50 million a copy, or twice what Saudi Arabia pays for the same plane built in St. Louis. The difference is borne by the Japanese taxpayer. It is obvious that MITI has decided that the value of acquiring aircraft technology, and of training the skilled workers who will eventually train others, is worth the cost. Mitsubishi builds one F-15J a month at their Nagoya plant, where they have already introduced a manufacturing refinement

McDonnell Douglas had not thought of. A gigantic cradle in Nagoya turns the assembled fuselage upside-down, permitting gravity to remove potentially dangerous extra parts or discarded tools.

Mitsubishi, one of the restructured prewar *zaibatsu*, was founded in 1857 as an ironworking company in the service of the last Tokugawa shogun. Now an enormous, diversified company, it began building aircraft before World War II. Its improvement of a British-designed plane became the dreaded Zero fighter, and its 'Betty' divebombers sank U.S. battleships at Pearl Harbor. On its board of directors is the younger son of Hideki Tojo, Japan's World War II prime minister who was hanged as a war criminal. The son, Teruo Tojo, is chairman of Mitsubishi Motors. Mitsubishi's warplane factories turned out 18,000 planes and 52,000 engines before they were destroyed by U.S. bombers during the war or dismantled by General MacArthur during the occupation.

The present company traces its aviation capabilities to the early 1950s, when North American F-86 fighters, the victors of Korean War air battles, were produced in Japan under license. 'The F-86 is the father of our present industry,' is the way Mitsubishi's chief engineer, Akira Ikeda, puts it. Mitsubishi is now established in the manufacture of several types of aircraft. Its fleet includes the Diamond I, an executive jet that cruises at 500 mph and carries eight passengers with great fuel economy and considerable luxury. The Diamond I, which has already captured about 10 percent of the U.S. market, is powered by twin Pratt & Whitney engines produced in Canada. Mitsubishi's sales literature boasts that the Diamond I's wings are computer designed. The company's other civilian aircraft activity includes two twin turboprop 'commuters' and past subcontract work on the Boeing 747 and the McDonnell Douglas DC-10.

In the military aircraft field, Mitsubishi is building the fuselage of the Lockheed P-3C, which is used for antisubmarine patrols, and a large helicopter for Japan's naval self-defense forces. Mitsubishi, which once built the U.S. F-4 Phantom and the F-104 Starfighter series under U.S.

licenses, has designed and built its own supersonic plane, the F-1, a close-support or attack fighter.

'It's better even than the British Jaguar,' Mitsubishi's Hideo Ogata boasted as he drank chilled juice of the *mikan* – the Japanese version of the mandarin orange – served by silent, uniformed hostesses in the ground floor visiting room of Mitsubishi's central Tokyo headquarters. 'Because of our Constitution, this aircraft cannot be exported,' he adds. Under Article Nine of this document, Japan renounced war as an instrument of national policy and the export of military equipment is forbidden. But in the last few years, MITI has winked at the occasional sale of unarmed helicopters to Thailand and Saudi Arabia, planes later outfitted with guns and rockets by their purchasers.

When asked if Mitsubishi has plans for a greater presence in aircraft manufacture, Ogata became evasive. He rummaged through his 'talking papers,' consulted with Yuzuru Matsumoto, a Mitsubishi public relations consultant, and at length produced a prepared statement. 'Everybody asks about this,' he told me. He then produced reams of statistics to support his point: Aircraft manufacture is now a tiny percentage of Mitsubishi's business; aircraft manufacture is overwhelmingly dominated by American manufacturers; aircraft manufacture is a risky proposition which requires a huge investment.

It was the same disclaimer that MITI officials had produced a day earlier, one that is unconvincing to those who understand that the first requisite of Japan's targeting sequence – the acquisition of technology – is now being met. 'The Japanese are getting ready to learn how to develop commercial aircraft,' states William Purple, who heads the Bendix aerospace division of Allied Corp.

The second requisite, a domestic market that can be protected from foreign competition, already exists in Japan's three airlines. Japan Air Lines (JAL), whose largest stockholder is the Ministry of Finance, is today the second-largest airline in the world. It surpassed British Airways in 1983 with 4,318,000,000 tons/per kilometer in passengers, freight, and mail logged on regular international routes. All-Nippon Air, Japan's domestic carrier, has been flying internationally as well since 1971. A third airline, TOA Domestic Airlines, has not yet acquired international routes, but all flights are allocated by Japan's Ministry of Transportation, which has a history of transferring flights between lines as needed to keep a company in business.

Even though their combined fleet has only 250 aircraft, or 10 percent of the number of planes in all U.S. airlines, the Japanese airlines collectively represent more aircraft purchasing power than any *single* privately owned or national airline in the world. Their domestic market is large enough to take a Japanese-built airliner close to the break-even point, particularly if the existing aircraft building consortium put together by Kawasaki, Fuji, and IHI were to produce it. If Japan's pattern of targeting holds, an early step in their market share plan would be to expand their fleet, offering international travel at prices unsubsidized airlines could not afford to match for an extended period.

The lifespan of an airliner is perhaps thirty years. Some Japanese sources believe that MITI will have a Japanese airliner built and competing within ten to fifteen years. 'If anyone ever said "you can export to anyone and everyone," the Japanese aircraft industry would really blossom,' said Charles Mraz, a Tokyo-based McDonnell Douglas representative. 'It's my biggest worry. It would be like Hondas all over again.'

An important principle of war is called *mass*. The idea is to concentrate all, or most, of the available resources on a single target. This concentration makes the attacker's forces at the chosen point comparatively stronger than the defender's and often permits the rapid destruction of the objective. After the objective is secured, most of the forces are redeployed elsewhere.

MITI well understands this principle and has applied it to the economic campaigns waged against the West. 'They've managed to save their resources by not duplicating each other's effort in a particular spectrum of technology,' says Robert Rutishauser of Control Data. 'That turns out to be extremely important from a national point of view. To that extent, it's a different competitive world than it was five years ago.'

Office automation, which the Japanese call OA, is a classic instance of an industry targeted by Japan in which there is no wasted duplication. MITI's statistics show that Japan's OA manufacturing was an $8-billion business in 1980; they predict growth to $30 billion in 1990. 'In most of the advanced countries in the world, there is a steady flow of population from blue-collar jobs to white-collar jobs. This trend is most pronounced in the U.S., but Japan is no exception,' says a study on OA done for the Japan External Trade Organization (JETRO), the promotional arm of MITI.

Japan includes four categories under the white-collar classification: professional and technical workers; managers and administrators; clerical workers; and sales workers. During this decade white-collar workers in the U.S. will go from 50.9 percent of the total work force to 59.1 percent, or a market size increase of 14 percent. But in Japan it will grow from 43.4 percent to 47.4 percent, a growth of only 9 percent, making the U.S. the largest and fastest-growing market for Japanese office products.

It is this American and European market that the Japanese office automation industry hopes to dominate. 'It seems to me that if we don't do something different, the Japanese will be even more successful in information processing than they have been in steel, autos and electronics,' said Rutishauser.

OA encompasses an extremely wide range of products from the comparatively simple electric and electronic typewriters, to sophisticated, computerized document filing systems and ultra-highspeed facsimile transmission terminals, to Computer Assisted Design (CAD) equipment.

To design and build this equipment, the Japanese have sharply increased their supply of electrical engineers over the last two decades, training several hundred thousands since 1960. In that year Japan had fewer than half as many engineers engaged in R&D as did the United States, but today the Japanese are moving ahead of the U.S. Both nations have about 50 engineers and scientists per 10,000 workers, but the Japanese are turning out about 21,000 new electrical engineers a year, about 25 percent more than the U.S., according to Roland W. Schmitt, General Electric Corporation's vice-president for research and development.

The reason the Japanese expect OA to be a growth industry, and therefore worthy of targeting, is that while factory worker productivity increased by 90 percent from 1960 to 1970, that of office workers increased by only 4 percent. The need to do better will automate offices, points of retail purchase, homes, and schools by providing computer-assisted equipment that will not only make work more efficient, but enable workers to routinely perform tasks now only rarely done. By the 1990s, the 'office of the future' will resemble present offices only to the degree that today's offices resemble those of the 1930s. And 'offices' will come to exist in enterprises that never before had them.

At the headquarters of Toshiba, founded in 1875 by Hisahige Tanaka, who is sometimes inaccurately idolized as 'the Thomas Edison of Japan,' a company spokesman, Yuji Wakayama, viewed OA as part of the 'information industry,' which includes everything from office equipment to computers to telecommunications. The senior planning people of Toshiba, he says, feel that the industry is now worth $100 billion a year and by the end of the decade will be the largest industry in the world, grossing $800 or $900 billion in today's dollars.

At Toshiba there are dozens of new OA devices waiting to be marketed in 1984 in the U.S. and Europe. 'This is called TOSFILE,' explained Wakayama. 'It eliminates much of the paper used in offices.' TOSFILE is the world's first optical disk document storage system. It works by making a photocopy of each page, converting it to electronic impulses and storing them on tiny disks about five inches across. Each disk can store up to 10,000 sheets of 8½×11 inch paper. Filing even a large office's input and output of letters, memos, telegrams, and reports will take no more than a few minutes a month. As soon as a document is stored, the original piece of paper can be destroyed, saving space.

Retrieval takes seconds, with the information either printed out or displayed on a screen. With backup disks stored in other parts of an office the system is far safer than keeping paper records. And instead of filling offices with filing cabinets, which need to be emptied annually, the TOSFILE document disks for even a huge office can be stored in a single desk drawer. And most important, the only way to buy one is to do business with a Japanese manufacturer.

A MITI-funded study has placed the Japanese electronics industry ahead of the world in another vital OA area – that of human/machine interface. One device using this technology is already in production at Toshiba: a voice-activated word processor which recognizes individual phonemes – the building blocks of speech – and translates them into Japanese *kanji* characters at the rate of about 100 characters per second. The machine's input is words 'spoken with natural delivery,' as Toshiba says. While not yet available for English, it is easy to see how a machine that understands human speech and types it out instantly will eventually replace dictation to secretaries in an enormous world market.

Toshiba has also used optical character recognition to produce a high-speed mail processing unit that reads and sorts 27,000 envelopes and postcards an hour. At Fujitsu, I witnessed a new type of facsimile transmission device in operation. Most large companies now use facsimile to transmit urgent letters, maps, drawings, and charts from one location to another via telephone. But these systems are slow, taking 30 seconds to two minutes per page, and quality is less than acceptable for many documents. Fujitsu's machine – based in part on the same MITI-funded technology as Toshiba's TOSFILE – transmits a whole page in a fraction of a second, with quality very nearly as good as an ordinary photocopy. The machine also doubles as a photocopier. With such speed and quality, expensive courier service, now a burgeoning industry, will eventually become obsolete.

The Japanese have also developed a system to ensure security in document transmission. Fujitsu demonstrated a data encryption device that can transmit data in total security from one terminal to another, even if the terminals are in different companies. The transmitting and receiving stations each key in their secret code number; the device creates a one-time random number sequence which is the basis of encryption. This security system has a market of its own in police forces and governments by eliminating present weak links in data encoding. Every station on a system now has to have a highly sensitive list of numbers, called a key list, which needs to be constantly changed, secured, and inventoried. Even so, from time to time one series is compromised or presumed so, and another has to be substituted at great effort. All this is eliminated in Toshiba's system.

Fujitsu also pridefully showed me one of their newest developments, an infrared modem. Modems, which connect one computer or terminal with another, currently use bulky cables. Each time the office is rearranged, the cables have to be rearranged, as happens every time a new station is added to the network. With Fujitsu's device, the linkage is provided with infrared light. Each workstation beams its signals to and gets input from a dessert-dish-size device unobtrusively stuck to the ceiling.

These products, and others, will transform the way office work is conducted for a long time to come. If the transformation has a decidedly Japanese flavor, it will be because MITI has targeted OA as a growth market it intends to invade, has spent tax money for industry, and has organized, coerced, and managed accordingly.

Another kind of transformation has already begun, the impact of information technology on other industries. A few years ago, while driving from Los Angeles to San Francisco through the fertile San Joaquin Valley, I saw, and smelled, an astonishing number of cattle in pens near the freeway. It was a feed ranch, where upwards of 10,000 cattle of a half dozen breeds are fattened before being shipped to market, a hi-tech version of the old California spread, complete with cowboys, horses, hay, and bunkhouses. But in this New California version, everything is run by computer. A single desktop computer tells the foreman how much hay to order and when to order it; how much manure the cattle will generate; how many trucks he'll need to ship it off; when a batch of new arrivals will be at peak market condition; and what the latest prices are at slaughterhouses all over the country. It prints out the cowpuncher's paychecks as well.

In still another transformation of traditional industries, computers are changing the world of manufacturing. In addition to computer-assisted design (CAD), and computer assisted manufacturing (CAM) there is computer assisted engineering (CAE), which can improve nearly every type of manufacturing. 'From those industries comes the technology that boosts productivity in countless other industries, which provides a lift to the whole economy,' says John Diebold, a leading U.S. consultant on information processing.

Japan is ahead in CAE. Toshiba, Nissan, and Hitachi have invested substantially in CAE for their internal use and are now acquiring the expertise to market this experience as a product. Applications are nearly endless. How thick should the walls of a water pipe be? Are the coils in a bedspring the right thickness? Are they made of the right material? How many should there be per square foot of mattress? For that matter, could there be a better way to make a mattress, without the traditional coils? These questions can be studied on all products, from tea kettles to trucks, resulting in less expensive, better-designed, better-built products. 'We all know how to do this, but the Japanese have done more of it at an early stage,' says Stephen Spacil, a scientific observer for General Electric in Tokyo. 'The payoffs there should be tremendous.'

I caught a nasty cold on a trip to Japan. Ordinarily, I would stay in bed for a day or two, but this was out of the question. I had appointments to keep. I was staying in Tokyo, in a district of bookstores, near Meiji University, not an area where there are very many foreigners. When I did find a pharmacy, I didn't know what kind of medicine to ask for. Eventually, I named the one brand I could remember: Contac. The pharmacist brought out several packages, one of which was Contac. The others, I was made to understand, were just as good, and they were much cheaper. Their price was about half the price of Contac's 980 yen, or about $4.14 for a package of ten capsules.

The retail price for the same medicine in the U.S. is $2.29, half of what it was in Japan. The reason for the price differential is simple: The Japanese government protects its drug industry from American and European competition, the ominous first step in a Japanese world-wide assault on that lucrative industry.

Japan's domestic drug market is huge, second only to the U.S., with per-capita consumption even higher and growing as Japan's population continues to age. The Japanese protect this market without tariffs, simply by refusing to honor pharmaceutical testing data submitted by foreign manufacturers. Instead, it requires that all new imported drugs or medicines, prescription or otherwise, go through an exhaustive testing process by Japan's Ministry of Health and Welfare. This effectively delays introduction of any foreign pharmaceutical by up to several years; furthermore, the cost of testing is borne by the importer.

But drugs produced by Japanese manufacturers, while officially held to the same standard, are usually licensed solely on the basis of data submitted by the manufacturer. They are then rapidly introduced into the Japanese market. In practice, this has meant that new drugs of foreign origin can be frozen out of Japan's markets. Domestic companies design near-duplicates and get them on Japan's shelves before the government's exhaustive testing process of imported drugs is completed. The government then grants exclusive marketing rights for five years to the Japanese companies.

France correctly perceived this policy as yet another of Japan's ingenious nontariff barriers to imports. In October, 1981, they asked the Japanese government to give reciprocal treatment to foreign government certification of drug safety. The request was 'taken under advisement' but never granted by the Japanese.

The Japanese like to boast that they have been among the world's pioneers in microbe management, citing their centuries of brewing yeast fungi for beer, soy sauce, sake, and fermented bean paste. Indeed, 200,000 tons, or two-thirds of the world's amino acids, are produced by the fermentation process. Japan produces some 60 percent of them and 40 percent of all amino acids. Japan acknowledges that most of its modern biological scientific achievements, some of which are quite impressive, are dependent on the 1953 discovery of the structure of DNA by the American J. D. Watson and the Englishman F. H. Crick. But Japanese biological science has a far more sinister link with Americans and the British.

In 1931 General Shiro Ishii, a surgeon in the Japanese Army, set up a research station in Manchuria, a territory seized from China, established as a Japanese puppet state, and renamed Manchukuo. Ishii's task was to learn as much as possible about biological warfare; he instructed his doctors to infect their research animals with anthrax, bubonic plague, and a variety of other diseases. To make the research definitive, Ishii decided to substitute human beings for animals. His first subjects were Chinese prisoners, and a few years later, after Pearl Harbor, Americans, Dutch, British, and Australian prisoners became available for his human experimentation.

The prisoners were infected with deadly diseases. The Japanese researchers then expanded their work by inducing gas gangrene and freezing prisoners' limbs. After this they butchered their living subjects to study the effects of the diseases they had induced. Some prisoners who managed to survive even this savagery were simply murdered when their disease-laden bodies were of no further use to the scientists. In other cases, all of the blood of prisoners was drained, then replaced with animal blood while doctors monitored the victim's reactions. By the end of the war, this research was being carried on in at least three stations in occupied China. No fewer than 3,000 prisoners, including Americans and their allies, were murdered during the course of these experiments.

The results of this research were made available to the Japanese Army as it launched its all-out campaign to conquer China. Japanese planes swooped low over Ningbo, a city near Shanghai, and dropped plague-infected debris, causing many civilian deaths, a procedure they repeated with several other Chinese cities. They reported their attacks had met with 'moderate' success.

As World War II came to a close, the Japanese biological researchers fled to escape Soviet armies closing in on Manchuria, taking all their files and reports with them back to Japan. After the surrender, most of this material came into the possession of the American military. In a secret memo by Edwin Hill, an American military scientist, the Japanese experiments were described thusly: 'Such information could not be obtained in our own laboratories because of scruples attached to human experimentation. It represents data which have been obtained by Japanese scientists at the expenditure of millions of dollars and years of work.' Another top secret memo argued that the scientists who had participated in these experiments be granted 'immunity from prosecution' as war criminals. No Japanese were ever tried for war crimes in connection with these experiments.

The legacy of these Manchurian horrors was a huge stockpile of contagious microbes, disease-carrying equipment, and delivery systems. The U.S. military made a deal with the Japanese: There would be no prosecution if they would provide further information about their experiments. Many of these Japanese are still alive and are among the leading executives and researchers of the Japanese pharmaceutical industry.

The protected Japanese drug industry is now ready for its major expansion into foreign markets. In late 1981, stock analysts were already recommending Japanese pharmaceutical companies as having unusual growth potential. 'The analysts expect the Japanese to start any new export drive by first selling more of their drugs through established companies abroad, although some are starting to advance on their own into world markets,' the *Asia Record* reported. The drive has begun. In 1963, Japanese companies had only 350 patented substances in the U.S.; by late 1982 this number had increased to more than 1,700, a close second to West Germany.

In 1982, Shionogi, Japan's largest antibiotic maker, began to sell its Shiomarin broad-spectrum antibiotic through Eli Lilly, which controls 40 percent of the world market for antibiotics. Japan has begun to pull ahead in this hotly competitive and risky field. The reason for Japanese interest in antibiotics is both financial and technological. In 1982 more then $700 million in antibiotics was sold to hospitals and drugstores worldwide, a gain of more than 22 percent over 1981. New antibiotics are in constant demand because, over time, most organisms acquire defenses against the older ones, thus reducing their effectiveness.

Most antibiotics are naturally occurring organisms, modified from their natural state in laboratories. Some are synthesized by computer-assisted researchers who design molecular combinations with desirable traits, then attempt to create them from organic chemicals. Most natural antibiotics are found in the soil, and the Japanese have proven to be the best soil searchers in the world. Since 1970 most of the important antibiotic discoveries have come from Japan. Some of their finds have brought prices of up to $40 million for worldwide licensing rights, which was the industry estimate for the sale of Toyama Chemical's Cefobid to Pfizer.

Japan is not entering the world market with small, under-capitalized firms. Most of Japan's pharmaceutical companies are huge, diversified organizations with enormous assets. Takeda Chemical Industries, for example, Japan's largest pharmaceutical maker, has assets of $20 billion. It has close affiliations with the Sumitomo Group of companies; its two biggest stockholders are Japan's leading life insurance companies, and it has extensive marketing arrangements with Switzerland's Hoffman-La Roche. In 1982, Takeda announced a joint venture with Abbott Laboratories, and in 1983 it began to market one of its drugs in the U.S. and to expand its U.S. field trials of two new antibiotics, Pansporin and Bestcall.

Another Japanese bio-giant is Green Cross, Japan's leading maker of plasma derivatives, headquartered in Osaka. Green Cross has two subsidiaries, both named Alpha Therapeutic, one in West Germany and the other in the U.S:, and has strong ties to UCLA and Hokkaido universities. The company makes hepatitis 'B' vaccines, antiinflamatory and anticancer agents, and in 1983 announced the development of a second generation product called Fluosol-DA, an artificial blood.

With its 1978 purchase of Alpha Therapeutics Corp., a Los Angeles company, Green Cross became the first Japanese company to acquire a U.S. manufacturing facility. Several other Japanese firms have entered into joint ventures with American companies. For example, Smith Kline – makers of Contac – have teamed with Fujisawa. Fujisawa is the Sanwa Bank Group's pharmaceutical arm, one of the top Japanese companies in the field. It has been exporting technology under license to the biggest European and American biotech companies.

The success of Japanese efforts in the drug field are now evident. A two-year study by the National Academy of Engineering in the U.S. shows that America is rapidly losing ground to Japan in new discoveries, introduction of new drugs, and production of all drugs. The U.S. industry now lags behind Western Europe. The Japanese, who once produced only one-third as much as America, now have near-parity, with three-fourths of the U.S. volume of pharmaceutical business.

MITI officially recognized the growth potential of the entire biotechnology field – one that encompasses pharmaceuticals, molecular biology, and biogenetics –

when in June 1982 it established its Bioindustry Office. Japan's pharmaceutical companies, rich, diversified, successful concerns with comparatively little debt, no significant foreign competition and closely affiliated with the cash-rich insurance companies and the major banks, were going to receive government subsidies so they could develop technology to compete with the European and American pharmaceutical industries. The third phase of the classic target plan is now in place.

One of MITI's current R&D projects involves three types of bioindustries: Bioreactors, large-scale cell cultivation, and recombinant DNA. A bioreactor is a facility for the rapid growth of microbes under closely controlled conditions. Large-scale cell cultivation is the technology required to grow trillions of identical living cells. Most types of immunizations for childhood diseases are no more than the weakened cells of agents causing the disease. Large-scale cultivation of these, and other types of cells, would make cells much cheaper to produce.

'Recombinant DNA technology,' a method of creating entirely new organisms or cells by manipulating the individual genes of the DNA and replacing selected genes, is at the leading edge of medical science. Scientists have already created 'supermice' by replacing a certain mouse gene with the related gene of a larger species. One promise of recombinant DNA technology is the creation of entirely new organisms that will range in size from the microscopic to the gargantuan.

MITI will also coordinate the activities of eight government research labs, of which three are involved in microbe engineering. With microbe engineering, MITI's scientists hope to use the naturally occurring functions of microbes to accomplish specific tasks related to manufacturing.

MITI has made the biotech industry a prime goal for the future. In 1982, MITI says, R&D expenditures for biotech research were $203 million, up 20 percent from 1981 and representing more than 6 percent of all research in Japan. To encourage the acquisition of foreign biotech technology by Japanese companies, MITI has lifted most restrictions on licensing and joint ventures. Of the 12 projects the Swiss giant Biogen is undertaking with foreign partners, eight are with Japanese companies, according to *Nikkei Biotech*, a trade magazine. It was Biogen which patented the first form of 'bio engineered' interferon, a substance used in the treatment of cancer.

Vickers Da Costa, an international research firm, reported in 1982 that Japan was still 'four or five years' behind the U.S. in basic genetic engineering. But it is now swiftly closing the gap. MITI spent $30 million of government funds in 1982 just on recombinant DNA research, and in August of that year their planners persuaded the Ministry of Health and Welfare to lift Japan's ultrastringent laws governing genetic research. 'Commercially, we're trying not to lose out to advanced countries,' said Fumito Haga, a MITA Bioindustry Office official.

Apparently they will not. In 1982 Nippon Zeon Co. began selling the world's first artificial DNA. 'We are producing 87 different types of synthesized DNA fragments and custom synthesized long-chain DNA,' a company spokesman said. 'Simple types of synthetic DNA fragments are being marketed by some American companies, but complicated hereditary genes [synthesized long-chain DNA] are not available elsewhere on the market.'

Japan also has its sights on the enormous potential market in the virus-fighter interferon, which is considered a likely cancer-fighting agent. In August 1982, MITI approved 11 commercial gene engineering ventures, most of which are aimed at producing interferon. New license applications have also been submitted to MITI for production of Interleukin-2, a human biological protein that aids the growth of cancer-killing cells. 'The demand for interferons represents the most dramatic and well-publicized example of how new biotechnologies have impacted industrial and small business development in the last five to ten years,' said E. F. Hutton's Nelson Schneider and Hedy Sladovich in a 1983 report. 'We estimate that research expenditures will have grown from about $1 billion a year worldwide in 1980 to as much as $6 to $7 billion by 1987.'

Japan has shown that it will be responsible for a large share of these research funds. At the Fujisaki Institute in Okayama, about 350 miles west of Tokyo, researchers are producing human interferon from hamsters injected with human cancer cells. The hamsters grow huge tumors, which are surgically removed; then a substance called Sendai virus, developed in Japan, is mixed with the cancerous growth cells to produce a type of interferon. The institute is owned by Hayashibara Laboratories, which for a hundred years was one of Japan's premier starch manufacturers. The new process promises to produce interferon, now one of the most costly substances known, in commercial quantities and at much lower prices.

In late August 1983, another Japanese pharmaceutical company announced an interferon breakthrough. The Kyowa Hakko Co. said that its new fermentation process will produce about 2,000 billion units of the drug, enough to treat 5,000 patients, in a single 200-liter culturing tank. About the same time, Wakunaga Pharmaceutical reported it had used cell fusion to produce monoclonal antibodies from mice; when injected into humans, they are expected to produce cancer antibodies. This is a promising first step on the road to mass immunization against cancer.

Most of the advanced biotech work in the U.S. is being done by new, small companies like Genex, which was founded in 1979 with only $15 million in seed capital. In contrast, most of the Japanese companies are established giants in a better position to later control world markets through high production and price manipulation. 'It's not a venture business in Japan. New companies are not starting up,' said Hiuga Saito, director of Tokyo University's Institute of Applied Biology. The biggest firms, divisions of companies like Sumitomo and Suntory, Japan's premier distiller of a whiskey that tastes much like Scotch, and Ajinomoto, which makes monosodium glutamate, or MSG, a food additive, are setting up the ultramodern labs. 'This is the business of the future,' said Katsuhiro Utada, president of Ajinomoto, which recently developed a cell-fusion process to mass-produce 20 kinds of amino acids at a very low cost.

'Japan is just awakening,' says Bruce Kaplan, a City of Hope, California, molecular genetics researcher who lectures in Japan. 'The Japanese are very committed to not being left behind; they're willing to commit themselves to extensive training. They have fabulous long-term corporate planning. I see Japan getting stronger and stronger in the biotech field.'

Of all the near-future industries that Japan has earmarked, perhaps the most exciting is robotics. In 1967 when Japan turned to robots as a solution to their manpower shortages, they turned to the world's experts, the U.S. The first robots in Japan were imported from the U.S. Now there are 50,000 of them laboring in Japan's factories, some of them at work turning out more of their own kind. 'Japan emphasized the development of robots at a very early stage,' says Diebold. 'At the start of the 1970s that country was doing more than half of all the world's research in robotics. Sure as day follows night, the products flowing out of that research are beginning to be used widely in Japan and are being exported.'

There are many species of robots. There are the robots of early science fiction, anthropomorphic contraptions such as the intergalactic plenipotentiary of *The Day The Earth Stood Still*, a mechanical superman. Other fictional robots were capable not only of superhuman strength but of human evil. Or they appeared as engagingly human as the Tin Woodsman, or as fanciful as a mobile, onboard starship computer capable of astronavigation or death-dealing with cosmic weaponry.

Actual robots are of another sort. Some are being developed to go one day in man's place to the depths of the oceans, to the planets, or even on millennia-long voyages to the stars. But Japan's working robots are not of this sort either. Like the Japanese worker himself, they are uncomplaining drudges. If Japan's robots ever organize – and at Fujitsu Fanuc robots are now members of the company union with dues paid by management – their motto would be easy to divine: I work, therefore I am.

At a dreary factory near Matsumoto, about 200 miles west of Tokyo, I spent an evening with a dozen robots that were assembling computer circuit boards. Each robot consisted of an enormous feeding apparatus – three or four dozen narrow, curving stainless steel channels through which endless paper belts of transistors, diodes, capacitors, resistors, and other components were pulled – and an insertion apparatus, a complex linkage of arms and cams. The whole monster was controlled by a computer that could be reprogrammed to change the sequence of assembly, to change the types of components used, or to change its work to an entirely different purpose.

Blank circuit boards swooshed down a set of rails and paused while a clawlike arm shoved one component after another into just the right place and spot-soldered them at the rate of one or two a second. It was fed by another arm which picked up individual components from the feed belts, then rotated forward like a football quarterback. This arm handed off a resistor or transistor to the arm inserting components into the board. While all this was going on, the whole assemblage was sliding back and forth to select the appropriate component from one of the belts running up the stainless steel channels. To 'supervise' the room full of robots there was only one human worker, who kept a plodding pace restocking the belts with components and responding to the muted siren and flashing red lights of the occasional robot in distress.

Robotization has developed so rapidly in Japan that this nation of groups has already set up an organization devoted solely to classifying robots, the Terminological Standardization Committee of the Japan Industrial Robot Association (JIRA). According to JIRA's latest figures, in 1980 Japan had 47,000 industrial robots, while West Germany had 5,850, the U.S. 3,255, and Britain 185. By 1982, Japan had 135 manufacturers of industrial robots, with a human work force of about 4,500 producing them.

The pace of Japanese robot manufacture is far outstripping the U.S. By 1983, with their factories running at only about 50 percent of capacity, Japan's robot makers increased production by 83 percent over 1982. By comparison, U.S. robot manufacture increased by only 25 percent during this same period.

According to Keiji Ikehata, writing in *Japan Echo*, there are 'about 80 government or academic research laboratories employing about 300 researchers in the development of robotic technology.' Janji Yonemoto, executive director of JIRA, proudly declares: 'Japan is number one in the world in the diffusion of robots and the expansion of research personnel.'

To remain competitive in world markets, Japanese manufacturers are 'hiring' vast numbers of robots. In 1982, the *value* of Japan's industrial robot production rose 37.7 percent, to about $610 million. The electrical industry was the biggest single buyer of robots, replacing the vehicle industry, which is still the biggest user. Although the export of robots was up 250 percent from 1981, with sales worth about $104 million, most of Japan's robots are being sold in Japan; as part of MITI's protectionist policy, very few are imported.

Despite the global recession of 1981–83 and a drop in demand for all types of heavy machinery, MITI has continuously encouraged Japan's robot manufacturers to increase output. To foster a home market, MITI has designed a low-interest loan program for small and medium-sized firms that want to buy robots. With the average cost of an industrial robot about $44,000 (compared to $47,000 in 1971), MITI will loan the firm up to $48,000 per robot. About 25 percent of all Japanese small and medium-sized companies now own one or more robots, and MITI has set a goal of 50 percent within 'the near future.'

JIRA classifies robots in two categories: those that perform mechanical 'flexible moving functions similar to those of the moving parts of organisms' and those that perform 'intellectual' functions, operating in response to 'human request.' The robots that joined the union at Fujitsu Fanuc are a little of both; they are robots that build other robots at one of Japan's largest robotmakers. They were 'organized' because the union's treasury was becoming depleted as more and more robots were put to work, making it possible to hire fewer humans. It was a way to appease workers anxious about their jobs. Human productivity also seems to rise in robotized factories. Fearful that management will replace them with robots, workers produce even more efficiently after the first robots are installed.

Japan expects to increase robot production by a value factor of seven, between 1980 and 1990. The impact of robotization on Japanese companies will be a rapidly rising productivity. According to Dr. Yoshikazu Kano, a senior economist at the Research Institute of National Economy, this rising productivity will make Japan's goods even more competitive with those of Western Europe and the U.S. 'The success of the Japanese economy may intensify trade friction,' he said in an unwitting understatement. 'The electronics revolution will only augment the exports of Japanese machinery, thus forcing the United States and Europe to adjust their industries. At a time of massive unemployment like today, the danger of recurrent trade friction is very real.'

Anticipating increased furor between Japan and the rest of the industrialized world in the coming decades, Kano argues for special consideration of Japan's needs. 'Complying with unreasonable demands from abroad is not the way to deal with trade friction,' he said. 'Japan should explain to the world the reasonableness of its own position and urge the other industrial powers to join it in upholding the spirit of free trade.' But realistically, he realizes this will not happen without Japanese concessions, even minor ones. 'In order to preserve free trade, Japan must bear its share of the cost. Two steps Japan should take are opening its markets to foreign products and investing in the U.S. and Europe,' he said. Realizing the importance of the MITI protectionist policy, he adds: 'Probably the opening of the Japanese market will proceed more slowly than the increase in overseas investments.'

Japan's overseas investments, unlike those of other

industrialized nations, typically favor joint ventures in which the Japanese can gain direct benefit. One such plant, a joint venture between General Motors and Fujitsu Fanuc, will begin producing robots sometime in 1984 for sale in the U.S. Most of the robots, for the foreseeable future, will immediately go to work in GM's own automobile and other factories. GM, which produced the first industrial robot prototypes in 1961, would eventually like to sell robots as well as cars. But as John Holusha commented in the *New York Times*: 'Ten years from now GM may be the American affiliate of a worldwide automobile combine dominated by the Japanese, or it may be as important in robots and computer controls as it once was in tail fins and chrome.'

The Japanese have an enormous lead in robot technology, in sheer volume of new robot output, and in the robotization of its factories. If their established pattern of doing business holds true, they will maintain and increase it by every means available.

Like all aggressor nations, Japan, with its appetite for economic dominance, cannot be appeased by being offered industries to swallow. MITI is constantly searching for new areas to exploit. One of the latest is the heavy earth-moving equipment industry, most of which has previously been controlled by the U.S. and West Germany. But the same robot-intensive factories that can make cars and small trucks can make bulldozers, tractors, and scooploaders. And Japan has been building them by the tens of thousands.

The Japanese industry began in the early 1960s when a naive Caterpillar Tractor Corporation, the Peoria, Illinois-based world leader in earth-moving equipment, joined with Mitsubishi Heavy Industries to sell equipment to a Japanese nation just beginning to reindustrialize. MITI saw this move as an invasion of their home market, and not to be tolerated. Its own candidate was Komatsu, Ltd., then a relatively small company. Now Komatsu is number two in the world, and Caterpillar is an ailing giant that has lost about $450 million in its last two years. When Shoji Nogawa, Komatsu's president, told the *Wall Street Journal* that he thought of Caterpillar as 'a good competitor with the standing of an older brother,' the *Journal* reporter had to add, 'But a listener might find himself thinking of the deadly competition between the biblical brothers, Cain and Abel.' Make no mistake, Komatsu is out to slay Caterpillar.

Komatsu's 1982 sales were approximately $1.3 billion, compared with Caterpillar's $2 billion. Komatsu, founded in 1921, built its first bulldozers during World War II, copied from captured American models used by U.S. Navy Seabees on the Pacific Islands. Now Komatsu controls some 60 percent of Japan's domestic market, and, aided by a division that builds robots, has recently introduced new computer-assisted models. As a company, Komatsu is strengthened by sales of its factory automation equipment, which it claims is the most technologically advanced in the world. The company's other subsidiaries include a huge construction company, Komatsu Construction, and nine ventures spread from Singapore and Australia to North and South America and Europe. About 64 percent of its production is exported, significant amounts of it in recent years to the Soviet Union to help build its massive Siberian natural gas pipeline.

This was another MITI-arranged deal, worth about $1 billion, in which the Japanese set up a massive forestry program in the Amur River region of Siberia and agreed to buy 12 million cubic meters of timber between 1981 and 1986 from the Russians. The Japanese essentially bartered manufactured products for raw materials.

Caterpillar, meanwhile, was barred from bidding on these contracts by the U.S. government. In late 1982, Caterpillar's woes were exacerbated by a bitter, seven-month strike by its unionized employees. Komatsu responded to this opening by broadening its line from crawlers and loaders to a full range of products. In May 1983, Komatsu's 51 U.S. dealers began 'filling their lots with new machines, big, yellow, and pervasively copy-Cat in style,' *Fortune* commented. In addition to lower labor costs, in part the product of intense robotization, Komatsu's machines could be priced cheaper because of the artificially depressed value of the yen. Caterpillar's management said, 'Komatsu enjoys a 20 percent cost advantage over Caterpillar' because of the relative strength of the dollar and the yen alone.

Steve Newhouse, a Caterpillar spokesman, is angry at the cheapness of the yen and the price advantage it gives Japanese earth-moving machines. 'We feel there is a chronic problem with the undervalued yen, and that problem is not likely to rectify itself in the short term,' he points out. 'The free-market forces by which other world currencies operate are not applicable to the yen. It's not a free-floating currency, in the same sense that the deutschmark and the French franc or the English pound or the U.S. dollar is.

'There's clear evidence that Japanese government actions affect the yen. We're not arguing that they're sitting there manipulating the exchange rates against the dollar. But certain economic and political policies have the effect of controlling the range in which the yen continues to operate, and therefore is substantially undervalued, compared to the dollar.' One of these political policies, Newhouse explains, is the restriction placed on Japanese direct investment in overseas money markets. 'The net effect of the consistently low yen has given the Japanese an "unearned advantage" in price competition that has made it extremely difficult for us to compete in third-country markets.

'The world market has shifted,' Newhouse points out. 'Instead of U.S. companies being the predominant manufacturers – Caterpillar, J. I. Case, International Harvester, and so on – the number two competitor is Komatsu, number three is IDH of West Germany, number four is Fiat of Italy. We are still the world's leading manufacturer, but you have to go way down the list before you find another American company.

'To use Chairman Lee Morgan's expression, "We're looking for a level playing field." The playing field has been tilted in Japan's direction for a long time now. We don't have any hesitation about being able to compete with them otherwise.'

Newhouse believes that the Japanese government's actions, which help set the low value of the yen, amount to a kind of subsidy. 'It will require the effort of the U.S. and Japanese governments to recognize the problem and turn toward some kind of solution. Otherwise, of course, it invites the escalation of trade barriers and protectionist measures by free-trading countries, and we're opposed to that.'

Japanese manufactured products are now successfully competing in the wide-open American market. The first of 325 cars built by Kawasaki Heavy Industries for New York City's subway system was delivered in August 1983. These were the first foreign-built train cars ever used in New York, a contract worth about $305 million. Giant Hino Motors, an affiliate of Toyota, began assembling its first heavy trucks in the five- to seven-ton range at a Jacksonville, Florida, factory in the summer of 1983. Hino's spokesman said they expected to sell 500 trucks in 1984 – but 5,000 a year by 1990.

Although U.S. truckmakers still dominate the domestic market, there are signs of trouble. International Harvester, which builds both farm equipment and heavy trucks, lost $1.64 billion in 1982. In July 1983, it shut the doors of its Fort Wayne, Indiana, truck plant forever. The plant produced trucks for 60 years, employing as many as 11,000 people as recently as the early 1970s. Between 1978 and 1982, 6,000 workers, some with as many as 17 years seniority, were permanently laid off.

Part of the company's woes can be traced to shrinking sales of equipment to U.S. farmers, many of whom have been teetering on the edge of financial ruin since 1980. Much of Harvester's equipment is used to harvest corn and other livestock feeds, crops on which U.S. farmers have been losing money because of enormous surpluses and low market prices. The U.S. cattle industry could buy much more feed grain if they could export more beef. But the Japanese have restricted imports of American beef despite domestic Japanese beef prices of up to $35 a pound for prime cuts. The Japanese are not responsible for the plight of American farmers, but the Japanese import restrictions on beef have exacerbated the problem.

Even though American food products are not freely allowed into Japan, Japanese companies now profit from handling the sale of about 20 percent of the entire export grain trade of the United States. Six huge trading companies – Agrex, owned by Mitsubishi, Mitsui, C. Itoh, Marubeni, Sumitomo and Zen-Noh – have carved up a fifth of a market worth about $60 billion annually, a market which provides half the world's import needs for corn, wheat and soybeans, according to the U.S. Department of Agriculture. This Japanese-owned trade is not merely to Japan; it covers U.S. agricultural export all over the world. This stealthy entry into another U.S. market has been at the expense of established grain traders, including Louis Dreyfus, a French-owned firm, Bunge Corp., owned by Dutch and Argentine interests, and by Cargill, the American company that leads the international sale of grains.

Japanese companies have acquired more than 24 major grain storage elevators and large port facilities in New Orleans, Portland, Oregon, and Long Beach, California. Agrex will not disclose its total tonnage, but in 1981 it shipped more than 100 million bushels of grain out of Long Beach, alone, an increase of 80 percent from 1979, its first year in business. The Japanese achieved this market share with a well-tested device. 'They paid 20 to 30 cents a bushel over the market price to the farmers at first,' said Mayor Henry Robinson of Superior, Nebraska.

As another Japanese target for the future, no industry offers such great rewards – a generation or less away – than solar energy. Japan hopes to capture that future market and become the world leader in solar energy. And once again, their head start is being provided by American technology. Using processes patented by Stanford Ovshinsky, head of Energy Conversion Devices (ECD), a joint venture called Sharp ECD – 51 percent owned by

Sharp, 44 percent by ECD, 5 percent by Standard Oil of Ohio – is now producing a new solar energy device that can make electricity as cheaply as coal, oil, or nuclear energy.

While the devices are now being used exclusively to power calculators and other contemporary gadgets, the technology holds out the promise of both solar farms capable of mass producing large amounts of electricity, and smaller generating plants atop city office buildings and residences for local consumption. A Japanese joint venture between government and industry has developed what promises to be the first practical solar battery. Simultaneously, MITI has funded $46 million for a solar project being carried out by Sharp, Hitachi, Toshiba, NEC, and several smaller companies. 'I'm confident we'll soon be able to produce a watt of electricity from solar power for about $4,' said Kosuke Kurokawa, an official of Japan's New Energy Development Association. 'Japan's solar energy development is on the verge of a major breakthrough,' adds the economics trade paper *Nikkan Kogyo Shimbun*.

One of Japan's first growth industries was cameras. While their early models were little more than imitations of German and U.S. optical and mechanical technology, Japanese cameras improved rapidly. By the early 1960s all but a handful of West European camera makers quit the business, unable to match Japanese prices. By the late 1960s Japan clearly controlled the world market.

In 1968, I searched Tokyo's many large camera stores for an 8mm fisheye lens made by Nikon. But the search was futile. Nikon finally located a fisheye lens in an Osaka retail camera store and promised to ship it to me immediately. Why, I asked, was this item, readily available in the U.S. and Europe, not available at Nikon factory warehouses? The answer was that in their infancy, Japanese products are supported by export, not by internal consumption.

By the late 1970s, technology had produced cameras

that incorporated electronic shutters and automatic exposure control and focusing, all programmed by built-in microcomputers. But by the early 1980s, Japanese cameras had saturated their most affluent trading partners' domestic markets. To keep the lines moving and the Japanese work force stable, all the leading manufacturers' prices began to tumble; even Nikon was offering rebates and discounts. Clearly the Japanese could not continue their exponential increases in camera production. In 1982 MITI included cameras on their list of 'sunset' industries, those that would be scaled down, or would have to find other products to sell.

It was obvious that the same systems of microprocessors and optics used in 35mm cameras could find applications in other industries. By the early 1980s, Minolta, Canon, and Ricoh were marketing competing lines of photocopiers for offices and smaller versions designed for homes. Ricoh, which had been making copiers for several years but selling them in the U.S. under another brand name, severed its marketing relationships with the American firm and began selling copiers under their own name. They were joined by the companies which had been supplying them with their microchips: Toshiba, Fujitsu, Sharp, and others.

Suddenly mighty Xerox, the American company that had invented the copier and sold so many machines in the 1960s and 1970s that their company name had virtually become a generic noun and verb for photocopying, was competing with multiple copies of Japanese machines, all offered at prices well below their own. This fight is not yet over. Xerox has significant resources, including an edge in new technology, and has begun to diversify into other office automation products. But the Japanese have now heavily targeted this once exclusively American market. By mid-1982, Japanese copiers dominated the market for low- and medium-speed copiers, and Sharp was advertising as the 'best-selling small copier in America.' In a closely related field, Japan's exports of facsimile machines to the U.S. rose by 95 percent in 1982, to more than 65,500 units.

In the field of small typewriters, the Japanese victory is already complete. Of the five U.S. leading small typewriter makers, only Smith-Corona still makes its products in the U.S. One of the Japanese companies which defeated them, Brother Industries, is among the Japanese companies now seeking to enter the office typewriter market, a three-million-units-a-year U.S. business now dominated by IBM and Xerox. These companies annually sell 150,000 of the new electronic typewriters – machines with a relatively small built-in memory to permit erasure of mistakes before they are typed out.

In 1982, Brother, originally a Nagoya-based manufacturer of sewing machines, sold $43 million worth of electronic typewriters, a 500 percent increase over 1981. Brother is already the second-largest seller of typewriters used *outside* the office, and closing in on number one, Smith-Corona. The Nikko Research Center, a Japanese industry analysis firm, estimates Brother's sales of electronic typewriters will increase at a rate of 32 percent a year through 1986. Other Japanese companies in the market are Ricoh, Canon, and Seiko ('Silver Reed' brand). 'With the new technology, the market has opened up,' said Yoshihiro Yasui, a senior managing director at Brother. Adds Kenichi Ohmae, managing director of management consultants McKinsey & Company in Tokyo: 'The typewriter is becoming a Japanese game, and Brother seems to be the leader.'

But the popular electronic typewriter is merely an interim technological product, a 'pretty good bridge' to full word processing, in the words of Darrel E. Whitten, a Tokyo-based analyst with Bache Halsey Stuart Shields. In five years, improvements and rising sales volume will drive down the price of word processors, which are more efficient office tools, to the present prices of electronic typewriters. These will require printers of the sort now used with home and office computers. Brother is already in this business, competing with others Japanese companies that dominate the field: Oki, Seiko, C. Itoh, Tokyo Electric Company, NEC.

Epson, a division of the giant Seiko Group, is now

world sales leader in inexpensive 'dot matrix' printers. Mitsubishi is a late entry in this market, but this is by design. 'Our policy is to come out late with high quality products,' explained Yoshito Yamaguchi, president of Mitsubishi Electronics. Their new computer printer incorporates older technology but adds such features as seven printing colors and multiuser access. About the same time that Mitsubishi's printer entered the U.S. markets, another with similar capabilities appeared under the American Transtar label. Actually, it was built by Seikosha, another division of Seiko.

Japan's higher-priced, higher-quality machines, whose printing equals that of a good typewriter, are often sold as 'Diablo' compatible: able to use the same ribbons and printing wheels, and responding to the same computer or word-processor generated codes, as the Xerox-made product that introduced the heavy duty 'daisy wheel' printer to the world.

The Japanese have not yet captured much of the world market for personal and small office computers, but they have been slowly increasing penetration of components and peripherals – anything that plugs into or is connected to a computer. The Japanese are having notable success in disk drives, which are used to store data or software on thin recordlike disks.

In late 1982, Alps Electronics of Tokyo replaced the American firm Shugart Associates as suppliers of 5.25-inch, disk drives for Apple, simply by selling $50 a unit cheaper. Almost simultaneously, TEAC was awarded a contract for the same size drives with Digital Equipment Corporation. Sony signed with Hewlett-Packard for $30 million in business for their smaller, 3.5-inch drives, while Hitachi and Matsushita followed the Sony entry into the three-inch size drives. In 1982, NEC began monthly shipping of 1,500 units of the larger, eight-inch drives commonly used in business computers, at unit prices much below those of their American competitors. 'At the very low end, the three-inch and five-inch disks for microcomputers, the Japanese have been very aggressive,' says Rutishauser of Control Data. 'They were the first to show three-inch disks. They had obviously invested a good bit in their development.'

American-owned Control Data is becoming a casualty of Japanese underpricing in the computer disk field. CDC makes disk drives for machines ranging from supercomputers to home computers, but shortly after the Japanese entry into this market, CDC's disk drive sales plunged. In an effort to protect the jobs of employees at its 16 peripheral-making plants, CDC scheduled layoffs of from four to 12 days at all but one of its plants. At CDC's subsidiary, Magnetic Peripherals, Inc., all 2,300 part-time and supplemental employees were terminated; the company ended all overtime, and reduced subcontracting substantially.

For several years, leading American computer manufacturers have steadily issued a series of proclamations to the effect that, while Japan's achievements in computer hardware and components are indeed impressive, they and their companies have little to fear because the Japanese have always lagged behind in software design, a peculiarly creative American activity. Since it takes software – the programming instructions needed to direct a computer's functions – to make any computer salable, this refrain went, and since the Japanese have never done this well, there's nothing to worry about.

They were wrong, and Joseph Podolsky is worried. Podolsky is an information systems manager at Hewlett-Packard's Palo Alto, California, headquarters. After his colleague, Ilene Birkwood, returned from a 1983 visit to Japan, he became concerned. 'She described some things she saw in Japan which scared the hell out of me,' he says. 'Seeing what happened to Detroit in a relatively short period makes me think that the changes in the programming industry will be much more rapid than anybody realizes.'

What has Podolsky worried is that the Japanese have now developed a system for mass-producing high-quality software, while the rest of the world is still plodding along building individual programs one at a time. In Japan, he reports, 'thousands of trained people are manufacturing software with levels of quality, reliability, and productivity that are beyond the dreams of our software people in the U.S. They have a disciplined methodology, and they have turned programming into a repetitive process which can then be managed in the same way they do repetitive manufacturing. These organizations have been at these tasks for over three years, improving their performances as they proceed.'

One dimension of this system is the use of pretested program modules, which are made up of standardized codes. 'In the U.S. and Europe, programmers treat their codes as a private creation. In Japan, systems are constructed out of programs and routines that have been used before; they are much more likely to be correct.'

The Japanese are able to do this, Podolsky points out, because 'the nature of Japanese society is disciplined. That is their main leverage point. Here, when we tell people to use reusable code segments, for example, they say, "You are restricting my creativity," but in Japan they just say, "Of course, that's the way to do it." Our culture basically refuses to do this. We reinvent the wheel in coding every day, thousands of times over.'

Ilene Birkwood is the charming, London-born quality assurance manager at Hewlett-Packard's mainframe division. In the summer of 1983, she made a one-week 'technology exchange' visit to Japan, where she spent a few days at the three largest Japanese mainframe computer manufacturers. Like Podolsky, she is uneasy.

'I'm alarmed because the Japanese approach to software reliability is excellent, and I think that in a couple of years from now they're going to come out with software Hondas, while the American industry will still be developing Ferraris,' says Birkwood. 'We'll still need our "pit crews" to keep them running. The Japanese won't have to. They have taken all the techniques that the Americans and Europeans know very well, but they've put them all together and tried them out. It's a total approach. They are automating the whole process from design through release, so that code is generated automatically and test cases are generated automatically.

'They have large software engineering groups that are dedicated to automating the whole process,' she adds. 'They're taking the human error element out of software, that's the most impressive thing. They are very much into reusable code, they have libraries of reusable modules, which are well documented. As they design, they call up a library on their computer terminal, and then automatically locate whatever's available to perform whatever specific function they need.

'One of the things the Japanese do regularly, every six months, is to trot over here and interview all the software reliability professors in the U.S.,' Birkwood continues. 'Then they go back and try all their new theories, and if they work, the Japanese implement them in their "software factories." They do it all very systematically. My suspicion is that the Japanese pool all that information between themselves, between the big companies.'

One myth about Japanese software is that it is, and will always be, second-rate, because the Japanese lack the ability for genuine innovation. Birkwood doesn't agree. 'I think that's a nice thought, that we'd all like to be comfortable about,' she says. 'But I think they can innovate as well as anybody. Their education system tends to produce more copiers than leaders, their culture promotes that. However, I think that Japanese history will show that there are as many innovators there as America has had. America followed Europe, initially, and now leads the way. Japan has tended to follow the United States, and found a good market by taking American ideas and improving on them. But I think they're very capable of innovation – and right now they're turning out more engineers than we are.'

Podolsky concludes with a frightening picture. 'I see unemployment offices sprouting along Massachusetts Route 128,' he warns. 'I see apricot and prune orchards returning to what was Silicon Valley. I see planes filled with Japanese software crossing over the Golden Gate from the Far East, and returning from the U.S. with cargo bays empty.' Podolsky was not being facetious. He is truly worried.

As the computer revolution proceeds, it has divided itself into two categories – personal and business. 'Personal computers are expected to turn up in four out of five American homes by 1990,' United Technologies predicted in 1983. As time progresses, the line between personal and business computers is blurring. 'I think that in seven years, or perhaps sooner, there will be only two types of computers,' comments Dr. Peter Gregory, VP for corporate planning for Cray Research Corporation, who notes the increasing speed of computers and the gradual merging of functions performed by both computers. 'There will be only very large computers for scientific research and military applications, and desktop-sized computers for homes, offices, businesses, and even data processing,' he says.

But Takayoshi Shiina, president of SORD Computer Corporation, second-largest manufacturer of small computers in Japan (after NEC), thinks that there will be a third type, the personal, portable, go-anywhere computer. It will be able to exchange data or software easily with desktop machines. Shiina is that rarest of Japanese animals, the self-made man, very much like the resourceful American entrepreneurs of Silicon Valley. The son of a Japanese Army officer, he was born in China during World War II. In 1970 Shiina, at the age of 27, started SORD with $2,000 and one employee – his mother, who still does some accounting for the firm. Now the company, the fastest growing of all 600,000 Japanese companies surveyed, is headquartered in Chiba, about an hour from Tokyo.

As his company grew, Shiina faced one of the major problems of entrepreneurs in clubby Japan: Where to find the best and brightest employees in a nation where only the very largest firms can offer lifetime employment. Shiina solved the problem by hiring younger people – the average age of his work force is 26 – and by going back to his alma mater, Tokai University, to recruit the best students. SORD now has thousands of employees, factories in Singapore and Dublin – where Shiina is introducing Ireland's first authentic Japanese restaurant – and 1983 sales estimated, conservatively, at over $85 million. When not traveling, Shiina, a talkative, nattily dressed man, hangs his hat at the company's sales headquarters in a Tokyo skyscraper near Japan's largest martial arts school. Japan's personal computer makers now collectively share only 7 percent of the U.S. market, but Shiina is out to change this. From 1977 to 1979, he attempted to sell his machines in the U.S. without success. Now he's trying again.

'The name "SORD" comes from S.O. for software and R.D. for hardware,' he explained when interviewed in Tokyo. 'We make the software first, then build a machine to perform up to its requirements. That's exactly the opposite of what everyone else does.' Another Shiina innovation: a magazine about SORD products and applications, along with new type-them-in-yourself programs. The magazine is in English but distributed primarily in Japan. In August, 1983, another version was produced for distribution in the U.S. and Great Britain.

As part of a careful plan to build a U.S. users' base, SORD's new machines for U.S. customers have a wide range of software adapters available for conversion to other manufacturers' software. 'A customer will be able to use IBM programs, or Apple, or most CP/M software,' he said. This would allow more than 80 percent of all existing programs to run on the SORD machines, a giant competitive advantage. At present, few U.S.-made computers can use other manufacturers' software. Some companies sell plug-in boards for IBM personal computers which also permit the use of Apple programs. Other machines, built to accept a widely used American-designed operating system called CP/M, can use adapters to run some versions of CP/M made for another manufacturer's hardware. But a machine like SORD's, which can accept IBM, Apple, and all CP/M programs, will enter the American market with a great advantage. 'We are marketing machines in the U.S. with a range from $200 to about $7,000 now,' Shiina told me.

Shiina thinks his first attempt to penetrate the U.S. market in 1977 failed because it was made too early. He now expects to succeed by exchanging stock with two small, but active, U.S. firms. 'First I must complete my scouting of America. Like in a war, you must know everything about the land,' Shiina says. 'It's so important to have an American distributor to support the customer after the machine is installed.'

SORD's family of computers use Zilog Z80A or Z80B central processors, and some use Intel or Motorola chips. The hardware comes from a small, closely held Massachusetts company, Charles River Data Systems; Shiina bought 7 percent of its stock in mid-1983 and sold a piece of SORD to Charles River. He is now negotiating a similar deal with Envision Technology, another closely held company based in San Jose, California. Envision makes printers and terminals, and has been supplying SORD with color graphics for its machines. This gives SORD a base on both U.S. coasts, where most computers are sold, and it gives the two American companies outlets in Japan, Singapore, and Ireland. It will also provide Shiina with a way to service the 32,000 business computers he hopes to sell in the U.S. during 1984. 'At this time we have two regional offices, in New York and Los Angeles. But soon we should have offices in Houston, San Francisco, Chicago, maybe Atlanta,' he said.

Besides SORD, at least one Japanese manufacturer is attempting to wedge open the lucrative American computer market: Epson. Epson is a division of the Seiko Group, which is part of the even larger K. Hattori trading company. Epson's production facilities are in Nagano Prefecture, about 200 miles west of Tokyo, but light years distant in temperament. The region, an enclave of craggy peaks within Japan's main island of Honshu, is so isolated that it was unknown to the West until after the turn of the century, when Walter Weston, a British clergyman and mountaineer, first toured this relatively obscure area.

Nagano is the heart of the Japanese Alps, a region where sawtoothed mountains crowd the horizon and miniature vineyards produce a passable imitation of a dry Chablis. Watchmaking and fine instrument manufacture tucked away in small, neat factories on the outskirts of its villages moved there for safety during World War II and remained. Throughout Japan, the people of Nagano have a reputation – in a nation of overachievers – for a special tenacity. It would be a mistake to underestimate Epson's commitment to carving out its own segment of the American home computer market.

In April 1982, I spent two weeks touring most of Epson's Nagano factories. Unlike SORD and other Japanese computer makers, Epson makes many of its components, including microchips and liquid crystal displays (LCDs), and sells them to other Japanese manufacturers. Epson has already become a familiar name to home computer buyers because of its highly successful and innovative line of inexpensive printers, which are the best-selling in the world and have taken 40 percent of the U.S. market. Since late 1982, Epson has been advertising its QX-10, which is either a smallish but expandable business desktop or a top-of-the-line home computer; and a first-of-its-kind miniature 'notebook' computer, the HX-20.

In 1983, Epson made a distribution coup: It convinced Computerland, the largest U.S. retail computer chain, to handle its products nationwide. It also established a national network of 12 distributors who can be reached via tollfree telephone numbers. Epson allows its dealers 45 days to pay for their computers, and gives subsidized, below-market interest rates on unsold inventory after that. In an advertising blitz in 1983, Epson spent more than $13 million using the talent of three top U.S. advertising and public relations agencies. Epson's management sees a way into one untapped market: American women. They selected the Bohle Company as its P.R. agency because it is one of the few in the U.S. owned by a young, innovative woman, and largely staffed by women.

Epson is also making gains with American software makers. On the strength of its excellent built-in Valdocs operating system, designed by a small California software company, the company has attracted about 200 sophisticated software packages from several U.S. makers, adding to the system's appeal. 'We think we'll sell 100,000 QX-10s and about that many notebook computers as well,' predicted Susumu Aizawa, an Epson senior managing director.

Japanese attempts to take the American home computer market are accelerating as the field expands. Determined to penetrate the U.S., the Japanese turned to a traditional technique: the collective assault. In June 1983, Microsoft, a large American software manufacturer, took full-page ads in the *Wall Street Journal*, the *New York Times*, and several other newspapers and trade publications. Their bold announcement was that Microsoft and Spectravideo, a U.S. manufacturer of videogame playing machines and home computers, along with 14 Japanese companies, including Hitachi, Matsushita, Mitsubishi, Toshiba, Sanyo, and Sony, had joined together to announce a new computer software standard, the MSX. From now on, proclaimed the ads, *all* computers made by *all* 15 companies would use one type of software, Microsoft Basic. Any program or game which would run on one machine would run on all of them. It was a stunning accomplishment for Microsoft and a tremendous marketing edge for the 14 Japanese companies, including several, such as Canon, Casio, and Pioneer, who do not yet make computers.

The standard required all these Japanese computer-making companies to use one type of microprocessor based on the Zilog Z80 design. Just as a record does not care which brand of phonograph is playing it, programs written to a standard would not care who made the computer. In Japan, mighty Matsushita's corporate spokesmen were already talking about a 500 percent increase in sales of home computers based on the MSX standard. 'When Matsushita starts to manufacture an MSX computer, everyone will follow,' said Kazuyasu Maeda, in charge of Matsushita's personal computer development. The announcement sent shock waves through the American computer community. 'You have a group of companies that haven't been able to succeed in this market individually trying to succeed collectively,' said Steve Greenberg of Commodore, the leading small computer maker. But most U.S. companies – Atari was a notable exception – said they would *not* adopt the new standard.

Almost immediately, three leading Japanese home computer makers – NEC, Fujitsu and Sharp – pointed out that they would not accept the new standard. 'We're studying other proposals for standards as well,' said NEC's Atsuyoshi Ouchi, senior VP of Japan's leading home computer company. News reports said that NEC and Sharp, which share 60 percent of the Japanese marketplace, backed out at the last minute. It was a move that embarrassed the Bellevue, Washington-based Microsoft and set the stage for round two. It took only a few days for the Japanese to come out of their corner, swinging.

'We are Japanese, and so we should develop a truly Japanese standard,' said Akihide Sue, speaking for the Japan Electronics Development Association. The association, representing all Japanese computer makers, is working on a standard of its own. 'Microsoft is too expensive,' said Masayoshi Son, chairman of Nihon Soft Bank. Son, a 26-year-old third generation Japanese-Korean, is a Berkeley-educated *wunderkind* who started Japan's largest software distributor with the $500,000 he got for selling a patent on his English/Japanese and Japanese/English translation computer to Sharp. 'Microsoft wanted $250,000 for a license and three or four dollars for each machine sold,' Son explained. Not so incidentally: Soft Bank has its own standard, reportedly offered at a tenth of the price of the Microsoft MSX. 'It's all secrecy, but I believe NEC and Sharp and others are thinking about their own standard too,' said SORD's Shiina.

There *is* a move for standardization in the computer swampland afoot. 'There is no way that there can go on being eight different noncompatible computers in the U.S.,' said Ken Williams, president of Sierra On-Line, a leading U.S. game and program manufacturer. 'The U.S. industry is headed for doom if it doesn't standardize.'

But such companies as Texas Instruments, Commodore, Tandy, Apple, IBM, and others with proprietary software systems for their machines have huge investments in them, a stake in maintaining a base of satisfied customers for repeat buying or trade-ups, and stockholders to satisfy with continuing quarterly profits.

There is also considerable flux in the state-of-the-art. Scarcely a month goes by without the announcement of some new hardware, some new approach to solving an old problem. American companies, glorying in their image as innovators and aware that fortunes have been made on new devices, are unwilling to give up the chance to achieve breakthroughs by adopting a standard that would fix technological development at present capabilities for years to come.

It may be years before the major U.S. companies feel comfortable about agreeing on a standard. But the disagreement may be academic: they may never get the chance to resolve it. Far more likely, Japan's major manufacturers will soon achieve consensus on what the standard will be. And it won't carry a made-in-U.S.A. tag.

These Japanese companies have worked closely together in the past to target other U.S. markets. It became obvious to them, especially to NEC and Sharp, that adopting an American standard would open the huge Japanese domestic market to American software, and later, perhaps, to American hardware. Clive Smith, a Boston-based analyst for the Yankee Group, a market research firm, believes that when the Japanese companies do adopt a standard – and he is sure they will – they will first use it to increase their domestic sales base, almost concurrently expanding to Western Europe. There are far fewer firms to compete with in Europe, and no talk of a standard for a continent where each of the four largest markets – Britain, Germany, France, and Italy – speaks a different language.

The Japanese have already laid the base for a computer invasion of Europe. 'Almost all Japanese computers can be programmed and operated and their output printed in either character-based languages or in languages that use the Latin alphabet,' said Mark Fruin. Fruin is a professor of economic history at California State University, Hayward, and a director of Oxford Stanford Corp., a Vancouver, B.C. (Canada) computer marketing firm. 'No other major computer manufacturing country worries as much about character generating abilities,' he stated recently in *Infoworld*. 'By providing a variety of functions in the same machine, Japanese computer firms can achieve economies of scale in a relatively narrow line of products [microcomputers] by serving the needs of many markets simultaneously.'

In late 1984, Clive Smith predicts, the Japanese computer makers will target the U.S. market. 'The Japanese got ahead of us with sex appeal in cars,' said Robert M. Bozeman, marketing director for Altos Computer systems. 'If they get ahead of us on the sex appeal of computers, we're dead. But they aren't going to do it by standardization.'

The book is still open on the standardization issue, but the Japanese may be writing it. 'They're hard to see, in part, because they are everywhere,' says Fruin. 'They're coming at a carefully measured and monitored pace. Look inside your CPU [central processing unit], printer and monitor, and you are likely to find them chock full of Japanese integrated circuits, circuit boards, switches, and connections. And not merely in small parts. Floppy disk drives, printers, monitors, and LCD readouts, for the most part, also originate in Japan.' Adds Koichi Ogawa, a Daiwa Securities Co. analyst: 'The most interesting way to look at this is that in consumer electronics, the Japanese companies dominate; so there's no room to expand. In industrial electronics [computers and peripherals] there's plenty of room for Japanese companies to expand their market share.'

But this low-key presence behind-the-panels of computers is not the whole story. Many large Japanese firms have marketing agreements with American manufacturers. Amdahl markets Fujitsu's machines, and Fujitsu sells to European customers through Siemens and ICL. According to Fruin, in 1983 Fujitsu increased production of two of its small models to 30,000 machines per month, and prices are rapidly falling. Hitachi's U.S. connection is National Advanced Systems, while in Europe, Italy's Olivetti and Great Britain's BASF handle Hitachi's hardware sales.

'What your best friends won't tell you is that the Japanese are here already, even if their presence is shielded for the moment by the casings on your machines and by the reputations of local firms with which they are associated,' adds Fruin. In July 1983, the *Asahi Shimbun* reported that 'exports of Japanese personal computers this year are expected to double from last year with NEC Corp., Fujitsu Ltd., and other major makers striving to expand shipments to the U.S.' *Asahi* noted that personal computer exports of 12 member companies and eight trading houses totaled 34,363 units in the first four months of 1983, a 95 percent increase from last year's corresponding period. About 60 percent of these went to North America. *Asahi* also reported that the 1982 totals for Japan's personal computer exports were more than 73,000 units, about half to North America.

The Japanese have adopted a stealthy approach to marketing in part as a defense against 'trade friction.' This is a Japanese euphemism for the dawning international realization that Japan is out to monopolize markets all over the world while protecting its own. The Japanese do not want protective barriers raised in countries they have targeted. Another reason for treading softly is that while the U.S. and North America are giant markets for computers, they are not the only ones. Japanese-style totalitarian economics demands continuously expanding markets, and the Japanese are now eyeing Southeast Asia as well as a place to sell their computers in the decade ahead.

The computer market they seek to capture is huge. The Japanese estimate a $30 billion market in office automation by 1990. School purchases of small computers in the U.S. alone will become a $3 billion market by 1987, according to DataQuest, Inc., a San Jose market research firm. DataQuest also says that auxiliary supplies, including service contracts and peripherals, will be a $4.5 billion market by that time. If United Technology's estimate of a computer in 80 percent of American households by 1990 comes true, that could be worth between $40 and $80 billion, including peripherals.

The breakup of AT&T into smaller companies has revealed yet another industry targeted by the Japanese: telecommunications. 'A lot of what the local operating companies are going to be buying from sources other than Western Electric [AT&T's own equipment maker] are the low-cost, high-volume products the Japanese traditionally excel at making,' says an industry analyst. Japan's own massive, nationalized telephone company, NTT, bought $3 billion in equipment in 1982. But NTT, whose upper management is filled with retired MITI officials, bought only $30.4 million from U.S. suppliers – only 1 percent – and most of that in a single purchase from Motorola. Japan has assiduously protected NTT from foreign competition because it is Japan's single largest domestic market for Japan's huge electronics companies.

In 1981, under pressure from the U.S., Japan supposedly 'lifted purchasing restrictions' to 'encourage foreign imports.' But once again, it was an empty gesture. The net effect of this ruling was to double the U.S. electronics industry's 1982 Japanese trade deficit by nearly $1 billion. 'It's like the semiconductor industry. As long as the Japanese telecommunications industry can hide behind their government's wall of protection, there is a zero American competition for telecommunications in Japan,' a U.S. diplomat stationed in Tokyo recently confided. 'The practice gives Japanese companies a protected market to serve, and that finances their drive to serve the world's telecommunications market and puts American manufacturers at a major disadvantage.'

An example of this in action: NTT refused to buy Corning Glass's optical fibers when Corning produced the only such commercially available materials. Instead NTT waited while Sumitomo, Fujikura, and Furukawa, using technology pirated from Corning's Japanese Patent Office applications, developed their own fibers. These three

Japanese companies are now producing about five times more than the amounts required by NTT. The rest is being exported at bargain rates, chiefly to Europe.

MITI denies they have targeted U.S. telecommunications. 'We Japanese want to grow,' MITI's Kazuyuki Wakasone told the *Wall Street Journal*. 'But we have no interest in increasing our share of the international market.' Despite this bald assertion, the value of Japanese exports of fiber optic equipment, including cables, connectors, and optical elements, tripled between 1978 and 1981. In July 1981, Japan's overseas telecommunications monopoly, Kokusai Denshin Denwa (KDD) launched a project to lay the world's first optical fiber cable across the Pacific, a contract to be completed by 1986. It will result in a trans-Pacific telephone capability of 10,000 circuits, compared with the combined capacity of only 1,000 circuits supplied by the two existing copper cables.

'Today, as more of communications has moved to digital and optical technologies, Japan's strengths have been magnified,' said Osamu Hayama, in charge of industrial economic studies at Nomura Research Institute. In 1982, Japan passed West Germany, Sweden and the U.S. to become the leading exporter of telephone and telegraph equipment. U.S. industry experts believe that Japan, which has a new marketing agreement with N. V. Phillips, the Dutch telecommunications giant, will soon overtake Europe's combined sales in telecommunications equipment.

Already, NEC has replaced General Telephone (GTE) as the world's largest supplier of satellite earth stations. Oki's private automatic branch exchange (PABX) equipment, the compact switching systems used by businesses to route phone calls within several offices or a complex, now account for over 75 percent of all sales, worldwide. 'The Japanese have pushed hard and leapfrogged a few of the technologies we used to think of as our own,' says John A. Fullenwider, an Arthur D. Little consultant.

'The Japanese don't have to necessarily wipe everybody else out of the game,' says Robert C. Rutishauser, vice president of Control Data Business Advisors, a subsidiary of Control Data Corp. 'They don't expect to be the world's *sole* source of computers, office automation, and so forth. They'd be happy with about 55 percent of the market. But they would clearly be the leaders, the dominant supplier in the world, and if they are the dominant suppliers, it clearly says that we are at best number two. Perhaps farther down than that. It is not a good position for America if we're going to be the leader of the Western Alliance and rely primarily on technology as opposed to numbers of weapons to maintain our military edge.

'If the Japanese should for some reason decide, with a given kind of computer, that they'll sell serial # 1 to the U.S. and serial # 2 to the Russians, and serial # 3 to the U.S. and serial # 4 to the Russians, then our advantage over the Soviets in military technology is eroded seriously,' Rutishauser adds. 'The only reason we can maintain 10,000 tanks in Western Europe and the Russians 40,000, and still have some sort of equivalence, is because of the superiority of our weapons. Once that superiority is lost, it's a question of whether you can withstand a four-to-one disadvantage. It's important to the whole Western Alliance for the U.S. to continue to be the leader in the economic area as well as in the military area. And the key to that is in information technology. Once we allow ourselves to slip into second place in that, where the other countries look to Japan as their leader of technology, I think we've effectively lost our ability to lead the Western Alliance, not only economically, but militarily.'

Rutishauser sees the Japanese threat in terms of American and Western Alliance power, which is one measure of the problem. Another is simple domestic economic health, the sense of affluence that comes with strength in the marketplace, a feeling of security that may desert us faster than we believe possible if Japan is permitted to continue its plan to target one Western industry after another.

7 Super Knowledge Equals Superpower: Supercomputers and the Fifth Generation

TSUTOMU HOSHINO'S thick, rubbery features contorted as he laughed so hard that he had to clutch the doorknob to keep from falling. He was immediately joined in laughter by his assistants who, like Hoshino, are doctors of electronic engineering and who, also like him, wear open-neck shirts and American-style 'bolo' string ties. All four computer scientists held their sides, gasping as they laughed, then stopped abruptly when Hoshino stopped. In the spotless corridor outside his laboratories on the second floor of a computer science building at Tsukuba University in Japan's modern Science City 37 miles from central Tokyo, passersby paid no attention, evidently quite accustomed to unusual behavior on this floor.

When Hoshino could speak, he apologized. 'We didn't laugh at you,' he said to me, 'but at your statement that the new Cray supercomputer being built in America will have 16 processors. Come and meet our PAX.' He led the way into a spotless lab, where after exchanging our shoes for special indoor slippers, Hoshino proudly displayed what looked like the guts of the telephone line distribution closet found in large office buildings.

PAX is an entirely unimposing assemblage. It consists of a hollow square of green circuit boards, measuring about four feet on each side. Hoshino took out a foot-square green circuit board with various items of hardware soldered to it. 'This is a microcomputer,' he explained, pointing out the components. Minus cabinet, keyboard, screen, and disk drives it was little different than an ordinary TRS-80 Radio Shack microcomputer except that the board was replicated over and over on PAX. The outside of each panel of the square held 16 microcomputers, in four rows of four each. Inside the square, back-to-back with the outer sides, were four more squares of 16 micro-computers each.

In the center was an obsolescent Texas Instruments minicomputer – about the size of a large studio-type reel-to-reel tape recorder – that was hooked up to program each of the microprocessors, either sequentially with different programs or simultaneously with the same. Each processor was connected to its four next-nearest neighbors in each direction. Hoshino explained that one 16-computer cell of this arrangement is called a Parallel Array Computer (PAC). Together the arrangement was first referred to as PACs, which made an easy transliteration to PAX, Latin for 'peace,' which Hoshino said symbolizes his hopes for its uses. Hoshino's creation, a stunning demonstration of parallel architecture, is a supercomputer with 128 CPUs, or 'brains.'

Hoshino's 128-processor machine, which was running in early 1983, processes at an average speed of about four hundred million FLOPS – a measure of computer calculating speed – or about 75 percent as fast as the speed announced for the Cray II, which is still undergoing development at one of America's two successful super-computer manufacturers in Minneapolis. 'Because of its architecture, the Cray can't achieve much more than an average of 50 percent of top speed for most applications,' explains Hoshino. 'PAX runs at about 98 percent of maximum speed because of its parallel architecture. So in actual usage, our PAX is equal to the new Cray machine for most applications.'

The Cray is made in a factory and will sell for $10 million, perhaps more; Hoshino built his PAX 128 in a university lab for a mere $30,000 using off-the-shelf components. Because of a law of physics called the linear scaling law, the Hoshino design, inspired by a 1968 MIT machine called ILLIAC-IV, is capable of far greater size and speed. Indeed, Hoshino and his team have already begun their next project, an assembly of 4,096 processors, each incorporating the latest in VLSI chips. It will run at *four billion* FLOPS, and the cost of a single, handmade machine will be only 'a few million dollars.' But the new chips it will use are still relatively expensive, and Hoshino is only building one machine.

'The ratio of performance over cost is about ten to 100 times better than conventional computer architecture,' said Hoshino. The applications of such a computer are identical to many, though not all, of the present uses for supercomputers. 'PAX 4096 will have the speed necessary to model nuclear fusion, for example, so we can design fusion power plants,' Hoshino adds in passing.

By the early 1990s Hoshino expects to have built and tested 'Super Freedom Simulator PAX,' a supercomputer with a million processing units. It will perform at over a trillion FLOPS. 'We think this design approach will do for Japan's scientific computers what the microcomputer did for general-purpose machines,' he says. Hoshino heads only one of several Japanese teams studying supercomputer architecture, all supported by massive government funds administered by MITI. Whichever design is ultimately chosen by Japan, their new machines may make the best American-made supercomputers look as if they were modest microcomputers.

Japan's computer makers have now achieved technological parity with the U.S. in critical areas of semiconductor manufacture, and are rapidly approaching it in several others. Through collusion and predatory, cartel-like marketing operations the Japanese have driven many of America's most innovative semiconductor makers out of business, or forced them to merge with huge diversified companies, many of which are owned or controlled by foreign interests. But as important as microchips are, they are only the beginning, the building blocks for an array of highly sophisticated products that are changing modern society.

The next move in Japan's plan to control the knowledge-intensive industries is to achieve dominance in computers. In 1982 and 1983, media attention focused on Japan's announcement of two costly, ambitious national undertakings, the *supercomputer* and Fifth Generation computer projects. The U.S. computer industry, which had largely ignored these Japanese research projects, is just beginning to acknowledge the threat to their leadership.

'The Japanese recognize that whoever controls the information revolution has, in effect, some form of increased geopolitical control,' says Michael Dertouzos, director of the Massachusetts Institute of Technology's famed computer laboratory. While Japan's two computer projects are separate, with individual goals, the manner in which MITI has structured them makes it inevitable that technology developed for one will enhance the other.

The Fifth Generation computer has received more publicity, but the project more likely to first become a reality, is the supercomputer. It will make Japan's computer science, and ultimately all of its science, competitive with that of the U.S. and Europe. Or more likely, it will move Japan ahead of the Western nations.

'Basic research for the national supercomputer project began in 1981 in the fields of architecture, software, and materials,' said Soichi Nagamatsu as he pushed a stack of photocopied papers across a tiny table. Nagamatsu is deputy director of MITI's electronic policy division, a serious-looking scientist in his late thirties. The papers he offered outlined the broad, publicly announced outlines of MITI's imaginative and heavily financed national plan for the superfast computer. Nagamatsu's office, buried in the bowels of the squat MITI building in central Tokyo, is 'too busy to meet in,' he says. Instead the meeting is conducted in uncomfortably low chairs in a corner of the severe office belonging to Koichi Kujirai, councillor to the minister, one of MITI's top bureaucrats.

'The basic research phase will continue until mid-1983,' Nagamatsu continued in rough but serviceable English. He then sketched out MITI's plan for building the new generation of supercomputers that Japan expects to have available by 1989. 'After the basic research phase ends in 1983, we will begin drafting the final specifications and designing the system to be built. This phase will continue until 1987, when we will begin building and testing the supercomputer.' The supercomputer, says Nagamatsu, will be 'at least 100 but possibly 1,000 times' as fast as the fastest one now in existence.

The 'super' in supercomputer is an indication of the *speed* at which the machine performs. The original use of supercomputers was to perform lengthy scientific calculations, which are now indispensible for national defense, for devising and breaking cryptographic codes, for exploration of outer space, and for advanced weapons. Only supercomputers can rapidly handle the complex calculations required for weather forecasting, simulating chemical reactions, nuclear fission and fusion experiments. Present supercomputers are now used to construct mathematical models of such concrete objects as airplane wings, automobile bumpers, and underground petroleum reservoirs. Even rubber tires, microwave ovens, or an innocent piece of pot roast can be represented mathematically by equations that simulate how they will perform under given circumstances.

A supercomputer is used to perform tasks that would be too dangerous, too time-consuming or too expensive to accomplish using actual objects. While the fastest machines now available can mathematically simulate only small portions of such complex objects as commercial airliners, the new breed will be capable of simulating an entire aircraft in a fraction of the time currently needed. 'If you can mathematically simulate something as difficult as an airplane, and then test its capabilities in a great many ways before you actually build one, you not only cut years off the design, you're able to evaluate several designs and pick the best before you ever have to actually build one,' explained an American supercomputer expert at Cray Research. There is little doubt in the minds of industrial researchers: Whoever builds the best supercomputers will have an invaluable lead in the designing, building, and selling of advanced products in the decades ahead.

The secret is in the speed of the computer, which is measured by a unit called FLOPS. A FLOPS is a 'Floating Point Operation Per Second,' the mathematician's slang for the time it takes to process a string of calculations in which the position of the decimal point changes. For example, if you multiply the number 1.2345 by 100 it becomes 123.45; if you divide it by 10 it becomes .12345. The decimal point moves back and forth from one operation to the next; it 'floats.' One FLOPS is the time it takes to make that calculation.

Most of today's best desktop minicomputers run at speeds of about half a million FLOPS, while IBM's newest data-processing computer, the 3081, averages between five million and ten million FLOPS. Cray Research's current top-of-the-line supercomputer peaks at a little better than 160 million FLOPS. Cray has new machines on its drawing boards with announced goals three to four times as fast, up to half a billion FLOPS. But the Japanese plan is to build a computer that will run at a speed of at least *ten* billion FLOPS. Some of Japan's supercomputer research teams are convinced that their work will lead to machines much faster than even the one MITI has announced.

The Japanese supercomputer teams are in somewhat the same position that the U.S. semiconductor industry was a decade or more ago. But there are three important differences. The first is that the creation of this new technology relies very heavily on computers, and today's computers are far more sophisticated than any available even five years ago. The second is that one part of the supercomputer project is the development of new materials, some of which are already available to researchers. Finally, unlike the venture capitalists and corporations of America, the Japanese researchers are unconstrained by any profit consideration.

MITI has announced $130 million in government grants to provide operating funds for the supercomputer project. Six private firms – Fujitsu, Hitachi, Toshiba, Oki, NEC, and Mitsubishi – are investing additional tens of millions, and are providing personnel and facilities. Most of the technology obtained during the process, especially the semiconductor technology which is ongoing, will be useful to each participating company in more immediate ways. The new technology will improve all of Japan's computers long before their national supercomputer project is completed.

'The technology achieved by the project will be owned by the Japanese government, and that's completely proper,' says MITI's Nagamatsu. 'Then it will be shared with the participating companies on a license basis.' Will foreign countries be allowed to obtain licenses? Nagamatsu deferred that question to his superior. 'It has not yet been decided,' said Kujirai the MITI councillor. He smiled. 'Do you think America will need Japanese technology?'

'There are two ways to approach the high-speed computer system. One is a system approach, power processing to make the computer run faster. The other is a device approach, develop a device with high performance,' explained Dr. Hisao Hayakawa, 42, chief of cryolectronics in MITI's Tsukuba electrotechnical laboratory. Other teams at the electrotechnical lab, and still others at each of the six Japanese computer companies that are part of the supercomputer project, are researching such new materials as gallium arsenide to make faster semiconductor devices. Another is a promising, Fujitsu-developed device called HEMT (High Electron Mobility Transistor). Before the end of 1985, MITI will decide which new device will be chosen.

While new devices are being tested and developed, other teams of software engineers and computer 'architects' are investigating new approaches to supercomputer design. In the meantime, Dr. Hayakawa, one of the world's leading authorities on an arcane device called the Josephson Junction, is hoping MITI will choose his speciality for use in Japan's supercomputer.

'The Josephson device is not a semiconductor, it's a *super*-conductor,' Hayakawa explains. 'It speeds up the flow of electrons, a quantum mechanical effect. But the most important advantage of the J-Junction is that its switching speed is very fast, about ten pico seconds.' A pico second is ten to the minus twelfth power, a trillionth of a second, a thousand times faster than the nano seconds at which today's best semiconductor devices operate. With a switching speed of ten pico seconds, a J-Junction is eight times faster than the latest experimental gallium arsenide devices.

In 1983, Fujitsu, Hitachi, and NEC, all participants in the superspeed project, announced performance figures for their first supercomputers. These machines range in speed from 500 million to 600 million FLOPS, competitive with those that Cray Research, the leading American supercomputer maker, is hoping to have by late 1984. In June of 1983, NEC announced the development, though not production, of its SX-2 supercomputer with 16 processors capable of running at speeds up to 1.3 *billion* FLOPS.

Wheat, once king of the Minnesota prairies, has abdicated to the new knowledge and information industries taking over the office buildings of Minneapolis's burgeoning, skyscraper-studded downtown. The former Pillsbury Building, seat of power for generations of flour kings, is now a renovated highrise. On its twelfth floor is the headquarters of Cray Research Corporation. Cray's offices are tunnels of winding corridors bathed in ultramodern lighting, branching off into private offices with adjacent, glassed-in conference rooms playing greenhouse to forests of hanging ferns. One of these offices belongs to the erudite, jovial Dr. Peter Gregory, British-born and educated, with a doctorate in mathematics. Cray and its crosstown competitor, Control Data Corporation, are the two most important U.S. supercomputer makers.

'We take Japanese competition very seriously,' said Gregory. 'We don't know what the total marketplace is, but we know that our success has attracted competition. The Japanese have said they see a market for about 30 machines. Today there are only three supercomputers in Japan, two of them made by Cray. It will be very interesting to see if we sell another machine in Japan.'

It will also be 'interesting' to see if Cray sells any more in Europe, which now accounts for 30 percent of its market. As Gregory explains it, a fateful business decision was made by the Europeans about eighteen years ago. 'De Gaulle wanted a supercomputer for his atomic energy program, but the U.S. government said, "No, we won't supply it." All the European governments said, "My God, this technology is the key to the rest of the twentieth century, and we're going to have to go for it, cap-in-hand, to the U.S. Government. If we won't do what they want us to do, they won't let us have it. The hell with that. It's much too important a technology to be a hostage to anyone." They all set up national computer projects and spent hundreds of millions of dollars over the next ten to fifteen years, trying to equal IBM. They've never been able to cut it, but now the Japanese are providing the machines that will give them freedom from dependence on the U.S.'

The companies set up by the leading European nations are not merely buying Japanese computers. They are distributing them as their own. 'International Computer, Ltd. (ICL) markets under the English banner,' said Gregory. 'At the moment, they're taking a machine from Japan, unloading it on the dock, changing the label, and marketing it under the British government's protection as a British product to nationalized industries who have a "Buy British" policy. That's very insidious. They're selling it as the ICL Atlas Computer and Fujitsu is building a component plant in the U.K.'

In August 1983, Fujitsu signed an agreement to sell its new FACOm VP-200, the fastest production supercomputer in the world (about 600 million FLOPS), through ICL in England. Simultaneously they announced a similar agreement with Siemens, the giant West German electronics firm. Quoting Fujitsu sources, the Japanese wire service Kyodo stated: 'The Fujitsu-ICL-Siemens alliance is aimed at challenging the dominant European position held by Cray.' Fujitsu has already announced its plans to make and sell 40 supercomputers over the next five years.

Cray's chairman, John Rollwagen, and its founder, computer designer Seymour Cray, believe firmly in the forces of the free market and in Cray's tradition that the best technical innovation is achieved with the least possible bureaucratic management. Cray provides its technical staff, unrivaled in quality, with laboratories, equipment and funds to innovate in a climate of intellectual freedom. 'In our experience, which goes back twenty-five years, the greatest advances in computing come when you have very small groups of people working with very little interference, with no external standards, no external bureaucracy, no external ties,' says Gregory.

It is true that this approach has thus far served them well. But it has served them in a market with only one real competitor, Control Data, a company that, like Cray, is constrained by the rules of the marketplace. They are both companies that work hard but play by the rules. The Japanese, meanwhile, are rewriting the rulebook in their own favor, and the management of Cray Research could be in for a brutal, irreversible surprise.

In contrast to the innocuous shades of gray or blue that most Fujitsu executives seem to prefer in neckties, Shigeru Sato's ties are bold statements in striped color. He moves and speaks with unusual forcefulness, a scaled-down sumo wrestler of a man who carries two business cards. The first introduces the deputy general manager of Fujitsu's computer systems division. The second, produced with a flourish, proclaims that he is chairman of the technical committee of the Scientific Computer Research Association (SCRA).

Sato's job is to keep everyone in the six Japanese companies that make up SCRA moving harmoniously toward the national goal of a new super-fast supercomputer. Sato insists Fujitsu's portion of the project is 'a secret,' but a careful study of Fujitsu's annual reports and other promotional material provides some clues. It is likely that Fujitsu will provide the central processors, which will be new types of logic chips, and build the processing units.

'The systems people are anxious to begin now,' Sato explains. 'But the device [semiconductor] people say "give us more time and we will give you better work." We asked MITI for $250 million for the superspeed computer. But we didn't get everything we asked for. Each company will have to spend some extra money,' he says. 'In the

VLSI project, MITI turned the semiconductor technology which was learned over to each company to develop whichever products they thought to make. But in this case, there isn't enough money available, and the market for supercomputers will be too small for more than one product.'

Because of this, Sato explained, the final result of the superspeed computer project will not be several different competing machines, each produced by one of the participating companies. There will be a single 'Japan Brand' supercomputer, *one* collection of components, each manufactured by a different company. It will be a national machine, a product of state capitalism unlike any ever produced.

Though the Japanese government's contribution is less than the six companies asked for, MITI's input cannot be measured only in dollars. The $130 million does not include the considerable cost of running the government-owned university labs participating in the project. Mainly created for other computer-related projects, their start-up costs were amortized long ago. While Japan's super-computer researchers number only 'a few hundred,' each team's tasks are carefully orchestrated by MITI to avoid duplication, and essential information is shared between industry and government at regular quarterly meetings of the team chiefs. As Japan's VLSI Project proved, $1 million invested in this way is worth up to $5 million invested in traditional U.S. R&D.

Japan has another not-so-secret weapon. All of Japan's supercomputer researchers – indeed, almost all Japanese technocrats – tend to work very long hours. Twelve-hour days are not uncommon, and six-day weeks are the norm. Japan's supercomputer project will get as many as 60 productive hours a week for less than the cost of a 40-hour week at Cray, Control Data, or IBM. This devotion to duty at first seems to be a product of national temperament, of a work ethic that shames Calvinists by comparison. In part, it is, but there is more to it. Many Japanese spend so much time at their place of work not because of *bushido* devotion but because life is far more pleasant at work than where they live. Most Japanese homes are dismal, and at Science City, at least, it can be shown that the Japanese government made them that way.

The offices and laboratories of more than 50 government and privately-funded research labs – representing more than 40 percent of all government-funded research in Japan – are in Science City in Tsukuba. The 'work' buildings are handsomely designed, well built, sparkling clean, well-appointed, and comfortably furnished. Until 1970, when construction began, the ground on which they stand was rice paddies and orchards. The entire Science City, an area half as large as Tokyo but with less than 140,000 people compared with Tokyo's 8.5 million, was built from scratch. Because of the relatively low population density, there is a California-like quality of spaciousness, with broad, landscaped, lightly traveled avenues. In good weather, almost everyone rides a cycle of some sort to work.

Nearly everyone who works at Tsukuba, except students at the university, lives in one of the blocks of new apartments which were erected at the same time as the spacious buildings of the institute. In a free market economy, the apartments would have been built by private enterprise, which – because of the forces of the marketplace – would have had to provide some amenities. But the system does not operate that way in Japan. The housing at Tsukuba was built by the government, which leases units to the researchers who work at the attractive university and research institutes.

The government subsidizes the rent. A typical apartment like the one rented to university researcher Tetsuro Muto, 32, costs only about $30 a month, a small fraction of his $500 monthly salary. The government has been generous with subsidies, but in Science City it has spawned a vast slum alongside the showpiece university and laboratory. Muto's building is squalid and dreary, its outer walls streaked with water stains, the crumbling sidewalks and brick walls covered with soot. Undernourished lawns are strewn with trash and worn thin with neglect. On closer inspection 'hedges' turn out to be forests of ragweed, which are in stark contrast to the manicured lawns of the university and institutes. The apartments are minuscule, hundreds of units crammed into each 15-story building. Most of these one- and two-bedroom apartments have a lilliputian shower and tub and have inadequate central heating systems. To survive in the bitter Japanese winter, researchers are forced to buy portable electric heaters.

The dormitories at the university are dingier still, four-story anthills without central heating, and with no plumbing except a communal toilet on each floor. These dwellings are monuments to the low priority MITI sets on human values. Does Muto mind living in such a place? 'I'm never home,' he shrugs. 'My office is warm in the winter, and the university buildings are airconditioned in summer. I just sleep in the apartment, that's all. If I invite friends over, we'll go out somewhere.' Muto often works more than 65 hours a week. 'There's always a lot to do.' MITI has discovered a new twist on Parkinson's Law: 'When a dwelling is uncomfortable, extra hours at work are preferable to unpleasant time spent at home.'

American researchers are not sitting still as the Japanese move rapidly forward; they too are seeking the new technology for the next generation of supercomputer. But at this writing, the Japanese are well ahead. Cray, IBM, and others are investigating 'parallel architecture,' a computer system with more than one central processing unit, CPU. This is considered essential for achieving greater speed of calculations.

Present computers use a system architecture designed in the 1940s by a Hungarian-born American, mathematician John von Neumann. Von Neumann computers essentially accept program instructions one step at a time. They process each number sequentially, storing the interim results in their memories, then take them out again to use in the next calculation. Parallel processing, which uses more than one processor, speeds up calculations by dividing the tasks among processors.

A supercomputer build by Denelcor, a Colorado

company, already uses four processors, and the new Cray II machine, which will be available in late 1984, will also have four and will operate at between 500 and 600 million FLOPS. 'The obvious simple uses of these four CPUs would be to put four jobs through the machine,' says Peter Gregory of Cray. 'But the problem we really are committed to solving is providing the software to enable multiple CPUs to be used on a single problem. That's the direction we think the industry must go. It's going to be a process where we learn from experience. What we're doing now is putting out a machine that has the capability of making that experiment interesting.'

America's academics are beginning to stir as well. Two MIT professors are planning to build a 'data flow' computer that will use 256 processor units to speed up the calculations. Computer scientists at England's Manchester University are working on a similar machine. A University of Texas professor, James Browne, has built and is using a prototype with four processors and nine memories.

Control Data Corporation is helping to subsidize a small research-oriented company to compete with the Japanese in the field of supercomputers. 'Supercomputer development historically and currently comes from small "skunk works" rather than big corporations,' explains CDC spokesman Bill Shaffer. 'Each succeeding generation of machines has come from a small entrepreneurial group in one form or another.' Since Control Data is itself a giant, its chairman announced at the Los Alamos Scientific Lab conference of supercomputers in 1983 the formation of a new company, ETA Systems, Inc., in which CDC will hold a minority position. Lloyd Thorndike, CDC's supercomputer development executive, has taken his nucleus of research engineers off to form this new company with Control Data's blessing and financial support.

Shaffer points out that the initials of the company's name, 'ETA,' are meant to convey something especially unpleasant to the Japanese. The *eta* are Japan's untouchables. 'Until ETA is operational, which will be 1986 when their first machine will be delivered, we will continue to market and support Cyber 205 at 800 million FLOPS, the fastest current commercially *installed* machine,' says Shaffer. The 205 costs between $7.5 and $10 million.

There are also a few signs that the complacent American technology firms are beginning to wake up to the larger designs of the Japanese – that they are being targeted for a carefully integrated assault that includes using the best American graduate schools to train the Japanese scientific competition. To fight this, Control Data chairman William Norris has called for the expulsion of Japanese computer science and electronics engineering graduate students studying in America. 'Norris has no fight with graduate students, but he doesn't like the Japanese government's policies,' says CDC spokesman Shaffer. 'They have imposed quite stringent barriers on their export of technology, but it's grab and run with whatever they can get here. "Go out there and rape and pillage, but don't let anybody see our girls," is their attitude.

'They don't let technology flow this way out of Japanese labs, but they take for granted the technology that is flowing to Japan from U.S. labs and university research,' Shaffer adds. 'Though many of these students do go on to work for U.S. companies here, their government tells them to return to Japan and many of them obey.' One example is Dr. Kaneyuki Kurokawa, who worked in the Bell Laboratories in New Jersey for twenty-five years, and who now holds a key position at Fujitsu. 'They're bringing in all the old eagles,' says Schaffer.

Robert G. Rutishauser of Control Data concurs. Rutishauser, 52, is a tall, well-dressed Missourian with the stern, thoughtful mien of a minister. 'They have access to the basic technology that comes out of some of our leading universities,' he says. 'In my judgment, the Japanese are far more effective at picking up U.S. technology and moving it to Japan than the other way around. Our efforts are fragmented and not very effective, not well coordinated. The bulk of foreign graduate students remain in this country – but my impression is that the Japanese are a clear exception to that. Japanese students come over here, get their advanced training, learn everything they can, and for the most part, go back to Japan.'

Super Knowledge Equals Superpower

It is reassuring that some American industry leaders are waking up to the Japanese threat in supercomputers, but as in television manufacture and semiconductors, the Japanese system of massive government research and subsidies, plus targeted marketing and dumping seems likely to ensure that the American effort – although ingenious and scientifically courageous – will once again be an object lesson in too little, too late.

The surprise cinema success of the summer of 1983 was a low budget film called *War Games*. It involves a teenage boy with a home computer who manages to tap into the powerful computer controlling all U.S. nuclear forces. In a benign, sometimes appealing way, the computer seems almost human. It talks to the boy over a telephone, either by typing out words on a video monitor or speaking aloud in colloquial English. But if humanoid, it is also childlike, an *idiot savant* with enormous powers of logical reasoning and information processing, yet exhibiting loneliness and another human quality, boredom.

Not knowing what the computer really does, the boy innocently asks it to play what he imagines is a new videogame, 'Global Thermonuclear War.' Playing the game launches a process that, if not interrupted, will cause the computer, which cannot distinguish between the simulated missiles of its programmed 'game' and the real missiles it will launch, to start World War III. The planet is saved because at the penultimate moment the kid thinks of a way to teach the computer, through the example of Tic-Tac-Toe, that 'Global Thermonuclear War' is a no-win game.

The computer in *War Games* is only a fictional device. No computer is now able to learn from experience, able to teach itself new skills, able to infer the general from information about the specific, able to expand its own knowledge base, or able to communicate with people through ordinary speech. But such a computer is in the scientific imagination of MITI, which has already mobilized the Japanese nation to build the world's first Fifth

Generation computer, one that will boast 'artificial intelligence,' or AI. MITI has brought together Japan's leading computer companies and will back them in a ten-year project to create computers beyond a scriptwriter's scientific fantasy.

'The project is divided into three stages, with the initial stage starting in 1982 and ending in 1984. The second is from 1985 to 1988. The third from 1989 to 1991,' says MITI's Soichi Nagamatsu. 'The budgeting will be totally from the government, 10.5 billion yen, in the first phase. All the direct costs of R&D will be paid by our ministry.' In 1982, MITI acknowledged that funding for the Fifth Generation computer would be $200 million, a sum they have since announced has been enlarged to $500 million. The true figure could be considerably higher, with portions buried in other government budgets.

The project is being carried out by the Institute for New Generation Computer Technology (ICOT), headquartered on the 21st floor of the Mitsui Kokusai building in a section called Minato-Ku, the Tokyo version of Park Avenue, complete with exclusive shops and elegant glass-and-steel office buildings. ICOT has bought or ordered 25 American-made Symbolics 3600 computers, the best machines now available for artificial intelligence research. Project leader Dr. Kazuhiro Fuchi, one of Japan's rare, genuine individualists, heads a team of 50 experts in software, computer architecture, and symbolic logic, many of whom have studied in the United States. Forty are from private industry, representing Fujitsu, NEC, Hitachi, Toshiba, Mitsubishi, Oki, Sharp, and Matsushita. Additional researchers are from Nippon Telegraph and Telephone (NTT), Japan's huge nationalized communications utility, and from MITI's Electronic Technology Laboratory (ETL) at Tsukuba.

Unlike the supercomputer project, which aims at building a single 'Japan Brand' system, the Fifth Generation computer project will not produce a single machine. It will result in a plethora of technological advances, a series of patented inventions licensed to Japanese companies. These will radically change the ways *all* computers are made and used, and will change the kinds of people who will use them. The computers of the Fifth Generation will be accessible to virtually anyone, including illiterates.

'Toshiba has sent five or six engineers to ICOT, young men,' says Yuji Wakayama, a Toshiba spokesman. 'Their job is to develop a general purpose Fifth Generation computer whose central processing unit's functions approach those of the human brain and which can understand human languages, read graphics, characters, letters, understand information from photographs, and handle several different jobs at the same time. This will give Japan leadership in this new technology. In a few years we will replace these men with newer people.'

'People who go back to their mother companies will continue with development at their company bases. That is our expectation,' adds MITI's Nagamatsu. When asked why Japan had embarked on such a costly, and perhaps risky, project, he answered: 'Of course, we know it is a very ambitious and risky R&D effort to meet our goals. But we still believe it is possible. We must try, because in the 1990s, informatization will penetrate into every aspect of our society.'

Tokyo University's Professor Tohru Moto-Oka, who designed the program, further explains Japan's reasoning: 'In the 1990s, when Fifth Generation computers will be widely used, information processing systems will be a central tool in all areas of social activity, to include economics, industry, science, culture, daily life, and the like, and will be required to meet those new needs generated by environmental changes,' he said.

Nagamatsu of MITI clarifies the Japanese national goal. 'Four requirements will be met by the Fifth Generation computer. The first is problem solving, and inference function. The second is a knowledge-data based function to support this inference function. These two are a package,' he says. Such a package would indeed be a giant step forward. It would enable machines – in this case Japanese machines – to accomplish the last two requirements of the Fifth Generation machine: intelligent interface functions and intelligent programming. It will make it possible for computers to take over many of the most difficult and time-consuming tasks now performed laboriously by people in every agency or company in industry, government, the military, and academia. It will be a stunning accomplishment.

Japan's Fifth Generation computers will not only be able to compute information, but to deliver expert *opinions*, based on knowledge acquired and stored almost anywhere in the world. It will allow planners in every field the luxury of being able to quickly act on information obtained from widely divergent sources and present it in an understandable summary, together with computer-originated recommendations for a course of action. A Fifth Generation computer may become a business's most valued advisor, an expert who never needs a vacation, who has no personal interest to conflict with the company's best interests.

Similar expert knowledge-based inferences may also be made in such fields as engineering, law, and medicine. Such a system, in relatively simple but usable form, already exists, it is a hardware/software package called *Internist/Caduceus*, developed at the University of Pittsburgh by Jack Meyers, an M.D., and computer scientist Harry Pople. This system now covers about 80 percent of all internal medicine and is familiar with about 500 diseases and some 3,500 sets of symptoms for these illnesses. But Japan's Fifth Generation computers will make it seem rudimentary.

'We will design inference machines that doctors can use as though they were friends, colleagues, someone to consult with on difficult cases,' said MITI's Nagamatsu. Obviously, such a system would be in immediate demand for space exploration and in rural areas where doctors could get expert advice almost instantly. One machine, accessible through remote terminals and telephone lines could serve a large area, making it economically feasible.

Other 'expert' systems already in use include one at Elf Acquitaine Oil designed to deal with one of the most serious, recurring problems of oil exploration. What does one do when a drill bit snaps a couple of miles below the earth? This system was designed by Teknowledge, a Palo Alto firm, which conducted a long series of painstaking interviews with Elf Acquitaine's leading drilling expert, Jacques-Marie Courte. His practical experience, or 'heuristic' knowledge, was recorded by engineers and programmed into a computer.

When a drill bit snaps, someone on the rig can access this computer by telephone, or even radiotelephone. The computer then goes down Courte's checklist of questions, and as the drilling crew answers, the information is processed by the computer. At the end, the computer gives its recommendations, which can include graphs or images drawn on a terminal screen. A drilling rig and crew can cost upwards of $50,000 a day, and a snapped drill bit can take a week to repair. Elf Acquitaine expects to recover its investment in this expert program the first time it is used.

Other uses for expert systems are for 'assistant pilots,' especially on complex military aircraft; locomotive repair; researching complex issues of law, thus saving weeks of an attorney's time; and such widely diverse jobs as dental prostheses design, spotting stock market trends, and designing insurance policies.

The third goal of the ICOT project is a 'natural language interface.' Nagamatsu explains: 'This means we can talk to the computer and it can listen, understand and respond in natural spoken language.' The last goal is an automatic programming production mechanism. The computer will be able to program itself to solve any problem a user defines, and it will continue to query the user until all necessary parameters of the problem are defined. If Japan can develop a computer with the ability to accept and impart information through spoken language, through the use of pictures and symbols, even through gestures, it would be the most important of the four ambitious goals ICOT has tackled. It would, for one thing, help speed the process of bringing computers into virtually every home, the first stage in what the Japanese already call the 'informatization' of life.

'In 1978 only about 9,000 homes in Japan had a personal

computer,' says Yasuhiko Ohmori, president of Nihon Soft Bank, Japan's largest computer software distributor, which handled about 9,000 different programs as of mid-1983. 'But by the end of 1983, there will be more than two million computers in Japanese homes.' By the end of the decade, Japanese marketing experts predict, more than 97 percent of all Japanese households will have at least one computer. Since ordinary telephone lines do not permit rapid computer communications, NTT, Japan's telecommunications company, has already begun a ten-year program to link most of Japan to an optical-fiber, data-quality telecommunications trunk line. When it is hooked up to the millions of home computers then in place, most of Japan will be able to communicate directly with high quality computer data exchanges.

The main drawback to using the present generation of computers is the time it takes to learn how to use them. Almost any reasonably intelligent person can learn the correct commands required to direct a computer, but shifting from one task, such as word processing, to another, such as adding a column of figures, requires the operator to learn a whole new set of commands. Of the thousands of software programs now in use, nearly all require unique sets of operating instructions that have to be typed in on a keyboard.

It is a slow process in English. In Japanese, with some 10,000 *kanji* pictograms required for a technical or scientific vocabulary, it has proved virtually impossible. Even the use of either of Japan's two phonetic alphabets (*kana*) involves 48 characters each. A computer that understands and speaks natural language would speed up the entry of commands and data. Even more important, it would make the computer available to virtually everyone.

A computer that could scan written material, then store it in memory, would be another forward move, and the Japanese have already taken the first steps in this direction. A nine-year MITI project which concluded in 1980 taught Japan's computer companies much about the recognition and processing of pattern information, including characters, speech, pictures, and objects. Some of this information has already led to products and technology which, when developed further, will form the basis for realization of the Fifth Generation goal.

Fujitsu, Ltd., Japan's largest computer company, is heavily involved in both the superspeed computer project and ICOT. Fujitsu's headquarters and research facilities are hidden away in the dingy Tokyo suburb of Kawasaki, where they are already producing some of the first Fifth Generation prototypes. Dr. Kaneyuki Kurokawa, director of Fujitsu Laboratories, was proud to show me around his basement laboratories, but I learned that his English is perfect only after my own interpreter's translation of Kurokawa's explanations began to founder on the shoals of high-tech jargon.

Kurokawa led the way to a large computer terminal where a technician laboriously typed in the *kanji* from a page of a Japanese technical manual. 'It will take some time, perhaps a minute,' he told me. 'The computer we're using just now is several years old, not the fastest available.' Nevertheless, in just over 60 seconds the screen cleared and then immediately filled with an English translation of the page.

Fujitsu software engineer Jun Ibuki had another surprise: a large-vocabulary voice-input machine that translates spoken English into spoken Japanese (as well as vice-versa) while storing both input and output. 'It works by analyzing the input sentence, not merely its vocabulary but its conceptual structure,' said Ibuki. 'We know we need higher quality than at present, but we're working on this now.' Since 1980 Fujitsu has been selling Japanese word processor conversion machines which first translate typed-in characters from either of Japan's two phonetic alphabets, then store and print out the *kanji* ideographs. Fujitsu also has a new optical character reader in the works, a device that already recognizes 2,000 handwritten *kanji* characters.

Elsewhere in the labs were prototype devices that analyze and store information derived from a closed-circuit TV camera. The device is now being used to teach a computer to recognize the intricate shapes of tools and mechanical parts. After the computer has learned them, it will call up a complete series of images which depict the object from any point of view as soon as it is shown any single view of the object. It is the first step in establishing non-language computer inputs.

Other Japanese research laboratories are also working on Fifth Generation types of input/output devices, including one that will enable people to talk to their computers. Sharp has announced a single-chip voice recognition circuit for 'nonspecified' users. The machine will recognize the voice of any person speaking any of the commands in its memory. 'This chip is able to take into account the various changes in pronunciation resulting from regional accents, differences in age, sex, and physique,' a Sharp spokesman states. 'It will recognize about 90 percent of the possible ways to pronounce a word in its memory. If it doesn't recognize, it rejects, thereby eliminating most errors from having any effect.'

This device is an improvement over one Matsushita announced a year earlier with a 64-word memory capacity. It will be used to start, stop, and control a wide variety of home and office machines. Fujitsu has already produced experimental 1,000-word vocabulary speech processors, and with only a slight stretch of imagination, we can contemplate the time when computers will talk, listen, and respond. But more and more, it looks like they will be Japanese computers.

The American response to Japanese strides in computer technology is a strange mixture of anxiety and complacency, the latter a knee-jerk reflex of presumed American superiority, one not unlike that which afflicted Detroit before the great Honda invasion.

Some Americans play down the Japanese goals, particularly in Fifth Generation research. 'I've been in the field for twenty years and I think the proposal is pie-in-the-sky,' says Martin Goetz, senior vice-president of Applied

Data Research. 'My feeling is that the Fifth Generation is simply a beautiful wish.'

Other American computer experts are truly concerned about the Japanese. When Cray's Dr. Peter Gregory and I spoke in the late spring of 1983, he seemed not unduly worried about the two Japanese projects. But by the end of August, his attitude had changed considerably. 'My initial reaction was that the Japanese government, anxious to establish a strong position in the world computing community, had been sold a bill of goods by an ambitious research lab working in AI,' said Gregory.

'Now I feel that it is a highly desirable objective. Even if they only go 30 percent of the way by 1990 they will have achieved something that no other computer manufacturer is even contemplating. Most others are struggling with the problem of ease of use, worrying about command languages, interactivity, how to get the systems programmer out of the computing shop. All of those things are aimed at taking a vast body of software written in the last twenty years and simplifying it. The Japanese are attempting to break out of that, throw everything away and start over again. They are asking how the computer can be humanized. That, I think, is real impressive stuff.

'If you could take speech recognition today and plug it into a von Neumann machine you would have a very useful machine,' he adds. Gregory thinks that a Japanese success in this field will have shattering results. 'The Fifth Generation project may look very appealing as an opportunity for sharing research, but I believe the end product is a master plan to try to dominate the computer world with a capability nobody else will be able to come within miles of. If they have extracted the ideas of our people in the meantime, just as they have emulated IBM's machine designs, just as they have emulated Cray and CDC machine designs, they will pick up the idea, turn it into a product, and market it as successfully as we all know they can.'

Does Gregory see the Japanese project as a challenge, a catalyst, or a blueprint? 'As a threat,' he said. 'They're very consistent. They declare what they intend to do eight or ten years ahead of time, then they spend the next eight or ten years doing it. What the Japanese have attempted has always sounded outlandish at first. No one believed they were serious in the camera industry, in the auto industry, in shipbuilding. They were not believed to be a serious computer systems supplier, and yet today they make an IBM-compatible machine that is twice as fast as the fastest machine IBM makes. The Fujitsu 380 is as fast as an IBM, but the IBM has two engines [processors]. The Fujitsu has one. I can't remember an instance when they said they were going to achieve a dominant position and didn't do it. The major concern I feel is that the large U.S. computer companies have become complacent,' said Gregory, who might well have been speaking of his own firm.

One of America's leading computer experts, Professor Michael L. Dertouzos, did not have to be awakened to the threat. He saw it early and was the first prominent computer scientist to give the clarion call to his complacent colleagues. A native of Athens, Greece, he came to the U.S. in 1954 as a Fulbright Scholar and entered Massachusetts Institute of Technology as a graduate student in computer science. Dertouzos is both a scientist and a capitalist; in 1968 he founded Computec, a manufacturer of computer monitors and other peripherals, a company in which he later sold his interest for 'a few million dollars' in order to return to pure science. Today he heads MIT's Computer Laboratory, where some 350 researchers, about half foreign-born, work on advanced computer technologies.

In 1982 Dertouzos spoke to a computer industry meeting at Orlando, Florida, about the need for an American research organization to rival the Japanese work on superspeed and Fifth Generation computer projects. 'Originally the computer companies wanted to set up the Microelectronics Computer Corporation [MCC] entirely as an electronics project. I was very upset and concerned about the Japanese Fifth Generation project, and in 1980 I wrote to Bill Norris at Control Data,' Dertouzos says.

The MCC has evolved as the first joint research activity of 13 competing American electronics and computer firms, a non-governmental response to the overwhelming power of Japan's MITI. This privately funded organization is headed by retired Admiral Bobby Inman, former deputy director of the CIA, and will be headquartered in Austin, Texas. MCC will have an annual budget of from $50 to $100 million once the new company is up and running. It is small by MITI standards, but it is a beginning, if belated, challenge to Japanese ambitions. 'We're starting off with four projects, and it will take quite a bit to get four projects off the ground and do them well, but it's better than doing twice that many and doing them poorly,' says Control Data's Rutishauser, whose firm is one of the MCC partners.

The first of MCC's four initial goals is the development of software productivity tools. This is similar to the Japanese Fifth Generation goal of creating self-programming computers. Another goal is a quest for quantum improvement in computer-assisted design (CAD) and computer-assisted manufacturing (CAM). Both are essential in making better products more efficiently, a critical cornerstone of the American success in both domestic and world markets.

The third objective is advanced computer architecture, which parallels one of Japan's superspeed computer projects. This will investigate new approaches to computer design, with an objective of greatly speeding up processing operations. Parallel processing techniques have been selected as the approach most likely to bear fruit. The fourth goal is 'packing,' MCC's terms for finding ways to shrink the size of computers, and thereby expand their capabilities. One of the problems MCC will have to solve is the physical size of present wire matrixes, which places an absolute lower limit on the size of components. MCC will attempt to crack this barrier with new materials and techniques.

One of the MCC's greatest problems – as is often the case in challenging Japan – is the U.S. government and its archaic antitrust laws. At present, the Justice Department is looking the other way as the companies start their joint research. But unless legislation is written by a newly enlightened Congress, any antibusiness administration in the White House could close MCC.

Dertouzos has some hopes for MCC, but he is not convinced that it is an adequate answer to the Japanese. 'I think MCC could be quite effective. The jury is still out. My position is, I'll help put it together, but I'm very watchful. I think it's going to lose power if it focuses on the short range and if it tries to be a "yes man" to the corporations that own it – doing basically what these corporations see as important in the next one, two, or three years. I think the power of the MCC will come if it focuses on the long range research, just like the Japanese.

'But, take a company that wants to participate in all four MCC programs. It's got to shell out $70 million for three years, either on top of or in lieu of its other research. A company that's going to shell out $70 million over a three-year period, under our current business philosophy, is going to expect some results pretty damn quickly, wouldn't you say? The fault may lie not so much with MCC as with the whole orientation we have towards short-term results. I think that's where our problem is,' Dertouzos stresses.

Rutishauser of Control Data is pleased that MCC has been created, but he too sees problems in America's late start. 'There's not a sense of crisis, but there is a sense of urgency,' he says. 'The Japanese are working while we're organizing. Every day that we spend getting our act together is a day that they're working and we aren't. It's going to be 1984 before any serious technology work is done at MCC. We're aiming at technology to come out of the pipeline in three years. Then it will be another year or two before the companies can take this technology and incorporate it. This program will not have much impact on the competitiveness of the MCC shareholders for at least five years. It's something that needed to be done, but it isn't a panacea for 1985 problems. There's not going to be any tangible results in terms of products shipped, balance of trade, before '86, '87, '88 or beyond.'

The Japanese project has been staffed with mostly

younger engineers, under 35 years old. 'History would say that younger people, 25 to 35, are those that are in their most creative years, in terms of technology,' Rutishauser adds. 'At MCC, we expect to employ large numbers of relatively young Ph.D.-type individuals, in the early stages of their careers, rather than rely exclusively on more experienced people. But we've got to have some kind of a mix.

'The number of people in the country qualified to do this sort of work are in the hundreds, or low thousands,' he adds. 'We could do as much with 250 people at MCC as the 13 participating companies could do individually with 650, or 50 at each company, because we won't be inventing the same products over and over. It's very important that our national resource – these electronics engineers – not be squandered, as it is in my judgment by companies duplicating each other in more generic type research. That's the leverage that MCC is trying to get.'

Rutishauser sees the competition not as a corporate, but a national one. 'It seems to me the Japanese have escalated the competition so that it is no longer a competition between companies for national markets but more between countries for world markets. The Japanese have saved their resources by not duplicating each other's efforts. It's a different competitive world than it was five or ten years ago. We're going to have to respond to that, because it's a new ballgame, one the U.S. hasn't been very adept at playing. What's required here is a level of investment in some of the advanced technologies that by and large only two U.S. companies – IBM and AT&T – have the resources to do. I think the other companies like Digital Equipment, Motorola, Control Data collectively could mount such an effort. A $50 million to $100 million investment in the advanced technology is required, *on top of* the investments the companies have to make in the proprietary technology that they need to stay alive. It's just more than most of the companies can afford.'

The goal has military implications as well, Rutishauser points out. 'It's the ability to do that very high speed modeling that has the U.S. military so concerned about the Japanese supercomputer project,' he explains. 'The machines we have available now can do a reasonably good job of modeling a piece of an aircraft, a wing for example, or a tail section, or the fuselage. But there isn't a machine built that can do a simulation model on the entire aircraft. Boeing has attained some very substantial improvements in their 757 and 767 models just by better design of the wing. The aeronautical engineers just drool at the thought of being able to model a whole airplane. Well, that requires a computer that's perhaps two orders of magnitude more capable than the ones we have now. That's where the leverage is in terms of economic and technical leadership; it's in those very large, very high speed machines. The Japanese announced goal is to build machines with a *three* orders-of-magnitude improvement.'

The need for a larger program to compete with the Japanese is obvious, both to solve the business dilemma of lack of capital and to override the obsession with short-term profits that afflicts America and most Western nations. This plus the need to protect the national interest, both economically and militarily, makes a government research program, in the magnitude of billions of dollars, seem increasingly sensible.

Dertouzos believes a U.S. government-funded research project is the answer. 'A government project is the proven method,' he says. 'Look at Defense Advanced Research Project Agency [DARPA], the agency that since 1963 has been funding advanced computer science research in this country. DARPA is the agency that is trying to push a $95 million government supercomputer project through Congress. It is the agency that has produced time-share computers, in 1964, computer networks, and a whole group of other things. If you look for one pioneering way that works, that's one. It goes to the industry circuit, and it goes through those universities that focus on the long range.'

Is there a threat if Japan gets a Fifth Generation system before the U.S. does? 'Absolutely,' says Dertouzos. 'I've been one of the first in this country to alert our leaders in government and in industry about what I perceive as the threat. It's geopolitical. In the same sense that the industrial revolution in England, France, and Germany gave them geopolitical strength because they had the factories, because they had the ability to utilize the industrial revolution's outcome. In that same sense, I think the country that is first in the Information Revolution will have geopolitical strength and dominance in the world.'

Dertouzos thinks the Japanese project particularly threatening because of the Japanese research in multiprocessor machines. 'The idea is that you take thousands of processors, small ones, cheap ones, and you hook them together, so that you have in effect greater power than a Cray machine,' he points out. 'It's the difference between having a thousand slaves working for you rather than one big powerful slave. One kind of computer architecture approach is the established approach, the Cray approach. The other kind is scaleable. You can go as far out in number of processors as you wish. The Cray approach is *not* scaleable, it has finite limits. It's a small market. It's important, but it doesn't affect society. The multiprocessor approach, if successful, whether developed by Japan or us, will affect everybody. The reason is that it will make possible the higher risk and higher payoff things like computer vision and hearing, and the artificial intelligence applications. And those will affect our society profoundly.'

It will also, he stresses provide Japan with a larger spectrum of new electronic products. 'Let's say they're successful in building a machine with a few hundred processors,' Dertouzos says. 'And let's say that they're successful in developing a programming language on it – PROLOG, perhaps. These engineers and scientists are going to go back to their companies – NEC, Fujitsu, Hitachi, Toshiba – and start saying: "How can we make some money out of this? Let's make our VCR [video cassette recorder] speak. Let's make our VCR understand commands. Let's build a little typewriter that converts speech to letters." In their own way, each will embark on

221

products which will use these basic ideas and expand on them. It's really an industry where all the key developments take place in Japan. I most definitely see a link between ICOT, the whole Fifth Generation project bureaucracy and its permeation into products. It's all very natural.'

Dertouzos believes that the U.S. could still win, *if* it moves quickly and effectively, without playing the corporate games that injure progress. 'The U.S. is in a very good position, but IBM cannot play the game they played with the Apple computer,' he warns. 'Apple went out, got into a business, and demonstrated you can make a hundred million bucks a year. Within one year IBM came out with a PC and is now sweeping everything out from under Apple. You can't play this game in the area of artificial intelligence or supercomputers. You must build a strength of people, over five, six, even ten years, people who understand what's going on. You've got to build architectures that take a lot longer to develop than a personal computer. So if in fact Japan succeeds in its leapfrog, and by the early 1990s they're coming out with computers that have vision and hearing, and we're still screwing around with the next thing for next year, and then start a crash program – an extreme scenario – that would take us another five to seven years to catch up. Meanwhile they'll have been building within their ranks what I call "leaders."

'Right now Japan doesn't have too many of these leaders. Maybe a handful, five or ten. But we've got maybe a couple of hundred in this country. I think they'll have built up a couple of hundred during that period, and it will give them increased dominance. Fuchi, who is in charge of ICOT in Japan, is organizing his people in a very nontraditional way. He's giving them more freedom, he's allowing small groups to work on whatever the hell they please, and he's got a lot of the same esprit we have here at MIT. If they're successful, they could have a tremendous effect and influence on the world.'

Surprisingly, as alarmed as he is, Dertouzos does not agree with Bill Norris and other computer executives who have called upon the U.S. government to bar Japanese graduate students from pursuing computer science studies at American universities. 'I think it would be a mistake to exclude the Japanese from our schools. When you have a system that works very well, you don't screw around with it. And the United States system, not just the educational system, has worked well with a free exchange of ideas and a free exchange of commerce over the past two centuries. Speaking as a European, that seems to be the main strength of this country. That's why I came here, to a country where your aspirations can be met. If you start screwing with that, and shutting it down in its extreme form, I think you shoot the U.S. – not in the foot – but higher up.'

Instead, Dertouzos seeks an open exchange of ideas and student transfer between the West and Japan, one in which Japan *truly* permits access to its knowledge. To expedite this, MIT is sponsoring a program to prepare U.S. students for study aboard, including electronics and computer study in Japan.

When the Japanese originally announced their Fifth Generation project they said they would share their information internationally, Dertouzos remembers. Later, in 1983, the Japanese reversed themselves. 'I asked this question of Professor Moto-oka [who oversees the project from Tokyo University], and the answer I got was that they wanted to first get their act together,' Dertouzos says. 'Recently I heard from Dr. Kazuhiro Fuchi, who heads ICOT, requesting a list of our publications and offering his own in return. I've passed that request to our executive committee, and I suspect they'll say "yes." We're in the business of the production of ideas, and the only kinds of controls we have are the ones that have to do with cryptography and other national security items.'

Another concerned American can be found on the campus of Stanford University at Palo Alto. Professor Edward Feigenbaum's offices are in Margaret Jack Hall, overlooking the lovely entrance driveway leading to Stanford's famed quad. The hoary Old California exterior conceals a modern building in whose bowels are massive mainframe computers, some connected to terminals inconspicuously evident in nearly every classroom and office. There is even a tiny terminal glowing in a corner of the snack room. Students and faculty tap in coded passwords, and sandwiches, soup, pastries, and drinks are automatically dispensed from vending machines. An appropriate sum is instantly debited to their monthly accounts.

A large red plastic machine – at first glance it appears to be an incongruous snail – guards the desk in Feigenbaum's outer office. A clue to its ostensible purpose is a neatly printed sign: *Take A Number*. No one ever does; the device is a joke, a monument to the futility of trying to systematize the human energy that crackles through this corner of the building. Telephones ring constantly and foot traffic is heavy: other professors, students and graduate assistants; knowledge engineers like Feigenbaum's Japanese-born wife, H. Penny Nii, secretaries, administrators. At times it seems as if the whole human race wants a piece of Dr. Feigenbaum.

Feigenbaum is a renowned computer scientist, one of the world's leading authorities on artificial intelligence (AI) and author of the book *The Fifth Generation*. He has been a leader in the small, vocal campaign calling for an American national effort to meet the Japanese Fifth Generation challenge. Tall and heavy, Feigenbaum observes the endless rituals of those who smoke pipes, and is given to casual dress in the manner of many Stanford dons. Overlarge, thick glasses magnify what might seem a baleful stare, one that is unintentionally intimidating, filled with intense, unbridled curiosity.

When the Japanese Fifth Generation project was announced in October 1981, it was at an international conference on artificial intelligence, held in a huge auditorium at the Japanese National Chamber of Commerce. Feigenbaum was there. 'It was like a Bar Mitzvah, a coming of age for Japan. They're very proud of this young kid that has grown up, the Japanese computer industry,' he says. 'The Japanese believe that you *can* have a vision about the future, and so they're acting as though for the most part the future has already been invented, or at least out to about a ten-year horizon. They've thought through what must take place. They're making the future happen.'

Feigenbaum has some ideas about what might result if the U.S. does not – rapidly – try to share that Japanese vision. 'We won't be a year or two behind Japan in the race for the Fifth Generation. Look what happened with video tape recorders. We Americans invented the VTR, but the Japanese created the product. Now they have the entire market. You can't buy anything but a Japanese-made VTR.' Pursuing the analogy, Feigenbaum thinks the first nation to bring Fifth Generation computers to world markets will be the only one to do so.

'If we don't get moving soon, we won't be in the business of information processing, which is the leading industry in the last part of the twentieth century, and will be for the first part of the twenty-first,' he warns. 'What's at stake is the economic future of America.'

8   MITI: The Japanese
Bureaucratic-Industrial Complex

UNLIKE THE West, Japan does not operate by business accident, or by the whim of eccentric, individualistic capitalists. It is a planned economy, one directed from an architecturally unappealing building near the small, delicate Hibaya Park, whose greenery relieves the glass, stone, and concrete density of central Tokyo.

The building itself is stark, made of grimy white limestone and smoked glass. It boasts few amenities, but as the headquarters of the Ministry for International Trade and Industry, MITI, and command post of the Japanese trade war it is appropriately guarded by several members of the Japanese national police, clad in dark gray uniforms and helmets, and carrying sidearms. The police salute as senior bureaucrats of MITI, the officers in this contemporary civilian army, enter the building.

I had come to MITI headquarters through an appointment arranged by a staff officer of the Japanese Foreign Press Center, Shigeyoshi Araki, who spoke perfect, if accented, English. He sent me to Kazuhiko Bando, vice director of the MITI Information Office, a man in his mid-thirties, whose office was on the third floor. Bando's office is like many in Japan, a large open area holding perhaps 20 desks in which Bando's own occupies the central command position near the window, from where he can keep an eye on everyone. Despite his authority, Bando – in typical Japanese fashion – does not have his own office. He sits at a utilitarian, unadorned steel desk no different from those of his subordinates.

Those used to plush Western corporate offices should not be misled by MITI's stark headquarters. From these airless, dim corridors and cheap steel desks orders in the form of 'recommendations' are issued to the barons of

Japanese industry, who convert the ministry's plans into billions of dollars in trade surpluses with virtually every advanced nation in the world.

MITI has been variously pictured by critics and admirers, American, Japanese, European. Some see it as a mysterious omnipotent organization, intruding into every corner of Japanese commerce, acting as puppet master to accomplish its ends. 'A spiderweb without a spider,' as one observer put it. Others dismiss the ministry as merely a *kyoiku mama* – a pushy mother. MITI's apologists, most of whom are Japanese, have drawn a different portrait. MITI is just one of many ministries in a democratically elected government, a dedicated corps of civil servants who, while generally favorable to Japanese business, have often been misguided, often less than effective, and often disregarded by industry. MITI, they say, is a faithful but toothless old dog.

MITI would very much like America to believe it is this enfeebled old hound. To promote this image of an inefficient bureaucracy, MITI has launched a public relations campaign to persuade Japan's trading partners in Europe and the U.S. that it is not very effective at getting Japanese industry to go along with its recommendations. 'Even if it were, so what?' asks MITI. 'In a way, the U.S. has an industrial policy. Such European nations as France, Britain, and Germany have an industrial policy. Why shouldn't Japan have one?'

MITI has disseminated a flood of documents in support of this contention. It has printed lavish four-color brochures replete with charts and graphs, written in excellent English, French and German and replete with statistics that indicate that Germany spends more on R&D than Japan, and that government contracts in a particular U.S. industry accounted for a larger percentage of spending than it did in Japan.

All MITI publications stress that Japan is committed, and always has been, to free trade and democratic capitalism. But, if necessary, MITI will invent statistics to support that false premise. Anyone making the effort to read the footnotes in MITI brochures and relate them to statistics available elsewhere might notice that the figures chosen for comparison in most charts are frequently not for the same years, and that the contents of the brochures often cannot be documented from any other source.

Feeling vulnerable of late, MITI has begun to take the offensive. In 1983, MITI started to claim that the *United States* is not trading fairly, that the United States has subsidized industries, that the United States is to blame for the deterioration in trade relations. Japan has singled out its largest and most generous victim for complaining about Japan's trade policies.

A May 1983 publication entitled *Background Information on Japan's Industrial Policy* claims that 'the industrial policy of Japan follows a soft-handed, indirect, and inductive approach. It offers fewer subsidies and imposes milder regulation than that of Western countries.' How can a country with 489 legalized cartels make that claim? The same document makes another spurious statement: 'In this country [compared to others] the government plays a smaller role in the nation's economic activity and its merchandise trade.'

This is also patently false. Japan has reduced its 432 import quotas to 27, but that is still more than most other industrial nations. But most significant is that Japan uses a myriad of subtle methods to block imports, including a semi-official 'Buy Japan' policy directed by MITI. For example, the huge nationalized telecommunications agency, NTT – despite years of promises – has yet to import significant amounts of foreign equipment. Yet Japan's bureaucrats continue to insist that their economy is open, that they are the world's fairest free traders.

The origins of MITI are in Japan's earlier history. After Commodore Perry sailed into Tokyo Harbor and demanded that Japan be opened for trade, Japan awoke. But the Tokugawa shogun lost face, and in 1868, the teenaged Emperor Meiji was restored to power by his chief vassals, and Japan rushed to join the community of nations, anxious to make up for its late start in science and technology.

It was eager to be accepted as an equal and determined to get on with Meiji's hundred-year plan of defeating the 'red-haired barbarians' and taking its rightful place as the leader of civilized nations.

In the 14th year of his reign, Meiji established the Ministry of Agriculture and Commerce. By 1925 its functions were divided between a Ministry for Agriculture and Forestry, and a Ministry for Commerce and Industry, the predecessor of MITI. One of the men involved in the latter ministry was a 29-year-old junior bureaucrat named Nobusuke Kishi, who only four years earlier had graduated from Tokyo University's law school at the head of his class. Despite his youth, Kishi found himself effectively in charge of the ministry in a few years.

Soon after Nobusuke Kishi was named vice minister, Japanese soldiers established a puppet state, Manchukuo, in the conquered Chinese province of Manchuria. In 1932, General Hideki Tojo, then head of the Kempei-Tai, the Japanese version of the Gestapo, was concerned about maintaining control of 30 million mostly unarmed, but decidedly hostile, Chinese with only tens of thousands of Japanese soldiers. Tojo decided that gainful employment would be the surest method of control. There were few factories in Manchuria, and although it had an abundance of raw materials, no foreign country would invest in Japan's seized territories. The army, which had conquered Manchukuo with no help from the *zaibatsu*, was reluctant to share the spoils. When Tojo became the military governor of Manchukuo, he sent for Kishi.

Kishi called on an uncle, Gensuke Aikawa, who had once been wealthy but had suffered a bankruptcy in the textile business. With Tojo's blessing, Aikawa set up an army-controlled industrial conglomerate, a company which he named Nissan. 'Only by courtesy could Manchukuo's economics be described as capitalist,' says Murray Sayle, an Australian journalist who lives in Japan. 'Operating capital was simply created by the army-controlled banks, thus eliminating capitalists with their tiresome demands for dividends. In an uncontrolled market, total bank finance is the high road to disaster (if sales slump, how can loans be repaid?); but with market shares guaranteed by the government, there is no risk. As general war in Asia came closer, Nissan and Manchukuo prospered on endless army orders for trucks, tanks, and guns.'

Today, Nissan, until recently known in America as Datsun, is a giant, the second-largest of Japan's automakers and highly diversified into aerospace and heavy manufacturing. Nissan has since rewritten its history, avoiding mention of its earlier career as the Manchukuo *zaibatsu*. 'Mr. Aikawa founded our company in 1933 to build cars. It was his ambition to establish a company to build an entire automobile, from starting to final assembly, to make cars which could be sold everywhere in the world,' says Shigeru Sawada, a Nissan public relations executive. Pressed, Sawada admits that Aikawa's sights were perhaps set higher. 'He was a very ambitious man, and he organized not only the motor industry but also established many heavy industries. Another field he was active in was to establish a very big heavy industry in Manchuria,' Sawada allowed. Asked if he, Sawada, was the head of his department at Nissan, he responded, 'Oh, no, I am just a soldier.'

Nissan's success in Manchukuo was to provide a model for the postwar growth of industrial Japan. In 1941, as plans for Pearl Harbor developed, Kishi returned to Tokyo to set up his wartime office, the Munitions Ministry. Using the Manchurian model, he attempted to reorganize Japanese industry for the war effort, but the *zaibatsu* were reluctant to relinquish any power, and he was only partly successful. After the war, Kishi was arrested by MacArthur and spent four years in Sugamo prison as a 'Class A war criminal suspect.' Released in 1949, he reentered politics, and in 1957 he became prime minister of Japan.

MITI is the direct descendant of Japan's World War II Munitions Ministry. Less than two weeks after Japanese leaders put pen to the surrender document page on the decks of the USS *Missouri*, the entire ministry changed its name to the Ministry of Commerce and Industry (which was to become MITI in 1949) and returned to work, minus only a handful of its top ranks. It was the same bureaucrats, in different uniforms but at the same desks, issuing the same orders disguised as subtle guidance.

Even the military parlance of MITI's World War II predecessor has invaded the consciousness of Japanese business. Companies secure new overseas markets by 'establishing beachheads,' learn competitor's strengths or weaknesses by 'scouting,' roll out a 'vanguard' of new products, and achieve dominant market position by 'attacking on a broad front' with lines of products, which often leads to rival businesses negotiating 'surrender' terms.

The *Pax Americana* of World War II was surely the most generous ever offered a defeated foe by its conqueror. America drained its own treasury to help the Japanese rebuild their industrial capacity, ironically granting Japan in defeat what it could not achieve by force of arms. America guaranteed Japan entry into world markets for manufactured goods, assured it supplies of raw materials, and maintained control of the seas around Japan and a strong American presence in Korea as prophylaxis against invasion from the Asian mainland by either China or the Soviets.

Under the terms of the constitution Douglas MacArthur forced on Japan, the *zaibatsu*, the giant cartels were abolished. The victor's rationale was that the quasi-feudal industrialists who led these cartels, and who had encouraged Japan to take the road of war, should be punished for their misdeeds. But the *zaibatsu* returned, if only in somewhat changed form. Some are still controlled by the same samurai-descended families; most are not. But in either case, the *zaibatsu* are stronger than ever. The directors of the recombined Mitsui *zaibatsu*, for example, all have offices in the same building with private corridors, private staircases and elevators, and a private telephone exchange connecting them. They continue to consult with each other on policy and on detail, and they are loyal to the wishes of the Mitsui family on management decisions.

But unlike pre-war Japan, the cartels are not all-powerful. The new *shinko-zaibatsu* are, in effect, controlled by MITI, which today assigns targets for the *zaibatsu*'s worldwide marketing strategy, focuses R&D, phases out uncompetitive industries, allocates scarce resources, and sets goals. MITI and its disciplined corporate adjuncts together constitute what the Japanese have themselves termed the 'bureaucratic-industrial complex,' the heart of Japan's state capitalism.

With the exception of the minister, who is by law a political appointee and a member of the Diet, all of MITI's 12,000 staffers are members of the Civil Service. MITI is organized into 12 bureaus, one for each strategic industry, each headed by a bureau chief. At the pinnacle is a vice-minister, the top bureaucrat, who theoretically reports to the minister. The political control is theoretical because the vice-minister, by long-standing custom, appoints his own successor. On a few occasions a politically appointed vice-minister has been brought in, but senior MITI officials have more than once retaliated, keeping the political appointee out of their deliberations by holding private meetings, and canceling others. Should the senior bureaucrats seriously differ with the political appointee, they can obstruct or ignore his guidance, a practice known as *menju fukuhai*, literally 'following orders to the superior's face, reversing them in the belly.'

Kishi filled the ranks of MITI and its ancestor agencies with the top graduates of his alma mater, Tokyo Law, or Todai, as its alumni refer to it, beginning a tradition that continues to this day. In 1965, for example, 355 of 483 – 73 percent – of all government officials at the department chief level or above were graduates of Todai; the percentage within MITI was even higher.

'Most students at Todai come from relatively well-to-do families,' said Ikuo Amano, a Todai associate professor. 'Over two-thirds of their fathers have college degrees, and over one-third of their mothers. Only 8 percent have parents with no formal education beyond elementary school. Fifty-five percent of their fathers are in managerial positions and 23 percent are in a profession. Almost a third are high-ranking bureaucrats or senior executives of large corporations. Family income is also very high, about twice the national average. After graduation from high school, 40 percent of Todai's students took a year off to prepare for the Todai entrance examination.'

Next to family and corporate ties, university affiliation, especially among members of the same graduating classes, is the strongest bond in contemporary Japan. One reason that businesses in Japan are anxious to recruit Todai law graduates is because it provides them with informal entry into the government bureaucracy manned by other graduates. In this way the leaders of Japan's largest industries maintain a close embrace with MITI.

MITI's senior bureaucrats are the best and the brightest of Japan's elite schools, nearly all of whom spend the bulk of their careers with the ministry. Positions in MITI are so valued that every year thousands of university graduates take competitive examinations for appointments to this and other government ministries. There are two classes of examinations. The 'A' or elite class is usually restricted to graduates of Todai and a few other top schools. The 'B' exam, open to all university graduates, is used to select the 350 or so men who can aspire to a 30-year career but will never go beyond the position of section chief. The elite exam selects only 25 engineers and 25 law or economics graduates annually.

In 1983, according to MITI, 1,370 took this exam to fill the small number of places. Those selected each year are the men from whose ranks eventually will be chosen half a dozen bureau chiefs and the vice-minister. Those who are not selected have an alternative. They become *amakudari*, literally, 'descend from heaven,' and are welcomed into the executive ranks of Japan's largest corporations, where they join their old college chums.

The bureau chiefs and the vice-minister of MITI usually serve two-year terms. When they retire, they either enter private industry or become politicians by running for one of the safe seats offered to them by the ruling Liberal Democratic party (LDP). In 1981, for example, Shoichi Akazawa, then 61, retired from MITI and joined Fujitsu, Ltd., Japan's leading computer maker, as vice-chairman.

Two years later he became president of the Japan External Trade Organization (JETRO), a government organization which works under MITI's guidance. In 1977, 27 percent of the House of Representatives and 35 percent of the House of Councillors were ex-bureaucrats.

Several of Japan's leading politicians have used the MITI portfolio as a stepping stone to greater power, including the present prime minister, Yasuhiro Nakasone, and former Prime Minister Takeo Miki. The most infamous connection between MITI and Japanese leadership was in the person of Kakuei Tanaka, Japan's prime minister from July 1972 to November, 1974, when he resigned after a scandal. Tanaka, who was considered the LDP's power broker and perhaps the most powerful man in Japan, was recently convicted of taking $2.2 million in bribes to assure the sale of Lockheed L1011s to Japan's airlines. It was Tanaka who selected Nakasone to succeed him as the MITI minister, and it was Tanaka who later maneuvered Nakasone into the Prime Minister's Office.

It is obvious that MITI's leaders, the leaders of Japan's principal industries, and the leaders of the Liberal Democratic party which has ruled Japan since the occupation, are essentially the same group of people. When MITI formally asks an industry or a company to do something or not to, it is, in essence, speaking to colleagues. 'There would be no punishment for turning down a specific invitation from MITI,' says Hiroshi Yamada, director of Fujitsu Laboratories. 'But in relations in this country, ties do not end with just one job. Over a long period of time, some adverse effects on business might be expected if an invitation is rejected.' Beyond this veiled threat there is a large inducement to conform. 'MITI bureaucrats are very competent,' adds Yamada. 'They have studied advanced technology well, and to go along with their judgment is generally not a mistake.'

Before World War II, the prevailing models of successful Japanese industry were the *zaibatsu*. There were four major groups – Yasuda, Mitsubishi, Mitsui, and Sumitomo.

Each consisted of a strong bank, which owned a substantial share of several large primary industries. The industries in turn owned substantial shares of the bank. Around each primary industry were clusters of subcontractors, affiliates, and partly-owned or totally controlled subsidiaries. A large trading company to merchandise the products from all the companies completed the group. Virtually all the shares and directorships of the companies were controlled by members of one extended clan.

A good example of the complete *zaibatsu* was Mitsubishi, which began when a samurai named Iwasaki, charged with running his *daimyo*'s business affairs in 1853, managed to hold on to them in his own right after the Meiji Restoration abolished the samurai class. When the new government gave him considerable business, he recruited the graduates of Keio University, one of the new schools established for the sons of the samurai, and formed Mitsubishi. The other great houses were created in much the same way.

General MacArthur dissolved the *zaibatsu*, but not long after the American occupation government departed Japan in 1952, MITI reconstituted them in a new form. The now independent Diet passed legislation that allowed MITI to subsidize the opening of foreign branch offices, to forgive bad debts, and offer tax deductions and outright grants to industry. Using its licensing authority, it assigned enterprises to the new trading companies. With its control over bank loans, MITI consolidated the 2,800 trading companies which were in existence during the MacArthur Occupation into about 20 huge concerns. Where the old *zaibatsu* had been totally interconnected by family affiliations, the new *shinkon-zaibatsu* were bound together by interlocking directorships and the bonds of shared schooling and background. By re-creating the *zaibatsu*, MITI had strengthened its hand in shaping their futures.

MITI's restructuring increased the influence of the *zaibatsu* considerably. Before the war the ten largest 'controlled 35.2 percent of the paid-in capital of Japanese business,' according to Komei Imamura, a respected Japanese economic analyst. The old *zaibatsu* families consisted of some 56 people controlling some 4,000 operating firms through 67 holding companies. But by 1971 the largest 'industrial groups,' which were now centered around the Fuji, Mitsubishi, Sumitomo, Dai-Ichi, and Mitsui banks, controlled 67.7 percent of Japan's corporate capital.

MITI's influence, like that of its brother ministries, does not end with guidance to industry. The vast majority of all legislation involving industry is introduced to the legislature by MITI at the cabinet level. There is some real deliberation on these bills, but it occurs before a bill is introduced on the floor of the Diet. To provide what the MITI Journalists Club describes as *kakuremino* – a magic fairy cape thrown over something – the ministries submit their proposed legislation to one of a couple of hundred 'civilian deliberation councils.' Council members are mostly retired MITI bureaucrats, senior officers of the industries which MITI is charged with regulating, and friends of the minister. Former MITI vice-minister Shigeru Sahashi has confided that as far as he is concerned, the councils are 'important primarily as a device to silence in advance any criticism of the bureaucracy.'

The infamous *yami karuteru*, or Black Cartel, case brought MITI perhaps its first barrage of unsilenced criticism. As Japanese housewives shouted *banzai*, the Japanese Fair Trade Commission indicted Japan's 12 leading oil companies, the Petroleum Association, and 17 senior executives on charges of price fixing, operating an illegal cartel, and withholding products from the market to drive up prices. The Japanese FTC charged that between December 1972 and November 1973, the group had met at least five times to work out the details of their conspiracy. The indictment was widely viewed as a direct attack on MITI's 'administrative guidance,' though no one at the ministry was charged. The FTC let it be known that MITI's involvement would constitute the heart of its indictment. These were the first criminal charges brought under Japan's Anti-Monopoly Law since its enactment.

MITI's involvement in this case began in March 1973, when it introduced a bill granting the ministry broad powers to control prices. Meanwhile MITI Minister

Nakasone restructured the ministry. A few months later, the leading Arab states attacked Israel to start the Yom Kippur War and Saudi Arabia and five other OPEC nations suspended oil shipments to countries that supported Israel.

The immediate result in Japan was panic; no other nation in the world is so dependent on imported oil. Nakasone and other Japanese politicians paid hurried visits to the Arab oil ministers, offering friendships, loans, massive construction projects, preferential trade terms – whatever it took to turn the oil back on. Market conditions were chaotic in Japan. Prices soared, commodities disappeared from the marketplace entirely. For a time there was no heating oil, no toilet paper, no dishwashing detergent. Japanese consumers were convinced that the cartels MITI had organized were taking advantage of the situation to reap huge profits. Nakasone and his bureau chiefs manned a special command post at MITI, dispatching emergency shipments whenever possible to calm the most outraged, and neediest, groups.

In this charged atmosphere MITI forced through the Diet two new laws enabling it to demand reports from wholesalers and retailers, to establish prices for specific commodities, to implement plans for distribution of products, and to assess fines for violations. MITI now had the legal power to back up what was previously 'administrative guidance.' It was with these powers that the petroleum industry was 'persuaded' to withhold certain products from the market and to raise its prices across the board. MITI's actions were a way of granting the petroleum cartels under-the-table subsidies against the probability that profit margins would later be reduced by OPEC's price increases.

The Black Cartel case took more than six years to proceed through the Japanese court system. In 1980 the Japan High Court ruled against MITI, declaring that the ministry was 'not authorized to cause companies to restrict production through administrative guidance.'

In 1974, shortly after the oil crisis, the JFTC and MITI faced off again when the JFTC attempted to pass an

Anti-Monopoly Law that would have given it the power to break up cartels. MITI fought the bill strenuously and won. The law the Diet eventually passed in June 1977 was considerably weaker than the one the JFTC had sought. The Black Cartel case had a sobering effect on MITI's top echelons, but only temporarily. It even served as the catalyst for a new scheme designed to expand MITI's influence, and became the blueprint for a new MITI. It was to create a MITI better oriented to the future, and in many ways a stronger force in Japan's international trade.

The plan, drawn up by the Harvard-trained Nobuyoshi Namiki, was MITI's blueprint for the coming decades. It spelled out in some detail what it called 'a knowledge intensive industrial structure,' calling on Japan to internationalize for its own good. It gave authority to a MITI department to coordinate budget priorities, make investment decisions, and decide on R&D funding for various high-technology industries. From this came a series of huge, government-funded R&D projects, the 'rationalization' – or more accurately the cartelization – of key industries, and the sheltering of these industries from free market competition.

In MITI's new plan of economic conquest, there were two strategic priorities. The first was to defuse foreign criticism of MITI's actions through the campaign of unrelenting propaganda. Since Japan is singularly dependent on international trade, if its trading partners were to reciprocate MITI's protectionist policies it would be disastrous.

The second point of strategy was to scale down the operations of Japan's declining industries. 'The most impressive thing about Japan's industrial policy is the way they manage the rational adjustment of their declining industries with a minimum of social pain and political obstruction,' observed Frank A. Weil, former deputy secretary of the U.S. Department of Commerce. MITI's methods are the same as those used to boost an ascending industry: They exert influence in numberless personal contacts among former MITI officials in the Diet and in industry and guide the key decision-makers toward their goals.

Japan's petrochemical industry, for example, has long had surplus capacity to produce ethylene, a chemical used in the manufacture of plastics and adhesives. As their raw material these Japanese plants use imported petroleum, which is more expensive than the natural gas North American manufacturers have available. Since these Japanese ethylene plants are inherently noncompetitive, MITI, in the summer of 1982, decided to scale down the industry.

They began with the custom of *nemawashi*, literally, root binding, a term borrowed from bonsai, dwarf tree cultivation. *Nemawashi* is a subtle way of feeling-out those involved in a project without taking strong stands on the issue or getting into arguments. Since MITI knew there would be great reluctance among petrochemical executives to commit business hara-kiri, they started with a 'research mission' to visit European manufacturers in October of 1982. On the trip were the presidents of 12 ethylene manufacturers, the chief executive of a company that made derivative products from ethylene, and a senior MITI official. 'While traveling together, eating together, drinking together, talking with each other, there came to be a feeling of trust within the group,' said one of the presidents.

The next phase was to set up seven 'study groups,' representing each of the 12 manufacturers. The groups met to study market projections and the common problems of the industry. MITI artfully circumvented anti-monopoly laws by insisting the groups were not acting as cartels but merely getting together to 'advise' MITI about a policy. But according to those who took part, most of their recommendations became MITI's policy.

That policy was to merge the firms and form three consortia from Japan's 12 ethylene makers and their six largest consumers. Each consortium would then reduce production by 36 percent and sell their products through a joint marketing company. Layoffs of workers would be avoided by transferring 'permanent' workers between divisions of the companies, and by attrition. The jobs of 'temporary' employees were not even considered. They would be slashed as required by declining capacity. As the companies moved toward consolidation and retrenchment MITI would reward the consortia with tax incentives, protection from foreign competition, and government subsidies.

MITI has coercive power, which it can use against those firms that refuse to cooperate. There is always the threat of cutting off an industry's bank credit. MITI has had some measure of control over Japanese banking since the twilight of the occupation, when Supreme Command Allied Powers (SCAP) opened the Export Bank in 1951. In 1952, when the occupation ended, the name was changed to the Japanese Export-Import Bank. One original source of funds was produced by the sale of U.S. aid products given to Japan; the Japanese government sold this food, petroleum, and medicine to its own citizens. The other source was the postal savings accounts of the populace, accounts that date from the time of Meiji and have more than once been expropriated by the government. In 1917 and 1918 they were used to redeem loans to China. But despite these defaults, the Japanese people trust the postal authorities more than the savings banks, and MITI has used these low-interest funds for loans to industry.

MITI was also instrumental in setting up the Japan Development Bank (JDB), created under SCAP in 1951. While the Ministry of Finance ostensibly ran the bank, once again MITI maneuvered itself into power by screening all loan applications and by influencing policy decisions with its advice on budgets. MITI further insinuated itself by getting several retired MITI officials appointed to JDB's board of directors, a practice that continues to this day. In 1980, for example, when Shiro Miyamoto retired as director of MITI's industrial policy bureau he was promptly appointed to the board of the Japan Long Term Credit Bank. In 1983, he resigned to become executive vice-president of JETRO.

As soon as the Allied occupation was over, MITI pushed the Diet into amending the JDB charter to permit removal of most loan ceilings. Simultaneously, the Ministry of Finance was prodded into diverting the money in the postal savings accounts into a vast pool of capital to be made available to the JDB and other government banks. However, it was specifically prohibited from using the funds for government social welfare programs. To encourage savings, Finance exempted from taxes the interest on the first three million yen (about $12,500 at 1983 rates) deposited in each savings account. To ensure that the money stayed there, interest rates for long-term certificates of deposit were pegged higher than bank rates, though somewhat lower than those in the U.S. during comparable periods. By 1980, the assets of the postal savings deposits were four times those of the Bank of America, the world's largest commercial bank.

Even this vast sum is exceeded by the investment capital that Japan's 21 major insurance companies and its seven trust banks control, almost $300 billion, almost all of which is invested in closely related Japanese businesses. The money managers at Mitsui Mutual Life and at Mitsui Trust and Banking receive their investment capital from insurance premiums, most of them paid by working-class Japanese.

Over the decades, Mitsui Mutual has invested the majority of its funds in the stocks and bonds of such companies as Mitsui Construction, Mitsui Engineering and Shipbuilding, Mitsui Mining, Mitsui Bank, Mitsui Mining and Smelting, Mitsui Real Estate Development, Mitsui Sugar, and Mitsui Petrochemical Industries, all parts of the same *zaibatsu*. Most employees of these companies have come to believe that buying life insurance from Mitsui Mutual amounts to an obligation. 'Japanese companies think about the historical relationship with an institution rather than performance,' said Sony Corporation General Manager Sumio Sano.

Far from being a toothless hound, MITI is full of vigor. For three decades it has pushed Japanese industry towards a command economy. It has made some mistakes. In the

1960s, MITI attempted to force the cartelization of the Japanese auto industry by merging its smaller, weaker companies into Nissan and Toyota. The auto makers resisted, fought back, eventually had their own way, and prospered. But in 1981, when the U.S. Congress threatened to pass a law mandating a rising percentage of American-made components in all imported cars, MITI cleverly pressured the car dealers into a 'voluntary' reduction of their exports to 1.68 million per year.

It was MITI which provided 'administrative guidance' to the car makers, and MITI which approved the plan that allocated market shares to the exporting companies. It was also MITI which told the car makers to increase their output of small trucks, which were not included in the cutback, to make up for their lost car sales.

MITI is not omnipotent, but it has largely had its way. Some Japanese businessmen will candidly acknowledge MITI's helping hand. 'I should also mention government intervention, which is not basically good in a free economy, but in the process of catching up it has been very helpful to business,' said Toshio Ozeki, a senior manager with Nikko Securities. He continued, 'Business sought this type of relationship and promoted it, because it has proved to be very helpful. In years to come, with Japan becoming a true member of the international community and the government paying more attention to social issues, we may have less of this kind of partnership between government and business; but so far it has worked.'

Not all Japanese business regards MITI and the Japanese bureaucratic-industrial compex as favorably. 'We cannot talk forever about "Japan as Number One," and rest on our oars,' said Isao Nakauchi, chief executive officer of Daiei, Inc., Japan's largest supermarket chain, in a September 1982 speech to the American Chamber of Commerce in Tokyo. 'We Japanese must change our attitudes toward trade. We cling to the notion that exporting is a virtue, and importing a vice. Japanese industrial structure should support exports and imports equally.'

242

He was obviously not speaking for most of Japanese industry, or for MITI. As the descendant of Japan's Munitions Board, MITI has other ideas and programs yet to be announced, but none of them include any change in attitude toward a war they are now winning.

9 The Exploited Japanese Worker

MUCH OF the success of the Japanese corporation has been attributed to the remarkable Japanese labor system. Hundreds of articles and dozens of books have paid homage to the myth of the close, compassionate relationship between the individual Japanese employee and the benevolent management team that directs the company's activities. All this, it is said, has provided wondrous increases in productivity that are the envy of the civilized world.

According to this prevailing view, Japanese workers enjoy lifetime employment, secure in their knowledge that their company will always have a job for them. Their wages, which compare favorably with those of most European and American workers, are augmented with huge bonuses several times a year. Their paternal companies provide them with subsidized housing, free medical care, and company discounts on purchases of major appliances and automobiles.

Unlike the West, where labor strife has often been bitter, labor relations in Japan are supposedly excellent. Japanese labor unions work alongside management and regularly participate in the decision-making process. Managers treat each worker with courtesy and individual attention. Decisions are arrived at through consensus, with everyone encouraged to speak their mind, and offer suggestions. Each company is one happy family, working together for the betterment of all. The Japanese worker loves his job, his company, the people he works with, and above all, his boss, who has provided him with the good life. The result is there for all to ponder: Japanese productivity, Japanese product quality, Japanese success.

The only flaw in this popular explanation is that it is a

distorted portrait of the true situation. It is another profitable myth perpetuated by the lords of the Japanese corporate fiefdoms. Like all such myths, it contains just enough truth for the Japanese to convince outsiders with illusory shadows. The Japanese are fond of telling everyone that they are a rich people in a poor country. The reality is that they are a poor people in a rich country.

Most Japanese workers live poorly by American and European standards. Japanese who travel abroad constantly express their amazement at the living standards of people in Europe and the U.S. 'When my husband and I visited New York, some friends took us for a ride in their car,' says Hiroko Horisaka, who has lived and traveled extensively abroad. 'We drove through a place called Harlem, and our friends said, "Look, this is not typical of the way most Americans live. This is a terrible slum, the people here are very poor, don't think that this awful place represents America." I looked around, and as far as I could see, these apartments weren't much better than ones we Japanese live in.'

The Japanese standard of living has been sacrificed in the name of increasing international trade surpluses. Since most Japanese are now urbanites, and more than 40 percent of the populace lives on only 1.5 percent of the land area, there is incredible crowding. Tokyo has its expensive neighborhoods, it has its slums, but most parts of the city are a mixture of both, a study in extreme contrasts. The wealthy live in oriental seclusion behind high walls, able to pay $350,000 for a 800-square-foot condominium – about half the size of a comparably priced American apartment – while next door workers occupy low-ceilinged apartments that cram three stories into a space in which American and European buildings have only two, and where residents usually manage without a private bath.

The typical Japanese apartment complex is four to ten stories high, an ugly, architecturally monotonous building with one-, two- and three-room apartments averaging only 450 square feet. Few buildings of less than six stories have an elevator. The halls are dark and narrow, and the public areas are often in need of paint. Not all apartments have telephones, and some families wait as long as two years for installation; due to population density, many telephone exchanges are overloaded.

The Japanese are sensitive about showing their homes to foreign visitors, but I have visited a few. Most employees of the larger companies and the government live in huge blocks of apartments appropriate to their seniority, at very low rentals. The apartments are owned and subsidized by their employer, but typically, they have no central heating. In the few buildings that do have furnaces, the heat supply is inadequate for Japan's frigid winters. In any case, the system is usually shut off between April 1 and November 1, when the Japanese survive on portable heaters.

Few of these apartments exceed two small rooms and a kitchen, and the entire family is often forced to sleep in one room until the children enter puberty. The kitchen is tiny, with a small refrigerator; with limited food storage space, Japanese housewives must shop for food nearly every day. Most apartments have a tiny balcony or porch, usually crowded with stored items. Closets are small, shallow, and narrow, and cannot accommodate the inhabitant's possessions, many of which are stacked on top of cabinets or under tables. Often, families devote as much as 20 percent of their apartment's space to the storage of electrical appliances.

Many of these apartments do not have either a bath or a shower, though in recent years the so-called luxury units have featured a tiny shower and a three-foot tub. Bathing requires a trip to one of Japan's tens of thousands of bathhouses. While public bathing has traditionally acquired social overtones – the bathing group often turns into an ad-hoc business meeting or a women's debating society – it requires at least an hour every day to go to a bathhouse.

Slightly larger apartments and small private homes are available in one of Tokyo's suburbs, and many Japanese are willing to commute several hours a day to keep them. Commuters who spend two or more hours traveling each way to and from work are not uncommon in Tokyo.

Frequently the homes they return to at night – after a ten-hour work day and four hours of commuting – are 700 square feet in size, with a garden not much larger than an office desk, and a roof-top 'solar' clothes drier.

But the Japanese are willing to commute because this is superior to anything they could find in Tokyo. Those in the West who live this poorly can move to a better environment if they have the money; the Japanese have sufficient money but cannot find better places to live. The reason is simple: the capital resources required to build decent housing have been allocated elsewhere. In Japan's totalitarian economy, the priority for capital investment, the priority for land usage, the priority for importing foreign construction technology and urban planning, and the priority for architectural and engineering development have always been given to the building of factories for export products.

When money is no object, Japan, like all countries, has its neighborhoods for the very affluent. The Japanese elite, the politicians, corporate *daimyo*, and movie stars live in high-walled isolation, many of them in such neighborhoods as Denen Cho-fu, in the Ohta-ku district, about 40 minutes southwest of Tokyo on the broad stretches of the Kanto plains, feudal Japan's richest rice growing fief. Now it is a community of narrow streets winding among mansions, the Beverly Hills of Japan, without the hills. There is no factory pollution of noise or smoke, and since few Japanese, aside from the families of its wealthy residents, have any reason to visit the secluded area, there is comparatively little traffic.

Other wealthy Japanese reside in nearby Meguro, almost due south of the central district of Tokyo. Still others live in Akasaka, a Tokyo entertainment district which has grown to a more sedate maturity. Once an area reserved almost exclusively for foreigners, large hotels, elegant restaurants and expensive night clubs, it now boasts high-rise condominiums. On the curving, cobblestoned inner streets of this district, small but luxurious units of 400 to 800 square feet sell for prices ranging upwards of $200,000. The location is favored by important business executives and many in the entertainment industry who can be close to their offices, and after an evening of carousing in the local nightclubs, can be home in minutes.

The upper middle class prefer such suburbs as Senkawa, an hour from central Tokyo by subway. This is a bedroom community, where the streets have no sidewalks, but behind the cinderblock walls, some topped with a few strands of barbed wire or with broken glass set in cement, are modern, wooden homes of perhaps 1,000 square feet. Many have gardens, if only tiny patches of green eight or ten feet square. This is a new neighborhood, with straight streets laid out according to plan and lofty streetlights illuminating intersections for the occasional automobile. Except for commuting times, when throngs crowd into the subway station, the streets are quiet and clean. Most of the residents are middle-management types, men with offices in the city who leave the running of their homes to their wives, and who can relish the weekend as a time to enjoy their comparatively spacious surroundings.

But few Japanese can live like families in Senkawa, or enjoy their job security. The privileged class of Japan are those with so-called lifetime employment, a privilege much heralded in the Western press. In reality, this status is held by less than a third of all Japanese workers, mainly in Japan's major industrial firms. Even for these most fortunate, 'lifetime' translates to a job only until age 55 and a pension that is insufficient to live on thereafter. The other two-thirds of Japanese workers, those who work in the service industries, in the myriad shops and the hundreds of thousands of small factories, in the subcontracting firms – where a sizeable portion of all Japanese automobiles are made – have no job security whatsoever.

The only wage scales which are comparable to Europe's and America's are those of the favored one-third. The other two-thirds make as little as 40 percent of the 'permanent' jobholder's wages. The vaunted 'bonuses' given out by management are actually withheld wages, involuntary subsidies to corporate treasuries. Highly-publicized company loans for big-ticket purchases are granted to the favored few, and serve to keep employees in extended company service in a nation where consumer credit is virtually unknown and interest rates can run over 100 percent. The Japanese labor unions are mainly company-controlled and do not even offer membership to the millions of part-time workers who have no job security and few benefits. In the Japanese 'worker's paradise,' unmarried factory workers often live in dismal dormitories with barrackslike discipline.

The fact is that underpinning Japan's economic system are the legions of the exploited, the workers who give far more to their nation's effort than they receive. Japan's national work force has been mobilized, trained, and deployed as an industrial army. They work hard; they march to management's cadence, but they are not, as some have suggested, happy drones. In fact, a 1983 Indiana University study reveals that they are a relatively dissatisfied, if submissive, army. Only 53 percent of Japan's workers said they were satisfied with their jobs, in comparison with 81 percent of American workers.

If the mobilized legions of Japan are unhappy, why do they work so hard? The answer is that the Japanese worker serves because he has been trained for just that since his birth. Unlike people in any other advanced nation, the workers of Japan – from the assembly line to top management – are obedient servants to the state industrial complex.

The current generation of Japanese has inherited a tradition of discipline from a feudal Japan that formally ended scarcely a century ago, but is still potent as a spiritual force. 'Many Japanese seem overburdened by the demands of duty – to family, to associates, and to society at large. . . . It is a clear continuity from premodern times, when the word used was *giri*,' says Edwin O. Reischauer, Japan scholar and former U.S. ambassador to that nation. *Giri* is the strong Japanese sense of duty which continually submerges the human feelings, which are called *ninjo*. This sense of spontaneity and individuality, so prized in the

West, is feared in Japan as a force that, once unleashed, could lead to personal and national chaos.

Discipline is what conquers *ninjo* and replaces it with *giri*. It is well developed in a Japanese child by the time he or she enters elementary school. 'Every Monday morning I can hear the loudspeaker from a nearby elementary schoolyard, hear the school master saying "Mae-e-Narae!"' says Kenichi Ohmae of McKinsey and Co., in Tokyo.

'Without being there today, I can picture the scene, for it has not changed since I went to school twenty-five years ago. The pupils are being told to line up straight. Those who fail to do so will be given a slap or at least made to stand outside the classroom for ten minutes. In high school, students are continually informed that if they sleep more than five hours a day they will not make it to a first-class university and hence will not make it to the top of the hierachy that follows.'

Fifteen years later, when the school child enters his country's work force, that early discipline has already paid off; it is as ingrained in him as obedience is in any good soldier. The Japanese worker has been socialized virtually from birth to the demands of a culture in which respect for authority is the highest virtue. The Japanese worker does not need external discipline; he has learned to impose it on himself. He knows that he must do what he is told to, that he will speak to certain people only when spoken to first, that he will work as long and as hard as he is asked to and for whatever wages are offered. If he complains – and he does sometimes complain out of earshot of the bosses – he will face punishment. He has accepted the wisdom of keeping his mouth shut.

Implicit in this formula of obedience is the Japanese worker's feeling that his value as an individual is less than his value as a member of his group, whatever that may be. As a loyal group member, he is expected to listen and obey. 'Learned commentaries on Japanese culture emphasize dominant values of *on* [obligation] and *giri* [duty] – the values promoted from above,' states B. Bruce-Briggs, a Hudson Institute analyst and Japan scholar. 'From below, however, the most relevant value is *gaman* – patience, endurance, putting up with it.'

With the Russians, the Japanese share a paranoia that drives them. In the case of the Soviet Union, the supposed fear of invasion has created a military monster continually seeking aggressive outlet. In the case of the Japanese the fear is that Japan is 'poor'; therefore they must continually strive to be richer than all other nations, including America and Western Europe, which are Japan's economic models.

Surprisingly, the Japanese do not feel rich as a nation even though their per capita income has now passed Europe's, and is only minutely below that of the United States. The reason is that Japan's work force has been brainwashed into believing that hard work is necessary for national survival. But why do Japanese workers put up with it? 'Because Japan is a poor country,' answered a young electrician at Fuji Electric. 'What do you mean, Japan is a poor country?' someone asked. 'Japan is a poor country because people must work very hard, and because there are very few holidays,' the worker answered. It is a case of a self-fulfilling national delusion, one calculated to make the Japanese work without protest, or end.

In the daily life of a Japanese worker, rewards are promised and occasionally even distributed. There is the notion of working your way up the pecking order. There is even a useful myth of entree to the oligarchy. If not for oneself, then perhaps it will be possible for one's sons, if they exhibit unlimited loyalty and skill.

But in actuality, most Japanese workers face a closed door. Promotions are based on two factors generally unrelated to merit: alma mater and seniority. Even for the supervisory ranks, says Kenichi Ohmae, promotions are 'governed by an equation in which his age and the name of the university he attended are the key variables.' Adds Arthur S. Golden, former managing editor of *PHP*, a Japanese English language magazine: 'Seniority is extremely important to the Japanese, and determines salary increases more than any other single factor.'

251

The Japanese like to think of themselves as members of a company 'family.' 'We don't say "worker" anymore,' Nissan spokesman Shigeru Sawada told me: 'Employees of our company are members of the Nissan family.' The roots of this attitude may be traced to the beginnings of Japan's industrialization. In the 1870s, as the first factories were set up, recruiters went from village to village, seeking young men and women to work in them. Their parents were reluctant to send them off without guarantees that they would have a place to sleep and enough to eat. Equally important was their insistence that the factories provide quasi-parental supervision.

The Japanese corporation offers that parental function, but along with it comes an equal degree of control. Unlike Westerners, Japanese parents do not allow children to come and go as they please, to decorate their own rooms, to associate with whomever they wish. In return for granting some degree of job security and a place to lay their heads at night, Japanese companies, large and small, expect the 'children' of their corporate family to conform to their parental notions including those involving after-hours activities. This is called *yokkakari*, dependence. 'By the end of his first year, the new employee will be made a spotless "company man,"' said Kenichi Ohmae.

This parental control gives unmarried Japanese workers the sense of an extended, overcontrolled childhood. Most unmarried factory workers, especially in the highly populated urban areas where Japan's heavy industries are concentrated, live in barracks-like dormitories. I have visited these grim, cheerless buildings of four or five stories without elevators, without central heating. None of the workers had a private bathroom. There was a communal toilet on each floor, but bathing required a trip to a bathhouse a quarter-mile away. The rooms were the size of a generous American walk-in closet, often windowless, with concrete floors covered with *tatami* matting. Workers slept two to a room, on *futon* bedrolls of thick padding stored during the day in a sliding-door closet. A single unshaded bulb dangled from the ceiling; only one electrical outlet graced each room.

The Exploited Japanese Worker

The rules of parental control were prominently displayed outside the entrance to one dormitory. The restricted life permitted inside was clearly spelled out on signs addressed to visitors.

I. No one except parents and relatives of dormitory residents are permitted inside.
II. Other visitors must register with receptionist and must obtain an entrance permit.
III. No visitors are allowed to remain after 10:00 P.M.

Inside each room there was another sign posted:

1. All electric appliances used in this room must be registered with the Dormitory Committee.
2. Electric capacity is 900 watts per room. Do not exceed.
3. Electric heaters must not exceed 400 watts.
4. Electrical heaters not permitted after March 31.
5. Heaters may not be used before work hours.
6. Extension cords are forbidden.
7. Ash trays must exceed 10cm in diameter and must be filled with water.
8. No smoking while walking.
9. Each room will be inspected twice daily to ensure all the above rules are obeyed.

Such regimentation extends to virtually every facet of an unmarried Japanese worker's life. It is impossible to have a lover in these rooms, not only as live-in roommate in the Western sense, but even for a casual sexual encounter. It is as if Japanese firms expect their single male and female workers to be celibate.

Since few can live that way indefinitely, single Japanese male workers usually find an emotional outlet in drinking, far from the workplace or dormitory. The Japanese are well aware of their low tolerance for alcohol, and drunks in Japan are forgiven almost anything, except drunk driving. 'Prime ministers are not held responsible for speeches made in drunkenness to the Diet, and crimes of passion are regularly excused in the law courts if intoxication can be proved in mitigation,' says author David Bergamini.

After work, many Japanese workers go out for a few drinks and like most Japanese activities, it is done in groups. After a whiskey or two, an employee can tell his superior what a jackass he thinks he is; since they're both drunk, everything is forgiven. 'The Japanese don't really trust a man who won't drink with them,' explains Robert Kirshenbaum, an American businessman living in Tokyo. 'They believe that if he won't drink, he's not being honest with them, that he's not revealing his true feelings.'

After everyone has had a few drinks, the group will break up into twos or threes and head for the 'Pink Light' district. Tokyo has several of them: the Shibuya, Shinjuku and Roppongi are among the busiest. Most weekday evenings by 8:00 P.M. the rabbit warren of streets on the east side of Shinjuku Station is filled with slightly tipsy salarymen seeking release from work pressures. The crowded streets are lined with neon signs, many of them slightly risqué. 'Pilots,' whose job it is to steer people to their establishments, stand outside and clap their hands sharply to attract attention. They sometimes bodily halt groups of passersby, barking out the joys and wonders within.

Inside, one can find everything from little whiskey bars with low lights and hordes of usually attractive hostesses, to R-rated, relatively tame live 'sex shows.' Mostly harmless flirtation and touching, plus some actual sex goes on in these establishments, and occasionally, a salaryman will fall in love with one of the hostesses. If he is affluent enough, and she is willing to probably forego marriage, he may take her for his mistress. But as in most societies, the ordinary worker cannot afford a mistress.

The single worker can usually find sex in some of these establishments, but only by making discreet arrangements with the manager. A man living in a closet-sized room and facing eight or ten hours a day of toil on the shop floor often finds it impossible not to. By ten o'clock, however, the streets start to clear, and by eleven, when the price of taxicabs rises, nearly everyone is back in the subway or on their *tatamis*.

Much of Japanese corporate paternalism is exaggerated, particularly when the worker's welfare costs money. Should a worker be injured badly on the job, for example, most large Japanese companies are unwilling to take financial responsibility if they can avoid it. Legally, they are obliged to pay an indemnity to such workers, but some Japanese companies have devised an array of evasive strategems.

'If an accident occurs, the ones responsible for the group have their next bonus reduced: 40 percent for the team chief, 30 percent for the foreman, 20 percent for the general foreman, and 10 percent for the section manager,' explains *Municipal Administration Study Monthly*, detailing how one Japanese firm penalizes everyone connected with the victim. Since the company cannot legally deduct money from an employee's salary, the money is instead taken from 'bonuses,' which are actually wages. By calling this part of the wage a bonus, a voluntary management contribution, it can be withheld at corporate whim. In both accident control and general worker discipline the 'bonus' is an effective method of enforcing management policies.

The practical effect of this draconian system is to encourage the chain of command not to report an accident. As a result, the company is rarely forced to officially acknowledge responsibility, especially when the injured party is a part-time, temporary, or probationary worker. A well-known case involved Kisaburo Onoe, who went to work for Toyota after serving with an affiliated firm, Toyota Auto Body.

When a Japanese worker leaves one company and goes to another, even an affiliated firm, he usually loses all seniority and starts over again at the bottom. During the 15 months of Onoe's 'probationary' period, his job was to stack auto roofs which had been stamped out of sheet metal. When he became a 'regular' worker he was given the job of running the press which stamped the roofs. He came to work on May 9, 1969, and was told to run his machine slowly since it had been operating erratically since the previous shift. Meanwhile the automatic crane feeding his machine was running at normal speed, delivering sheets of metal three times as fast as he could stamp them out.

To keep up, loyal worker Onoe had to hold two 35-pound roofs in his right hand while operating the machine with his left. After six hours of this labor he experienced a sharp pain shooting from the lower part of his back and right arm up to the back of his head, and was unable to stand upright. He returned to work the following day and was given lighter work. After three days of light work, Onoe was sent back to pressing hoods, which are slightly smaller than roofs. Still in pain, he asked to be taken off the line, a request that his foreman refused. He stayed out sick for a few days, then returned to work, using only his left arm.

Onoe asked his general foreman to give him written recognition of his occupational disability, but there was a safety campaign, 'Five Million Safe Hours,' underway, and the Toyota foreman refused. Nobody wanted to be known as the individual at fault if the company failed to achieve its goal. Because he had not followed regulations and reported his accident within three days, his case was disqualified. There followed a struggle that lasted several years while Onoe tried to win recognition for his injury, as a basis for compensation. Despite medical certification, his applications were rejected by Toyota. He went to the government Labor Standards Inspection Office in Ozaki, near Toyota's factories, and asked for a hearing.

At the hearing Toyota introduced as evidence photos of better automatic machinery which had been installed after Onoe was injured, and the government turned down his claim. He appealed to his union, which declined to get involved. In the end, Onoe, a tall, physically imposing man, was reduced to doing odd jobs around the factory while his fellow workers shunned him as a 'troublemaker.'

Despite his obvious inability to perform the same kind of work, Toyota has never recognized Onoe's occupational disablement.

No Japanese phenomenon has received more extensive praise than the QC, the quality circle of workers, which has helped change Japan's image from the junkmakers for the world to producers of quality goods. In actuality the quality control circle is still another example of a Japanese adaptation of a foreign – in this case, American – management technique. Ostensibly, the QC circle is a volunteer activity, but in practice, QC circles are often coercive. Workers are expected to attend meetings on unpaid time, sometimes during their breaks or lunch hours, but most often after regular working hours. Management exerts pressure downward through the company ranks to extract as many suggestions as possible from individual workers. Typically, scrip good for a few dollars in merchandise at the company store is paid for suggestions actually adopted. Once in a great while a real prize – often a car – is awarded with fanfare.

Nissan claims that suggestions from its 4,000 QC circles saved the company $60 million in 1980, but fails to mention that little of that was passed along to members of its 'family.' There is constant, at times enormous, pressure to produce the volume of suggestions needed to justify the time spent in these meetings. The Japanese press periodically publishes reports of workers hospitalized for stress-induced mental illness, or even driven to suicide by the relentless demands for more QC suggestions.

In 1981 there were 130,000 QC circles in Japan, with a membership of one million, registered with the Union of Japanese Scientists and Engineers. Throughout the nation, there are several hundred thousand groups with more than three million members, according to the newspaper *Asahi Shimbun*. Hajime Karatsu, a Japanese QC expert and former managing director of Matsushita Communications Industrial Company, claims that workers are drawn to QC by faith in industry, or he says, 'like a new religion promising miraculous benefits, QC spread from factory to factory around the country.' He fails to mention that the greatest enthusiasm is demonstrated by the priests of this new religion, the topmost rank of Japanese management.

The reluctant but typically obedient acolytes do not always share this faith. 'The fact is, the circles do not work very well in many Japanese companies,' says Robert Cole, director of the University of Michigan Center for Japanese studies. 'Even in those plants recognized as having the best operating programs, management knows that perhaps only one-third of the circles are working well. . . . For all the rhetoric of voluntarism, the workers clearly perceive the circle activity as coercive.'

What really happens at these QC workers meetings? At the Nagasaki shipyards of Mitsubishi Heavy Industries in July 1980, workshop QC groups decorated their lunch rooms with bamboo sprigs to prepare for the Festival of the Weaver. They were told to intersperse the sprigs with safety slogans. One such slogan stated: 'For safety's sake I'll always watch my footing while at work.' But 30 employees refused to write the slogans. 'It was not the safety program they objected to, but the none-too-subtle coercion,' an *Asahi* reporter said.

A spokesman for the dissident workers, Mitsuyoshi Kusano, told the press: 'We were told to write the pledges because they said the whole group had decided to do it. But would a grown man voluntarily write such nonsense? When a guy gets hurt on the job, then he'll be told he broke his pledge. It's another way for management to clamp down.' Such incidents of wholesale refusal are comparatively rare in Japan, where the average worker is too well disciplined to raise objections. But the revolts are no longer isolated events. 'The unconverted regard QC as a device to squeeze unpaid labor from workers,' said another *Asahi* reporter.

For an outsider, about the only way to penetrate the quasimilitary security blanket around Nissan's factories is to take 'the tour.' This involves an introduction to Nissan's public relations apparatus, where bona fides and motives are examined. Properly screened, the visitor will then have an opportunity to view that which Nissan would like to show him. I wanted to see one of Nissan's automobile production plants, especially the one at Atsugi. 'We are very sorry, but just now no one is allowed to visit any production plants since we are in the process of retooling for the new model year,' said Shigeru Sawada, one of Nissan's immaculately groomed public relations staffers. Instead, he offered to show me a videotape of the revamped production plant at Oppama and invited me to Nissan's Tokyo headquarters for a private viewing.

Nissan's headquarters complex is a collection of spotless, spacious, modern offices near the Ginza, 'Tokyo's Broadway.' They are as Italian-marble and plush-carpet opulent as those of any giant multinational manufacturer, but surprisingly posh for Tokyo, where space is dear and few companies invest much beyond the facade to impress foreign visitors.

Every Nissan employee wears a uniform, or a badge, which shows not only his name and department but his rank in the company, an important detail in an organization that began its existence as the manufacturing appendage of the Japanese Army. Sawada is a charming man in his late thirties, and he apologized again for not permitting me to visit a manufacturing plant. The videotape, he explained, would be 'better than a visit,' since it would show me places I wouldn't be permitted to enter if I visited in person. Before my visit, I had read the reports of Satoshi Kamata, author of a book about his six months as a 'temporary' Toyota assembly line worker, and of John Junkerman, who wrote a disturbing magazine piece on working conditions at Nissan's plants.

According to these sources, the workers were driven to produce at ever-higher levels, often forced to forego their break time or to arrive early to do setup or other preparatory tasks; they were spied upon by management; their union was totally ineffectual in representing their rights; any worker dissent was ruthlessly stamped out; living conditions in company dormitories and family housing were poor; and in general, working conditions were abysmal.

When I raised some of these points to Sawada he told me 'everything will be clear from the videotape.' As the tape progressed, it was clear that whoever wrote the script had used the Kamata book and the Junkerman article as a framework. Point by point, the allegations were refuted. Here were the happy Nissan workers, attractive young men and women in spotless new uniforms, playing volleyball in the sun during their lunch hours and eating delicious food in their cafeteria. Here was a senior Nissan worker, in his peaked cap with stripes of rank, telling of the pleasures of working at an automated plant. Here was the quality circle meeting, with intense workers tripping over their tongues to explain an ingenious, cost-saving suggestion.

The tape went on for half an hour, in English. Since Nissan became a huge international company, with sales offices and production facilities all over the world, they have made progress in understanding the nuances of modern public relations. Would I ever be able to visit a manufacturing plant? 'That will not be necessary, now that you have seen the videotape. Don't you agree?' asked Sawada.

Fortunately, I have visited several Japanese assembly plants on my own. Conditions do not match the Nissan idealized view, except superficially. In the spring of 1982 I visited a factory that is part of a division of K. Hattori, a massive diversified Japanese trading company. The day there begins with a 'voluntary' period of light calisthenics 15 minutes before the start of the shift; almost no one misses it. A few minutes before eight, everyone is quietly standing by his work station, getting tools and assembly parts lined up, turning on and testing soldering guns or test equipment, adjusting stools and preparing for a day of uninterrupted toil.

Before the shift starts, everyone sings the company song, to the accompaniment of music from a loudspeaker. Then it is all action. For the next two hours, work continues without pause. No one leaves to smoke a cigarette, to go to the bathroom, to drink a cup of coffee. No one talks to his neighbors, either, or to a supervisor, unless there is a problem or the supervisor asks him something. About 10:00 A.M. the loudspeaker plays gentle chimes, the assembly line stops, and the workers put down their tools.

For three to five minutes, everybody stretches, turns, bends, and bounces. Anybody who *must* use the bathroom streaks off and returns before the music ends and the shift resumes. At midday some 700 workers walk to a single, enormous cafeteria-style dining room. Inside of six minutes, every single person in the plant has entered the cafeteria, picked up his food, paid for it with company scrip, charged to his wages, and found a seat. By the end of another 20 minutes, the dining room is emptying, as though by command. The workers have 45 minutes to eat, go to the toilet, and perhaps stop by a company-owned convenience store to pick up a few items they will place in their lockers before returning to the assembly line. Five minutes or so before the shift starts, everyone is back in place, sitting or standing at their work station, repeating the same preparations they did in the morning. 'Not a minute is wasted,' a supervisor told me. That was quite obvious.

This particular plant – and several others in nearby cities – produces computer printers under the Epson brand, the best-selling small printer in the world. To meet production quotas, each line has a device that automatically keeps track of every printer coming off the line, and the numbers are prominently posted on a chart which shows how many units make up the goal, and how many are actually produced. 'We have always exceeded our target,' a quality control supervisor beamed.

'Japan's labor movement is impotent,' Shigeki Hijono, editor-in-chief of the Japanese *Encyclopedia Britannica Yearbook*, exclaimed as we spoke. 'It hasn't been a force in national issues in a very long time.'

Japan's labor unions, which cooperate openly with

management, to whom they are usually obsequious, hardly compare with their American or European counterparts. Unlike labor in the United States or in Western Europe the Japanese unions are fragmented and ineffectual. The basis of all organized labor in Japan is the enterprise union, an organization encompassing only the workers at a single location. If a large company, like Toyota, has several plants at several different locations, each one has a separate union, with its own officials. The officers of these unions and the shop stewards are frequently lower-level management personnel. In Japan – totally unlike the West – one of the best ways to rise in management is to get involved with the union and show your boss that you can handle the rough job of keeping workers productive and in line.

Because the unions are enterprise unions, the management of, say, Honda, can appeal to its workers on wage and benefit issues by pointing out that its competitors, Toyota and Nissan, have only been given 5 percent pay increases in a particular year. To stay competitive, the management says, they need to keep the increases below that range.

There are a number of federations of enterprise unions, such as the General Council of Trade Unions, known as Sohyo and the Japanese Confederation of Labor, or Domei. Together these two largest unions represent some 7.5 million workers, as well as several lesser union confederations. But they are only umbrella organizations and lack the economic or political power of the American AFL-CIO. What they can, and try to, do is to present a unified front on social issues and 'guidelines' for the *Shunto* or Spring Offensive, the annual negotiations for wage increases. They have no power in the governing Liberal Democratic Party, the LDP; their only political leverage is within the Japan Socialist party, which has been the opposition since the end of the occupation.

In 1983, a new 'superconfederation' of labor was formed. Zenmin Rokyo includes affiliates from the four existing national confederations as well as 'neutral' and unaffiliated unions, representing about 4.9 million workers.

This organization is still in the formative stage and has yet to announce firm policies or obtain reliable funding, but it is aiming to be a force in the 1984 *Shunto*. 'Roughly speaking, the initiative of the next *Shunto* will be taken either by Zenmin Rokyo or the metal workers' group,' Yoichi Yamada, director of international affairs for Sohyo, explains.

But only some 12.5 million Japanese workers belong to any union, or about 30.5 percent of all salaried employees, a category that includes most hourly American workers. Not counted in the 'salaried worker' category, and not represented by unions, are the millions of part-time, seasonal, and temporary workers, some of whom have been in that unfortunate category for ten years. They cannot join the enterprise unions until they become employees. There are no union hiring halls in Japan, and attempts at organizing these workers have largely failed.

'Part-time workers are mostly female workers – housewives – or they are farmers who seasonally come to town to work under contract,' claims Sohyo's Yamada. 'They are not willing to participate in the union movement. Temporary workers also don't seem to want to participate. Secondly, the industrial structure of Japan's economy is changing very rapidly, and the tertiary sector – the service sector – are very much small-scale enterprises. Among those enterprises, the employers do not like the workers to be organized. The employers are hostile to the union movement. So it's very difficult to organize these workers. We are trying to organize them, but very frankly speaking, we are not successful.'

American labor experts are skeptical about the motives of most leaders in the Japanese union movement. 'The workers are being exploited, and they know it, too,' says Lester Slezak, a labor expert at the American embassy in Tokyo. Lester Slezak is tall and avuncular, a gentle, plain-spoken, middle-aged, bespectacled man. 'They're willing to pay the price in exchange for having pretty much a guaranteed job in the large firms. That's the quid pro quo.'

The American embassy in Tokyo is in Akasaka, a district known for its nightclubs and world-class hotels. The embassy is on a side street, across from the office building that houses the Japan External Trade Organization (JETRO). The embassy building is a cantilevered structure of warm, reddish-brown brick and glass, its severe angles mitigated by a walled courtyard and the steeply sloping hillside it nestles against. Marine guards in dress uniform are stationed at the entrance, and the visitor's bona fides are examined through bullet-proof glass in an airlock-type lobby.

Inside, the embassy is light and airy, in welcome contrast to most Japanese office buildings. Slezak met me in a modest solarium, and after a brief discussion we opted for lunch at the embassy's basement cafeteria. It is one of the few places in Japan where genuine American fare is offered, and at prices considerably below those prevailing elsewhere in Tokyo.

Slezak is sophisticated about Japanese worker-management relations and is candid about the failings of the trade unions. 'In the economically dynamic corporations, most of the unions have been put off by political unionism, and have openly taken the point of view that their number one interest is retention of jobs,' he explains. 'The moment you start from that point you have economic identity with the company.'

Slezak sees the Japanese tradition of paying more to older workers as another major obstacle to true unionization. 'One of the problems now is that seniority has been the sole or principal basis for wage scales, and with the rapidly aging work force that's driving up company costs,' he explains. 'So now they're trying to lighten the seniority factor in the wage computation, trying to change it to only 50 percent of the calculation and make other factors the remaining 50 percent. The medium and small companies are saying, "we can't afford these high wages."'

James N. Ellenberger, an AFL-CIO official who specializes in international affairs, takes an equally skeptical view of many aspects of Japanese trade unionism. 'There's only one union that's organized in the Western sense, and that's the Japan Seaman's union, Kaiin Kumiai,' Ellenberger told me. 'They have contracts which cover multiple employers, so in a sense it's like our seaman's union. The other unions are enterprise unions. These are not unions in the American or Western European sense, but neither are they unions like the American company unions in the twenties and thirties.'

He, too, sees the greatest failing of the unions as their unwillingness to organize the millions who are not 'permanent' employees. 'Japanese trade unionists can be very vocal and self-critical of the failures of their own organizations to organize temporary workers, part-time workers, casual workers,' Ellenberger points out. 'The unions by and large are representing those workers who enjoy long-term employment or "permanent" employee status. Often times people have been temporaries for ten years or so. They don't have any union representation at all.' Ellenberger goes on to explain that it is a Catch-22 situation, with an exclusionary twist. 'Union representation for a Japanese worker is a sort of knighthood. It means you're a permanent employee. But, in many cases you're not eligible for membership unless you're a permanent employee.'

The giant Japanese enterprises, which employ some 25 percent of the nation's labor force and pay the highest wages, have their own company unions, which function more as an arm of management than of the workers. Being a company union member is not unlike being in the army. Just as an army truckdriver can be turned into a machine gunner, or a cook into a rifleman at his commander's whim, any employee may be assigned to any task in a Japanese company. In like manner, workers can be sent where they are needed, even if it is to locations hundreds of miles distant.

Nor is it uncommon for one company's workers to be 'loaned' to another company. A Japanese worker will work hard wherever he is sent; his allegiance is to his company, not to a union or to his fellow workers. In April 1983, for example, Nippon Steel was asked for a 'dispatch of support forces' to swell the overextended ranks at

Nissan's Kanda factories, where export goals had risen beyond capacity. Nippon Steel sent 130 steelworkers for a six-month stint on the assembly lines. Later 60 more were dispatched to Nissan's Oihma plant, and an additional 75 workers to the Isuzu plant at Fujisawa. Yamaha has in the past sent idle employees to Toyota, others to Pioneer Electric, and transferred still others to its retail and whole-sale outlets to work in sales, warehousing and after-sale maintenance.

In America and Europe, we typically think of labor and management as being represented by men who dress, talk, and think differently and seldom share political views. In Japan, it is quite the opposite. Union officials and company management men are indistinguishable. They have the same goal – Japanese industrial power. In fact, they are frequently the same people. 'Companies are reluctant to discuss the presence of so many former union leaders among top management, and few will admit how many there are,' stated Masayoshi Kanabayashi, a *Wall Street Journal* staff writer.

In violation of accepted Western trade union ethics, Japanese union officials are often rewarded with promotions to high management positions, clear evidence of the management collusion to the detriment of workers. Among the companies whose presidents were former union leaders are Dai-Ichi Kangyo Bank, Kanebo, Ltd., Sumitomo Chemical Co., and Nisshin Steel. A 1981 survey showed that three-fourths of the 313 major companies responding had one or more executive directors who had previously served as labor union leaders. The same survey revealed that one in six of all directors at the responding companies were former union executives.

Is this an indication of upward mobility by blue-collar workers? Hardly. Nearly all these directors with former union experience are college graduates who entered the company as white-collar workers and assumed union leadership at the upper-echelon level. Most company unions may properly be viewed, then, as mere extensions of management. Their task is to act as lightning rods, to absorb worker discontent, to wear down those who complain by putting their protests through layered bureaucratic channels, to keep workers working, to stop them from disturbing management's *wa*, the peace of their corporate households.

Three Harvard professors, authors of *Industrial Renaissance*, point out that 'the fact that first-line supervisors, lower-level managers, engineers, salespeople, office workers, and other staff personnel are all union members – these conditions help make Japanese unions more like an arm of a company's personnel department than (as is the United Auto Workers) a steady, if sometimes cooperative adversary.'

This state of affairs has not escaped the workers, who may be well-disciplined but are far from stupid. Unions are 'useful only for people who want to ascend to hierarchy,' a Toyota worker named Takahashi stated. 'The general impression is that the union constantly betrays workers' interests.' But, he added, no one thinks things will ever change.

Japanese unions have elections, but they are more like exercises in one-party Soviet-style government than democracy. Company management makes it known which people are acceptable to them as union leaders, using the subtle pressure the Japanese understand so well. The result is that the nominating process is strictly controlled, and those at the helm remain in power. 'In the last ten to fifteen years, I can't remember a single labor union president who was forced from office or lost a reelection attempt,' says Lester Slezak.

This is not to say that Japanese unions have always been arms of management. 'Before World War II Japan's labor movement was highly influenced by politics but not very effective in winning much for the workers,' Slezak explains. 'After the war, Article 28 of the Japanese Constitution guaranteed the rights to organize and conduct collective bargaining.' But the ruling bureaucrats and industrialists twisted this statute to permit any group 'of two or three people' to organize its own union.

'Divide and conquer, that was business's strategy,' Slezak says. 'It obviously worked. After the war the only large, organized union group was controlled by the Communists, and when they called for a general strike in February 1, 1947, it alarmed the real ruler of Japan, General Douglas MacArthur. On January 31, MacArthur issued an order to the Japanese authorities that a strike would not be tolerated. That broke the back of the labor union movement in Japan.' Slezak adds that it has never recovered.

Once a year there is a national pretense of trade union aggressiveness when hundreds of labor unions launch their 'Spring Offensive,' or *Shunto*. In the opinion of many, *Shunto*, which almost always results in a wage increase only slightly higher than what management publicly offered beforehand, is less forceful than it seems. Despite the public pageantry of union power what little real bargaining exists takes place in private.

'The first week of *Shunto* all the workers will wear armbands to express solidarity,' says Robert Kirshenbaum, president of Pacific Photo Service. A tall, affable, American with a wide circle of Japanese friends, he has lived in Japan for more than twenty-five years and speaks fluent, idiomatic Japanese. His company employs some 30 Japanese. 'As negotiations proceed, the union will hang out their red banners, and maybe, if they want to put a little extra pressure on the employer, they'll rent a sound truck and harangue the public for a couple of hours a day,' Kirshenbaum explained at his office.

'Then maybe they'll strike. For one hour. After the strike, if they still haven't got what they want, they may refuse to work overtime for a few days, for about a week. That involves real financial hardship, so it means they're getting close to a settlement. At that point, management gives a little, the union gives a little more, and everything is settled. But it's always settled a little bit more to management's benefit.'

After the Spring Offensive of 1983, the first in more than two decades without an accompanying strike, working members of Japan's largest corporate 'families' received the smallest average pay hike since 1955 – only about 5 percent. While Toyota's reported profits were the highest in the company's history, the company rewarded its 'family' of workers with raises of 5.1 percent. Nissan similarly recorded an increase in profits of 17.6 percent, but granted its work force only a 5 percent increase. Both were less than the national average for annual raises, which since 1958 have always exceeded 5.6 percent.

Matsushita's wage increase averaged 4.9 percent, which is typical for the electronics industry. These increases represented about a third less than those of 1982. The rationale for these small settlements was that the world recession had caused Japan's unemployment levels to rise to 2.4 percent. Unemployment in the U.S. at this time was slightly higher than 10 percent, while European nations averaged over 11 percent.

Keeping the Japanese worker down is not difficult, for unlike Americans and Europeans, he does not openly press for higher living standards. In terms of striving for a better life, the Japanese propensity is in inverse relation to that of the West. In Japan, the goal is not to 'keep up with the Joneses,' but to 'stay down with the Suzukis.' Therefore, families do not want to be the first in their community to acquire some new gadget; only when a few have turned up in neighbors' homes will everyone rush out and get one. Like Westerners, they will then buy one even if they do not really need it, and sometimes if they cannot afford it. In their world of ultimate conformity, it is hardly surprising that, when asked, Japanese will almost always answer they are middle class. But within the framework of the Japanese working forces, everyone is not equal, not nearly equal.

One factor that dramatically separates one worker from the other is job security. Western accounts extol the Japanese worker's 'lifetime employment,' but the myth is exploded by experts on Japanese labor. 'The very term "lifetime" employment is inaccurate and misleading,' says James Ellenberger. 'It might better be called "long term" employment.'

Since wages in Japan rise primarily with seniority, the highest paid workers are rarely the most productive workers. When someone has to be let go, the old, higher-paid workers are 'encouraged' to take early retirement. Workers are sometimes forced out even before the usual mandatory age of 55, a policy that exempts only those who rise to the managing director level or above. The impact of retirement on individual workers is enormous. Japanese firms have pension systems, but most are lump-sum distributions of two to three years wages, and Japan's social security benefits are considerably lower than most other industrial nations.

As a result, most retired workers do not have enough income to maintain their standard of living. They must take another job, starting all over again at the bottom of the seniority ladder. *Asahi*'s senior research editor, Mitsuo Tajima, says that over 80 percent of all men between the ages of 60 and 64, and 45 percent of men over 65, are still in the work force – and reduced to working at entry level wages. 'These figures are by far the highest in the industrial world,' he adds.

The indifference of the Japanese business world to their retired people results in the lack of work dignity for men like Jimpei Kamuro. Kamuro is 69, a tiny, wizened man still possessed of great energy. From 1937 until 1972 he worked for the Japan Express Company, the largest trucking firm in the country. When he retired, Kamuro was a relative success: the chief assistant to the director of the company's Yokohama office. Now, six days a week he is a hotel handyman, working long hours and at labor not befitting a man his age.

Kamuro rises about five every morning at his home in Kanagawa Prefecture. After tea, he hurries to the Japan National Train Station for an hour's commute to the small hotel where he works, a four-story building with 40 guest rooms rented mainly to visitors on business. Kamuro's duties are undefined and broad. He sweeps and cleans the lobby, shines the brass, helps guests with their suitcases, mans the check-in desk, helps out in the kitchen. He works from six in the morning until six at night, when he walks about a mile to Ochanamizu Station and takes the trainride to his home, his wife, and his daughter, 30, an elementary school teacher.

Kamuro considers himself fortunate. With his government pension, plus what he has saved from a lifetime of toil and the tax-free interest he earns from post office savings accounts, together with what he now earns from the hotel and what his unmarried daughter contributes, his family is able to live almost as well now as they did before he 'retired.' He also considers himself fortunate to have originally found a job with one of the companies that did offer so-called lifetime employment. 'I got a little more of a pension than most, because I was able to advance to the rank of chief assistant,' he told me.

Most of Japan's workers cannot hope for as much, and will be forced to live out their declining years on the charity of relatives. One reason is that even at the larger companies many workers never become 'permanent' members of their corporate families and are therefore never eligible for full benefits. They will always be less equal than regular workers.

At Nippon Steel's Kimitsu Works, for example, Robert Wood, a writer who studied Japan's wage system, reported that the regular workers, who wear silver helmets, 'receive higher pay, have cleaner jobs, work shorter hours, are eligible for company fringe benefits like housing, transportation, vacation packages, etc. and are considered "permanent."' Temporary or subcontract 'yellow helmet' workers 'work longer, are paid less, receive few benefits, and do the dirty work of climbing under hot oxygen furnaces to clean them, bending over short shovels to recondition the tracks where hot metal will flow, and work close to ear-splitting noise.'

Even these exploited yellow-helmet workers are still better off than those in 'grandchild' subcontracting, in which smaller firms congregate around the larger companies they supply. 'Male workers in these small companies earn only 71 percent of the wages paid in "big" companies and receive far fewer benefits,' James Ellenberger reveals. They also work longer hours. Japanese who work for firms employing only ten to 99 people work an average of 32 hours per month more than employees of larger firms.

There are '7,400 regular employees at the Kimitsu Works and something less than 9,000 subcontractors within the mill's gates,' Wood says, adding that another 10,000 work as 'grandchild subcontractors' in the area. 'That means,' he concludes, 'that of a total employment roster of perhaps 26,000 people, just over one in four wears the privileged silver hat.'

A common practice of large companies is to send their retiring seniors to smaller affiliates for postretirement jobs. The top ranks of smaller companies are thus full of 'retired' executives who will work for another six to ten years before leaving. Meanwhile, other employees of the smaller company are denied advancement because the upper ranks are filled from the outside. Management of these smaller companies are mindful of their vulnerability to the larger firm that buys their products, and they take whatever steps necessary to maintain that relationship, including accepting the larger firm's 'retirees.' Frequently, this also means they pay their own employees much less. Typically, in a company with fewer than 100 employees and one with more than 1,000 there is a 40 percent difference in wages.

Perhaps the most common method of exploiting Japanese workers is to use them as part-timers, making them ineligible for extensive fringe benefits. Over four million of Japan's 58.3 million workers are part-timers, an increase of 21 percent from 1978. Many are actually not part-timers, but only considered as such on payday. A recent survey by *Zensen Domei*, a Japanese business organization, revealed that 70 percent of 'part-time' workers actually work a full day, yet do not receive fringe benefits. They are given only 65 percent of the wages paid 'permanent' employees doing the same job, and lose both benefits and the hope of long-term employment.

This dependence on part-time and contract labor for much of the work force begins to put Japan's much vaunted productivity figures in a different light. Increasing robotization and the benefits of computer-designed manufacturing have helped Japan manufacture cheaper products. But it is not the whole story. Japanese productivity figures are not really accurate, for they do not reflect part-time work or the rising use of subcontractor companies.

Subcontracting is increasing in Japan, to the overall detriment of Japanese workers. In 1980, one third of all Nissan and Toyota vehicles were assembled by other companies. 'The Japanese automotive industry is the world's biggest cottage industry,' states the British publication *The Economist*. AFL-CIO spokesman Ellenberger adds that while Nippon Steel and U.S. Steel's sales volumes are comparable, Nippon Steel's 'regular' work force numbers only 42 percent that of U.S. Steel. 'The statistics, however, only take into account the permanent employees of Nippon Steel and do not include the much larger group of temporary and subcontract employees,' Ellenberger stresses. 'The large Japanese advantage in steel productivity is unquestionably due in great measure to the difference in the way workers are categorized.'

Japanese workers work harder, and often for lower wages, but they also get less rest than most Western laborers. Most Japanese work a five-and-a-half-day week. By the early 1980s, when unemployment began to be a problem in Japan, the government encouraged shorter work weeks. Today almost 90 percent of large companies indicate that they have some form of two-day weekend; but that usually means that once or twice a month workers are not required to come in on Saturday. Less than 10 percent of the companies regularly give their employees a full two-day weekend. And when pressure is on for production to move ahead, even less time is given to workers. Work shifts are extended, national holidays are ignored, and individual vacations postponed. Sick leave is traditionally paid only after the first three days of an illness, so most workers take vacation time instead when they become ill.

Japanese management even exerts subtle pressure to keep employees from taking their legitimate vacations. Added to this is peer pressure, fostered from the top down, that keeps many Japanese workers on the job instead of on the road. The Japanese Ministry of Labor confirms this trend, reporting that Japanese workers are obtaining more holidays from management but using them less. Says a U.S. embassy report on Japanese labor: 'Workers in 1981 used only 55 percent, or 8.3 days, of their annual leave entitlement of 15 days, compared with 61 percent (8.8 days out of 14.1) in 1980.' In most shops, factories, and offices workers who take their full, authorized, vacations know that their supervisors are watching. They will penalize them in some way, whether by delaying a promotion, denying a future request, or, most frequently, by increasing their workload.

'In thirteen years, my husband never took a vacation,' reveals Hiroko Horisaka, whose husband, Kotaro, worked for several years as the Latin American correspondent for *Japan Economic Journal*. 'Everytime he would start to hint about some time off, all the other people in the office began to complain about how much work there was to do. Then his boss asked him if he couldn't help out a little more and restore peace in the office,' she told me. 'If you take your vacation, when you come back everyone will grumble that you're lazy and they are having to do extra work. So nobody ever takes their vacation. In the end you feel cheated, but there's no help for it.'

Another way in which Japanese management controls the worker is by the threat of withholding much of his wage. In America and Europe, wages are the worker's and can only be taken away if the worker is fired or laid off. But Japanese workers have traditionally been paid by a combination of methods. In addition to 'regular' wages, overtime pay is a significant part of most workers' income, especially in manufacturing. An additional 40 percent of total annual income is paid in bonuses, two or three times a year. There is no legal obligation to pay bonuses; since they are usually based on a worker's seniority and his *group* performance, management can withhold them at will.

At its most insidious, this system of group bonuses is applied to manufacturing teams. If production goals set by management are not met, the team works overtime until they are. If overtime then rises significantly beyond management's tolerance, bonuses are reduced or eliminated. Overtime pay is in effect subtracted from the bonus. The result is an accounting manipulation in which workers wind up being paid piece rate instead of a salary.

The bonus system generates billions in income for Japanese firms by allowing them to withhold substantial amounts of workers' wages for several months at a time. Workers receive no interest on the money withheld, enabling the company to reduce its capital needs or add to its profitability, or to sell its goods abroad at lower prices than a foreign competitor. In bad times, bonuses are reduced or eliminated. Japan's exploited workers are thus exposed to the downside of corporate enterprise, but unlike stockholders – most of whom are found in the top echelons of management, or who are the directors of closely associated firms or banks – they are denied a real share in the upside, increased profits.

Japanese workers save about 20 percent of their income, three times as much as American consumers. Since private pensions are notoriously small and limited to lump-sum payments, and government social security pensions are totally inadequate, the Japanese save for retirement. They also save because the government makes it difficult to borrow money, even for the most worthwhile purpose.

Japan supplies capital to its corporations at cut-rate interest but is reluctant to extend credit to workers and consumers. Instead of rationing credit by interest rates, as free-market capitalist systems do, the Japanese system of totalitarian economics allocates most of its available credit to major corporate borrowers at rates below what they would pay in world money markets. To get this money, the government sucks it out of the workers. It has built an enormous pool of capital from the savings of the people who work in the factories, offices, and shops. It pays them considerably less interest than world rates but cleverly exempts the interest from income tax.

Japan achieves this fiscal magic in several ways. First it keeps strict controls on foreign access to its money markets. If individual Japanese investors could buy shares in a U.S. money market fund, they could earn much higher rates, but this is not permitted. If it were, Japan would be forced to raise domestic interest rates to competitive levels. But Japan does not permit the free flow of capital, as do most Western nations.

Since nearly all the available credit is diverted to business from workers' savings, there is little left for consumers. 'We can't borrow from banks,' a Japanese friend told me. 'They only lend to people who don't need to borrow.' Japanese banks charge high fees for all services, one reason why most companies pay salaries in cash. Personal checking accounts are not common in Japan: just to transfer money from one account to another can cost about $1.70. A transfer to another bank costs about twice that. There are no credit cards of the type now ubiquitous in Europe and the United States. Instead, there is a recent proliferation of bank debit accounts and automated teller machines, which allow a consumer to pay a merchant by using the debt card instead of a check, or to get cash without going to a bank. With no bank loans and no credit cards, Japanese consumers, until recently, had only two ways to borrow money: *shimpan* and *sarakin*.

'Fifteen or twenty years ago, Japan started to form *shimpan* companies to finance retail purchases,' says Bill Yates, 53, a tall, heavy-set man with horn-rimmed bifocals and a graying crewcut. Since 1978 he has been president of Avco Financial Services, Japan, headquartered in Tokyo. 'At first, merchants financed customer purchases of very expensive items, like wedding kimonos, but in the last few years the *shimpan* expanded to finance the purchase of cars, TV sets, appliances, and so forth. This was the beginning of "buy now, pay later," for Japan.

'*Shimpan* offer fairly low rates – about 14 percent, annualized – but limit themselves to short-term loans, always less than 24 months,' Yates adds, pointing out that 14 percent is about ten times the passbook saving rate and twice the post office certificate of deposit rate. 'They finance only purchases, and unlike American systems do not offer the convenience or flexibility of revolving credit.'

Five American finance companies began operations in Japan in 1978. Before that Japanese consumers had only one option for a cash loan, *sarakin*, or salary loan companies, which were allowed to charge as much as 109.5 percent annual interest. 'People would come in to the *sarakin* and borrow, say $50 or $100, and pay back in 59 days or less,' says Yates. 'Under those circumstances, you can't look at the interest rate, because it's a small amount and a short term, and it costs something to make a loan. But now they're lending as much as $2,000 – at the same rate. That's unconscionable.'

After investigating Japan as a possible new market for years, Avco, the third-largest consumer finance company in the world, started its Japanese venture five years ago. 'We're pretty much agreed that the salary loan business had gotten out of hand, and for that reason, the Japanese government decided to allow foreign companies to come in and reform the industry,' says Yates. 'If we could show the Japanese how to make consumer lending into an ethical business, it might push the *sarakin* into straightening themselves out. Meanwhile, some of them would undoubtedly go belly-up, but all the public criticism could be directed at foreigners.' At the press conference announcing Avco's first office, Japanese reporters asked Yates, 'How many Japanese businesses do you think you'll bankrupt in your first year?'

The great appeal of the *sarakin* is their confidentiality. In contrast to American loan companies with brightly lit offices and high-visibility locations, the *sarakin* are usually on side steets, and often on upstairs floors of nondescript office buildings. 'There's a stigma attached to borrowing money in Japan,' explains Yates. Any Japanese salaryman can go to a *sarakin*, bring his driver's license or national identification card, and walk out in 20 minutes with up to $2,000. In 1982, ten million Japanese made *sarakin* loans, leaving about $12.5 billion on the *sarakin* books at any time, resulting in nearly $80 million in profits for 1982.

'The *sarakin* don't do a credit check. They may have an

idea that the fellow owes money elsewhere, but they don't care if he does,' Yates continues. 'So, at those interest rates, it's pretty easy to fall behind. What happens frequently is that a guy will borrow from one *sarakin* to pay off another. The interest mounts up pretty quick, and he may try to win the money by gambling or investing in a speculative stock. Most of the time, the poor guy loses. Then he has to try to find another *sarakin*, borrow more money. It breaks up families, it causes divorces, suicides, murders. Most of the time, the guy doesn't tell his wife, he doesn't tell his employer. If he can't pay, they usually send someone around to his employer,' adds Yates. 'Then, since the man who borrows money must obviously be of poor moral character, they always fire him. After that – suicide, or murder, or both, and I mean you see these things in the paper almost every day.'

Indeed you do. Between January 1, 1983 and April 1, 1983, government statistics recorded at least 19 murders attributable to failing to repay loans; more than 400 suicides; and 7,000 families driven from their homes after being unable to repay *sarakin* debts. One was an insurance saleswoman in Toyama who owed $40,000 and couldn't repay it. She loaded her children into the family car and drove it into the sea, drowning all of them. Another, 36-year-old Takao Terada, a mid-level official of the Omiya city government, tried to break into a golfclub's office to get the $8,300 he owed to a *sarakin*. Driven off by a burglar alarm, he hid in the woods for nine days without food before turning himself into the police. Another Tokyo salaryman accepted a murder contract in lieu of repayment of $4,000. After he killed a young woman, he, too, turned himself in.

American firms like Avco offer rates of 18 to 29 percent, about the same as American loan companies, but much lower than the *sarakin*. But so far the five American companies have had a tough time staying in business. 'The Japanese banks won't lend to us,' said Yates. 'And most people who come in for loans don't like to be asked where they work, and they don't like it when we ask them to bring their spouses in to cosign the loan application. Since the Japanese lenders will not share credit information with us, we can consolidate a person's debts, get him out of trouble – and he can immediately go out and borrow from a *sarakin*. The biggest problem with our customers is they don't want their companies to find out they've borrowed money, because they'll probably lose their jobs.'

The high-interest borrowing, and the misery it brings, is the price the Japanese pay to keep low-interest capital flowing to their companies. 'The low-interest-rate level in Japan stems from the inability of the Japanese to lend or invest abroad readily,' said James A. Abegglen, Boston Consulting Group's top Japanese economic expert. 'If the yen and Japanese lenders were part of the world market, the current level of interest rates in Japan could not be maintained and the current very substantial under-valuation of the yen could not be continued.' It is the undervaluation of the yen that makes American products more expensive in Japan, and makes Japanese exports far less expensive in world markets.

Numerous factors, from tradition to business ethics, monetary policy to a system of virtual state capitalism, have made Japan a threat to world economic health. But in the final analysis, without the exploitation of servile Japanese labor, none of its enormous advances would be possible. The giant industrial empire of Japan operates like an army, on the back of its foot soldiers, the over-worked, abused and underpaid Japanese worker.

10 The Other Exploited: Women and Minorities

CHINATSU NAKAYAMA is a tiny, nervous woman, with wavy, shoulder-length hair, delicate hands and feet, a musical voice and a ready smile. As she speaks, her face becomes animated and her hands flutter to emphasize her attitude. She has been variously described as 'the Gloria Steinem of Japan' and 'the Jane Fonda of Japan,' while others have said, less kindly, 'the Jane Fonda *and* the Tom Hayden' of Japan. In 1980, at 31, she became the youngest person ever elected to either house of the Diet. She admits that her election victory was probably due to her celebrity. At age nine, she launched a stage career as a singing actress; by the time she was twelve, she was one of Japan's brightest stars. In her teens she turned to TV roles; at the age of twenty Nakayama was already a TV news anchorwoman. In her late twenties she became the hostess of a popular TV talkshow. Throughout her entertainment career she acquired a reputation for publicly expressing her unorthodox views on many subjects.

Women like Nakayama are rare in Japan, as are politically active women. In the House of Representatives, there are only nine women out of 522 members, or 1.76 percent of the body. In the upper house, the House of Councillors, which has more influence than power in the Japanese political structure, there are 18 women out of 252 members, or 7.14 percent. Together, women represent 3.5 percent of the parliament. After visiting the U.S. Senate in 1981, Nakayama told a Japanese reporter that she greatly admired the genuine floor debate that takes place there, revealing that in the Diet real decisions are made by a handful of male powerbrokers operating behind closed doors.

Her office is in a modern building across the street from

the Diet's unique obelisk-topped-by-a-ziggurat, and a few yards from Kokkai Gijidomai subway station, a name that aptly translates to 'Place where Japan's representative leaders gather to debate national problems,' in central Tokyo. Access to the severe office structure is restricted to those with appointments by armed, uniformed guards. Her office, two tiny rooms off a sterile corridor on the third floor, consists of an outer reception area with space for scarcely more than two chairs facing a receptionist's desk and her 'private' office, which she shares with her other staff member.

At Nissan headquarters spokesman Shigeru Sawada had told me that no women in the Nissan 'family' work on the assembly line 'because women are not strong enough.' I pointed out that women were working in an upholstery plant. They did the same job as the men they worked with, but they were not paid nearly as much. Why was that? 'Women don't require such big wages,' Sawada answered without a trace of irony.

I asked Japan's most famous woman politician about the Nissan attitude. 'It's very queer,' said Councillor Nakayama, who is now 35 and still the youngest member of the Diet. 'Legally, it is not allowed to pay men and women working under the same conditions differently. However, the management always finds some reason to slow down the promotion of women. It is a widespread practice in industry to keep women's wages low by coming up with various reasons. Therefore while a woman might have been working for the same length of time as a man, she will get paid less.' Nakayama is hopeful that some changes may occur in Japan because her nation is participating in the United Nations Decade for Women.

Do most Japanese women accept flagrant discrimination? 'Those who think their present job is a lifetime profession do object, quite strongly,' Nakayama explained. 'But the majority of women in Japan think of work as a temporary situation, until they get married, then, after their children have grown up and they don't have to stay at home all the time, they can return to work, part time. So, although the people who do protest are serious about their protests, and they're getting some help from women's organizations, the general fact is that these movements don't have any power to change anything.'

Japanese male workers are often exploited, but many women in the workplace suffer even greater indignities. As recently as 1981, the public policy of Sohyo, the Japanese union council, toward women read like the Japanese version of the Dred Scott Decision: 'Women are entitled neither to lifetime employment, nor to seniority wage rates, and are customarily considered to have resigned the day they marry.'

The Ministry of Labor's own statistics on women reveal a grim picture of wholesale discrimination. According to their *White Paper on Women Workers*, the percentage of women in the work force rose to 34.5 percent in 1981, the latest year for which full statistics are available, up from 34.1 percent in 1980. At the same time, women's wages *dropped* for the third straight year, to 53.3 percent of men's wages. The average man in Japan earned $1,430 per month, the average woman $760. In the manufacturing area, the disparity in wages between men and women was the largest measured among 19 nations surveyed by the International Labor Organization.

I asked Nakayama if there were any women involved in the labor movement who could fight this inequity. 'Very few, perhaps ten or 15 in the country, have any kind of position of authority in labor unions,' she said. 'The big unions tightly control who is allowed to run for office, who will be elected, and so forth. It's all agreed beforehand. In unions in private firms, I've asked several times why there are so few women in positions of authority. They told me, "We have to have our meetings and do all our organizing in the evening, after we've finished work for the day. Generally, the great majority of women would prefer to go home and do their housework or shopping, or just enjoy themselves." I asked a lot of women if this was true, and I got the same answer. There were only a few women really interested. In Japan, it's rather uncomfortable for a small number of women to join a large group of men to discuss things. The women are made to feel intimidated.

'Men don't consider women as partners, as complete equals in a discussion,' Nakayama continued. 'Therefore women tend to try not to offend male members of those groups. And women on the whole are not very good in those kinds of groups – they don't do it often enough. They find they can't speak up so much. They find it makes them uneasy.' Nakayama candidly says that she has found it hard to be effective in the Diet. 'Because I am a young woman among older men it's even worse. And since I'm the youngest member, it sometimes makes it terribly difficult even to deal with older women in the Diet.'

Discrimination against women extends to every corner of the Japanese society, especially in the workplace. A scan of employment ads in newspapers reveals that for white collar and for public-contact jobs, including many that have little public visibility, Japanese employers demand that female job applicants submit photographs of themselves along with their resumes. 'This is very embarrassing, and violates our privacy,' said Tomoko Yamamoto, an attractive, fashionably dressed Tokyo secretary who works in an office with some 30 men and women. 'This seems to me very old-fashioned, but still most employers require it. *Men* are not hired on the basis of their photographs, but on their qualifications for the job. It makes me angry, but I cannot say anything, because every place you go, it is the same.'

In 1983 the written guidelines for hiring female part-time employees for Kinokuniya, one of Tokyo's largest bookstore chains, fell into the hands of the press, which published them. They read: 'Don't hire divorced women, women who live alone in apartments, wives of writers or teachers, or women who wear glasses. At all costs, avoid hiring ugly women.'

Japanese employers find most of their part-time workers among females, who then face double discrimination – as women and as less-than-permanent employees. At many manufacturing facilities, special shifts have been set up for such women. In 1982, I visited a plant in Nagano where Liquid Crystal Displays, LCDs, are made. These are the electronic signboards found in calculators, watches, and clocks, photographic meters, hand-held electronic games, test instruments and, quite recently, in tiny TV sets. The workers were all women, most in their late thirties or older, while the supervisors were men. The work they do requires skill and concentration. They are dealing with very thin sheets of glass upon which a matrix of tiny dots is laid down, either by a method similar to silk screening or by a photographic process similar to offset printing.

About 2:45 in the afternoon the women started to clean up their individual work areas. At a few minutes before three, the airlock doors to this high-tech area opened, and in poured hundreds of men, the second shift. They took the places of the women, who quickly left. I wondered aloud to a supervisor why their shift was over now while the rest of the plant changed at 5:00 P.M.

'Their children will be coming home from school about five, so the women must go home to their families,' a supervisor told me. 'They must do their shopping, then they must make a meal for their husbands.' In the morning, he explained, the women had to make breakfast for their families and see their children off to school. 'So they can't work before nine; therefore we make special arrangements for their working.'

A quality control inspector told me that fewer of the LCDs turned out by the women's shift at this plant were rejected than those made by men. But later I learned that the women were paid only about a third of the hourly wages paid to the men; and when demand slackened women were the first to be laid off. According to the Ministry of Labor, women working part-time, 35 hours a week or less, made up some 20 percent of the total Japanese work force in 1981. Their wages averaged only three-fourths of those paid to full-time female employees, or 40 percent of the average male wage. At the bottom of the wage scale are women working in their homes, the cottage industry work force. There are 1.4 million 'cottage workers,' 92 percent of whom are women, and who average only $1.30 an hour.

Analysts at the U.S. embassy in Tokyo attribute this wage gap to several factors. One American spokesman says that in addition to the layers of prejudice about female workers, the male seniority on the job increases the disparity in pay. 'The male-female wage gap has also been attributed to the fact that, as men work longer at the same job, they gain the higher pay derived from seniority,' he says. He adds, however, that the situation is changing. This factor has declined in importance as more women remain in their jobs after marriage and return to them after brief maternity leaves. As in America and Europe, women in Japan are staying on the job longer. The Ministry of Labor reports that only about 21.7 percent of pregnant workers 'resigned' in 1981, while half did so in 1965.

The low status of women in Japan is rooted in the country's recent feudal past. Women in today's work force are not protected or sheltered from hard work; on the contrary, they are expected to do a full day's work *and* go home and serve their families. While the European tradition of feudalism relegated women to inferior roles, the clear distinction in status between men and women was softened by notions of romance, which at their best sought to provide women with more comfortable lives. But there has never been a cult of chivalry in Japan. Japanese women have always been expected to be as tough as Japanese men, but without the compensation of rights, privileges, or power.

The inferior status of Japanese women was demonstrated in a thousand small ways, explains Susan J. Pharr, a University of California Japan scholar. 'Women showed deference to men of their own as well as higher classes through the use of polite language and honorific forms of address, through bowing more deeply than they, walking behind their husbands in public, and in numerous other ways deferring to men.' She adds: 'A new bride coming into the house was expected to acknowledge her inferior status in a number of ritualized ways: getting up first in the morning and going to bed last at night, taking her bath only after all other family members had bathed, eating after other family members and taking the least choice servings of food.'

Supported both by custom and by law until Japan's defeat in World War II, women were totally subject to the authority of their husbands. The head of the household was almost always a man, and a woman could act in no legal matter without his permission. Until she married, the head of the household was either a woman's father, or, if he were dead, an uncle, a grandfather, or her oldest brother. After marriage, if her husband died, the oldest son became legal head of the household when he was of age. Civil law favored husbands over wives. While a judge might award some share of property to a woman after divorce, there was never a question of alimony. If the man wanted custody of the children, it was usually granted by the courts. It is small wonder that despite the reforms of the MacArthur reign, women today are often still treated as third-class citizens.

The progress of women in Japan since the end of the feudal period has been slow. While Japanese women undoubtedly enjoy more rights and privileges now than ever before, conditions are still more as they were in feudal times than in any other industrialized nation. A wife's first duty is still to please her husband. She must rise early, make a meal for her family, get children off to school and husband to work, and be home for both with a meal at day's end. If she has a job, even a full-time job, her homemaking responsibilities remain her first priority.

For most Japanese women, the days revolve around their children's education and their husband's comfort. 'Her job is to maintain *wa* or peaceful harmony in the house,' says Keiko Kadota, 29, traffic manager for Nippo Marketing and Advertising, who has lived in Los Angeles for six years. 'And as far as her husband's social life, the housewife doesn't have any part of it.'

The story of Kadota's own mother illustrates much about the Japanese male-female relationship. 'My father is an electrical engineer and he has his own small company in Tokyo; my mother was the bookkeeper. My father's mother, my grandmother, raised me. There were three generations living in one house,' explains Keiko. 'My grandmother did everything around the house. At that time I really felt my father wasn't treating my mother right. He gave her no respect whatsoever.' Keiko adds that this is not unusual for men of her father's generation.

'He worked very hard on his business, so he wasn't home most of the time, which is very very typical of the Japanese businessman's behavior,' Keiko continues. 'I didn't see him much, and when he came back he was always drunk, from entertaining. My mom had to wake up at two o'clock in the morning and serve him tea and sake, and so forth. She must have suffered from such a hard time. She had a couple of nervous breakdowns. She complained to me a lot but never to him. But somehow, after my grandmother passed away, my parents' relationship became much better. It's now a perfect relationship. As long as my father's mother was in charge of the house, my mother was kind of secondary.'

This is a classic example of the Japanese marriage as it has come down from feudal times. Even under the reformations provided by the nineteenth-century Meiji Constitution, which governed postfeudal Japan until 1945, a husband could divorce his wife if she did not show proper respect and deference to *his* parents. But if these same people abused her, even physically, which was often the case, it was no grounds for granting *her* a divorce.

The male-female role in Japan continues to conform to tradition in most areas of contemporary life. Like men in all previous generations, Japanese husbands today take almost no part in maintaining their household; the average time a Japanese husband performs household chores, according to government official calculations, is less than two minutes a week. 'My husband doesn't do housework a bit,' said Kadota, who is married to an account executive with a film production company. 'The house is all *my* responsibility.'

The low status of Japanese women is demonstrated in their sex lives, where the old double standard still reigns. Elaborate systems have been established to satisfy the needs of men, while women are considered to be sexually indifferent. Japanese executives are granted expense-account-paid visits to gaudy 'love hotels,' some constructed to look like Arabian palaces or landlocked ocean liners, many with rooms equipped with mirrored ceilings and rotating elevator beds. Since prostitution officially became a crime in 1958, the love hotels are expensive places, available only to those who can afford them. Authorities look the other way and satisfy public opinion by periodically arresting Koreans or Chinese who run brothels for the masses, usually in sleazy hotels or massage parlors.

Each year a million Japanese men leave home temporarily to seek pleasure on expensive sex tours to Bangkok, Seoul, Manila, or Taiwan. They stay at Japanese-only bars and brothels, spending upwards of $200 a day in sexual escape. Other Japanese men sign up with such enterprises as *The Mistress Bank*, which, for a fee of about $800, provide an introduction to a prospective mistress. These are young women, typically university coeds, shopgirls, or office workers, who negotiate the terms and conditions of their relationships on their own. The women pay about $200 to be listed at the establishment. While the mistresses profess to feel no shame about their professional sex services, they usually do not tell their families, boyfriends, or employers. To do so would probably end all prospects for a decent marriage later on.

Japanese wives prefer not to know about their husband's sex lives and take the requisite steps to ensure their ignorance. A Japanese wife will never question her husband about where he has spent the evening – or the whole night. Since she is expected to remain loyally at home waiting for his return, she rarely has an opportunity to 'accidentally' find him with another woman.

Before marriage, the same double standard prevails, although there has been some change in attitude toward a woman's having premarital (but not *extra*marital) sex. 'I think this is changing very rapidly in Japan,' ventured Kadota. 'I am not your average Japanese woman, but I think men are starting to accept it if a woman has had sex before marriage.' But she admits that the older generation has not made that adjustment in attitude. 'A few years ago, when I was in college, the younger generation didn't condemn a woman for having sex before she got married.

But for the families – as long as they didn't find out, everything was okay.'

According to one study, some 12 percent of young Japanese are sexually active, while most of the remainder are not. One of the problems for an unmarried woman wishing to have sex is *where* to have it. Most live with their parents until marriage, or in school, or in company dormitories or company-owned apartments where their comings and goings are closely observed by neighbors, all of whom work for the same firm. Most unmarried men also live in dormitories or company-owned apartments, or with parents or siblings.

While men can go to 'love hotels,' the only way a Japanese woman can regularly have sex outside of marriage is to find an apartment of her own, a move which her family and many friends might regard with suspicion. It is also made difficult by a severe housing shortage, especially in the urban areas where most Japanese live. The result is that while men can enjoy sex in or out of marriage without difficulty, women are given little opportunity.

Japanese men prefer women who are not assertive, who defer to them in all things. About half of all Japanese marriages are still arranged by matchmakers called *nakodo*. Before computers, a *nakodo* was generally an old woman who knew most of the children in a village or a community. Today, the *nakodo* has been partially replaced by some 500 computer-assisted matchmaking services in Japan. Large firms such as Mitsubishi frequently have them for their own employees.

The qualities men seek in marriageable women still center on their being good mothers and housekeepers. A 1981 survey of 265 engaged couples showed that the five most commonly expressed requirements for a 'good wife' were that she

(1) do housework properly
(2) be kind and considerate
(3) stay healthy and pretty
(4) get up earlier than I do
(5) let me rule my home.

After a child is born, sex in most Japanese marriages is deemphasized. Many Japanese men seem unable to express romantic feelings toward their wives, and their wives, for the most part, are resigned to it. According to Reischauer, 'In Western eyes, husbands frequently treat their wives coldly and with disdain.' This behavior, however, is mostly for public consumption. The usual relationship is that of *amae*, or warm dependency. 'For example, a husband may act in a childish way as a sign that he wishes his wife's indulgence,' says Barbara Gewirtz, director of the Tokyo Community Counseling Service, which assists troubled marriages between Japanese and foreigners.

But *amae* discourages most notions of sexual equality. In any case, most Japanese men are unconcerned about their wives' sexual satisfaction. Sara Siegler, a young American woman who lived and studied in Japan, reports several conversations with Japanese women that show an extraordinary ignorance about the possibility of a satisfactory sex life for a woman. 'They didn't know it was possible to like sex,' Siegler says. 'They had read or heard about American women's sexual experiences, and they were amazed that women liked it. That's not to say the Japanese women didn't like sex, but what they were amazed at was that it could take place for longer than three minutes. They were also amazed that there could be any aspect of romance and seduction, and that a woman could behave in other than a passive way.'

Women in Japan do have one important right, that of abortion, even if they must falsely plead that it is being done for 'economic reasons.' The law has been in effect for some time, but Japan's leading party, the Liberal Democratic party, was joined by more conservative groups in a 1982 attempt to repeal Article 14 of the Eugenics Law, which first made abortions legal. The official position was stated by the Minister of Health and Welfare, Motoharu Morishita: 'Now that Japan's GNP has reached that of a prosperous nation, there is no need to allow abortions for economic reasons.'

Women's groups in Japan were responsible for defeating

the proposed abortion repeal in 1982. Although, as Chinatsu Nakayama explains, it is rare for the women in Parliament to vote together, they joined forces on this one issue. 'The men tried to change the law to make abortions more difficult, or even to ban them,' Nakayama recounts. 'Even though the male members of the LDP brought it up, all the women – including members of the LDP – went against it and crushed it.'

As in the West, virtually any Japanese woman can get an abortion on demand, but, surprisingly, abortions have been decreasing each year since the late 1970s. There were 600,000 in 1981, a low point since the present law has been in effect. At the same time, however, the number of abortions by teenagers has risen to some 20,000 – only a fraction of the Western statistics, but still a significant factor for traditionally conservative Japan.

The male arbiters of Japanese-style democracy have had less difficulty in excluding women from virtually all influence in major government decisions. Since government and business are so intimately linked in Japan – where it is often difficult to distinguish one from the other – female workers have nowhere to turn when they seek redress. Women were totally disenfranchised until the occupation, when the MacArthur Constitution guaranteed them the right to vote. Since then, the percentage of women voting in all elections has consistently been higher than that of men. This may be traced to the extensive, multimedia campaign launched by the occupation authorities in 1946, which sought to persuade women to exercise their new rights by equating voting with a patriotic act. Despite their impressive voting record, and the fact that women of voting age outnumber men of voting age, their success in winning office is appallingly low, and retrogressing. While 8.4 percent of the seats in the 1946 House of Representatives went to women, the current percentage is only 1.7 percent.

These percentages are roughly comparable with national legislative bodies in the U.S. and Western Europe, but for women in the West the traditional path to national elective office has been through local and regional office. In Japan, less than 1 percent of these elective posts are filled by women, while more than 6 percent are held by women in the U.S.

This same male dominance operates in appointive office. In Japan, a nation run more by appointed bureaucrats than by elected officials, the 'Old Boys' are not about to relinquish power to an underclass. As late as 1983, female government employees in Nara were required to report to work 30 minutes early every day so they could prepare tea or coffee. They received no pay for the ten or 12 extra hours a month this required. According to a 1982 survey by the Japan National Personnel Authority, only 34 women, or 4.6 percent of the total, occupied senior government posts.

'After this survey was conducted the Finance Ministry for the first time appointed a woman as director of one of the nation's 509 district tax offices, a post considered as an essential stepping stone to senior positions in the single most powerful ministry,' states a U.S. embassy document. 'However, the female official involved is not herself one of the "elite" of the ministry. She did not enter by means of the most competitive exam, and she is near retirement, rather than at middle level.'

The woman involved was in fact 55 years old, and will be forced to retire at 58. In other words, the appointment was either a reward for years of service, or one used to placate the impotent women's groups that have been hounding the bureaucracy for reform. A 1983 Japanese government report admits that 'the number of women holding the post of section head and above still accounts for only 0.5 percent of the total.'

More Japanese women are graduating from college than before, but the record still does not compare with the West. A recent study showed that while almost 40 percent of the men had completed a four-year college course, only 10 percent of the women had full college degrees. Once women graduate, finding work commensurate with their training is even more difficult. More than 80 percent of all

Japanese firms in 1982 said they had no plans to hire even one female college graduate. Collectively, the 1,734 companies listed on the Tokyo Stock Exchange hired only 4,100 women college graduates, less than three each and a decline of 4.5 percent from 1981.

Japanese firms are allowed to administer a battery of tests to prospective employees, and while men are sometimes excused from this trial, women are not. Those who do get hired, reports *Asahi*, do not make it solely because of good grades on company exams. The women taken on by top firms are those with either family connections in the company or with influential patrons. 'Female graduates without "pull" are not hired no matter how well they do in the examination and interview,' said Keiki Fukuzawa, editor of a job-hunter's handbook for college women.

One recent graduate with a degree in political science was offered a sales job by a large real-estate company in Tokyo. In addition to her other duties, she was made to understand that she would have to prepare tea and 'help make life pleasant for male coworkers.' When she complained about this to the recruiter, she was told the company was 'a favorable place to find a husband.' Twenty-three-year-old Eiri Bessho turned the job down. 'They didn't care that I would be an able saleswoman,' she said. 'They just wanted intelligent, well-educated women to marry company men.'

Some Japanese observers believe higher education actually hurts the chances of some women. 'While women have more opportunities for a university education today, in some ways this hurts their job opportunities far more than it helps,' says Takako Doi, a member of the House of Representatives. 'If you're a university graduate, no one will hire you for the sort of jobs that high school graduates take. And if you're a woman with a university degree, most of the bigger companies won't hire you for junior management jobs, because they don't like to have a woman with authority over men. They also think that after three or four years, a woman will get married and then quit, and they'll have put a lot of time into training her for nothing. It's really much easier for a woman to find a job if she *doesn't* have a university degree.'

Despite formidable odds, a very few managerial jobs have opened for Japanese women in the last few years, though rarely in manufacturing or in those industries where the lower ranks are staffed by men. There were 182,300 Japanese women in jobs classed as managerial in 1980, the Ministry of Labor reported, or about 6.7 percent of the total. But these women teeter on the edge of daily failure in a society where working for a woman is somehow a slur on a man's masculinity. 'My male subordinates are afraid people will say, "This guy worked for a woman, so that's proof that he's incompetent," ' said Kisako Kimura, a computer sales company manager.

Discrimination in female employment even extends to the hours she is permitted to work. Rigorously enforced regulations prohibit women from being hired for jobs which require them to be on the job between 10:00 P.M. and 5:00 A.M. There are a few exceptions: telephone operators, nurses, those working in agriculture or fishing, and actresses. But female astronomers cannot take observations late at night. Taxi drivers, night shift workers, reporters for morning daily newspapers, airline ground workers are all male by law. A woman in Saitama Prefecture made the news in July 1983 when she tried to take the more lucrative graveyard shift as a taxi driver. She has two children and a disabled husband to support, but the Labor Standards Inspection Office forced her to quit. The official explanation is that allowing women to work at night is detrimental 'to the protection of motherhood.'

The unmarried woman is the least protected person in Japanese society, which practices selective discrimination against them, particularly as they get older. There are three million unmarried women near or at retirement age in Japan. About 600,000 of these were never married, mostly because of the 3.1 million men who died fighting Japan's Great Pacific War between 1937 and 1945. The unmarried women support themselves, working for discriminatory wages in a variety of professions, but in many companies they are forced into retirement at 50 to make room for the next generation, while men are allowed to stay until 55.

Even in housing the single woman is penalized. Japanese housing, which is abysmal by Western standards, is governed by several statutes, one of which was amended in 1980 to allow women over 50 to live alone in the smallest apartments. But a nationwide survey by *Asahi Shimbun* revealed that most officials automatically shunted applications from older women for such units to the least desirable available. 'In our society, women are often treated as half-persons,' commented Shoji Yabushita, an *Asahi* staffer.

In 1608 the master carpenter Gembei completed eight years of work on Japan's most striking structure, the masterpiece called White Heron Castle, in Himeji. According to legend, Gembei's wife took the occasion to point out that the castle's *donjon* – fortified central tower – sloped unmistakably to the southeast. Gembei, inconsolably distraught that a mere woman had pointed out his mistake, climbed to the roof and leaped to his death.

This tale strikes at the real problem for women in Japan, one highlighted by a survey taken in 1982. Tokyo's *Sankei Shimbun* asked prominent Japanese: 'What would happen if women were to hold 50 percent of executive positions?' The answer from Bunpei Ohtsuki, president of the Japanese Federation of Employer's Associations summed up the national attitude: 'That would deprive men of work and cause social unrest. By nature, women are better suited for raising children and domestic responsibilities.'

The Japanese self-image is one of an extraordinarily homogeneous nation, a huge, extended clan, where if roots are traced back far enough, everyone will be related to everyone else. The Japanese have difficulty comprehending a group of people with disparate ethnicity that calls itself a nation, and take pride and great comfort in the racist notion that theirs is a 'pure' people, totally unlike the ethnically mixed West. 'The Japanese are a people that can manufacture a product of uniformity and superior quality because the Japanese are a race of completely pure blood, not a mongrelized race as in the United States,' Toshio Soejima of Nippon Telegraph & Telephone (NTT) told an American reporter.

The Japanese have a sense of racial superiority that leads them to regard the relatively small number of non-Japanese living in their midst as inferior people, outsiders allowed to live in Japan only on sufferance. 'We have not shed the mentality of a nation that was isolated from the world for centuries,' said Kaname Saruya, professor of international relations at Tokyo Women's Christian College. 'Insularity is so deeply ingrained in us that we do not realize it, and it makes us discriminate on the basis of skin color, nationality, religion, and political beliefs. This prejudice is manifested not only in Japan's foreign policy, but in domestic affairs as well.'

This attitude affects Westerners who live and work in Japan, but for public relations reasons, Japanese are careful to display their disaffection with Americans and Europeans only in the privacy of their homes and clubs. But no such politeness is extended to Japan's largest group of 'foreigners,' the Koreans.

In 1905 Japan humbled Russia in naval and land battles, and with the assistance of U.S. President Theodore Roosevelt won territorial concessions solemnized by the Treaty of Portsmouth. Japan took the southern half of Sakhalin Island and the Manchurian railroads, and was allowed to place a strong military force in Korea. A folk proverb has it that 'Korea is a dagger pointed at the heart of Japan.' On the other hand, each of Japan's repeated invasions of China has been launched through Korea. An ancient Korean proverb states that 'Korea is as China's courtyard.'

In 1910 Japan annexed Korea, ending the 519-year reign of the 27 kings of the Yi dynasty. To integrate the peninsula kingdom into its 'Greater East Asia Co-Prosperity Sphere' Japan forcibly uprooted most of Korea's mandarin class and resettled them in Japan. The Korean royal pretender, whose parents, many Koreans believe, were murdered by the Japanese, was married off to a high-spirited Japanese princess once rejected by Emperor Hirohito. Later, as Japan's armies spread throughout the Pacific during World War II, Japan experienced a severe shortage of industrial manpower at home. More Koreans were brought to Japan to work in munitions factories.

When World War II ended, most of these Koreans, their descendants, and others who had been conscripted into the Japanese Army, remained in Japan. Since most now had families living in Japan, they had no strong incentives to leave; the Soviet occupation of the northern half of Korea provided an additional reason to remain. The result is that there are now 664,000 Koreans living in Japan, most descended from people forcibly brought there. But under exclusionary Japanese law, neither they nor their children – even though born in Japan – will ever be Japanese citizens, unless they intermarry with Japanese. Until 1984, only the children of Japanese fathers could qualify for Japanese citizenship; after 1984, children of Japanese mothers will also qualify. But most Japanese, following the racist traditions of their country, despise the Koreans in their midst, and the number of intermarriages is small.

The Japanese industrial empire demonstrates widespread discrimination against Koreans. They are all but totally denied employment by the biggest companies and offered the least attractive jobs elsewhere. To avoid discrimination, many Japanese-born Koreans have attempted to change their names to one of the more common Japanese family names, such as Suzuki or Nakamura, or take the Japanese translation of the Chinese-style *kanji* characters for their names in place of the Korean. 'This doesn't usually work for them,' explained Hiroko Horisaka, who has a far less insular view of Japanese culture than most of her countrymen. 'Japanese names have two characters each for the given name and for the family name, while the Koreans use three Chinese characters.'

The escape route for Koreans is to pass as Japanese, an idea that offends many Japanese. Years ago I dined with Michi Nakamura, who was the secretary for the public affairs office of the American military command headquartered in Tokyo. In a taxi en route to a restaurant, it occurred to me that I didn't know her last name even though we had often met before, and I asked her, in English. 'Nakamura,' she answered. When the taxi driver glanced into the rear-view mirror at hearing this, she hastened to explain. 'But my family is *real* Nakamura. We've always been Nakamura.' She repeated this in Japanese, for the benefit of the taxi driver.

I asked why she felt compelled to make this point. 'There are many Koreans living in Japan who don't want to be known as Koreans,' she told me. 'They try to pass as Japanese, but their names give them away. So they will often take a very common Japanese name, and use it. A lot of them choose Nakamura. But *I* am a Japanese, and our family has always been Nakamura.'

A dozen years later, on a flight to Tokyo, my seatmate was a charming young Korean woman, the daughter of a Protestant minister. She was living in the San Fernando Valley and had started college at California State University. She was on a summer vacation trip to Japan, where she had spent most of her life, and to Korea, where she was born. She told me of her plans to spend time with her relatives in Osaka and with her friends in Tokyo. After we chatted a bit, she invited me to call her in Tokyo, at a friend's house, or in Osaka, at an aunt's house. Then she wrote the numbers down and scribbled a name by each, both in Hangul, the language of Korea. The names were different. The Osaka name was obviously a Korean name, the one with which she had introduced herself. The other was a Japanese name.

'In Osaka, everyone I know is family, or is Korean, and so I use my Korean identity there,' she confessed. 'But in Tokyo, I am Japanese. My friends are Japanese, even if some of them know I am a Korean. Their parents wouldn't allow them to become friendly with me if they knew I was Korean, so I am Japanese in Tokyo, and a Korean in Osaka, and it's okay.'

She told me that many Koreans, especially young

women, try to pass as Japanese, because it is the only way to meet the better class of Japanese men. 'Someone from a working-class family would never marry a Korean, he's got too many problems already, and his family wouldn't allow it. But someone from a wealthy family won't have to worry about his job. His family will take care of that for him, and as long as it's all kept in the family, it isn't such a problem. They can say that the woman's parents died, or they live abroad, so they can't make the wedding. That way her children will become Japanese, since their father is.'

Some Koreans can physically pass as Japanese but Japanese and Koreans can usually tell each other apart, which makes it difficult for most Koreans to share in the pursuit of Japanese-style happiness. The case of one young Korean man has been heavily publicized in the Japanese newspapers. 'He passed all the written examinations to be employed at a major electronics firm,' Hiroko recalls. 'After three months, the probationary period, they fired him for no reason except that he was Korean. They wouldn't say so publicly, but they were afraid if one Korean worked there, others would want to. Japanese workers would make a big fuss about how foreigners were taking their jobs. I am deeply ashamed for my country.'

A bookkeeper for a small Tokyo company detailed another example of the prejudice Koreans encounter in their search for employment. 'One of my friends from school, Miss Kim, didn't try to conceal her Korean identity and was never able to find a good job, even though she had the same education as me,' says Kayoko Kudo. 'Finally, she moved to Korea, where she has relatives, because she couldn't earn a living here.' Another Japanese woman told me about her neighbor, a Korean born in Manchuria and conscripted at age 18 into the Japanese Army. 'After the war, he couldn't return to Manchuria – the Communists would have shot him. So he stayed here. His wife is Japanese, he no longer remembers how to speak much Korean, but his three kids are never going to be Japanese citizens. It's very unfair.'

'Although the Japanese are a mixed race – if you go

back 20 centuries or so – the government tries to keep out anyone not of the Japanese race,' says Diet member Chinatsu Nakayama. 'This is a racist policy, a "pure race" policy. Koreans and minorities in general don't have the rights one supposes they should have by living in this country, but they have all the obligations. For example, all foreign residents must at all times carry the alien registration card, even to the bath house. They must submit their fingerprints, which is the same as for criminals. One person refused and he was arrested and put in jail for several days. They are often victims of atrocities by the police. Because of this, they are very weak and don't have the vitality to organize an effective protest. I think the Japanese need to have a general understanding of the whole unfortunate Korean situation. As it is, relatively few people really know how bad their situation is. If more people did, perhaps they could force the government to do something.'

Under Japanese law, Koreans are officially divided into two groups: those who came to Japan before World War II, which is by far the largest group, and those who came afterward. Japan initially granted citizenship to the prewar arrivals but withdrew it after signing the 1952 Treaty of San Francisco in which they renounced all right to Korea. About half the Koreans who came before the war were granted permanent resident status by a treaty between South Korea and Japan, but many of those with ancestral homes in the north – perhaps then hopeful that there might one day be a reconciliation between the two Koreas – refused South Korean citizenship and were permitted to remain as 'stateless persons.'

These stateless Koreans are further divided into three sub-categories. Those who arrived before the San Francisco Treaty are 'first-class' Koreans, and must carry an alien identification card at all times. The card must be renewed at three-year intervals. The children of these people are 'second-class' Koreans, even though they have been born in Japan. When they go to renew their alien cards, they undergo rigid screening to see if they have sufficient reason to stay in Japan, even though they have no other homeland. The bureaucrats of the Foreign Ministry are the sole arbiters of who is permitted to stay. Anyone who arrived after 1952 is a 'third-class' Korean and has to get his card renewed every year.

In all cases stateless Koreans may take only two trips abroad during their lifetime if they wish to remain Japanese residents. They are permitted one when they marry, a 'honeymoon' trip, and the other when they reach 60. 'It's simply not good enough to allow us to stay unless we are assured of equal opportunities and treatment by the society at large,' said Han Il-Shin, a member of Mindan, a pro-South Korean organization. In January 1982, Japan lifted some of the legal restrictions on Koreans, but continued to insist on taking fingerprints of all Koreans applying for passports, including those born in Japan. Fingerprints for Japanese are not required.

'This change of heart for legislators did not come as voluntary action that sprang out of the goodness of their souls,' says Yoshiko Sakurai, a Japanese reporter. 'It was an offshoot of the Indochinese refugee problem. The argument was that if Japan could demonstrate the human compassion shown to the refugees, there was no reason to deny the same to the Koreans in their midst.'

Japan is a signatory to the United Nations Convention on the Status of Refugees. Under this agreement, Indochinese refugees living in Japan have the same legal rights as its own nationals. Japan, a nation of 119 million, demonstrated its lack of concern by absorbing only 2,152 Indochinese refugees and limiting the total of future arrivals to 3,000. Of the 2,100, 742 were already in Japan studying in various technical schools. To put this in context, Canada, with a population of 25 million, and France, with a population of 54 million, each accepted 80,000 Indochinese; Australia, with a population of 15 million accepted 60,000, and the U.S., population 232 million, took in 640,000.

'To my regret, almost no big companies have offered job opportunities to refugees,' said Yukio Imagawa, then director of the Foreign Ministry's Refugee Affairs Division. Comments Kenji Suzuki, a *Mainichi Shimbun* editorial writer: 'Large corporations look the other way, and the established religious sects sidestep the issue, refusing to lend a hand. Members of the Diet are indifferent to refugees, because they have no vote.'

The Koreans are a visible problem, but the largest minority group in Japan is not only the victim of the most onerous discrimination it is also the least discussed in 'polite' Japanese society. These are an estimated three million *eta*, an underclass of the same race as other Japanese, who have been condemned to the most outrageous discrimination for at least 400 years. The *eta* are the untouchables of Japan. They are sometimes known by the euphemism *burakumin* – literally, hamlet dwellers – a reference to the appallingly poor ghettos they were once forced to live in and where most even now continue to dwell.

Under the Tokugawa shogunate which began 259 years before the coming of Commodore Perry, society was classified in four parts: samurai, peasants, artisans, and merchants. Those belonging to a fifth category, the *eta* and *hinin* outcasts, which numbered about 5 percent of the population, were outside all society. The *eta* were those people engaged in any trade that involved touching dead animals. Before the Meiji Restoration of 1868, Buddha and Shinto doctrines taught that eating meat was barbaric, as was disposing of dead animals or people. The dying were often removed from their homes so others in the household wouldn't have to suffer the indignity of touching them after they were dead.

The irrational curse of *eta* fell not only on those who handled the dead but on those who slaughtered animals, cobblers who made shoes of leather, those who made hides and tallow, even those who made musical instruments – whose strings were made of animal gut. The craftsmen who created weapons for the samurai were also classed as *eta* simply because they used leather to make bowstrings and other weapons.

Over the years the ranks of the outcast were enlarged

to include prostitutes, beggars, circus and carnival people. *Eta* became a hereditary caste system; outcasts who moved to such 'cleaner' occupations as farming, fishing, or weaving still retained their *eta* or *hinin* status. Later the hereditary ranks of the nonhuman were stretched to include criminals and even those who merely violated custom. For example, lovers who survived a double suicide pact were designated as outcasts, as were common criminals who survived jail terms or whose death sentences were commuted. They, as well as their descendants for all time, became *eta*.

Before the Meiji Restoration the outcasts were the subject of the most brutal discrimination. 'They were not treated as human beings, they were not allowed to wear any footwear but had to go about barefoot,' wrote Japanese author Mikiso Hane. Tetsu Tsuchikata, an *eta* himself, described the plight of his ancestors. 'They could use only straw ropes as belts, and only straws to tie their hair. They were forbidden to leave their hamlet from sunset to sunrise. They were not allowed to associate with other people. When it was necessary to see others, for some business reason, they had to get on their hands and knees before they could speak.'

The legal system did little to punish those who harmed the outcasts. An *eta* youth who tried to enter a Shinto Shrine in 1859 was beaten to death by townspeople. When the head of the *eta* community appealed to the local magistrate, he was told 'the life of an *eta* is worth about one-seventh the life of a townsman. Unless seven *eta* have been killed, we cannot punish a single townsman,' Hane reports.

With the installation in 1868 of the boy-emperor Meiji, whose remarkable reign brought Japan into the modern world, Japanese leaders began to have contact with Westerners. The eating of meat was officially endorsed, and Meiji issued a government decree removing all legal restrictions against the *eta*. But while peasants were pleased to see the samurai's special privileges removed and the lands of the *daimyo* distributed to the tenant farmers, they refused to recognize the outcasts as equals.

Many were killed in the 11 anti-*eta* riots which took place in the 1870s, when in Okayama Prefecture villagers burned or destroyed 400 *eta* homes and killed 18 of these people. Later the same year peasants in Fukuoka Prefecture burned or wrecked more than 2,200 *eta* homes. The lands of the outcasts were taken without compensation, and they were forced to become city dwellers. The only housing permitted them was near garbage dumps, crematoriums, slaughter-houses, hospitals for contagious diseases, jails, or human waste disposal sites.

The eta, or *burakumin*, are physically indistinguishable from other Japanese. They are, like all other Japanese, descendants of the Korean and Chinese immigrants who 2,600 years ago left the mainland and mixed with the aboriginal inhabitants of the archipelago, the *Ainu*.

That the supposed sins of the *burakumin* ancestors occurred hundreds of years ago seems not to matter to Japanese today. Unlike the modern Australian, who will boast that his forefathers were sent in chains from England, the Japanese do not forgive these ancient sins, nor do they forgive the descendants of the sinners. The merest hint that someone may be even partly descended from a *burakumin* leads to elaborate attempts to trace his ancestry, to prove he is an outcast – and to cast him out.

The *burakumin* are still very much *hinin* – nonhuman – and therefore virtually untouchables, condemned to live in the meanest circumstances. About 17,000 *eta* reside in 12 of their ancestral *buraku* in and around the ancient capital of Kyoto, the largest concentration of *eta* in Japan. Since their names are nondistinctive, the Japanese go to great lengths to make sure that no *hinin* slip through to enjoy a normal life.

Japan's employers, particularly, take elaborate precautions to keep *eta* out of their work forces. According to Katsuhiko Namoto, executive officer of the Federation to Liberate Burakumin, more than a hundred organizations, including Japan's leading employers – banks, security agencies, life insurance offices, automobile makers, and universities – have purchased all of at least ten books of lists identifying both the hamlet locations and the

names of people with *burakumin* origins. These constitute
a blacklist that allows corporate labor relations staffs to
screen out *buraku* applicants. Namoto says that there is no
legal recourse in Japan to being denied a job because of
your ancestry.

In private life, most families of prospective brides or
grooms will hire a private detective to investigate for any
trace of *burakumin* ancestry. Often, anonymous postcards
are mailed to a family, accusing the intended spouse of
eta ancestry. Since the postcards are read by those who
deliver them, that itself can end the engagement whether
there is a shred of proof or not. According to Namoto, this
type of harassment occurs at the rate of about 50,000 a
year. 'Many of them don't regard us as human beings,'
lamented Shoji Kinoshita, a 22-year-old *burakumin* who
learned that he was somehow different on his first day of
elementary school.

There are always rumors that some prominent Japanese
person is actually an *eta*, and speculation about the presence of *burakumin* blood in certain well-known persons –
especially film and TV personalities – is the subject of
frequent gossip. Despite this, no Japanese would permit
a member of his family to associate with a known *burakumin*. While they were confined to their ancestral
villages, it was relatively easy to determine which people
were *burakumin* by inspection of birth records. Until 1968,
in fact, the birth certificates of those with *burakumin*
fathers were stamped to indicate this ancestry. But today the
burakumin are not confined exclusively to their villages and
live all over Japan. The Japanese seem concerned that
this will make them harder to identify.

Not only are they the subject of intense discrimination
in employment, education, and housing, it is even considered impolite to mention the word *burakumin* or *eta* in
public, except perhaps among very close friends. So complete is this conspiracy of silence that a Japanese acquaintance, a 20-year-old from a prominent banking family who
spent most of his childhood in London, had never heard of
them. Only after he had asked and had been told by his
father about them, did he believe they actually existed.

To avoid saying the unspeakable name of the *eta* aloud, the Japanese use a hand gesture. They drop their hand, and while hiding the thumb splay the four fingers out perpendicular to the ground, as though they were four feet. 'If you do that to a *burakumin*, or to someone you think is one, he'll get very angry,' explained Osamu Sakashita, a Tokyo University student. The four 'legs' refer to their ancient – and modern – professions of animal slaughterers and leather makers.

Some Japanese mothers tell their young children about the *burakumin* in ways calculated to perpetuate the ancient slanders against them. 'When I was a little girl, my mother used to tell me and my sister about them. She would make the "four feet" sign and say, "You cannot marry one of their kind, or *your* children will have four hooves – like a cow, a horse, or a pig,"' says a middle-aged Japanese woman married to an American.

The Japanese conspiracy of silence was made clear to Sara Siegler when she lived in Kyoto, teaching English and studying Japanese. 'I was watching a TV soap opera,' she explains. 'I didn't speak Japanese very well, and I was getting maybe every third word. In the last scene, one of the characters whispered the word *burakumin*, which raised expressions of shock from the other characters. This was followed by a dramatic musical chord, the screen went dark and the episode ended. I had no idea what that word meant, so I wrote it down.' Later Sara spoke to her friend, the woman who had sponsored her visit to Japan. 'I asked her what that word meant, and she got very upset with me. "Don't ever say that word out loud," she said. "With me it's all right, for we are good friends. Other people will not be so understanding. It's a very bad word." I tried to find out a little about these people, but everyone refused to talk about it,' recounts Siegler.

They still refuse to talk about it. Even Chinatsu Nakayama, who is particularly liberal, did a conversational sidestep when I raised the subject. 'These people [she wouldn't use the word] are Japanese, of course, and they are very well organized. But if you want to know about *real* persecution, let's talk about Koreans,' she told me.

The Other Exploited: Women and Minorities

No one wants to talk about the *burakumin*, for to do so would invite the opprobrium of other Japanese. Condemned for the sins of their distant ancestors – sins that today would not be sins, or even misdemeanors – the *burakumin* suffer from the silence of their oppressors.

There has been some government action designed to integrate the *burakumin* into Japanese society. While a few *buraku* have been the beneficiaries of modest public-works projects, like bridges and high-rise apartments, more than a thousand of their hamlets have received no aid at all. Elementary schools in many communities have been integrated, but several school masters and teachers have taken their own lives after being subjected to unmerciful pressure by parents of non-*burakumin* children. After that the integration program was put on hold. Says Namoto of the Burakumin Federation: 'The prevailing tendencies among government officials and bureaucrats is to believe that the *buraku* issue is only the problem of those assigned to solve it, and therefore anybody else may remain uninvolved.'

But the Japanese government has found it convenient to remember the *burakumin* when dealing with foreign economic competition. Intensive discrimination has forced more than 80 percent of the *eta* to remain in their historic professions, as leather workers eking out a marginal living in small tanneries, as shoemakers, and as livestock slaughterers. When American trade officials asked Japan to open its domestic markets to leather imports by reforming Japan's archaic distribution system, the Japanese reply, from Tomio Tsutsumi, a high MITI official, was ironic: 'Dropping quotas on leather imports is regarded as politically impossible because it would hurt the "*burakumin*" outcasts who are the only people in the tanning business.'

11   Farmers, Votes, and Food

SINCE WORLD WAR II, Japan's GNP has grown at an astounding rate, the product of an economy totally committed to exporting high-volume, high-quality products to the rest of the world. The bounty of this export economy has been a phenomenal rise in Japanese per-capita and disposable incomes to a level only a few hundred dollars less than those of Americans. Japan's phoenixlike recovery from its 1945 defeat has been called 'the Japanese Miracle.' But despite this so-called miracle, the average Japanese family, whose regimented toil has produced that astonishing GNP, does not share a standard of living commensurate with their income. The Japanese work very hard but their money does not buy what Westerners would consider a decent lifestyle.

Nowhere is the gap more glaring than in the price of that most basic of human requirements, food. I have spent many hours in small shops and supermarkets in Tokyo and in Nagano Prefecture, watching and learning. Two of the main attractions in the best well-stocked supermarkets are the meat counter and the vegetable bins, where I was struck by the amount of time Japanese housewives put into shopping for their food. I have seen the same scene recur many times, with only minor variations. A shopper looks at every banana in a pile of several hundred, and eventually selects just two or three, a process that can take up to half an hour. At the meat counter, housewives queue up for their purchases, waiting ten to 15 minutes for their turns, then usually buy only 500 grams, a little over a pound of beef, and perhaps that much pork or chicken.

The reason for this deliberate approach to shopping is that beef, usually a medium-quality cut such as a rib, butt, or shank, sliced into razor-thin strips, costs upwards of $11 a pound, three to four times what it would cost in a California supermarket. Prime beef cuts, which sell for some $6.50 per pound in the U.S. sell, as we have seen, for as much as $35 a pound in Japan. Imported Central American bananas are priced three times higher than they are in North America. A broiling chicken costs $2.50 a pound, or three times what an American consumer pays for the same chicken. Eggs are $1.40 a dozen, compared to $0.85 in the U.S. Fresh milk is over $1.00 a liter, compared to $0.59 in an average American supermarket.

When a family has to spend 25 percent of its income on food, as do Japanese families, it is clear why a housewife would spend half an hour shopping for something as ordinary as bananas. American households, by contrast, spend only about 13 percent of their incomes on food, an amount that buys an average daily intake of 3,420 calories. The Japanese 25 percent buys only 2,520 calories; Japanese consumers are paying more than twice as much per calorie as their American counterparts, a disparity that is particularly wide in meat consumption. According to the U.S. embassy in Tokyo, the average Japanese annually consumes a total of only 49 pounds of beef, veal, pork, lamb, mutton, and poultry. Americans eat 207 pounds. 'Most families would like to eat more meat,' explains Hiroko Horisaka. 'But meat prices are just too high. So we buy only a little, and we cut it up very small and mix it with our other foods.'

While the Japanese consumer must pay exorbitant prices for domestic beef, the Japanese government has set strict quotas on the import of less expensive foreign meat, a policy that has cost American and European farmers billions in lost income. For years, American officials have asked the Japanese to raise import quotas or to abolish them. In response, the Japanese have increased quotas an average of 20 percent a year between 1978 and 1982, which effectively doubled the amount of beef imported. The Japanese point to this measure as proof of their credentials as free traders, but in 1982 the total value of American beef and veal imports to Japan totaled only

$238 million dollars, less than 11 percent of Japanese consumption. In the same, period, Japan's trade surplus with the U.S. came to more than $21 billion.

The average Japanese seems unaware of this imbalance, partially because of a misleading reason. Since McDonald's opened its first franchise hamburger store in the Ginza area of Tokyo in 1971, the chain has grown to 350 stores. 'What do you mean, we don't import enough American beef?' a Japanese economist asked. 'What about all those McDonald's hamburger shops, they're everywhere,' he said.

McDonald's may be an American franchise, but the beef is Japanese. 'McDonald's won't say where they get their beef, but I happen to know that about two-thirds of the McDonald's hamburger comes from Japanese Holstein dairy cattle that have been slaughtered because their milk production was too low,' explains John Child, an agriculture expert with the U.S. Embassy in Tokyo. 'So two-thirds of the hamburger are old milk cows, and the remaining third is the "black steer," Kobe beef. Once in a while they put in some low-cost Australian beef,' Child adds. 'Everything else in the place, from the furniture and the buns and catsup to the printing on the wrapping paper – and the paper itself – is grown or manufactured in Japan. McDonald's gets a franchise fee for every new store, but we're not doing a thing about the trade imbalance by selling McDonald's hamburgers to the Japanese.'

Most of the sacrifices made by the Japanese consumer in paying for high-priced food can be attributed to various policies promulgated by the government of Japan. The Japanese could import food at much lower world market prices. They could buy much of this food from the United States, as a start on restoring balance to bilateral trade. But the Japanese government prefers not to do so, forcing its citizens to pay for their trade surplus through their rice bowls and meat plates. According to the Japanese National Institute for Research Advancement, a leading Japanese think tank, import restrictions for eight major agricultural commodities – including beef, pork, dairy products, wheat, rice, potatoes, and sugar – cost Japan's consumers $16 billion extra at the retail level. Instead, these funds are funneled into Japan's agricultural and food distribution systems in the form of enormous subsidies.

The primary purpose of these subsidies is to maintain the political power base of Japan's postwar rulers, established at the close of the MacArthur occupation. 'Without farm subsidies most Japanese farms would be unprofitable,' says a U.S. Department of Agriculture report. 'Many different types of payments are made from the government to farmers and farm groups in Japan, including production subsidies, rural development assistance, price stabilization payments, and special bonus payments.' In the Japanese fiscal year ending March 31, 1981, $10.6 billion in farm subsidies was paid, equal to 54 percent of Japan's total farm income.

Japan does buy some $6.6 billion worth of agricultural commodities from the U.S., and is in fact our best customer. 'But 85 percent of that figure is for feed grains that Japanese farmers buy for their livestock,' John Child clarifies. 'Only about $1 billion is consumer-ready.' Thus the jobs required to make a raw material into a consumer product are Japanese jobs; the profits from the value added is a Japanese profit. Most of the American feed grains imported into Japan are handled by the giant Japanese trading companies, to their considerable profit. Still more Japanese profit comes from reselling grain bought at low world prices to Japanese millers. In 1981, for example, the Japanese Food Agency, administered by the Ministry of Agriculture, Forestry and Fisheries (MAFF), earned $350 million this way. This money comes out of the Japanese consumer's pocket and goes into Japanese government's coffers, where, in turn, it is used to offset part of the massive subsidies paid to Japan's wheat farmers.

The reason for these massive subsidies is that the Japanese farmer, unlike his industrial cousin, is inefficient. The size of Japan's 4.6 million farms, which average only 2.9 acres each and cultivate only 13.4 million acres of land, does not begin to compare with American agribusiness. The average American farm, of which there are only 2.4 million, is 429 acres, and there are 365 million acres under cultivation. Despite these disparities, the average Japanese farm income in 1982 was $24,800. Highly efficient American farmers earned only $25,583 per family.

The Japanese farmers' survival is ensured by the enormous, consumer-financed subsidies that Japan's government pours into their pockets. Despite official claims to the contrary, Japanese farmers are not poor, nor are they distressed. Protected by tariffs and quotas, they are the recipients of a hidden tax paid by Japanese consumers in the form of high food prices, and by American workers in the form of jobs lost. But the Japanese government's largess to its farmers, in the form of subsidies and protection, is not the result of altruism. It is a major side effect of the unusual political environment of post-MacArthur Japan.

Since the American military forces withdrew in 1952, Japan has been run without challenge or interruption by a partnership of industrialists and the government bureaucracy. Each of the succession of prime ministers and their respective cabinets have been the leaders of the Liberal Democratic party (LDP), which has held a parliamentary majority since it was created from the merger of the Liberal party and the Democratic party in 1955. But in Japan, few things are really as they seem. Peer behind the *shoji*, and the LDP emerges as neither liberal, democratic, nor even a real political party.

The LDP is the agent of business and Japan's government bureaucrats who enforce economic totalitarianism, plus a small but politically potent group, the farmers. 'A wide range of groups stands behind the LDP, including big business, small businessmen, farmers, and implicitly but nonetheless definitely most career civil servants,' said the late Herman Kahn, director of the Hudson Institute. Building the framework of political rule in postwar Japan began in 1945 with the formation of the Japan Liberal Democratic party, 'a conservative party despite its name,'

312

says Yuichi Sato in a Tokyo daily newspaper. The party was built around elements of the Japan Progressive party, another conservative party organized soon after the war's end.

The merger of these two parties occurred in 1955. 'The conservative merger was forced, first and foremost, by the reunification of the Japan Socialist party,' explained Sato. The Japan Socialist party represented the interests of Japan's independent trade unions. 'The second reason prompting the conservative merger was pressure from business. Japanese business, having got back on its feet thanks to windfall profits from the Korean War, was facing the need to reestablish itself on a firm base as American aid began to decrease,' Sato explains.

The platform of the new LDP, which remains unchanged today, included the usual vague references to 'perfecting Japan as a cultural and democratic state' and 'upholding the universal justice of humankind that aspires to peace and freedom.' But its true goals have been economic. As the LDP itself says: 'The party will rectify and regulate international relations in order to achieve Japan's complete sovereign independence. . . . The party will plan and administer a comprehensive economic program.' The goal, as long as thirty-eight years ago, was first to rehabilitate the economy, then transform Japan into the world's leading economic power.

The LDP is not a genuine political party in the Western sense. 'The LDP is less a political party than a loose coalition of mini-parties grouped around individual leaders, who in turn maintain their power through their ability to mobilize political funds and dispense patronage in the form of pork-barrel projects or official posts [such as cabinet portfolios, parliamentary vice ministerships, and party officerships],' stated Kahn. Within the LDP are cliques, or factions, each with broad agreement on goals but with diverging views on ways to achieve them. Control of the LDP has therefore passed back and forth between the leaders of the largest factions, the bureaucrats and the professional politicians.

If the LDP is not truly a party but a coalition of political

313

bosses jockeying for supremacy, neither is it truly democratic. Constitutionally, the Diet makes its own rules of conduct for all of its integral institutions and members. The rules set by the LDP are clearly designed to maintain them in power. In the Diet, for example, the party with the parliamentary majority chairs all committees. Committees normally parallel government ministries, and the vast majority of the bills submitted are developed within the bureaucracies and submitted through their respective ministers, who virtually control the committees since the chairmen are all senior LDP members.

In 1978, the Fukuda Cabinet, for example, boasted it had passed 90 percent of the 82 bills it introduced. But to achieve such a record requires more control than democracy permits. 'In response to opposition delaying tactics, the administration and ruling party resort to railroading,' said Akira Matsui, an editorial writer with the influential *Mainichi Shimbun*, Japan's third largest daily. 'In forcing the passage of a bill in committee, a member of the ruling party moves for immediate termination of deliberations and a vote. In some cases, the Liberal Democrats unilaterally call a plenary session, attend it alone, and pass the bill.'

The mechanism that has kept the LDP in power since 1955 has not been public approval but the prop of apportionment, what Americans call 'gerrymandering.' In Japan, it is through the manipulation of the farm vote – using its cherished food tariffs – that the LDP stays in power. 'In 1956 the Ichiro Hatoyama government presented a bill to the Diet proposing a small constituency system of a single seat per constituency. Through such a revision the government party hoped to secure a two-thirds majority in the House of Representatives to make amendment of the Constitution possible,' explained Yoshio Sakuma, an editorial writer for Fuji Telecasting. 'The redistricting plan proposed in the bill was so blatantly in favor of the government party, however, that it drew sharp public criticism and Hatoyama was accused of trying to "Hatomander" the constituencies.' The bill was shelved.

The period after 1956 was one of rapid, sustained

economic growth in Japan. Millions of new jobs were created, most in the narrow corridor between Tokyo and Kobe, which includes the densely populated cities of Yokohama, Nagoya, and Kyoto. It was accompanied by a population shift from rural to urban areas. While 45 percent of all Japanese lived in rural areas before 1956, by 1980 this number had dwindled to less than 13 percent. The shift from farm to factory represented a threat to the LDP. As the number of urbanized salarymen increased, so did the sophistication of their political perceptions. 'Since the inauguration of the LDP in 1955 . . . practically every general election has seen the LDP's share of votes decline,' said Kenzo Hemmi, former dean of agriculture at Tokyo University. After decades of LDP rule, many of the LDP's most enthusiastic political supporters were rural people, those who were farmers or who made their living serving farms or farm communities.

The threat to the LDP came from the Public Offices Election Law, which required that voting districts be reapportioned every five years in accordance with the most recent census. In order to comply with this law, the LDP would have had to give more Diet representation to the heavily populated urban areas, to the workers in the burgeoning factories created by their economic policy. The LDP should be as popular there, but the party is unwilling to chance democracy. Instead, the LDP has simply ignored the law as it applied to rural areas, mandating only token reapportionment in some urban districts.

The LDP's failure to allow reapportionment for the country as a whole has enormously magnified the strength of rural voters. A typical example for the House of Representatives is the Fifth District of Hyogo Prefecture, a farming area, which elects a Diet member for every 80,000 voters, while it takes 285,000 voters to elect one in the Fourth District of Chiba Prefecture, a crowded urban area. Thus one vote in the country is worth more than 3.5 votes in the city. For the upper house, the House of Councillors, the contrast in representation between a rural district like Totori and an urban one like Kanagawa is even more dramatic: over fire to one.

'The share of [LDP] parliamentary seats won is always greater than the share of the votes won, usually by a wide margin,' adds Hemmi. 'It would not be an exaggeration therefore, to cite this as the single, albeit sometimes obscure, factor that has enabled the LDP to maintain its singular hold on the reins of power despite the fact that its share of the electoral votes has long since slipped below the 50 percent mark. . . . It may be assumed that when and if the LDP can no longer compensate for its weakness in the urban areas with its strength in the rural areas, the era of single-party government by the LDP will come to an end.'

In 1983, the LDP strengthened their hand in the House of Councillors by pushing through a change in the election process, one cloaked as a reform. Since the MacArthur Constitution, members of the House of Councillors have been elected from two kinds of constituencies. One hundred seats were filled with candidates elected from the nation at large, while 152 were elected from prefectural election districts. The LDP could not control the candidacies of those who ran for the at-large seats, places generally filled by Japan's most famous people. Some were celebrities from the entertainment world, but most were either Japan's intellectuals or special interest groups seeking the public vote which the LDP had denied them in the lower house. To fill these 100 elusive seats with those they could control, the LDP made a temporary truce with their principal rivals, the Socialists. The Socialists, trying to keep smaller parties or splinter groups from eroding their own numbers, joined with the LDP to push a deceptive election law through the Diet. The new system is called 'proportional representation.' It has the ring of the democratic process, but by most Western standards, it is not.

Under so-called Japanese proportional representation, the voters can no longer mark candidates' names on their ballots, a regulation that critics believe is a violation of the MacArthur Constitution. Instead they must write in the name of a political party or organization, which then receives a share of seats proportional to its vote. The party allocates its seats to candidates whose names appear on

316

lists drawn up before the election. The party determines which names will go on the list and the order in which the candidates are listed. Seats won are filled from the top of the list down.

Only certain political parties may participate in these elections for the House of Councillors. To qualify, a party must have at least five members already in the Diet and have received at least 4 percent of the total vote in the most recent Diet election. To keep individuals out of the running, only political parties may conduct campaign activities. The party is required to file a four million yen ($16,000) deposit for each candidate before the election. Fielding a full slate requires a minimum deposit of $166,000. If a party fails to get half as many seats as they have candidates, they forfeit the fee for each person not elected. And how will the LDP select the names it will put on its list, and in which order? 'According to an understanding within the party, an incumbent wishing to be listed has to recruit 50,000 or more new members to the party and a nonincumbent 100,000,' explains a Japan Foreign Press Center booklet. 'Party members are required to pay an annual fee of 3,000 yen, although actual payment falls to the aspiring candidate. Thus a nonincumbent candidate has to donate at least 300 million yen ($1.25 million) to the party.'

The new system will not only strengthen the established parties, especially the LDP, it will force such outspoken Diet members as Chinatsu Nakayama to choose between being frozen out of the political system or being coopted into a party whose goals are not her own. 'In Japan, generally, interest in politics is much, much lower than it is in the United States or in Europe,' Nakayama explains. 'For example, a waitress or a waiter in France, or a store clerk in the U.S., is quite willing to speak up on how they feel about the way the President is doing his job, or not doing it. In Japan, you'd hardly ever see that.

'Originally I did not intend to become a member of the Diet,' Nakayama adds. 'From the time I was about 20, I was a TV newscaster. I thought that to make the political system in Japan really effective, it's important for everyone to show interest. If a person like myself would get involved, perhaps more people would begin to show some interest.' Under the new proportional representation system Chinatsu will not be allowed to seek reelection to the Diet unless she is accepted on the list of a major party.

To appeal to the gerrymandered rural prefectures and maintain political power, the LDP has adopted an agricultural and rural policy that heavily penalizes Japan's overwhelmingly urban population. The railbed for Japan's famed *shinkansen*, or bullet train, is a recent example. It was completed at the staggering cost of $60 million per mile, money which mainly went into the rural prefectures that maintain the LDP. In the obscure mountain town of Urasa, population 15,000, the bullet train stops on its way from Tokyo to Niigata at a station that cost $100 million to build, or more than $6,500 for every person in Urasa.

The station also allowed local farmers to get rich by inflating the price of land in Urasa by 50 times its erstwhile value, according to Koji Miyazaki. Miyazaki used to be a farmer, before he and 120 other farmers put together 79 acres of their land and sold it to the government for $64 million, or $810,000 an acre. The LDP is very popular in Urasa. To keep it that way, a new international university is being built nearby, on more land purchased from farmers. The LDP will be popular in Urasa for some time to come.

To comprehend the magnitude of the sustained spending that transfers wealth from urban factory workers to rural farmers, shopkeepers, and a multitude of special interests, we must consider that Japan's 1982 national government deficit was a third of the entire budget, $70 billion, or 6.4 percent of its entire GNP. Japan is a country whose GNP represents a tenth of the world's total production of goods and services, but a country which spent only $11.5 billion on its own defense, less than 1 percent of its GNP, shifting the financial burden for that obligation to the United States, its most exploited trading partner. As a result Japan, a nation with half the population of the U.S., a nation with one-twenty-fifth the land area, consumed more cement than did the U.S., much of it in the construction of public works projects.

Paying for government projects does not affect everyone equally. The Japanese have a national income tax, but not everyone pays. Salarymen have little choice, because not only is the money withheld, but their employers actually file their tax returns. In 1982, 91.5 percent of all salaried workers had tax returns filed for them. But proprietors of the omnipresent small retail shops (Japan, with half the U.S. population, has 100,000 more shops) have never been required to keep business records. Nor have rural mill owners or farmers. In 1982, according to the Ministry of Finance, only 40 percent of Japan's shopkeepers paid any taxes. An estimated 86 percent of all farmers paid no taxes at all. Obviously, in urban areas where the LDP is weakest its staunchest supporters are shopkeepers and small businessmen.

Ultimately, it is the housewife who pays for the LDP's rural policy. 'Ask a Japanese housewife if she's tired of paying outrageous prices for food,' says John Child. 'Lots of people are now saying, in effect, "We want a choice about what kind of food we can buy. Why are we paying twice as much or more for food than we have to?" I think attitudes are changing. I think the Japanese politicians will have to answer some hard questions soon.'

Outspoken Chinatsu Nakayama agrees, adding that high food prices are the result of a government policy that does not even benefit the farmer. 'Often, the consumers in urban areas and the farmers quarrel about food prices,' explains Nakayama. 'But I think the fundamental problem lies in the agricultural policy of the LDP. Even if the government raises the price of rice, the farmer's profit doesn't increase. In fact, although consumer prices are quite high, the farmer's profits are very low. So a lot of farmers come to the urban areas to look for part-time jobs – road work or casual labor – during the winter, just to make ends meet. Yet the agricultural policy has the government trying to persuade farmers to reduce the acreage they have in rice in exchange for subsidies to start other crops – vegetables, and so forth. But that's not solving the problem.

'I think the extent to which Japan can feed itself is very low, and the result of the government's policies will be to reduce it still further,' she adds. 'The LDP's policies are killing the farmer's incentives to work. If the crop is bad, the government gives them money anyway. Since the government is trying to reduce rice acreage, farmers get paid for leaving the field fallow. If there's overproduction of vegetables, the price goes down. In order to prevent that, sometimes the farmers are forced to leave their vegetables to rot in the field, or plough them under – in a country that can't feed itself – to keep the price high.'

The small size of Japanese farms contributes to farm inefficiency, but prices of consumer commodities are propped even higher because of the nation's archaic food distribution system, one that has been maintained by the LDP. The system provides hundreds of thousands of jobs, most of them in the farming communities where LDP candidates are elected. Farmers receive low prices for their crops, consumers pay very high prices, and most of the profit goes to middlemen and distributors.

'The consumer and the farmers are very good people, and their demands are reasonable,' Nakayama comments. 'The people in the middle are the ones getting rich at their expense. For example, a farmer harvests his apples, but before they get to the consumers, they go to many places. Each time they stop and are unloaded or reloaded, the price goes up. The same thing is true with fish. We're a nation of islands, surrounded by seas, and you'd think that we could eat a lot of fresh fish. But in general we eat mostly frozen fish, and fish that's been frozen for a long time. When the fishermen return with their catch, it's sold to the distribution monopolies. They freeze it, then wait until prices go up because there isn't any fish on the market. In the meantime it goes from one storehouse to another, and each time it does the price goes up some more.'

Japanese consumers could buy food at half the prices they presently pay if Japan's rulers would allow more food to be imported from nations with a more efficient agricultural system, nations such as America, Australia, and France. Not only would it benefit Japanese consumers, but it would reduce Japan's enormous surplus trade imbalance. The scarcity of beef, and its high price, is a continuing national scandal in Japan. 'The reason is that the size of an American cattle ranch is typically hundreds of animals, compared to maybe three or four for the Japanese,' explains Child. 'The American rancher will keep an animal only about two or two-and-a-half-years, until it's about 1,400 pounds. He feeds it grain for only the last nine months or a year before he brings it to market, and grass before that. But the Japanese "rancher" has no grass. So he feeds his cattle on grain, all of it expensive. He keeps the animal three to four years before going to market, when it weighs between 1,600 and 1,900 pounds. And there are a lot of Japanese farmers who have just one animal at a time. It's an inefficient system; there are no economies of scale as there are in other countries.'

The cost of raising a beef animal on the hoof in Japan is much higher than raising one in the U.S. But this alone does not account for the difference in price between the two countries. John Child and the American embassy staff have documented that en route between the farmer and the consumer, Japanese domestic beef makes as many as 14 stops as it moves through the distribution system. 'Sometimes they just drive an animal from one side of town to the other, take it off one truck, put it on another. Everytime they do that, somebody makes a little money,' Child reveals. 'The same people who control the supply and distribution system for domestic beef are in control of the channels for imported beef.' Child points out that they can raise the price of imported beef so that it is no longer competitive with the domestic variety, effectively keeping imports out.

The same frustrating situation exists with citrus fruits, especially oranges, which could be imported cheaply in vast quantities from America, Israel, and elsewhere. In Japan, orange juice costs about three times what it does in other nations. It is almost impossible to find pure orange juice in supermarkets, because the Japanese mix imported concentrate with locally grown *mikan*, a variety of tangerine. By itself, the juice of the *mikan* is too tart for most tastes. But every time the government raises the question of increasing imports of beef or tangerines, farm groups express their outrage by holding highly publicized protest rallies in prefectural capitals.

'We call the farm life "*san chan nogyo*," said Hiroko Horisaka. 'It sums up how we who live in Tokyo regard the country people. It means a household where an old couple live, a grandfather and a grandmother, and their daughter-in-law. The son also lives there, but he's actually a salaryman. The old folks and his wife work the farm.' This is a fairly accurate picture of much of Japanese agriculture. According to the Japanese Bureau of Statistics, in 1982 only 599,000 families, or 13.1 percent of all Japanese agriculture households, were primarily engaged in farming. Only 5 percent of the total work force were in agriculture or forestry.

My conversation with Horisaka occurred on the way to Shizuoka Prefecture, about two hours by bullet train from Tokyo. At Shizuoka we changed to an ordinary JNR train for the half-hour trip to Shimada, a tiny place whose 'downtown' shopping area replicates, in miniature, Tokyo's more affluent districts. There were new cars on the streets, dozens of shops and smart restaurants which offered both traditional Japanese fare as well as passable imitations of pizza, spaghetti and hamburgers. From Shimada we took a taxi about five miles into the countryside, traveling on a well-kept asphalt highway that winds between endless terraces of manicured tea bushes, *mikan* in neat groves, and greenhouses tucked away on unpaved but well-graded farm roads.

Our destination was the home of Tadao Kitagawa. He is 63, tall for a Japanese, an angular, balding, brown-skinned, bifocaled Japanese version of 'American Gothic' immortalized by the painter Grant Wood. Kitagawa lives with his wife; his oldest son, Yuichi, 32, and Yuichi's wife, Tomie, 29, a grocery checker in a Shimada supermarket; and his aged parents, both over 90. Tadao's other son,

Hiroichi, 28, lives in Shizuioka where he is a salaryman, a junior architect for a construction company.

The family lives in a large, spacious home, parts of it more than a hundred years old. The Kitagawa clan has lived on this land for nine generations. This household, at least, does not appear to suffer from the poverty Japan claims afflicts its farmers. The farm's fleet includes two identical, late-model pick-up trucks and two cars. One is brand new, a Nissan that is one of the largest four-door sedans made in Japan. The Kitagawa homestead is filled with electronic gadgets, including TV sets, a stereo receiver, a huge Sony portable stereo radio-cassette recorder, and other appliances.

The Kitagawas, like most in this area, grow both tea and *mikan*, as well as a little rice. 'Until 1965 we grew only rice,' explained Tadao. 'Then the government built a dam across the O-oi River. To get water to us, the river had to pass through a long tunnel beneath the mountain, and it became too cold to grow rice. The government wanted everyone to switch to other crops. They paid 70 percent of the cost of converting to tea and *mikan*.' Tadao is a director of the Shimada Agricultural co-op, which markets *mikan* and tea. He sells his own *mikan*, however, direct to consumers on a route he has developed in Shimada, and receives almost twice the price of those who sell through the co-op.

Tadao Kitagawa is not an average farmer. He is a local notable, one of the half-dozen men who run things in this tiny rural district. He complained to me that the government had not raised the price of *mikan* in five years though production costs had gone up. This is, he says, because too many *mikan* are being produced; many are grown in greenhouses which yield a summer crop months before the outdoor groves have ripened. 'Perhaps we'll try navel oranges next year,' he told me, if the expected government *hojokin*, or subsidy, comes through. His son, Yuichi, blames the low prices of *mikan* on food imports. 'Every time the government wants to export more cars, they have to allow more oranges to be imported,' Yuichi says. 'One hundred percent of the farmers feel this way.

We've given up on getting government help.' Nevertheless, he and his family have worked to reelect their LDP Dietman for the last ten years.

Though the Kitagawa family truly believe their fruit is being sold at lower prices because of increased imports, the facts do not support their claim. In 1982, according to the Japan Customs Bureau, only 82 tons of oranges were imported, while *mikan* growers produced 2,864 tons of fruit. Imported oranges, which amounted to less than 3 percent of the Japanese *mikan* production, are hideously expensive. Five medium-size Valencia oranges with a decorative ribbon sell for upwards of $4 in Tokyo in summertime, and as much as $10 in winter. The Kitagawas, of course, cannot be blamed for believing what their Dietman tells them, nor for passing this misinformation along to the other members of their agricultural co-op.

According to Professor Hemmi, the LDP's political organization in the rural prefectures and the agricultural business organizations and co-operatives are virtually one and the same. These groups do not represent the interests of the majority of the rural population of poor, subsistence-level farmers. They are concerned with the interests of the more affluent distribution organizations which, through government indulgences, have a monopoly on the sale and distribution of farm products. These organizations – and thus the LDP – have a direct economic stake in restricting the import of food products from the United States and elsewhere. A true reform in the food distribution system and greater availability of food at lower prices would put them out of business.

Since these organizations buy the output of the small farmers, and often lend them money to finance a year's production, they have a stranglehold on the community. If a co-op director calls upon the farmers to don their demonstration headbands and placards, they have no choice. Japan's *eggu oh*, 'egg king,' Hikonobu Ise, who has five million egg-laying chickens, the largest such enterprise in Japan, found himself the target of one of these well-organized demonstrations in front of the Diet building in 1979. Ise was inside testifying that he could not see why the government should provide price support subsidies to egg producers in a protein-hungry nation that needs eggs. But outside a thousand farmers were calling him names, none of them kind, for daring to say that the market should dictate egg prices.

This is not the only example of farmer exploitation by distributors. An investigation by the Agricultural, Forestry and Fisheries Ministry of Japan showed that it took an average of 140 days for government subsidies to be distributed to the farmers after the distribution co-ops were themselves paid. The ministry also reported that 32 of 55 producers' organizations inspected failed to make the subsidy regulations clear to their members. If Japan's archaic and convoluted distribution system were abolished and domestic producers of beef and *mikan* could sell all they produced, farmers' income would probably rise and consumers could afford to buy more of the foodstuffs that other advanced countries take for granted.

But it will not happen. 'The Japanese use the distribution system as a mechanism to absorb excess workers,' explained labor expert Lester Slezak at the U.S. embassy. The leaders of the distribution companies, with disproportionate representation in the Diet, will not allow the LDP to do what would be best for the nine out of ten Japanese who do not live in a rural prefecture, and what, in the long run, would be best for the farmers themselves. The LDP knows that their continued domination of Japan's economy is now hostage to these rural prefectures.

As long as the LDP can ignore the constitutional requirement to reapportion the Diet, that party will continue to exercise control of Japan's affairs. While opposition parties and a few private groups have pointed out the illegality of the LDP's inaction, and a few lawsuits have challenged it in the courts, they have gotten nowhere.

As their popular support has dwindled, the LDP has increasingly turned to ultranationalism as a prop. In 1982 the government revised school textbooks, provoking howls of protest from China and Korea. The new textbooks minimized or ignored World War II, the unprovoked attacks on Japan's Asian neighbors, and the attrocities committed by the Japanese Army. The government also exerted its influence on the new Tokyo Disneyland, which opened in 1983 on land reclaimed from Tokyo Bay. One of its most popular attractions is a highly attended multi-media presentation of Japanese history. When the presentation reaches the 1930s, the lights are dimmed and a childlike voice from the distance declares, 'It's so dark in here.' Japan, in darkness, disposes of its debt to inform children of the consequences of its aggression.

In the Japanese view, the LDP has accomplished an economic marvel in bringing Japan back from defeat after World War II to its present position of economic power. But in manipulating its farmers to maintain political leadership, the LDP has added another imbalance to world trade. By refusing to import low-priced food for its people, food other nations have in abundance and are ready to export, Japan continues to add to its excessively large trade balance, one that may soon topple of its own weight.

12   How to Deal with the Japanese Conspiracy

WHO WILL lead the Western Alliance? As Japan's imbalance of payments increases in lockstep with its GNP, one industry after another in America and Europe falls before its totalitarian economics. Free-market trading and the industrial health of the United States and Western Europe are ever more threatened.

If this equation is not altered significantly, we may well envision the time, perhaps as soon as the earliest decades of the twenty-first century, when the American economic relationship with Japan will somewhat resemble that of a colony to its colonizer. In return for certain raw materials, energy and food, the output of Japanese factories will be sold to Americans, on Japanese terms. Europe, strongly dependent for its strength on America, will suffer in tandem. It is not a pleasant future to contemplate.

But this equation has implications even more ominous for the competition between the Soviets and the West. Can second-rate American and European technology maintain a credible deterrent to the global ambitions of the Soviet Union? Could Japan provide the technological, moral, and military leadership that now serves to counter Soviet power? Hardly. It is not within the Japanese tradition to view cooperation in international affairs as desirable. We cannot allow Japan to dominate the Western economic alliance, nor even allow her to determine the nature of the global economy.

The web of plots and secret agreements, the concerted acts and duplicitous maneuvers, the vast conspiracies that have served Japan's goals ever since World War II ended have become that nation's *modus vivendi* only because they have worked. Conversely, the Japanese conspirators will not alter their behavior unless – and until – it can be demonstrated that their nation will be better served by adopting a new attitude.

But before abandoning what has worked so well, Japan's leaders must believe that the cost of changing to more acceptable behavior will be less than the pain suffered from counterattacks of America and Europe. 'We're asking the Japanese to shoot themselves in the foot,' opined Jerry Sanders of Advanced Micro Devices. 'They're not going to do it, unless we can demonstrate that if they don't, we'll shoot them in the head.'

The Japanese must trade to live, as they are acutely aware. If Japan's trading partners counter Japan's protectionism with trade barriers of their own, the whole world will suffer. But in the long run, no nation will suffer more than Japan. This message must be repeated over and over to Japan's leaders. It will take a long time to force the Japanese to change their ways, a long period of dogged negotiation and relentless punishment of each incident of anticompetitive behavior. It will be a period during which the United States, above all nations, must demonstrate a firm and coherent national policy towards Japan.

And it will take toughness. Toughness like that shown by Norman Larker. After an undistinguished, six-year baseball career with the Dodgers and the Astros, Larker, a utility outfielder, signed with a big-league Japanese team in the late 1960s. He joined a small number of American players who found they could play more often for larger salaries because Americans, who are comparatively bigger and stronger than the average Japanese baseball professional, are valuable to Japanese teams.

Many Japanese players resent them. On Larker's first turn at bat, the opposing Japanese pitcher hit him in the head with a baseball. Hurting but unwilling to quit, Larker got up and trotted down to first base. As he did so, the pitcher removed his cap and bowed deeply. On his next turn at bat, Larker took the first pitch, then hurled his bat toward the pitcher's mound, narrowly missing the pitcher's head. He then ceremoniously removed his own cap and bowed even more deeply than had the Japanese pitcher. Larker went on to enjoy several years of considerable success playing in Japan. Never again did a pitcher try to hit him with a ball.

On the field of international trade, the Japanese have repeatedly thrown beanballs at the heads of the Americans and Europeans. They have doffed their diplomatic caps and bowed deeply in apology, but each time the West comes to bat, Japan throws still another beanball, followed by yet another deep bow. As we have seen, the Japanese have repeatedly 'liberalized' their trade practices, yet the imbalance between what Japan sells to the U.S. and Europe and what it buys from them continues to increase, and at an accelerating rate.

The Japanese have demonstrated that their definition of the ethics of free trade are not ours. They have also shown that a concerted, covertly organized industrial plan will defeat any number of lone competitors constrained to obey the rules of the market-place. But their success in selling to the free markets while simultaneously protecting their own with subtle but effective barriers, has caused the industrialized world to reconsider free trade as a philosophy.

By ignoring reciprocity, the Japanese threaten to destroy the system. We need to fling a baseball bat at Japan. We can then remove our national cap, bow deeply, and get on with a game where both sides respect the same rules. The type of pressure to apply has been the subject of increasing debate across the United States, and in the nations of the European Economic Community. What follows are some ways to deal with the Japanese conspiracy.

❋

The first step is to speak candidly. We must tell Japan that if we are to continue to trade with them, they must change their system to conform to that of other nations. That will require a transformation of the Japanese business and industrial world as revolutionary as their economic 'miracle' of the last generation.

The initial move will be to insist that the Japanese allow the yen to become an international currency like the American dollar, the German deutschmark, and the pound sterling. *All* restrictions on foreign investment in Japan should be lifted. This would serve to remove much of the insulation Japan has selfishly wrapped around its enormous pool of savings capital. It would end the era of an artificially under-valued yen that has enabled Japan to export goods at prices well below their real value. A fairly-valued yen would also lower the price of all foreign imports sold in Japan, increasing the demand for foreign goods. Making the yen into an international currency, thereby integrating Japan's financial establishment with the rest of the industrialized world, would go a long way toward removing many other trade barriers as well.

Japan's amoral and uncharismatic leadership will not go along with this plan unless compelled to. One way to force the issue is to deny them access to *our* capital markets. While Japan has a huge pool of capital in postal savings accounts and savings bank deposits owned by the working class, these funds are used by business to finance expansion. By law they cannot be borrowed by the government for social programs. Japan's porkbarrel politics have resulted in enormous, ever-increasing government deficits. Japan's banks and insurance companies have been force-fed government bonds to the point of choking, requiring the Japanese government to go abroad to borrow. They now sell their bonds in London and New York, depriving Western nations of capital needed for their own industries.

Japan has also increased its access to American savings funds. Large Japanese banks have been able to absorb smaller American ones, obtaining direct access to American deposits, much of which they have legally siphoned off to finance Japanese business activities in the U.S. Meanwhile, the 1,000 American companies doing business in Japan have rarely found Japanese banks willing to make them loans. Internationalizing the yen would make it far easier for foreign companies to operate in Japan, and this, too, would ease import imbalances.

The counter-conspiracy plan? Let's keep the Japanese from borrowing in our capital markets until we can borrow in theirs. Let market forces determine who borrows from whom, and how much. Let's have a fair game, or no game at all.

Secondly, we must break Japan's protectionist policy, once and for all. The West could sell the Japanese people a great many products, from Swiss cheese to American plumbing, if the Japanese government would let them. As we have seen, they could import enough low-priced American foodstuffs – grain products, beef, citrus fruits – to eliminate perhaps half their U.S. trade surplus, simultaneously providing their citizens with a more nourishing diet. But to do this, they need the courage to remake their archaic agricultural distribution system, one whose political power is paradoxically tied to its inefficiency.

Over the past decade, the Japanese have replied to repeated requests to remove *non*tariff barriers to imports by asserting that 'there is little which Americans or Europeans make that we Japanese want or need.' This is quite untrue. The Japanese masses are forced to huddle in cramped and miserable homes. All but the wealthiest lack adequate central heating and the basic amenities which make American homes comfortable. Few Japanese apartments even have bathing facilities. Yet America and the European nations, if allowed to sell their expertise in designing, building, and furnishing homes, could transform Japan into a far more livable country.

Instead of spending vast sums – and incurring vast deficits – for public works jobs that buy a few crucial votes in the underpopulated rural prefectures, a Japanese national program to upgrade housing would give private enterprise, both Japanese and foreign, the opportunity to make a legitimate profit. The surplus workers Japan has absorbed into its industries and agricultural distribution system could find new jobs in the housing industry.

A rise in national living standards would help redress some of Japan's social inequities. The Japanese have only to admit to themselves that it is no longer necessary to live like a nation of beggars while accumulating enormous trade surpluses and capital funds. They could then become accepted as equals in the international community. It is time for the Japanese to accept a lower balance of payment surplus in exchange for a better life.

We should also require the Japanese to pay for the defense of their own country. Japan presently spends less than one percent of its GNP for defense.

We should make it clear that the $1 billion which Japan estimates is the annual worth of bases provided to the U.S. military is an inadequate contribution to our joint defense. The U.S. spends more than that on the payroll for its 45,000 troops, its thousands of Japanese employees, and locally procured merchandise. While American security interests in the northern Pacific are served by these Japanese bases, the primary beneficiaries of the American military presence are the Japanese themselves.

Japan should pay for its protection; the amount should perhaps be tied directly to the trade imbalance between the two countries. If Japan insists on exporting $30 billion a year more than it buys from the U.S., the Japanese government should pay perhaps 20 percent of that to the United States Government, in cash. This would reduce the size of U.S. defense budget and cut the federal deficit. In turn, more American capital would be freed for investment, which would increase productivity and the competitiveness of American goods abroad. If Japan's trade surplus declines, their defense contribution will decline proportionately. Surely the Japanese cannot rationally object to paying for part of their own defense. But in any case, the alternative of buying more American goods will be far more palatable to ordinary Japanese citizens and politicians alike.

Japan must be made to recognize the truth: that their present actions endanger the world economic system, from which they have profited handsomely. To make amends, the Japanese must voluntarily seek to undo much of their 'bureaucratic-industrial complex' and return business to the free enterprise mold of other nations.

The Japanese must be induced to do the following:

(1) Discontinue the cartelization of industries, which

creates a handful of large, effective organizations able to overwhelm foreign competition. The Japanese must institute true anti-monopoly legislation with teeth. It is time, after almost forty years, to break up the reconstructed giant *zaibatsu* that General MacArthur thought he had permanently destroyed.

(2) They must end all subsidies from the Japanese government, open or covert, and force individual Japanese firms to make it on their own. These subsidies include *hojokin*, disguised government allowances in the form of virtually interest-free loans paid back only when a company shows a profit.

(3) The Japanese must discontinue 'targeting.' Individual firms can go after whom they please, but when the Japanese bureaucratic-industrial complex targets an industry overseas, it attacks it as a quasi-governmental unit, with all the power of a soverign state.

(4) The Japanese government must prosecute domestic firms that illegally appropriate foreign technology. They must police the violation of licensing agreements, the lifting of foreign patents from the Japanese patent office, and especially the outright theft of technology from foreign firms. At present, the Japanese government winks at, even encourages, such unethical business behavior.

(5) 'Dumping' is a systematic Japanese activity which must be stopped. Since firms in the 'victim' nations are often willing to secretly accept cheaper-priced foreign goods, the Japanese must police themselves. The Japanese Fair Trade Commission should be armed with legal sanctions to make it into a true fighting force to prosecute Japanese firms selling goods in Japan at inflated prices in order to subsidize predatory pricing in foreign markets. This action would involve prosecution of senior bureaucrats who contribute to this practice.

(6) Sharing of proprietary technology by Japanese firms, through the government conduit, makes them unfairly competitive with Western companies who must finance their own R&D. This must end. The government should remove itself from non-defense research, particularly in such areas as the giant, MITI-financed superspeed

and Fifth Generation 'artificial intelligence' computer programs. The alternative is for the United States, perhaps working in concert with all other Western countries, to conduct their own national research efforts on behalf of private business.

(7) Most important, Japan must show that it is willing to play by Western rules by having MITI commit administrative hara-kiri. This formidable organization of 12,000 must be dismantled. It must forfeit its command of Japanese industry. Japan needs to dismiss at least 10,000 MITI bureaucrats without placing them elsewhere armed with the same powers. With MITI's shadowy conspirators consigned to history's trash heap, Japan can once more compete as an equal in the world trade arena.

If the Japanese will listen to reason, if they will take the serious and painful steps required to eliminate the inequities they have fostered for most of three decades, they can take an active and responsible role in the technological transformation of the world and help provide the basis for many more decades of affluence and peace. Japan can sell its goods abroad at fair prices, and Japan can buy from its trading partners what it cannot efficiently produce itself. Japan could earn the respect of the world if it would put its own house in order and accept the status of an equal partner in the world trading community.

But while we may ask the Japanese to alter their totalitarian tactics, to conform to the same ethical constraints and legal obligations that the West takes for granted, they probably will not. They enjoy their new position, no matter how improperly gained.

If the Japanese will not reform themselves, economic catastrophe for the whole world may eventually result, a catastrophe on the same scale as the Depression of the 1930s. Japanese practices must inevitably touch off a worldwide wave of protectionism which will cripple or destroy many national economies, particularly those of the United States and Western Europe. But none will suffer more than Japan, for they must trade to live.

Fortunately, this need not happen. The nations of North America and Western Europe will not much longer stand idly by while their domestic industries are ruined, while their laws are flouted, while their jobs are siphoned off to Japanese factories, while their technology begins to falter.

The United States and Western Europe, collectively, or even the U.S. alone, have the power to end the Japanese conspiracy. They have no critical need for any Japanese products. There are no manufactured goods that America, or Europe, cannot produce domestically. The West has the capability to make as many high-quality, fuel-efficient automobiles as it needs. It has the capability to manufacture computers, large and small, microelectronics of all descriptions, office automation equipment, pharmaceuticals and other biogenetic products, photovoltaic batteries, machine tools and everything else the Japanese make, including motorcycles, TV sets, and consumer electronics items. Indeed, virtually all the technology used by Japan to manufacture these goods is American or Western European technology.

Since the United States does not need Japanese goods, and manufactures products competitive with them, it has simply to decide not to buy any more Japanese products until they reform their system.

'We have been suckers,' says Clyde Prestowitz, acting assistant secretary for international economic policy in the U.S. Department of Commerce. 'I'd start with making it very tough for them to import cars or VCRs. We should order the U.S. Customs Service to inspect every Japanese car. They would back up to Yokohama. It would be like the French at Poitiers with Japanese VCRs. You can do that without breaking the rules; the customs service now expedites procedures for the Japanese, but it doesn't have to. You can tell the customs service to work the rules, or you can transfer a few customs agents, so there aren't enough to do the job. There are lots of administrative things that can be done to harass them until they get the point.'

Prestowitz's remedies go considerably further. 'I wouldn't

335

do military coproduction,' he adds. 'We transfer a lot of technology to them that way. They build F-15s in Japan, in coproduction with us. I wouldn't do that. They have a choice: They can build their own airplanes, or buy them from us. If they buy from us, it costs them about a third of what it would cost them if they built their own. I think aviation coproduction is a very poor deal for us.

'Mind you, I would do all this for a quid pro quo. We have competitive industries, too. Our telecommunications, petro-chemical and pulp-and-paper industries are competitive. So there should be trade-offs with Japan. It ought to be made clear to them that unless our petrochemical industry, which has a 40 percent cost advantage on theirs, gets a 20 percent share of their market, then their auto industry, which has a 40 percent cost advantage on ours, is not going to get 20 percent of our market. I would do things on a much more reciprocal basis,' Prestowitz says.

'I wouldn't let U.S. software companies export software to Japan without checking first with the Commerce Department. I would make the transfer of software technology to Japan a matter of license. And I think we ought to take a much harder look at reciprocity in the academic areas. We have something like 200 Japanese at NIH [National Institute of Health] and there are zero Americans at Japan's equivalent. We should take a look at that. Japan has a program to develop its own space launching capability and its own telecommunications satellites. Virtually all of that technology has been transferred from the United States. We are creating a competitor for ourselves in space launches and in satellites. I wouldn't do that. Instead I'd tell the Japanese they can have the satellites if they buy them from us,' Prestowitz adds.

How could the United States of America, the leading economic power since its triumph over the forces of fascism in 1945, have allowed the Japanese to succeed for so long when so many of their tactics have been both obvious and odious?

The answer is complex, yet it can be summarized simply: Democratic and Republic administrations have cooperated in a bipartisan policy of short-sightedness. Successive American governments refused to acknowledge that Japanese success could threaten the Western economies. Administration after administration has refused to recognize the issue for what it really is: the economic equivalent of war, a worldwide trade battle.

'It's ironic that a Republican Administration, which normally would view big business as its natural constituency, is setting about really unwittingly, but with almost wanton recklessness, the deindustrialization of the United States,' says attorney Richard Copaken, who supervised the Houdaille investigation of the Japanese machine tool industry. 'They do so because of the call of ideology, not the call of common sense or pragmatism, or even of constituent concern. Yet the alternative being offered up by the Democrats, a so-called industrial policy, is really no closer to the mark. It's attempting to emulate an approach that is crafted brilliantly to fit the personality and sociology of the Japanese people, but not our own. What nobody seems willing to do is to use our marketplace as a strategic weapon and to gain a degree of moderation where our real interests are at stake.'

The real interests of America and Western Europe require the maintenance of a strong industrial base. First, independent of what Japan does, or fails to do, the West must take a hard look at the competitiveness of its own industries. If we are not to invite the day when we *need* Japanese technology, we must begin a program of national involvement in high-technology education and research.

The knowledge-intensive industries in which Japan is investing billions will provide most of the world's economic growth for the rest of the century. For America to compete will require changes in federal statutes. For example, the foundations of our present anti-trust laws were laid in the era of the robber barons, nearly a hundred years ago. They were intended to keep finite resources – land is one good example – from being taken over by a few powerful interests at the public expense. They were also written to protect consumers, in a nation which was then primarily agrarian, from those who sought to monopolize basic industries.

We are now dealing with an entirely new resource, information – knowledge. Unlike land, knowledge is an *infinite* commodity. While the American public still needs protection against price fixing and collusive practices, the American information and knowledge-intensive industries, undreamed of when the Sherman and Clayton Acts became law, need the freedom to maximize the returns from their R&D by avoiding needless duplication in fundamental areas. They need legislation that will permit competitors to jointly engage in certain fundamental types of research activities without fear of anti-trust prosecution no matter which American political party happens to control the Justice Department.

And we need to give substantially higher tax incentives to American industry for research and development in high-risk technology, but only when the investment goes beyond normal R&D expenditures. In other words, we should reward with a bigger tax break companies willing to stick their neck out a little further than others. Given the relatively short time in which high-tech production equipment becomes obsolete, a system of accelerated depreciation for these investments should be enacted.

At the same time, we need to strengthen laws regulating unfair trade practices, particularly by foreign companies. For example, the present law mandates a maximum fine of $10,000 per count for dumping or theft of trade secrets. This penalty is hardly a deterrent to Japanese companies, which often use these schemes to increase their market shares or to illicitly obtain technology. They accept these fines as a minor cost of doing business.

We must educate the next generation of specialists by at least doubling our production of engineers and scientists. America, paradoxically, now spends a fortune educating Japanese and other foreign scientists who make up a large percentage of our graduate science classes. It would not be extravagant to spend some money to assure our own economic survival. A national program endowed by the government is the only answer to the production of more, and better, scientists and engineers to provide the technology for tomorrow.

Some of this energy must be expended to produce teachers of science and engineering. At the university level, many doctors of English literature and the other humanities cannot find suitable employment in academia, while doctors of computer science cannot be found to fill available positions. They are instead working in industry, where they can usually expect to be paid far more than they would by a university. The shortage of Ph.D. computer scientists in universities is comparable to the situation of the farmer who eats his seed corn instead of planting it for the next year's harvest.

To remedy this imbalance, some academicians must be offered salaries commensurate with the supply and demand situation. If we will pay a person with a Ph.D. in electronic engineering as much to teach his knowledge to others in a university as industry will pay him to design circuits, we will soon have more of the highly qualified researchers America needs to maintain its technological leadership. If we won't, we will be buying licenses for technology from the far-sighted Japanese by the end of the century.

America, when it can, properly favors the private sector. But there are some things that only the government, acting on behalf of all the people, can best endow. One of these is a national computer research project for Fifth Generation and superspeed computers. We need multidisciplinary national programs designed to assure our continued technological supremacy in computer science. For the design of safe, cheap power from nuclear *fusion*, for cryptographic applications, and for future generations of advanced weapons development, a national superspeed computer project is essential.

To achieve breakthroughs in artificial intelligence and to bring simplified computer access to every economic sector and to every citizen, to give the entire economy the benefits of the computer's ability to rapidly process vast amounts of information, we need an American version of the Fifth Generation project, a marriage of academia and industry with a generous government dowry. This is a proven approach that has been successful in the space program and will undoubtedly be equally effective here. America needs a NASA for the computer sciences, and needs it now.

Positive domestic action by America and Western Europe will have some effect on the Japanese onslaught. But only the Japanese can decide if they are willing to take the West to the brink of economic ruin before they understand the danger of their obsessive mercantile war.

The Japanese people have shown a remarkable ability to make tremendous adjustments, even radical changes, when their leadership demands it. And they will have to make another major change in the 1980s and 1990s in the way they do business with the world. It would be a severe injustice to believe they are incapable of responding; if the change is mandated from above, the Japanese will respond as they always have. They will display the same energy and spirit they used to transform their defeated nation from a shattered ruin in 1945 to an industrial powerhouse in the 1980s. Provided with the right kind of incentives, and the right kind of threats, the Japanese are perfectly capable of adapting their behavior in the trade world to acceptable standards of conduct, quite capable of transforming Japan into a nation that enjoys the respect and friendship of the West.

However, they will not feel the need for this radical change until America and the West demonstrate the courage to insist on it. Should Japan transform itself, there will be no need to make the ultimate threat, one which would return Japan to a second-rate power.

That threat is not protective tariffs, for duty walls only punish the consumer – as in Japan – by keeping out goods that are decently priced. The threat that America and the West can make, and enforce, is the *quota* – 'voluntary' or otherwise – on every type of Japanese product, from autos to computers to machine tools to earth-moving equipment.

340

How to Deal with the Japanese Conspiracy

By using the quota device, America and Europe can protect their domestic markets, permit consumers who want to to buy Japanese goods, and simultaneously let the Japanese insistence on high quality and reasonable price act as a competitive goad to domestic manufacturers. The auto industry is a perfect example. The threat of a domestic content bill, which would ultimately have required that 90 percent of all car parts be made in the U.S. forced the Japanese to agree to a 'voluntary' quota of 1.68 million cars, now about 20 percent of the market. Meanwhile, the Japanese inundation of the market frightened American car makers, who are now far more competitive and regaining their strength.

Twenty percent is an arbitrary figure and might be too high in certain industries, as in aircraft or drugs, or too low in others, such as inexpensive radios. But quotas, from perhaps 10 to 30 percent of market share on *all* Japanese goods would not only check the Japanese conspiracy but be a great stimulant to domestic industries, both in the United States and Europe.

There are some products, for example, that the West does not now make, but very well could. It is impossible to find an American-made video cassette recorder (VCR), for example. The reason is that Japanese 'borrowed' American technology to make them in Japan and took a stranglehold on the American market before any U.S. firms could bring out competitors. But if there were no imported Japanese VCRs, or only a few, American companies would quickly compete. Existing giants such as Zenith, RCA, and General Electric would be able to manufacture VCRs competitive in quality and price with any made in Japan.

If we could create an entirely new American industry in the wake of Japanese quotas, the same could be done to rebuild those industries which the Japanese have crippled or destroyed. Why not make all, or most, of our own TV receivers? To keep prices competitive, we could work in concert with our Latin American neighbors. Factories could be built in depressed areas of America, in Puerto Rico, in Mexico, and in Central America to do much of the most labor-intensive manufacturing. The same is true of computer peripherals, small electric typewriters, motorbikes, radios, and other fields which the Japanese have seized, or are now taking over.

America and Western Europe are the two largest consumer markets in the world. They seem mesmerized by the Japanese conspiracy, watching numbly as Japan becomes *itchiban* – number one. In international trade, the power of the marketplace is everything. America and Europe, together or individually, can use the power of the market quota to readjust the proper balance of trade, one that will ensure prosperity for all, not for Japan alone.

The Japanese must end their industrial, bureaucratic and mercantile conspiracies. They must have the vision, and the courage, to contemplate a world where trade is truly reciprocal, where the ethics of capitalism and the dynamics of the unfettered marketplace make prosperity available to every nation. If they will not or cannot reform, Japan will – unless the West is as morally weak as many Japanese believe – find itself a trading pariah, a nation isolated from its neighbors and doomed to penury in a world of plenty.

Notes

Chapter I

In addition to the sources noted below, information for this chapter is drawn from the author's personal interviews with Jon Woronoff; Richard Copaken; Doi Takako; Kazuhiko Bando; Koichi Kujirai; Soichi Nagamatsu; Arnold Kalman; John Nevin; Shigeki Hijino; John Zysman; Tom Hinkleman; Tom Howell; John Calhoun; Clyde Prestowitz; Bill Shaffer; Robert Rutishauser; Michael Dertouzos; Peter Gregory; John Child; and Lester Slezak.

'Japan's trade surplus': *New York Times*, April 17, 1983.

'What is an onion, anyway?': *New York Times*, April 17, 1983.

Japanese barriers to American cigarettes: *Fortune*, Feb. 21, 1983; *Los Angeles Times*, April 27, 1983; *Wall Street Journal*, Sept. 30, 1982.

Japanese food: Interview with John Child; USDA unofficial report on Japanese Agriculture, 1982.

Japanese deserve their success: *Los Angeles Times*, May 22, 1983.

Economic totalitarianism: coined by Bill Shaffer of Control Data Corporation.

Bureaucratic-Industrial Complex: *MITI and The Japanese Miracle*, by Chalmers Johnson, Stanford University Press, 1982.

Defense subsidies: *National Review*, March 4, 1983.

Opinion Research Poll: *Congress and U.S. Trade Policy*, The LTV Corporation, Dallas, Texas, 1983.

Mercantile Image tarnished: *The Asia Record*, May, 1982.

Reminiscent of ABCD and December 1941: Ibid.

Chapter II

Connor, visa cancellation: Interviews with Connor with Jack Latona; excerpts from Connor's personal diary; Connor's passport; Letter from Hill, Gross, Simpson, Van Santen, Steadman & Simpson, July 26, 1977, to Consulate General of Japan, Chicago; Letter, Consulate General of Japan, Chicago, Aug. 17, 1977; Letter, Embassy of Japan, Washington D.C.,

The Japanese Conspiracy

by Koichiro Matsuura, Counselor, Aug. 15th 1977; *Vol. II, Official Report of Proceedings, U.S. International Trade Commission*, Aug. 18, 1977.

Yamazaki litigation: Interviews with Connor, Latona, Copaken; *Petition to the President of the United States*, Houdaille Industries, Inc. May 3, 1982; Letter from Hill, Gross, et. al., to Office of U.S. Congressman Abner Mikva, Aug. 19, 1977.

Strategic & military value of machine tools: *Weakness in the U.S. Defense Industrial Base*, CIA internal memorandum (unclassified) OGC 81-10280, 3 Dec. 81; Testimony before *subcommittee on Trade, House Ways and Means Committee*, 14 Oct. 1980; *Technology of Machine Tools*, U.S. Air Force (Wright Aeronautical Laboratories, Machine Tool Task Force), 1980; *Defense Economic Impact Modeling System (DEIMS)*, Office of the Secretary of Defense, Jan. 1982, tables 271 and 272.

Market data, impact on U.S. industry: *Petition to the President of the United States*, Houdaille Industries, Inc. May 3, 1982; Interviews with Joseph Franklin, statistical manager, National Machine Tool Builder's Association; and with Jack Latona; Congressional Record, Dec. 15, 1982.

'The most serious challenge to the very continued existence of MITI . . .': Letter from Copaken to R. T. McNamar, Deputy Secretary of the Treasury, April 12, 1983.

'to counter the imports . . .': 'Character and Future Application of Plan of Financing of Domestic Deferred Payment Sales of Machinery,' *Machine Tool News*, Takeo Sato, Heavy Industry Division, Heavy Industry Bureau, MITI, Issue #33, 1963.

Mergers and cartelizing of Japanese Machine Tool Industry: Ibid.

Tax incentives to Japan's Machine Tool Industry: Ibid.

Japan Co-operative Association Law: Ibid.

'MITI . . . pressed Japanese machine tool manufacturers': Testimony of Phillip O'Reilly to ITC, June 15, 1983.

Sugar subsidies: *Petition to the President of the United States*, Houdaille Industries, Inc. May 3, 1982; Japan *Extraordinary Measures Law for Promotion of Specific Electronic Industries and Specific Machinery Industries*; MITI *Notification No. 304*, reprinted in #65, *Machine Tool News 10*, 1969; interviews with Latona and Copaken.

Copaken's investigations: Interviews with Copaken; *Petition to the President of the United States*, Houdaille Industries, Inc. May 3, 1982.

Bicycle and motorcycle race wagering subsidies: *Petition to the President of the United States*, Houdaille Industries, Inc.

May 3, 1982; Interviews with Copaken; Letter from Copaken to Jeanne S. Archibald, Assistant General Counsel, U.S. Trade Representative, Sept. 13, 1982; Japan Bicycle Race Law No. 209 of 1948, as Amended; Letter from Copaken to Donald DeKieffer, U.S. Trade Representative, Nov. 10, 1982; *Bulletin of Japan Keirin (Bicycle Race) Association, Extra Addition, April 9, 1982*, Budget of MITI Mechanical Engineering Laboratory (FY1982).

Cooperative Association Law: Letter from Copaken to R. T. McNamar at Treasury, April 8, 1983; *The Medium and Small Enterprise, etc., Cooperative Association Law (#181, June 1, 1949); Law Concerning Prohibition of Private Monopoly and Maintenance of Fair Trade Law, #54 of April 14, 1947; MITI* commentary on Third Extraordinary Measures Law (Law for the Promotion of Specific Machinery and Information Industries), #84 of 1978, Article 6. *Petition to the President of the United States*, Houdaille Industries, Inc. May 3, 1982.

Japanese machine tool inventories in U.S.: *American Metal Market/Metal Working News*, June 28, 1982; Letter from Copaken to Archibald of U.S. Trade Rep., March 10, 1983; Report by Akimitsu Ohko, Research Director of Japanese Machine Tool Builders Assoc., June, 1982; *Machine Tool News (Japan)*, Sept., 1982. *Petition to the President of the United States*, Houdaille Industries, Inc. May 3, 1982.

Leak to Japanese on Cabinet findings: Interview with Copaken.

Nakasone as MITI Minister: *MITI and the Japanese Miracle*, Chalmers Johnson, Stanford Press, 1982, pages 293–298.

Tanaka as Nakasone's MITI predecessor: Ibid.

Chapter III

In addition to the sources cited below, information for this chapter came from the author's personal interviews with Arnold I. Kalman, Herbert Hoffman, John Nevin, William Nail, Stuart Chemtob, Masayoshi Sakisaka, Larry Norris, Shigeki Hijino, Chuck Signor and Leonard M. Shambon.

'don't argue among ourselves': Interview with Sakisaka.

Meetings of Tenth Day Group: 513 F.Supp 1100 (1981); *Appellant Brief, Zenith Radio Corp. and National Union Electric Corp. (D.C. Civil no. 0000189, Third U.S. Circuit Court of Appeals).*

Palace Group: Ibid.

Palace Preparatory Group: Ibid.

Okura Group, Matsushita's involvement: Ibid.

'We are a social group': Ibid.

Japanese companies began to dump: *U.S. International Trade Commission Report to The President on Investigation No. TA-201-19*, USITC Publication 808, March 22, 1977; Interviews with Kalman, Hoffman, Nevin, Nail. *Appellant Brief, Zenith Radio Corp. and National Union Electric Corp. (D.C. Civil No. 0000189, Third U.S. Circuit Court of Appeals)*.

'stage by stage assault': Interview with Kalman.

Employment losses: Interview with Nevin; *U.S. International Trade Commission Report to The President on Investigation No. TA-201-19*, USITC Publication 808, March 22, 1977; Interviews with Kalman, Hoffman, Nevin, Nail.

Zenith lawsuit: Interviews with Kalman, Nevin, Nail, Hoffman; *513 F.Supp 1100 (1981); Brief of Appellants, Zenith Radio Corporation and National Union Radio Corp.; 518 F.Supp 179*, 1981 *Third U.S. Circuit Court of Appeals, D.C. Civil No. 0000189 MDL;* U.S. v Sears, Roebuck & Co., Inc., Appellate Brief, Ninth U.S. Circuit Court of Appeals, D.C. No. CR 80–183 MLR.

Check Prices: Ibid.

Matsushita response to U.S. Customs: Ibid.

'If you buy that one I have a bridge. . . .': Interview with Kalman.

Sanyo argument: Interviews with Kalman, Hoffman, Nevin; 513 F.Supp. 1100 (1981).

'Sears' motives. . . .': Interview with Kalman.

Warwick driven out of business: Interviews with Nevin, Kalman; *Journal of Legislation*, U. of Notre Dame Law School, pp 13, Vol. 6, 1979.

Ijima note: *513 F.Supp. 1100* (1981).

Midland memo: Ibid.

Zenith tries to sell in Japan: Interviews with Nevin, Kalman, Nail; *513 F.Supp 1100* (1981); *Report by The Comptroller General – U.S. – Japan Trade: Issues and problems,* September 21, 1979.

Motorola, Alps, Sharp, etc.: Interviews with Kalman, Nevin; *513 F.Supp. 1100,* 1981.

Motorola deal with Matsushita, Aiwa and Sony venture: Ibid.

American TV makers forced to liquidate: Interview with Nevin; *Journal of Legislation*, U. of Notre Dame Law School, pp 13, Vol. 6, 1979.

False billing: Interviews with Nevin, Kalman, Hoffman; *518 F.Supp, 179,* 1981, U.S. v. Sears, Roebuck & Co.

Japanese TV plants in Taiwan: Interview with Nevin.

Notes

Covert promises to Japanese: Ibid; interviews with Nail; Washington *Star*, May 4, 1979.

Marshall Plan mentality: Interview with Nevin; *Journal of Legislation*, U. of Notre Dame Law School, pp 16, Vol. 6, 1979.

Actual value of sets dumped: Interviews with Nevin, Kalman, Hoffman; *518 F.Supp 179*, 1981, U.S. v. Sears, Roebuck & Co; *513 F.Supp. 1100*, 1981.

Fines reduced: Ibid.

Difficulties with government's case against Sears: Ibid; Interview with Hoffman.

Criminal charges reinstated: *518 F.Supp. 179*, 1981, U.S. v. Sears, Roebuck & Co.

Ovshinsky and Matsushita: Interviews with Norris; Hijino; *Electronic News*, July 18, 1983.

Z80 chip: Interview with Chuck Signor; *Los Angeles Times*, June 26, 1983; *Business Week*, July 4, 1983.

Reverse Engineering: Interview with Ronald Billings; Chuck Signor; *Christian Science Monitor*, July 21, 1982.

List of Japanese dumping findings: Interview with Chemtob; *Internal Justice Dept. Memo (unclassified) Oct. 19, 1982.*

Steel dumping: Ibid; interview with Hoffman; *Wall Street Journal*, Feb. 7, 1973; Feb. 15, 1973; March 23, 1973; July 22, 1982.

Mitsui Steel: Interview with Hoffman; *Time*, Aug. 2, 1982.

Marubeni and Tanaka: Interview with Hoffman; *Wall Street Journal*, Oct. 12, 1983; *Los Angeles Times*, Oct. 12, 1983.

Cement dumping: *Japan Times*, July 19, 1983.

Electric Typewriters: *U.S. News & World Report* April 26, 1982.

Kobayashi interview: *Bungei Shunju*, September, 1982.

MITI and computer companies out to displace IBM: Ibid, *Wall Street Journal*, July 7, 1982.

Amdahl leaves IBM: Ibid.

Fujitsu laboratory at Amdahl: Ibid.

Description of Hayashi: Interview with Hoffman.

Maxwell Paly and Hitachi: *Fortune*, March 7, 1983; *New York Times*, June 26, 1982.

Paly and IBM: Ibid.

IBM sting operation: Ibid; interview with Hoffman; [Selected] Transcripts of Tapes made by FBI, Operation PENGEM, Hitachi Video Transcript Vol. I, II; Hitachi Audio Transcript; *New York Times*, June 24, 1982; July 23, 1982; May 16, 1983; *Wall Street Journal*, Sept. 27, 1982; *Los Angeles Times*, May 17, 1983; *U.S. News & World Report*, May 9, 1983.

Japanese Press reaction: *Asia Record,* Aug., 1982; *Wall Street Journal*, Aug. 2, 1982.

'An old trick of con men': *Yomiuri Shimbun*, translation in *Asia Record*, October 1982.

'A new era in international business': from Kobayashi interview: *Bungei Shunju*, September, 1982.

Chapter IV

In addition to sources noted below, information for this chapter is drawn from the author's own interviews with W. J. 'Jerry' Sanders III, Elliot Sopkin and Dr. James Cunningham of AMD; Thomas Hinkleman and many of his staff at SIA; Rebecca Wallo and John Calhoun of Intel; Lennie Siegel of Pacific Study Center; Shigeru Sato, Dr. Kaneyuki Kurokawa, and Koicho Endo of Fujitsu; Yuji Wakayama of Toshiba: Fujiya Yamagata of Japan External Trade Organization; Thomas Howell and others at Verner, Liipfert, Bernhard and McPherson; W. J. Kitchen of Motorola; John Zysman of the University of California, Berkeley; Clyde V. Prestowitz of the Department of Commerce; Ronald L. Billings of Nihon Soft Bank; and Lloyd Thorndike, Bill Shaffer and Robert Rutishauser of Control Data Corporation.

'Dynamic RAMs lead MOS technology,': *Electronic News*, July 18, 1983.

VLSI project: *The Effect of Government Targeting on World Semiconductor Competition*, Semiconductor Industry Association, Cupertino, California, 1983.

'Crude oil of the 1980s,': Interview with Sanders.

'The few ICs . . . brought to market by Japan . . .': *The Effect of Government Targeting on World Semiconductor Competition*. Semiconductor Industry Association, Cupertino, California, 1983.

Noyce and Moore, founding of Intel: *Electronic Design*, Oct. 14, 1982.

History of microprocessors: *IEEE Micro*, Feb., 1981.

Wolff's speech to SIA executives: *Public Policies and Strategies for U.S. High Technology Industry,* proceedings of SIA Long Range Planning Conference, Monterey, California, November 22, 1982.

'16K chip a photographic ripoff': Interview with Calhoun.

'Japanese have every reason to collude,': *Public Policies and Strategies for U.S. High Technology Industry*, proceedings of the SIA Long Range Planning Conference, Monterey, California, November 22, 1982.

Notes

'Whole U.S. economy basically flat . . .': Interview with Tom Hinkleman.

Financing of VLSI project: *The Effect of Government Targeting on World Semiconductor Competition*, Semiconductor Industry Association, Cupertino, California, 1983.

Silicon Island: *Now in Japan*, #34, 'Technopolises,' JETRO, Tokyo, 1983.

Nodaichi Soy: Ibid.

Haraseiki: Ibid.

'Dominance in Memories': Interview with Sanders.

'Brute force product . . .': Interview with Calhoun.

'We screwed up': *Electronic News*, July 18, 1983.

Semiconductor prices: *The Effect of Government Targeting on World Semiconductor Competition*, Semiconductor Industry Association, Cupertino, California, 1983; *SIA Yearbook and Directory*, Cupertino, California, 1980; *Electronic News*, June 1979–July 1983, inclusive.

'learning curve . . .': Interview with Kitchen.

'. . . our industry . . . deprived . . .': Interview with Sanders.

'sell your company to save it': Interview with Hinkleman.

'University of Intel': Ibid.

'starved for cash': Interview with Rebecca Wallo.

'playing a different game': Interview with Sanders.

'nobody in America coming out with 256K': Interview with Howell.

SRC: Interview with Tom Hinkleman; *SIA Yearbook and Directory*, Cupertino, California, 1980; *Public Policies and Strategies for U.S. High Technology Industry*, proceedings of the SIA Long Range Planning Conference, Monterey, California, November 22, 1982.

256K chip market: *New York Times*, June 3, 1983; *Business Week*, May 23, 1983; *Los Angeles Times*, May 24, 1983; *Electronic News*, January–July, 1983, inclusive.

Transfer of 256K technology: *The Effect of Government Targeting on World Semiconductor Competition*, Semiconductor Industry Association, Cupertino, California, 1983.

U.S. 256K chips: Interview with Calhoun, Hinkleman.

Toshiba 256K chips: Interview with Wakayama.

Japanese ventures into other chips: numerous publications of JETRO; *Science & Technology in Japan*, October 1982–July 1983; *Japan Economic Journal*, December 1982–August 1983.

CMOS technology: *IEEE Micro*, Feb., 1981. *The Effect of Government Targeting on World Semiconductor Competition*, Semiconductor Industry Association, Cupertino, California, 1983.

New Japanese chips: Interviews with Wakayama, Kurokawa, Dr. Hayakawa of MITI Electrotechnical Laboratory (Tsukuba); *Toshiba Towards 2000*, Toshiba Corporation Tokyo, 1982; Fujitsu Annual Reports (1982, 1981); *Science & Technology in Japan*, October 1982–July 1983; *Japan Economic Journal*, December 1982–August 1983.

U.S. 256K chips: Interview with Calhoun, Hinkleman.

Toshiba 256K chips: Interview with Wakayama.

Japanese ventures into other chips: *Business Week*, May 23, 1983; numerous publications of JETRO; *Science & Technology in Japan*, October 1982–July 1983; *Japan Economic Journal*, December 1982–August 1983.

New NEC Chip plant: *Japan Times*, July 20, 1983.

New Toshiba Chip plant: *Asahi News*, July 18, 1983.

Firms that gave up in frustration and disgust: Interview with Tom Howell.

'it's going to be hard to stop them . . .': Interview with Cunningham.

Chapter V

In addition to the sources noted below, information for this chapter is drawn from the author's personal interviews with: Jon Woronoff; James Ellenberger; Robert Kirshenbaum; Chinatsu Nakayama; Shigeki Hijono; David Jampel; Richard Copaken; Yuji Wakayama; David L. Cocke; Tomoko Tsutsiya; Robert Paolinelli; Hiroko Maki; Tetsuro Muto; Osamu Sakishita; Kumhiro Morita; Hiroko Horisaka; Yoshio Taketomi; John Boccellari; and William Yates.

'Things the way they should be . . . and truth.': Interview with Woronoff.

Japanese language: Ibid; Interviews with Woronoff and Kirshenbaum; *Japanese Manners & Ethics in Business*, by Boye De Mente, Phoenix Publishers, Phoenix, 1981; *The Japanese*, Edwin O. Reischauer, Harvard University Press, 1981; *Asia Record*, July, 1982.

Written language: Ibid.

Belly talk: Ibid; *Japan's Imperial Conspiracy*, by David Bergamini, Wm. Morrow, New York, 1971.

Hirohito's defeat speech: *Japan's Imperial Conspiracy*, p. 119.

Speaking to seniors and subordinates: Interviews with Ellenberger, Woronoff, Kirshenbaum; *Japanese Manners & Ethics in Business; New York Times Magazine*, Dec. 5, 1982.

Notes

Samurai's education: *Imperial Japan*, Livingston, Moore and Oldfather, eds., New York, Random House, 1973.

Samurai concentrated in towns and cities: Ibid.

Oishi: *The Rising Sun*, by John Toland, page 14. Random House, New York, 1970.

Japanese assassins often admired: Ibid; *Imperial Japan; Japan's Imperial Conspiracy*.

Japanese Brain: *Science 80*; December, 1980; *Time*, Aug. 1, 1983, March 28, 1975; *Time*, Aug. 1, 1983; *Fortune*, Nov., 1977; *Theory Z*, William Ouchi, Addison-Wesley Publishing, Reading, Mass., 1981.

Aggression directed at someone else: Interview with Woronoff; *The Japanese Mind*.

'why the Japanese want to win': Interviews with Ellenberger, Woronoff.

Lessons from the shoguns: Ibid; *World Press Review* Sept., 1983; *The Book of Five Rings; Imperial Japan; Japan's Imperial Conspiracy; The Rising Sun*.

Kanrisha Yosei Gakko [Management Training School]: LIFE, Sept. 1983.

Meiji's 100 year plan: Interview with Hijino; *Japan's Imperial Conspiracy; Imperial Japan; The Japanese; The Rising Sun; At Dawn We Slept*, by Gordon Prange, Penguin Books, New York, 1981.

Japanese racial purity: Interviews with Hijino, Nakayama, Doi; *The Japanese; Japan before Buddhism*, J. E. Kidder, Jr.; Frederick A. Praeger, New York, 1959; *Peasants, Rebels & Outcastes*, Mikiso Hane, Random House, New York, 1982.

Boccellari's contract: Interview with Boccellari.

Villagers and five-man groups: *Imperial Japan; Peasants, Rebels & Outcastes*.

Ringi: *Japanese Manners & Ethics in Business; Theory Z; Fortune*, Nov., 1977

Dead wood in Japanese corporations: Ibid; interviews with Woronoff and Ellenberger.

'My father died 10 years ago.': Interview with Yajima.

Promotion in Japanese companies: *Technology Review*, Jan. 1975; *Theory Z; MITI and The Japanese Miracle*, by Chalmers Johnson, Stanford University Press, 1982.

Japanese president's powers: *Commerce*, January, 1981; *Time*, Aug. 1, 1983; *Fortune*, Nov., 1977.

amae, indulgent love: Interviews with Woronoff, Ellenberger; *Japanese Manners & Ethics in Business; The Anatomy of Dependence*, Takeo Doi, Kodansha, Int'l, Tokyo.

Japanese personality mechanisms: Ibid.

MITI bureaucrats: *MITI and the Japanese Miracle.*

Revenge: Interviews with Woronoff, Hijino, Jampel, Ellenberger; *Japanese Manners & Ethics in Business; The Anatomy of Dependence*, Takeo Doi, Kodansha, Int'l, Tokyo.

Feudal vassals lose heads: *Peasants, Rebels & Outcastes.*

Introductions: Interviews with Woronoff, Jampel, Slezak.

'let their hair down with me at night': Interview with Copaken.

Vexing customers in petroleum industry: Interview with Cocke.

Negotiations: Ibid, interviews with Woronoff, Ellenberger, *Japanese Manners & Ethics in Business; New York Times Magazine*, Dec. 5, 1982.

'opportunities are a precious commodity': *The Asia Record*, Sept. 1982.

Bushido and negotiation: *The Book of Five Rings.*

Japan's national straight jacket: Interview with Hijino.

Rape of Nanking: *Japan's Imperial Conspiracy.*

Revising the textbooks: Interview with Hijino.

Inferiority complex: Interviews with Ellenberger, Woronoff; *Japan Unmasked; Japanese Manners & Ethics in Business.*

Chapter VI

In addition to the sources noted below, information for this chapter is drawn from the author's personal interviews with Hiroko Horisaka; Hideo Ogata; Yuzuru Matsumoto; Yuji Wakayama; Shinsaku Sogo; Koichi Kujirai; Soichi Nagamatsu; Shigeru Sawada; Joseph Podolsky; Ilene Birkwood; Steve Newhouse; Robert Rutishauser; Peter Gregory;

Economic growth a popular religion: *The Japanese Challenge*, by Herman Kahn, William Morrow & Co., New York, 1979.

Aircraft industry a stationary target: *Fortune*, March 21, 1983.

Abilities carry over to defense industry: *The Wall Street Journal*, November 26, 1982.

Japan 10 to 15 years behind the U.S.: Ibid.

British joint venture: *The Economist*, May 28, 1983.

International Aero Engines: Ibid.

British aircraft industry force reductions: *Japan Times*, July 17, 1983.

Nissan will be Boeing's partner: Interview with Sawada.

Bullet train brakes: *Wall Street Journal*, November 26, 1982.

Mitsubishi licensed to make F-15s: Interview with Hideo Ogata.

Notes

F-86 is father of modern industry: *Fortune*, March 21, 1983.
'Better than the British Jaguar.': Interview with Ogata.
'Everybody asks about this.': Ibid.
Japan Air Lines: *Japan Times*, July 17, 1983.
All Nippon Air: *Business Week*, September 27, 1982.
TOA airlines: Ibid.
'Hondas all over again.': *Wall Street Journal*, November 26, 1982.
A different competitive world: Interview with Rutishauser.
Growth in Office Automation: *A Vision of Business Machines in the 1980s*, Japan Business Machine Makers Association, Tokyo, 1982.
Trend in U.S.: Ibid.
Japanese even more successful: Interview with Rutishauser.
Japanese turning out more engineers: *Electronic News*, May, 1983.
Productivity of office workers: *A Vision of Business Machines in the 1980s*.
Toshiba products: Interview with Wakayama.
Fujitsu facsimile machine: Interview with Shigeru Sato, Kaneyuki Kurokawa.
Document cyphering equipment: Ibid.
Infrared modem: Ibid.
Nontariff barriers to Japanese drug market: *Asia Record*, November 1981.
France demands removal: Ibid.
Japanese leadership in amino acids: *Research on Biotechnology in Japan*, #14, JETRO, 1982.
Germ warfare experiments: *Business Week*, June 20, 1983; *Fortune*, October 3, 1983; *Asia Record*, December, 1981.
Japan's huge biomedical firms: *Japan Times*, July 16, 1983.
Joint venture with Biogen: Ibid.
MITI R&D projects: *Research on Biotechnology in Japan*, #14, JETRO, 1982.
Trying not to lose out: *Japan Times*, July 16, 1983.
Interferon from hamsters: Ibid.
Monoclonal antibodies: *Japan Times*, July 19, 1983.
'Japan is just awakening.': *Japan Times*, July 16, 1983.
Organized robots: *New York Times*, May 4, 1983.
Electronics revolution augments Japanese exports: *Industrial Robots*, Japan Foreign Press Center, 1982.
Upholding the spirit of free trade: Ibid.
Chronic problem with undervalued yen: Interview with Newhouse.
Japanese in grain trade: *New York Times*, Sept 6, 1982.

Solar Energy: Interview with Larry Norris; *Asia Record*, March 1983; *World Press Review*, March, 1983.

'Our Policy is to come out late.': *Info World*, Volume 5, #3.

Alps replaces Shugart: *80 Micro*, December, 1982.

TEAC signs with Digital: Ibid.

Japanese have been aggressive: Interview with Rutishauser.

'scared the hell out of me.': Interview with Podolsky.

Japanese approach to software reliability excellent: Interview with Birkwood.

Myths about Japanese software: Ibid.

Two types of computers: Interview with Peter Gregory.

Rarest of Japanese animals: Interview with Shiina.

Sales of Epson computers: *Business Week*, August 1, 1983.

Matsushita starts to make MSX computer: *Business Week*, July 4, 1983.

Japanese computers can be programmed in other languages: *Info World*.

At best Number Two: Interview with Rutishauser.

Chapter VII

In addition to the sources noted below, information for this chapter is drawn from the author's personal interviews with Edward Feigenbaum; Robert Rutishauser; Michael Dertouzos; Lloyd Thorndike; Peter Gregory; Tsutomo Hoshino; Hisao Hayakawa; Yuji Wakayama; Koichi Endo; Kaneyuki Kurakawa; Bill Shaffer; Kazuhiko Bando; Koichi Kujirai; Shigeru Sato; Ronald Billings; Yasuhiko Ohmori; Soichi Nagamatsu; Tom Hinkleman and Kenzo Yanagida.

Whoever controls the information revolution: Interview with Dertouzos.

Mathematical simulation: Interview with Peter Gregory.

Technology owned by Japanese government: Interview with Nagamatsu.

Two ways to approach superspeed: Interview with Hayakawa.

MITI will decide by 1985: Ibid; interview with Nagamatsu.

Explanations of Josephson Junction: Interview with Hayakawa.

Taking Japanese competition seriously: Interview with Gregory.

European supercomputer programs: Ibid.

ICL marketing under English banner: Ibid.

'Japan-Brand' supercomputer: Interview with Sato.

Number of researchers: Interview with Nagamatsu.

Office warm in winter, cool in summer: Interview with Muto.

Notes

Supercomputer built by Denelcor: *Newsweek*, July 4, 1983.
American and British academics respond: Ibid.
Control Data's new venture: Interviews with Shaffer, Thorndike.
No fight with graduate students: Interview with Shaffer.
'Go out there and rape and pillage . . .': Ibid.
'They're bringing in the old eagles': Ibid.
Stages of Fifth Generation Development: Interview with Nagamatsu.
MITI budgeting: Ibid.
Forty researchers from private industry: Ibid.
Toshiba engineers to ICOT: Interview with Wakayama.
Continue with development at company base: Interview with Nagamatsu.
Four requirements of Fifth Generation computers: Ibid.
Opinions from computers: *The Fifth Generation*, by Edward Feigenbaum and Pamela McCorduck, Addison-Wesley Publishing, Stanford, 1983.
Internist/Caduceus: Ibid.
Doctors using machine as a friend: Interview with Nagamatsu.
Expert systems: *The Fifth Generation*.
Natural language interface: Interview with Nagamatsu.
Home computers in Japan: Interview with Ohmori.
Single chip voice recognition: *The Japan Industrial & Technological Bulletins [JITB]*, 1982.
'Pie-in-the-sky.': *Datamation*, July 1983.
'Achieved something no other computer manufacturer is even contemplating': Ibid.
Fujitsu as fast as IBM: Interview with Gregory.
Originally MCC was only an electronics project: Interview with Dertouzos.
Starting off with four projects: Interview with Rutishauser.
Objectives of MCC: [DRAFT], MCC Technology Programs, Sept. 1982.
Justice looking other way: Interview with Hinkleman.
Power of the MCC: Interview with Dertouzos.
A sense of urgency: Interview with Rutishauser.
Leverage in economic and technological leadership: Ibid.
Government project proven method: Interview with Dertouzos.
Fifth Generation Threat: Ibid.
A Japanese Bar Mitzvah: Interview with Feigenbaum.
The economic future of America: Ibid.

Chapter VIII

In addition to the sources noted below, information for this chapter is drawn from the author's personal interviews with Edward Feigenbaum; Jon Woronoff; Richard Copaken; Chinatsu Nakayama; Doi Takako; Kazuhiko Bando; Koichi Kujirai; Soichi Nagamatsu; Arnold Kalman; John Nevin; Shigeki Hijino; John Zysman; Tom Hinkleman; W. J. Kitchen; Tom Howell; John Calhoun; Clyde Prestowitz; Bill Shaffer; Robert Rutishauser; Lloyd Thorndyke; Michael Dertouzos; Peter Gregory; John Child; Lester Slezak.

Zaibatsu return: Zaibatsu Dissolution and the American Restoration of Japan, CCAS Bulletin, Sept. 1973; *Return of the Zaibatsu, Far Eastern Economic Review*, Aug. 6, 1973.

Mitsui *zaibatsu: Japan's Imperial Conspiracy.*

Bureaucratic-Industrial Complex: *MITI and the Japanese Miracle*, by Chalmers Johnson, Stanford University Press, 1982.

MITI heart of Japanese state capitalism: Ibid; *Background Information on Japan's Industrial Policy*, MITI publication, May, 1983; *Manhattan Report*, Oct. 1982.

Elite schools: *MITI and the Japanese Miracle [137]; Asia Record*, April, 1982.

Military parlance of Japanese business: Ibid; *Harper's*, Nov. 1982.

Legal Cartels: *Los Angeles Times*, May 23, 1983.

Japanese beef prices, quota: Interview with John Child.

Japanese barriers to American cigarettes: *Fortune*, Feb 21, 1983; *Los Angeles Times*, April 27, 1983; *Wall Street Journal*, Sept. 30, 1982.

Toothless dog that doesn't bite: *Los Angeles Times*, May 22, 1983.

Establishment of MITI: *MITI and the Japanese Miracle.*

Creation of Nissan: Ibid; Interview with Shigeru Sawada.

MITI organization: *MITI and the Japanese Miracle.*

Students from Todai: *Asia Record*, April 1982.

MITI examinations: Ibid; *MITI and the Japanese Miracle, Los Angeles Times*, May 23, 1983.

Zaibatsu before World War II: *The Japanese Economy*, by G.C. Allen, St. Martin's Press, New York, 1981; *MITI and the Japanese Miracle; Zaibatsu return: Zaibatsu Dissolution and the American Restoration of Japan*, CCAS Bulletin, Sept. 1973; *Return of the Zaibatsu, Far Eastern Economic Review*, Aug. 6, 1973.

Notes

Re-created *Zaibatsu*: Ibid.

Black cartel case: *MITI and the Japanese Miracle*.

Shiro Miyamoto retirement: *Japan Times*, July 20, 1983.

Capital controlled by Insurance companies, trust banks: *The Institutional Investor*, Oct., 1982.

Mitsui Mutual's investments: Ibid.

Chapter IX

In addition to the sources noted below, information for this chapter is drawn from the author's personal interviews with Jon Woronoff; James Ellenberger; Lester Slezak; Robert Kirshenbaum; David Jampel; Chinatsu Nakayama; Doi Takako; William Yates; Shigeki Hijino.

Japanese housing: *Asia Record*, July 1982.

'We drove through a city called Harlem.': Interview with Horisaka.

Myth of lifetime employment: Interviews with Woronoff, Ellenberger; *AFL/CIO American Federationist*, April/July, 1982.

Worker dissatisfaction: *Japan Times*, July 11, 1983.

'I hear the loudspeaker . . .': *Technology Review*, Jan., 1975

'Because Japan is a poor country.': *World Press Review*, July, 1981.

Seniority basis of promotion: *Technology Review*, Jan., 1975; *AFL/CIO American Federationist*, April/June 1982.

Japanese don't trust nondrinkers: Interview with Kirshenbaum.

Unprincipled work rules: *Japan in the Passing Lane*, by Satoshi Kamata, Pantheon/Random House, New York, 1982; *Mother Jones*, Aug., 1982; *The Progressive*, May, 1983; *Harper's*, Nov., 1982; *American Federationist*, April/June 1982.

Accidents and bonus reductions: *Japan in the Passing Lane*, Satoshi Katama.

Job-related disability at Toyota: Ibid.

Quality control circles: *Mother Jones*, Aug., 1982; *AFL-CIO American Federationist*, April/June 1982; *Asia Record*, May, 1981.

'A new religion . . .': *Asia Record*, May, 1981.

Only a third of QC circles work well: *AFL-CIO American Federationist*, April/June 1982.

Mitsubishi shipyard workers rebel at QC: *Asia Record*, May, 1981.

Sqeeze unpaid labor from the worker: *AFL-CIO American Federationist*, April/June 1982.

'Japan's labor movement is impotent.': Interview with Hijino.

Enterprise unions: Interviews with Woronoff, Ellenberger, Slezak.

'Roughly speaking . . .': Interview with Yamada.

Part-time workers not willing to unionize: Ibid; interviews with Woronoff, Ellenberger.

Workers exploited but know it: Interview with Slezak.

Only one union organized in Western sense: Interview with Ellenberger.

Temporaries for 10 years: Ibid.

Japanese workers loaned to other companies: Ibid; *Japan in the Passing Lane*.

Unionists from management ranks: Interviews with Woronoff, Ellenberger.

Unions like an arm of personnel department: *Industrial Renaissance*, Abernathy, Clark and Kantrow, Basic Books, New York, 1983.

Unions useful for ascending hierarchy: *Mother Jones*, Aug., 1982.

Japan's labor unions once highly political: Interview with Slezak.

Divide and conquer: Ibid.

Shunto: Interview with Kirshenbaum.

Jimpei Kamura: Interview with Kamura.

Silver helmets, yellow helmets: *AFL-CIO American Federationist*, April/June 1982.

Grandchild companies: Ibid.

Wage differentials between big and small companies: *World Press Review*, July, 1981.

Labor statistics: *Labor Trends in Japan*, American Embassy, Tokyo, 1982.

Zensen Domei survey: Ibid.

Subcontracting: *AFL-CIO American Federationist*, April/June 1982.

Getting more holidays, taking them less: *Labor Trends in Japan*, American Embassy, Tokyo, 1982.

Husband never took a vacation: Interview with Horisaka.

'If the foreman doesn't think you really believe . . .': *World Press Review*, July, 1981.

Can't borrow from banks: Interview with Hiroko Maki.

Finance companies: Interview with Yates; *U.S. News & World Report*, Aug. 1, 1983.

Make Japanese lending ethical business: Ibid.

Murders related to unpaid loans: *Business Week*, June 13, 1983.

Suicides: *U.S. News & World Report*, Aug. 1, 1983.

Notes

Saleswoman suicide in Toyama: Ibid.
Tried to break into golf club: *Japan Times*, July 15 1983.
'Probably lose their jobs.': Interview with Yates.
Low interest rates for Japanese business: *Forbes*, Jan. 31, 1983.

Chapter X

In addition to the sources noted below, information for this chapter is drawn from the author's personal interviews with Lester Slezak; Jon Woronoff; Kyoko Kudo; Osamu Sakishita; Hiroko Horisaka; Chinatsu Nakayama; Doi Takako; James Ellenberger; Tomoko and Nobuatsu Tsutiya; Sara Siegler; Hiroko Maki; Tomoko Yamamoto and Keiko Kadota.

Chinatsu Nakayama: Interview with Nakayama; *Asia Record*, April, 1982.
'This is embarrassing': Interview with Yamamoto.
Part-time women workers: *Present Status of Women and Policies*, 1983, The Prime Minister's Office, (translated by Foreign Press Center.)
Male-female wage gap: *Annual Labor Report – Japan (1982)*, U.S. Embassy, Japan.
Inferior status demonstrated in 1000 ways: *Political Women in Japan*, by Susan J. Pharr, U. of California Press, Berkeley, 1981.
Oldest son legal head of household: Ibid.
Homemaking first priority: *Women of Japan*, Foreign Press Center, 1977; *Annual Labor Report – Japan (1982)*, U.S. Embassy, Japan.
Maintain *wa* in home: Interview with Kadota.
Japanese male-female relationships: Ibid.
Japanese sex lives: *TIME*, Aug. 1, 1983; *The Japanese; The Japanese Mind*.
Arranged marriages: *Asia Record*, Aug., 1982.
Japanese abortion law revision: *Asia Record*, Oct., 1982.
No need to allow abortions for economic reasons: Ibid.
Women crushed revision: Interviews with Nakayama, Doi.
Women's voting records: *Political Women in Japan*.
Female government employees serving tea: *Annual Labor Report – Japan*.
Woman was 55 years old: Ibid.
More education but less job opportunity: Interview with Doi.
Woman taxi driver: *Japan Times*, July 19, 1983.
Unmarried women in Japan: *Asia Record*, Dec., 1982.
Women are treated as half-persons: Ibid.

359

The Japanese Conspiracy

If women held 50 percent of executive positions: *The Asia Record*, May, 1982.

'Deprive men of work, and cause social unrest': Ibid.

Restrictions on Koreans: *Asia Record*, Dec., 1981.

Attempts to change names: Interview with Horisaka.

Korean fired by Hitachi: Ibid.

Kim didn't try to conceal identity: Interview with Kyoko Kudo.

Couldn't return to Manchuria: Interview with Tomoko Tsutiya.

'A racist policy.': Interview with Nakayama.

'Not good enough to allow us to stay.': *Asia Record*, Dec., 1981.

Indochinese refugees in Japan: *Asia Record*, Sept., 1982.

History of outcastes: *The Japanese, Peasants, Rebels & Outcastes; Imperial Japan; The Japanese Mind.*

'had to go about barefoot': *Peasants, Rebels & Outcastes.*

Youth beaten to death: Ibid.

To cast them out: *Asia Record*, July, 1982.

Black lists: Ibid, April, 1983.

An acquaintance who never heard of them: Interview with Osamu Sakishita.

'Cannot marry one of their kind.' Interview with Dee Hoffman.

Conspiracy of silence: Interview with Siegler.

'Prevailing tendencies . . .': *Asia Record*, July, 1982.

'Dropping quotas is impossible': *AFL-CIO American Federationist*, April/June, 1982.

Chapter XI

In addition to the sources cited below, information from this chapter came from the author's personal interviews with Nobuatsu and Tomoko Tsutiya; William Yates; Hiroko and Kotaro Horisaka; Robert Kirshenbaum; Lester Slezak; John Child; Chinatsu Nakayama; Doi Takako; Tadao and Yuichi Kitigawa; Jon Woronoff; James Ellenberger; Lennie Siegel; Tetsuro Muto; Osamu Sakishita; Fr. Pius Honda, O.F.M., and John Zysman.

Food prices: interviews with Child, Slezak, Horisaka, Tomoko Tsutiya, Woronoff, Yates, Muto, Kirshenbaum and Sakishita; Statistical summaries provided by Japan's Customs Bureau, (Ministry of Finance); Office of the Prime Minister; Ministry of Agriculture, Forestry and Fisheries; and U.S. Agricultural Affairs Office, (USDA), Embassy of the United States, Japan.

Two-thirds of McDonald's hamburgers: Interview, Child.

Import restrictions cost $16 billion extra: *U.S. Embassy Attache Report JA1180*, Oct. 9, 1981.

Without farm subsidies Japanese farms unprofitable: Ibid.

Japan buys $6.6 billion in U.S. agricultural products: Interview with Child.

Subsidies to Japanese farmers: *U.S. Embassy Attache Report JA1180*, Oct. 9, 1981.

'A wide range of groups . . .': *The Japanese Challenge*, pages 73–77, Herman Kahn, Wm. Morrow & Co, New York, 1980.

'conservative party despite its name': *The Diet, Elections and Political Parties*, Foreign Press Center of Japan, June, 1979.

LDP platform: Ibid.

Fukuda Cabinet passed 90 percent . . .: *Diet, Elections and Political Parties*, Foreign Press Center of Japan, June, 1979.

'Hatomandering': Ibid.

LDP's share of votes declined: *Agriculture and Politics in Japan*, p. 222, by Kenzo Hemmi, Tokyo, 1982.

Public Offices Election Law: *Constitution of Japan*.

'share of (LDP) parliamentary seats': *Agriculture and Politics in Japan*, p. 224, by Kenzo Hemmi, Tokyo, 1982.

LDP changed House of Councillors' voting: *House of Councillors Election System Reformed*, Japan Foreign Press Center, June, 1983.

Lower interest in Japanese politics: Interviews with Nakayama.

Bullet train costs: *Forbes*, Jan. 31, 1983.

Japanese housewives tired of paying outrageous prices: Interview with Child.

Agricultural policies of LDP: Interviews with Nakayama, Doi.

Frozen fish scandal: Ibid.

Factors in raising beef: Interview with Child.

Supply and distribution system: Ibid.

Description of farm life: Interview with Horisaka; *U.S. Embassy Attache Report JA1180*, Oct. 9, 1981.

Kitagawa household, farming procedures, etc: Interview with Kitagawa, et al.

mikan production: Ibid; *U.S. Embassy Attache Report JA1180*, Oct. 9, 1981.

Egg farmer protests: *Wall Street Journal*, June 22, 1983.

Late payments to farmers: *Asia Record*, August, 1981; *Japan Times*, July 18, 1983.

Japanese food distribution system: Interviews with Slezak, Nakayama, Doi.

Chapter XII

In addition to the sources noted below, information for this chapter is drawn from the author's personal interviews with: Tom Hinkleman; John Nevin; John Zysman; Herb Hoffman; Jerry Sanders; Lloyd Thorndike; Clyde Prestowitz; Robert Rutishauser; Peter Gregory; Arnold Kalman; Michael Dertouzos.

'Shoot themselves in the foot.': Interview with Sanders.

Norman Larker: As related by Joe Garagiola to Don Drysdale.

Make the yen into an international currency: Interview with John Zysman; *Forbes*, January, 1983.

Japanese selling bonds in New York, London: Ibid.

Japanese banks taking control of American banks: *Los Angeles Times*, Aug. 24, 1982; *Wall Street Journal*, Aug. 24, 1983; *New York Times*, Aug. 24, 25, 1983.

'We have been suckers.': Interview with Prestowitz.

Customs should inspect each car: Ibid.

Prestowitz's remedies: Ibid.

'ironic that a Republican Administration . . .': Interview with Copaken.

Accept $10,000 fines as business expense: Interviews with Kalman, Hoffman.

Shortage of computer scientists: Interviews with Dertouzos, Hinkleman.

Buying licenses from Japanese: Ibid.

Index